COMMERCIAL LEASES
IN SCOTLAND

2nd Edition

COMMERCIAL LEASES
IN SCOTLAND

2nd Edition

By

Kenneth S. Gerber
Partner, Anderson Strathern LLP
Legal Diploma Tutor at University of Glasgow and
University of Edinburgh

W. GREEN

 THOMSON REUTERS

Published in 2013 by W. Green, 21 Alva Street,
Edinburgh EH2 4PS
Part of Thomson Reuters (Professional) UK Limited
(Registered in England & Wales, Company No 1679046.
Registered Office and address for service: Aldgate House,
33 Aldgate High Street, London EC3N 1DL)

ISBN 978-0-414-01862-4

Typeset by LBJ Typesetting, Kingsclere
Printed and bound in Great Britain by
CPI Group (UK) Ltd, Croydon, CR0 4YY

A catalogue record for this title is available
from the British Library

No natural forests were destroyed to make this product; only
farmed timber was used and replanted.

FOREWORD

The "all singing and all dancing" FRI style of lease arrived on the scene in Scotland in the 1970s and in a little over 30 years is well-established in Scottish commercial leasing practice. This is largely due to the fact that it is the occupational lease that creates value in a property investment transaction, and investors like uniformity. Accordingly, the traditional short form of lease which prevailed before the introduction of the English style of lease was no longer suitable.

The commercial lease is, in essence, a contract, and practitioners require to take care when drafting and/or revising such documents. There is little in the way of statutory overlay of the subject in Scotland and, if not effectively displaced, the common law will come into play in whole or in part.

The growth of commercial leasing as a discipline was not accompanied by the publication of any text books on the subject and, at least initially, decided case law was relatively rare. That has changed however, and there are now a range of different Scottish textbooks to suit most requirements.

This book was first published in 2009 and it has become an essential text for solicitors and students alike. This is largely due to the clear and informed commentary of the author, and the way in which the subject matter is presented. I was therefore not surprised to learn that a second edition was planned although, from a personal point of view, I do question the rush to produce new editions these days. Some of us can remember how out of date our textbooks were at University only some 30 or so years ago! There was, however, a clear need for a second edition of this book. The author has carried out an extensive review of the text and has added new chapters that enhance the overall approach of the book. Particular mention should be made of the new chapters on Rent Review—Procedure and Rent Review—Valuation (Chs 10 and 11); the separate treatment of these matters is beneficial. It is also good to see a review of lease obligations that bind successors (Ch.22) and a summary of the statutes that affect commercial leasing in Scotland (Chs 4 and 5). The vexed question of notices is another new and very welcome addition (Ch.21).

I was pleased to be asked to write the foreword to this second edition. Anyone who is brave enough to commit his/her thoughts on any subject to paper deserves admiration. When the result is a careful and studied analysis of the law and practice of commercial leasing in Scotland that will undoubtedly aid our practice and understanding of the subject, the author should be rightly praised. As was the case with the first edition, the book comes with a compact disc containing a selection of indicative styles—the most useful being the draft single occupancy and multi-occupancy leases as revised and counter-revised by the parties' solicitors. My one caveat in this regard is that readers should always ensure that they cross-refer to the underlying law as outlined in the book, when they are considering using a particular style or adopting a form of words for revisal.

I have pleasure in commending this book. I am confident that it will be a much-used text.

Professor Stewart Brymer
April 2013

INTRODUCTION

I have written this book for a wide readership. I hope that solicitors, surveyors, property managers and property investors who are involved in occasional or regular day to day, working with commercial leases, whether they are new to commercial leasing or are well experienced in this field, will find this book useful. The book is a practitioner's guide; it is not a fully exhaustive textbook on all legal aspects and cases relating to commercial leases, nor is it a simplistic entry-level guide.

The text deals with each element of the subject in a user-friendly, concise manner, using plain English. I hope it will be of assistance to all who are seeking an understanding and a working knowledge of commercial lease transactions. The book covers all the main aspects of the law of commercial leases in Scotland and, where appropriate, there is also a brief outline (as opposed to a full exposition) of the corresponding position in English law. The purpose of dealing with the corresponding English law provisions is in order to allow the main differences between the Scottish and English systems to be highlighted. I do hope this will enable readers in Scotland to appreciate the main differences between the Scottish and English systems in commercial leasing law, so as to be able to handle transactions more effectively where instructions come from a client or agent who is conversant with the English system, but who is unfamiliar with the Scottish system. This book should also allow those who are not solicitors, but who are involved in the property industry, to obtain a working knowledge and understanding of the law and practice of commercial leasing in Scotland.

Whilst this book is very much dedicated to the practitioner, there is commentary on relevant case law included within the text, and so it will hopefully be of some assistance to students.

The book contains a comprehensive treatment of the principles of common law, which provides default rules for many important aspects that apply to commercial leases. Rather surprisingly these rules are not always fully understood by those involved in the drafting and revisal of commercial leases.

The accompanying compact disc contains an example of an offer to grant a lease where a draft lease is to be annexed to the offer, a short-term lease comprising an offer to lease that has all the terms of the lease contained in it, a single occupancy lease, and of a multi-occupancy lease, each with suggested revisals by a tenant shown in "tracked changes", and as separate documents, the same leases counter-revised by the landlord.

I very much hope that you find this book helpful and as enjoyable and digestible as any book on law can be. I would genuinely welcome any comments and criticism by e-mail to ken.gerber@andersonstrathern.co.uk

Kenneth S. Gerber
April 2013

ACKNOWLEDGEMENTS

I am extremely grateful to the following people who have given me helpful comments and valuable guidance to allow me to produce and refine this second edition of the book:

Various people at Anderson Strathern have been of valuable help: these include Alan Menzies and Stephen McDonagh for input into the Scottish legal content of this book, Neil Farrell for input into the English law content, Deborah Lovell for her expertise in property tax law, Joan Devine on enforcement aspects, and Richard Hart for input on care home leases.

I am also grateful to Professor Stewart Brymer of Brymer Legal for his overview on various chapters.

When I was writing the first edition, I relied heavily on David Murdoch, who is now at Savills and Roddy Pearson of R.J. Pearson Property Consultants for comments and suggestions on treatment of content from the surveyor's and property industry's viewpoints. Their excellent input has been carried into the second edition.

Rebecca Standing of W. Green, publishers, for her kind help and presentational guidance throughout the formulation and writing of this book, and to all at W Green & Son for their help in bringing this book from rough manuscript to the finished article.

I could not have done it without the help of them all.

I proudly and lovingly dedicate this book to my wife Barbara, and to our three children Danielle, Joelle, and Adam.

CONTENTS

Contents of CD

Introduction to the contents of the CD
Offer to grant a lease
Short form missive of lease
Single occupancy lease
Single occupancy lease—revised by tenant
Single occupancy lease—counter revised by landlord
Multi-occupancy lease
Multi-occupancy lease—revised by tenant
Multi-occupancy lease—counter revised by landlord

TABLE OF CASES

TABLE OF STATUTES

ACTS OF THE SCOTTISH PARLIAMENT

TABLE OF STATUTORY INSTRUMENTS

SCOTTISH STATUTORY INSTRUMENTS

GLOSSARY OF LEGAL TERMS
RELATIVE TO COMMERCIAL LEASES IN SCOTLAND

Assignation

The transfer by an assignor to an assignee of the tenancy under a lease. The document effecting this is also called an assignation. In Scotland an assignation must be notified to interested third parties in order to be effective. For example, the tenant would be required to notify the assignation to the landlord.

Acquiescence

The loss of right to enforce an obligation if not challenged or objected to for a period of time by the party who is entitled to enforce it.

Books of Council and Session

A public register of deeds held by the Keeper of the Registers of Scotland in which a wide variety of deeds may be registered.

Building Warrant

Permission issued by a local authority under the Building (Scotland) Acts to allow works to be carried out to property.

Candlemas

A quarter or term day in Scotland, formerly February 2, but now by statute February 28, except where the old date of February 2 is expressly referred to in the relevant document.

Caveat Emptor

Latin term meaning "buyer beware". The buyer has to satisfy himself on certain points.

Charge

A security (or mortgage) which attaches assets (including the right in a lease where applicable) to give the chargeholder a preferred claim on the asset or proceeds.

Collateral Warranty

A warranty granted by a party (building contractor, members of design team), with whom there is otherwise no legal or contractual relationship, to a purchaser, tenant or lender warranting their work, giving the grantee a direct right to sue.

Conditional Missives

A contract that is conditional on matters, often outwith the direct control of the parties, e.g. obtaining planning consent.

Confusio

Where one party becomes entitled to two different interests in the same property, for example, both the landlord's and the tenant's. While both interests are held by the one party, payment obligations are suspended.

Date of Entry

The date on which a tenant takes possession of a property.

Debenture

English equivalent of a floating charge by which a lender has a security over the assets from time to time of a company.

Deed of Conditions

A deed that contains rights and obligations affecting the owners from time to time of a building or an area of land.

Deed of Servitude

A deed granting a servitude.

Disposition

A deed by which a seller transfers heritable or freehold property to another party.

Disposition

A conveyance transferring ownership, or "title", to land and buildings. The disposition is registered in Land Register of Scotland.

Ex adverso

Opposite to, or fronting.

Excambion

An exchange between two parties in one deed of heritable title to land.

Executed

Signed.

Extract

The officially issued print of a registered document, which has equivalent status in law to the original deed.

Floating Charge

A security held by a lender over the assets from time to time of a company, or of a limited liability partnership.

Foreshore

The area of land lying between high water mark and low water mark.

FRI Lease

A "full repairing and insuring lease", where the tenant is responsible for all repairs, reinstatement and rebuilding and the cost of insurance, and the landlord has no liability for repair other than making good insured risk damage.

Grassum

A lump-sum payment, sometimes referred to as a "premium".

Heritable property (also heritage)

Land, buildings, minerals and certain rights in respect of land.

Heritable Title/Interest

Ownership title to land/buildings.

Heritable Fittings & Fixtures

Items fixed or fitted in such a way that they are deemed part of the property, and if removed, would cause damage to the fabric of the property.

Hypothec

A security that exists in law for arrears of rent due by the tenant in a commercial lease, over goods in the premises belonging to the tenant.

Interposed Lease

A new lease that is granted to a third party by the landlord under an existing lease, so that the third party becomes the immediate landlord of the tenant in that existing lease.

IRI Lease

An "internal repairing and insuring lease", where the tenant is responsible for maintaining/repairing the interior of the property, but not for the fabric or structure of the building.

Irritancy

The Scottish equivalent of the English right of forfeiture, and the premature termination of the lease by the landlord, when the tenant has failed to comply with one or more of his obligations under the lease. The grounds for irritancy will almost always be set out in the lease; they usually include non-payment of rent, breach of one or more of the conditions under the lease and tenant insolvency.

Ish

The contractual expiry date of a lease.

Joint and Several Liability

If a tenant consists of more than one party, such as a partnership, and the lease imposes joint and several liability on all parties comprised in the tenant, the landlord can look to any one or more of them for performance of obligations. If the lease imposes joint and several liability on the tenant and on all assignees, the landlord can look to the existing or any prior tenant during the term for performance of obligations.

Keeper

The Keeper of the Registers of Scotland, who is responsible for maintaining the Land Register of Scotland and other registers including the Books of Council and Session.

Lammas

A quarter or term day in Scotland, formerly August 1, but now by statute August 28 except where the old date of August 1 is expressly referred to in the relevant document.

Land Certificate

The Land Certificate is evidence of an owner's title or right to heritable property in Scotland.

Land Register of Scotland

A public register of interests in land in Scotland based on the Ordnance Survey Map. Registered title (heritable or leasehold) carries UK Government indemnity (guarantee) of good title, provided there is no qualification to the indemnity stated.

Lease (of heritable property)

A contract hiring for a finite period land/buildings to a tenant, setting up rights and obligations of the parties.

Letter of Obligation

A letter, issued by a solicitor undertaking to produce something or giving other obligations. It is usually addressed to the solicitor acting on behalf of the other party to a transaction. Certain obligations are given by the solicitor as agent for and on behalf of his client.

Licence

A form of occupancy agreement that is not a lease.

Licence for Works

A document in which the landlord consents to works that the tenant wants to carry out, and which provides for obligation relating to the carrying out, and sometimes also the reinstatement, of the works.

Long Lease

A lease with a duration of more than 20 years, i.e. at least 20 years and one day. A lease that is shorter than a long lease cannot be registered in the Land Register.

Market Rent

The estimated amount of rent for premises at the date in question between willing landlord and willing tenant at arm's length, after proper marketing, and with both parties acting knowledgeably, prudently and freely.

Marketable Title

Where a proprietor has title to a property that is essentially good and is capable of being transferred to another.

Martinmas

A quarter or term day in Scotland, formerly November 11, but now November 28 except where the old date of November 11 is expressly referred to in the relevant documents.

Minute of Extension of Lease

A document that contains an agreement to lengthen the period of a lease.

Minute of Variation of Lease

A document that varies the provisions of an existing lease.

Minute of Waiver

A document where a party undertakes not to exercise, and waives, usually permanently, a right that they are entitled to exercise by law.

Missives

A written contract for the purchase, sale or lease of land and buildings; the missives consist of the offer and an acceptance, often with qualified acceptances in between the offer and acceptance, and are usually signed by the solicitors for the respective parties.

Notary Public

A person, commonly a lawyer, who is authorised to administer an oath.

Notice to quit

A notice in statutory form given by either party to a lease, indicating his or her intention to terminate a lease at the contractual expiry of the term or at the end of any period of tacit relocation.

Offer

An offer, usually to buy or lease a property, which forms part of the Missives.

Overriding interests

These are rights such as short leases and servitudes that bind owners of land and buildings, although they do not appear in the Land Register.

Personal Bar

Loss of the right to enforce an obligation or to object to a breach, due to the party's own actions or inaction.

Pre-emption

The right in favour of a party to match a competing offer or to buy an interest in land.

Premium

A lump-sum payment, usually by a tenant to a landlord at the start of a lease, or by an assignee to an assignor on assignation (transfer) of a lease.

Prescription

The operation of law to create or extinguish a right on expiry of a specified time period.

Prescriptive Period

The period after which a right is created or extinguished. There are different periods for different rights.

Probative/Self-proving

A document that has been signed in accordance with the Requirements of Writing (Scotland) Act 1995. Such a document will be considered valid in court, and the onus is on the party challenging it to prove it is invalid.

Property Enquiry Certificate (or Report)

A Certificate or Report that gives information about a property regarding the status of roads, drains, sewers, outstanding notices, etc. which can be obtained from private searching companies as well as from the local authority. There is no priority period in Scotland.

Public Right of Way

A right in favour of the general public to cross by a designated route land that is privately owned.

P16 Report/Property Definition Report

A report detailing any discrepancies between the boundaries of a property as narrated in the title or as shown on a deed plan, and the Ordnance Survey map used by the Land Register.

Qualified Acceptance

A letter forming part of the Missives accepting the terms of a formal offer or of a prior qualified acceptance, subject to further qualifications.

Quarter days

Candlemas, Lammas, Martinmas and Whitsunday. Also known as term days.

Real Right

A right to property (whether moveable or heritable) that is good against claims by a third party.

Register of Charges

A public register that shows details of any standard security, floating charge or other security granted by a registered company or limited partnership. The Register of Charges is maintained by the Registrar of Companies.

Register of Inhibitions and Adjudications

A register maintained by the Keeper containing details of entries that prevent the holder of an interest in land from giving good title or from granting a good charge.

Registered Proprietor

The person who is registered in the Land Register as the owner of an interest in property.

Register of Sasines

A register of property deeds (which is being replaced by the Land Register) which records title to property.

Registration Dues

The amount to be paid in order to have legal documents registered in the Land Register or the Books of Council and Session.

Registration for Execution

Registration for execution in the Books of Council and Session enables fast-track enforcement of payment of specific sums of money, and is equivalent to a court judgment of debt.

Rei Interitus

Where a property is destroyed or is so damaged that performance of the contract is no longer possible, with the result that existing rights and obligations cease. This rule is usually contracted out of in commercial leases.

Resile/Rescind

Where a party withdraws from a contract or missives on the grounds of material breach by the other party. The noun is "rescission".

Renunciation

This is similar to a surrender in England. However, in English land law, when a tenant surrenders the lease to a landlord, the landlord obtains the tenant's interest in the property, and any sub-leases remain in force. This is not necessarily the case in Scotland, where the sub-tenant's interest might be terminated, unless the landlord specifically consented to the sub-lease and acknowledged that it would continue even if the main lease has been terminated, or if the renunciation is subject to and with the benefit of the sub-lease.

Reverse Premium

A lump-sum payment, usually by a landlord to a tenant at the start of a lease, or by an assignor to an assignee on assignation (transfer) of a lease.

Seabed

Land below low water mark. Usually owned by the Crown Estate.

Section 75 Agreement

An agreement between a land owner and a planning authority to create planning conditions as title conditions. The planning authority can require such an agreement to be entered into before issuing planning permission.

SEPA

The Scottish Environmental Protection Agency, who protect the environment in Scotland.

Service Charge

A sum of money paid in return for provision of services, which are most commonly maintenance and repair services.

Servitude

A right exercisable by the owner of one piece of ground over an adjacent piece of ground, for example a right of access or a right to lay pipes or cables, with access for maintenance purposes. Known in England as an easement.

Solum

The area of ground on which a building has been constructed. An owner of a building will also own the solum, unless there is provision to the contrary, but will not necessarily own the mineral rights.

Stamp Duty Land Tax (SDLT)

Tax payable by the transferee or tenant on a purchase or lease transaction.

Standard Security

Equivalent to a legal charge or mortgage, it secures the land or the leasehold interest in respect of obligations of the granter. Statute has created certain standard conditions, most of which can be expressly varied.

Summary Diligence

If the lease contains a clause saying that the tenant consents to registration for execution, the landlord can do summary diligence, i.e. fast-track enforcement, without having to go to court, to recover any rent or other specific sum which the tenant has not paid.

Suspensive Condition

A condition which requires to be satisfied before a missive is to be performed.

Tacit Relocation

The continuation of a lease after its contractual expiry date by operation of law because neither party has taken steps to terminate the lease by giving sufficient notice, and then acting on that notice.

Tack

An old fashioned name for a lease in Scotland.

Tack Duty

An old fashioned name for rent.

Tenement

Another word for land but commonly now means a traditional building of residential flats or a building of shops on the ground floor and flats above.

Testing-clause

The clause that sets out details of when, where and by whom the deed was signed, and gives details of the witness.

Wayleave

Another word for servitude. It is usually used to create a right to cross or run services across land belonging to another.

Whitsunday

A quarter or term day in Scotland, formerly May 15, but now by statute May 28 except where the old date of May 15 is expressly referred to in the relevant documents.

Yield

The annual financial return from an investment expressed as a percentage of capital value or cost.

CHAPTER 1

DOING THE TRANSACTION:
COMMERCIAL AND PRACTICAL POINTS

Introduction

In this Chapter, we consider the more commercial and practical aspects of **1–01**
doing a lease transaction. Most of the material in this chapter relates to new
leases, but many of the points are also relevant for sub-leases and assignations.
It is helpful for each side to be aware of the issues involved and to anticipate
where delays may occur, and to set in motion the actions needed to overcome
the challenges and obstacles. We live in a commercial world, where landlords
want their property to be income producing as soon as possible and want to be
relieved of having to pay "empty rates", and where tenants do not want to be
held up from fitting out and opening for business. It is better to highlight to the
client the problems that will (or may) arise, so that they can budget their cash-
flow and opening timetable accordingly.

We deal with the legal aspects of various topics as follows:

Missives: Ch.6
Common law: Ch.3
SDLT and VAT: Ch.23

The client's background

Is the client well acquainted with lease transactions? If so, then much time will **1–02**
be saved and much respect gained by acknowledging to the client that you are
aware that he is familiar with the main concepts of leasing commercial property in Scotland, and thus not having to explain in full detail many of the things
with which he will be familiar. However, be wary of falling into the trap of
assuming he knows more than he does—therein lies the road to claims!

Clients who are used to dealing in England

Is the client used to dealing with property in England, and relatively new to **1–03**
dealing in Scotland? If so, then it is important to explain that in Scotland:

(a) the tenant has no right to renew a lease, other than a very limited right
   in respect of shops;
(b) there are very few statutory provisions and protections for tenants in
   Scotland;
(c) there is no privity of contract and no provision for authorised guarantee agreements. Some (mainly older) Scottish leases provide for
   joint and several liability (where the original, and each succeeding
   tenant is fully liable for all obligations of the tenant, with the landlord

being entitled to choose which to seek performance from, leaving that party to claim relief from the current tenant) but it is unusual to find this in a modern commercial lease;

(d) there is no implied term that the landlord is to act reasonably, except in respect of repairs;

(e) there is no obligation on the landlord to adhere to the service charge code, and

(e) generally, the law is very different to that of England, in the area of commercial leases.

Heads of terms

1–04 The heads of terms set out the main aspects of the transaction, such as the parties, the premises, the term (with any options), rent, rent review cycle, rent concessions, and permitted use. They do not set out the full legal obligations of the parties.

Very often, a schedule of condition will be provided for—this is a report in photographs and/or words, on the state of the premises, and is used to water down the tenant's repairing, etc. obligations. If a schedule of condition is provided for, then it is very important that the lease contains the relevant concession.

It is important to check with the client that he accepts what is in the heads of terms and to identify any inaccuracies, and any changes that may have been agreed since the heads of terms were prepared. As they are merely a summary of the main commercial points, they will not deal with the actual detail of the legal clauses that are to go into the lease. Although the solicitor on the other side will be surprised to see drafting that is directly contrary to what is stated in the heads of terms, he should not object to something appearing in the lease that is not provided for in the heads of terms.

Remember that the "deal is not done" until missives have been concluded or, if there is no missive, until the lease is signed. The heads of terms are merely the start of the transaction—they are not tablets of stone!

The parties

1–05 It is important to check that if the lease is a head lease, i.e. there is no lease above it, and it is being granted by the (supposed) owner of the property, that the landlord is infeft in the property (i.e. he is the registered or recorded title holder). If the lease is a sub-lease or a sub-under lease, etc. check that the landlord has a lease that can be traced up to the title holder. If what is being granted is not a head lease, then it is very important to understand the hierarchy of leasehold interests, as your tenant client may believe he is obtaining a direct lease from the owner, when in fact he may merely be obtaining a sub-under-lease. The validity and sufficiency of the granter's leasehold title should be checked.

If you are acting for the landlord you should check that the proposed tenant is correctly stated and is satisfactory—if it is a limited company, check the name—the proposed tenant's grandiose sounding name may merely be a dormant company within the tenant group. Be aware that companies often swap or change names, but that the registered number always stays with the company.

If the tenant is a company, is the landlord satisfied that the company is likely to have the funds to pay the rent and other sums, such as insurance premiums and the cost of exclusive as well as common repairs, and service charge, and to perform the other obligations of the tenant from time to time? If it does not appear to satisfy this requirement, the landlord should consider obtaining a guarantee from a suitable guarantor or obtaining a performance deposit from the tenant (see Ch.24), or some other security, such as a standard security over the house of the individual who is behind the corporate entity etc.

Guarantees

We deal with guarantees in detail in Ch.20. The main points to consider at this **1–06** stage are, who is the guarantor, and are they of sufficient means to be able to grant a satisfactory guarantee? Has your client seen evidence of their financial position, or is he just assuming that because the proposed guarantor is the shareholder or director of the company, or the parent of the tenant they have a wallet deep enough to meet all the obligations of the tenant—has any financial information on the guarantor been produced?

If the guarantor itself is a limited company, then it is necessary for there to be a commercial benefit to the company in granting the guarantee, otherwise it can be challenged by the shareholders of that company and by a liquidator, etc.

The other matters to be considered in respect of guarantees are the period of time for which they are to be in place, the amount of monetary obligations and any non-monetary obligations that are the subject of the guarantee, whether the guarantee is terminated on a permitted assignation of the lease, and whether the guarantee is available to anyone who buys the landlord's interest, or whether the guarantee is to be personal to only the initial landlord.

Premises

Are the premises correctly stated and, if they are shown on a plan, is the client **1–07** satisfied with the location, extent and accessibility of the premises? Are there any ancillary rights that should go with the premises, such as parking, and, if so, is it dedicated parking spaces or a right to park in a specified area, subject to availability of space at any time?

Term

How long is the lease to run for? The landlord will want as long a period as is **1–08** achievable, subject to any redevelopment intentions he may have. The tenant will want the flexibility not only of being able to walk away if the premises cease to be suitable or desirable, but also to stay on if he is trading well. Separately, if the tenant wants to grant a standard security over his leasehold interest, then the period must be a minimum of 20 years and 1 day, otherwise it is incompetent to grant a standard security over it.

For the past few years many tenants have been insisting on a break option, i.e. the right to terminate early. If a break option is to be provided then the landlord needs to consider whether any, and if so which, conditions are to be attached to the right being exercised, such as:

    (a) all rent and other payments have been paid up to date at the time the option is exercised;
    (b) all rent and other payments having always been paid on time;
    (c) non-monetary obligations have been performed in full;

(d) whether any one or more of the above are to be the position as at the date of service of the early termination notice and/or at the actual date of termination.

If the lease provides for a payment to be made by the tenant to the landlord in order to terminate early, then this may be unenforceable as being in the nature of a penalty. Many leases will try to avoid the "penalty" problem by stating the payment as being an agreed sum payable to the landlord as compensation for loss of future rent. The competency and effectiveness of such drafting has not been tested in the courts.

Some leases contain an option in favour of the tenant to renew or extend the lease, and once again, these may be subject to conditions—a landlord is unlikely to want to have the tenant stay beyond the originally contracted term if the tenant has not paid rent, etc. on time and has not performed his other obligations properly.

Options to break are full of difficulties (see Ch.18: Termination, and Ch. 22: Inter naturalia).

Stamp Duty Land Tax

1–09 We deal in some detail with Stamp Duty Land Tax in Ch. 23. However, it is worth focusing briefly, but very meaningfully, on SDLT at the initial stages. The tenant does not want any nasty surprises and it is worth explaining to him how much, if any, SDLT is payable. This of course depends on the amount of rent payable initially and during the first five years of the term, and on the duration of the lease. A helpful SDLT calculator function is available on HMRC's website.

In April 2015, Stamp Duty Land Tax will be replaced by Land and Buildings Transaction Tax. Details of how this new tax will be applied to commercial leases are not yet known, but the intention is that is will be a more straightforward tax than SDLT.

VAT

1–10 We deal with VAT in some detail in Ch. 23, but it is worth considering at this point whether VAT will create any difficulties for the tenant. Some tenants are not able to recover VAT, such as financial services, funeral directors, and insurance brokers, and so, if any of these tenants have to pay VAT on rent and other sums under the lease, they will not be able to reclaim or set-off that VAT. The VAT element will therefore be an extra cost to them. The Heads of Terms may be silent about VAT, but VAT may in fact be chargeable on rent and other sums. Even if VAT is not presently chargeable, then the landlord is entitled at any time to register the property for VAT and thus make VAT chargeable, unless the lease prohibits the landlord from registering the property for VAT.

Incentives

1–11 Has any incentive been offered to the tenant to take the lease, such as a contribution to fitting-out works or other payment of money or a rent free period? If not, should this not be suggested to the tenant and negotiated in to the deal (depending on the state of the market and the demand for the premises)?

If an incentive has been offered, then the tenant should be advised by a surveyor as to whether the amount of incentive is appropriate for these premises in the then current market.

From the landlord's point of view, a rent-free period at the start of the lease means that there is no income stream until the end of the rent free period. Many landlords want to "see the colour of the tenant's money" and they will insist on receiving an initial payment at the start of the lease, with the rent free period being dealt with by postponing the next payment of rent-until the end of the rent free period plus the pre-paid period.

Surveyor's input

The surveyor-agent's job does *not* finish when he issues the heads of terms. It **1–12** is important that the solicitor and the surveyor acting for the client liaise together on the main commercial terms of the lease, especially anything that could impact on marketability of the client's interest, such as rent review, assignation and sub-letting, etc.

The tenant should always be advised to have the premises surveyed so as to identify any wants of repair. If the premises form part of a larger building or other entity then some consideration should be given as to whether there are any wants of repair or defects in the common parts. In recent years many leases have included directly in the lease, or at least in a back letter, a schedule of condition, specifying the state of repair and condition of the property at commencement of the lease, with the purpose of excluding the tenant from liability to make good any wants of repair or defects shown in the schedule of condition.

If there is a managing agent or a factor for the larger entity then a letter should be obtained confirming that there are no repairs instructed but not yet carried out and that there are no major repairs or improvements contemplated.

Fitting out and alteration works

In many cases the tenant will want to change the premises so as to be suitable **1–13** for it to trade. It is sensible to ask the tenant at the start of the transaction for details of any fitting out works that it proposes doing. The tenant should be made aware that the following consents will be necessary:

(a) landlord's consent;
(b) head landlord's or any superior landlord's consent;
(c) the head landlord's or any inferior landlord's chargeholder's consent—most standard securities and floating charges will prohibit alterations except with the chargeholder's (lender's) consent.
(d) other proprietors in any building of which the premises form part, if the proposed works deal in any way with common parts. For example, if a flue is needed for extraction of cooking smells then the flue will invariably have to go through the back wall of the building and be attached to the wall and go above roof height. If the external walls of the building are common, then unless there is already a right contained in the title deeds for flues to be installed, the consent of the other proprietors of the building will be needed. This could be time consuming and, if not obtained, could make it impossible for the tenant to trade form the premises.
(e) building warrant;
(f) planning permission, and if the property is, or is in, a listed building, as well as in some other situations, listed building consent.

Title deeds

1–14 The titles should be examined so as to check that the granter of the lease is infeft (if it is a head lease) and to ensure that there is a good title to the premises as well as the common parts, and that there are no adverse title conditions that could adversely affect the tenant's proposed use of the premises or the hours of trading. The search in the property or land registers will show if there is any standard security over the landlord's interest (in which case consent from the security holder is needed), and the charges search will show if there is any floating charge or debenture, and if so then consent and a letter of non-crystallisation should be obtained.

Service charge and common charges

1–15 If the premises are part of a larger entity, the tenant should be made aware of the common charges or service charge regime, and be given details of payments that were required during the previous three years, as well as a budget for the current year, so that the tenant is aware of historical as well as, to some extent, imminent liabilities. The heads of terms may provide for a fixed or capped share of liability, or if not, then there may be the opportunity to negotiate this.

Pre-transaction information

1–16 The tenant should ask for a property enquiry report to check there are no outstanding notices or orders (although one should be aware that some older, yet unsatisfied, notices or orders may not appear on the report). He should also ask to see planning permissions, listed building consents, building warrants, completion certificates, notices of acceptance of completion certificates and relevant drawings. If the tenant does not see these items then he may have to make good any breach that has occurred in the past if a statutory notice is served after commencement of the lease.

Inter naturalia

1–17 We deal in detail with this matter in some detail in Ch. 22, but at this stage it should be remembered that only those obligations that are *normally* found in leases will be enforceable against successors of the landlord's/tenant's interest. Therefore, if you are putting any unusual or quirky provisions into the lease, you should only expect these to be enforceable by and against the original parties, so that if the landlord sells the property with the benefit of the lease, or if the tenant assigns his interest, the obligation will most likely fall away.

Softening of obligations for first tenant

1–18 Depending on the state of the market at the time, the location of the premises, and the negotiating strength of the parties, the tenant may be able to negotiate certain concessions that the landlord will agree to, on the basis that these are available only to the first tenant. It is normal for these concessions to be contained in a back letter, and if so, then the back letter should be stated to be for only the first tenant and to be incapable of being assigned (in which case the concessions will still apply if the tenant sub-lets) and that, if the landlord disposes of its interest, then it will ensure that any party to whom it does dispose will grant a back letter in exactly the same terms. If the landlord, having given such a "perpetuation" obligation, fails to honour it when he sells on, the tenant is left with a claim for damages against the landlord, who may no longer exist, or have disappeared, or be insolvent

The mechanics of the transaction

Normally the landlord will produce a draft offer and draft lease which are then **1–19** revised by the tenant, counter-revised by the landlord, and so on. There are some good reasons why we have missives—first, so as to provide for the lease and any ancillary documents, such as a licence for works, deposit agreement, back letter, etc. to be binding from the date of entry, even if they have not yet been signed and delivered; and secondly to deal with ancillary matters, such as production of searches, planning and other local authority documentation, any conditionality and the provision of any back letters. The missives will also provide for a timetable for the documents being produced, signed and delivered.

The landlord will usually produce the engrossments of the documents, and these will be signed by the tenant and by any guarantor, and then passed to the landlord's solicitors for execution by the landlord. The landlord's solicitors will then complete the details of signing and will register the deeds in the Books of Council and Session. If the lease is for longer than 20 years, then it does not matter to the landlord whether or not the tenant registers his lease in the Land Register of Scotland, and accordingly the tenant should provide for this to happen at the same time as the lease is registered in the Books of Council and Session. Alternatively the tenant could wait for the Books of Council and Session Extract to be produced and then proceed to register that extract in the Land Register of Scotland. However, he will not obtain a valid leasehold title, and will not be able to grant a good standard security over his leasehold interest, until such time as the lease is registered in the Land Register of Scotland. Accordingly he may be reluctant to wait for the Books of Council and Session Extract to be produced.

If the transaction is notifiable for Stamp Duty Land Tax purposes then the SDLT Return must be lodged no later than 30 days after the "effective date", which in most lease transactions will be the date of entry.

Insolvency before date of entry (settlement)

If either party becomes insolvent before the start of the lease, then the liqui- **1–20** dator, etc. can choose to not proceed with the transaction, leaving the other with a claim as an ordinary creditor for damages. If the insolvency occurs after the lease has started, then the parties are bound, which may be cool comfort! The lease document may not have been executed, but the missives may provide for the terms of the agreed draft to apply from the date of entry as if it had been executed and delivered.

CHAPTER 2

LEASES AND LICENCES

Introduction

2–01 It is important to know whether an occupancy arrangement is a lease or a licence, as there are significant differences between the two. There are common law rules and statutory protections that apply to leases, but these do not apply to licences. Just because a document is called a licence, it does not follow that it is indeed a licence. Even if a document states that it is not a lease, it may, in fact, be found to be a lease.

In this chapter, we consider the Scottish and then the English position on the difference between a lease and a licence to occupy commercial premises, and we look at how leases are created.

A—SCOTLAND

Lease or licence

2–02 If a non-permanent right to occupy or use land or buildings is being granted, it is very important to determine whether that right is a lease or a licence, as the law provides for significantly different rules for each of these.

Licences are often used for advertising hoardings, small kiosks in shopping centres and rights to park a vehicle in a car park, or if occupation is temporary or non-exclusive, such as in serviced office accommodation. The distinction is important—a lease will bind a new owner if the property is sold, will entitle the landlord to various remedies, and will give the tenant some measure of statutory protection.

A lease is subject to the various obligations, rules and warranties that are provided by common law,[1] except to the extent that these are contracted out of, whereas a licence does not have these constraints. A lease is usually enforceable by the tenant against any party to whom the original landlord has sold or transferred the property, whereas a licence is only enforceable against the original licensor.

There is no stamp duty land tax on a licence to use or occupy land.

2–03 A licence is a contract which grants a right to use land or buildings. The main aspects for identifying a licence include the express terms of the agreement and whether or not there is exclusive possession, whether or not an occupancy fee is charged and whether there is a defined or ascertainable termination date.

A document may be called a "licence", but may in fact be a lease if it has the elements required for leases, such as exclusive possession, a rent and an

---

[1] See Ch.3.

ascertainable termination date. In *Wilson & Co v Assessor for Kincardineshire*[2] it was held that an agreement between a hotel owner and an advertising firm that allowed the firm to put up an advertisement board in exchange for an annual payment for three years, but which could be terminated on three months' notice, was a lease.

However, in *UK Advertising Co v Glasgow Bag-Wash Laundry*[3] it was held that the right to display adverts in post offices for three years in moveable frames on the walls or in the windows of certain post offices for payment of a fixed annual sum for each advert and for the hire of each frame, and all subject to the approval of the Postmaster General, was not a lease, but was in fact a licence to use the spaces. One test in such cases is whether possession of any piece of heritable property is given and, if so, whether such possession is intended to be exclusive or only partial. If it is exclusive, the contract may be a lease, but if it is only partial, then the contract is likely to be a licence.

In *Broomhill Motor Co v Assessor for Glasgow*[4] premises belonging to **2–04** motor garage businesses comprising a large number of separate lockups were let for varying periods to private car owners at rents that included water, heat, light, washing facilities, etc. Each occupant had a key, but the garage company reserved a right of access for inspection and cleaning. Some of the lockups could be entered from the street, but others could only be entered through the garage premises. This was held to be a lease because it gave exclusive possession and there were no services provided. In *Chaplin v Assessor for Perth*[5] the owner of a piece of ground constructed wooden lockups, each with its own key, and he let these as garages to car owners under a verbal agreement for a weekly or daily payment. Either party could terminate at a week's notice and no services were given. It was held this was a lease, as each occupier had exclusive possession and there were no services included.

In *Mann v Houston*[6] an agreement stated that it was a licence, but the court held that in fact it was a lease, and that calling it a licence was an obvious sham, designed to avoid the legal consequences of being a lease.

In *Brador Properties Limited v British Telecommunications plc,*[7] a lease prohibited sub-letting except with the landlord's consent which was not to be unreasonably withheld; breach of the clause would entitle the landlord to irritate the lease. The tenant requested landlord's consent to grant a sub-lease and this was refused. The tenant then entered into agreements with various parties to provide services and facilities, including use of an allocated office room, with a right in his favour to change the location of the room on 14 days' notice. Each occupant was given a set of keys and an entry card. The court held that the arrangements were in fact sub-leases and that the tenant was trying to avoid the restrictions on sub-letting. One of the cardinal elements of a lease is the grant of certain and definite subjects, and the court held that the arrangements were leases even though the landlord was entitled to change the actual room that the occupant would use. The issue of keys and entry card implied exclusive possession.

---

[2] *Wilson & Co v Assessor for Kincardineshire*, 1913 S.C. 704.
[3] *UK Advertising Co v Glasgow Bag-Wash Laundry*, 1926 S.C. 303.
[4] *Broomhill Motor Co v Assessor for Glasgow*, 1927 S.C. 447.
[5] *Chaplin v Assessor for Perth*, 1947 S.C. 373.
[6] *Mann v Houston*, 1957 S.L.T. 89.
[7] *Brador Properties Ltd v British Telecommunications plc*, 1992 S.L.T. 490.

Creating a lease

2–05 A lease for less than one year or shorter does not need to be constituted in writing. In order to create a lease:

- there must be a landlord and a tenant;
- the parties must have reached agreement on the main terms;
- it must relate to occupancy of heritable property, i.e. land or buildings;
- there must be a rent payable (albeit only a very nominal rent). A capital sum paid at entry without any continuing rent is not good enough; and
- there must be a defined or ascertainable termination date.

Mere negotiations are not enough to set up a lease; it is not sufficient for the tenant to agree to a reasonable or market rent.[8] The term does not need to be defined as having an absolute end date, provided there is an ascertainable end date such as the occurrence of an event.

It has been held that co-proprietors cannot grant a lease to one of their number unless the tenant expressly divests himself of his co-proprietorship interest.[9]

2–06 A lease is a contract between two parties: the landlord and the tenant. The tenant will not obtain a "real right", which is good against all third parties, including in particular anyone who buys the property from the landlord, unless:

- the lease, if for more than a year, is in writing;
- the tenant's interest in the lease, if it lasts for, or is capable of lasting for, more than 20 years, is registered in the Land Register of Scotland, unless the lease was granted, or the tenant acquired his leasehold title, before the county in which the premises are situated became operational for land registration in Scotland;
- if the lease lasts for no longer than 20 years, the tenant has taken possession of the premises; and
- the landlord was the registered owner at the time the lease was granted, had the property conveyed to him after the lease had begun or has a valid leasehold title traceable back to the owner.

It does not matter to the landlord whether or not the tenant's interest is registered in the Land Register of Scotland. However, the landlord will invariably want to register the lease for execution in the Books of Council and Session, in order that the landlord can undertake fast-track enforcement against the tenant if the tenant is in breach of his specific monetary obligations under the lease.

If a lease is stated to run for a specified period of time, and thereafter from month to month, or year to year, etc. then the tenant has a real right, good against successor landlords, but only for the original specified period.[10]

---

[8] *Gray v Edinburgh University*, 1962 S.C. 157; 1962 S.L.T. 173.
[9] *Clydesdale Bank v Davidson*, 1994 S.C.L.R. 828, *Bell's Executors v Inland Revenue*, 1987 S.L.T. 625.
[10] *Campbell v McKinnon* (1867) 5 M. 636.

B—ENGLAND

Lease or licence

In England there is a vast body of statute law that gives protection to tenants, **2–07** and hence the practice grew for landowners to try and enter into arrangements that were licences, so as to avoid the protective legislation.

A lease gives an interest in land, but a licence does not give such an interest. A licence is merely a personal privilege, and its purpose is to make lawful that which would otherwise be unlawful.

Contractual licences do not bind a successor in title of the original granter.

It has been held in England that the grant of a right to erect an advertising hoarding on imprecisely identified areas of land[11] and display adverts on it is not exclusive possession of the land itself.[12]

Payment of rent is not an essential prerequisite to the grant of a tenancy, and it has been held that a lease may exist even though no rent is payable under it if there is exclusive possession.[13]

In England a licence can be granted for a fixed term or until the occurrence **2–08** of an event or until terminated on notice.

The leading English authority on licences is *Street v Mountford*,[14] concerning an agreement granting the right to occupy two rooms at £37 per week, subject to termination on 14 days' notice. It was called a Licence Agreement, and it contained a declaration that the grantee understood that this did not give her a tenancy which would be protected under the Rent Acts. The House of Lords held that where residential accommodation is granted for a term at a rent with exclusive possession and there is no attendance or services, then the arrangement between the parties is a lease. Exclusive possession is of first importance in considering whether it is a tenancy, but is not decisive, because an occupier is not necessarily a tenant if he has exclusive possession. He may be a lodger or a service occupier, or he may fall within other exceptional categories.

Creation of leases

A lease is defined as "the grant of a right to the exclusive possession of land for **2–09** a determinate term, less than that which the grantor has himself in the land".[15]

For a lease to exist in England:

- there must be a landlord and a tenant and premises;
- the duration must be sufficiently defined; and
- there must be an intention on the part of the landlord to grant, and on the part of the tenant to take, the lease.

Unlike in Scotland, there does not have to be a rent payable, although it is customary, if there is no monetary rent, for the rent to be stated as a peppercorn.

---

[11] *Clear Channel UK Ltd v Manchester City Council* [2005] EWCA 1304; [2006] L. & T. R. 7.

[12] *Ashburn Anstalt v WJ Arnold & Co* [1989] Ch. 1.

[13] *Ashburn Anstalt v WJ Arnold & Co* [1989] Ch. 1.

[14] *Street v Mountford* [1985] A.C. 809; [1985] 2 All E.R. 289.

[15] Woodfall, *Law of Landlord and Tenant* (London: Sweet and Maxwell), para.1.003.

In *Street v Mountford*[16] the House of Lords set out the principles that for a lease to exist there must be exclusive possession for a fixed or periodic term and either payment of a capital amount or periodical payments.

A lease for three years or shorter at the best rent reasonably achievable can be in writing or verbal. A lease for more than three years must be made by written deed, and this includes a lease for more than three years which can be terminated within the first three years. Since July 31, 1990, an instrument is not a deed unless it clearly states that it is intended to be a deed and is validly executed as a deed. The common practice in England is for a "part and coun-terpart" to be prepared. The landlord executes one print of the document and gives this to the tenant, and the tenant signs the other print and gives this to the landlord.

Deferred start date

2–10   In terms of s.149(3) of the Law of Property Act 1925, a lease will be invalid if the period of time between the grant of the lease and the date of possession is greater than 21 years. However, if the grant of the lease is preceded by an agreement for lease, then there is no limit to the period between the date of the contract and the grant of the lease, so long as the tenant takes possession within 21 years of the date of the grant.

Uncertain duration

2–11   Where a commercial lease is expressed to last for the lifetime of the tenant, it is deemed to be for a 90-year fixed-term lease, terminable before that date on the death of the tenant by one month's written notice on or after death.

A tenant who has entered into possession and has started to pay rent can get some protection through the creation of a periodic tenancy in default. An express periodic tenancy is where the parties agree to enter into a yearly tenancy or a tenancy from year to year. The lease will initially last for one year, but when this expires it will continue for another year and so on, until either party terminates by serving the appropriate notice. For shorter periods, the notice is at least one full period expiring at the end of a period. If a tenant wants to terminate a monthly tenancy, he must give at least one month's notice, ending at the end of the month. If there are either joint landlords or joint tenants, then any joint owner can serve a notice to quit.

In *Prudential Assurance v London Residuary Body*[17] a lease was granted for the period until the local authority landlord required the land for road widening, but the project was subsequently abandoned. The former council sold the land and the purchaser served notice to quit. The House of Lords held that the lease was void from uncertainty because the period of grant was an indeterminate term, but they held that there is a yearly periodic tenancy that could be terminated by the landlord serving the appropriate notice to quit, in this case six months.

2–12   If a lease is granted for a fixed term with an option in favour of the tenant to renew, the tenancy will end on expiry of the term unless the tenant exercises the option. If a fixed term with an option to renew is granted, then great care

---

[16] *Street v Mountford* [1985] A.C. 809.
[17] *Prudential Assurance v London Residuary Body* [1992] 2 A.C. 386.

should be taken to avoid any provision that the renewal is on the same terms, otherwise this will also contain an option to renew. This effectively creates a perpetually renewable tenancy, which by statute is converted into a 2,000-year, fixed-term lease. The courts have held that although the term of a periodic tenancy is not certain at the outset, either party has the right to make it certain by serving a notice to terminate at the appropriate time. In other words, the duration is within the power of the parties. Therefore the court will not allow any restriction on the power of either party to terminate the lease when the appropriate time comes.

A lease can be for any length of time short of perpetuity (unlike Scotland, where the maximum is 175 years unless authorised by an Act of Parliament). A lease for a lifetime or terminable on the marriage of the tenant, or formation of a civil partnership between the tenant and another person, takes effect as a lease for 90 years, terminable after the death, marriage, etc.

A lease can be limited to take effect immediately or from a future date within **2–13** 21 years of the grant of the lease. A reversionary lease is one that takes effect from a future date. This is different to a lease of the reversion, which is a lease that takes effect immediately but does so subject to and with the benefit of an existing lease.

A perpetually renewable lease (giving the tenant a right to renew the lease for a further period on the expiration of the term) is possible, but since 1925 such leases are converted into a fixed term of 2,000 years subject to the tenant's right to terminate the lease on 10 days' notice in writing on any occasion when the original lease would have expired, had it not been renewed. The landlord does not have a similar right to terminate.

A concurrent lease (or a lease of the reversion) is where a landlord has granted a lease to a tenant, but he then grants an interposed lease to another party of the same premises. The grantee cannot take physical possession because the tenant is already entitled to possession, so the new lease is seen as a lease of landlord's reversion on the tenant's lease. If the new lease is longer than that in favour of the tenant then the grantee of the new lease will eventually be able to take physical possession of the property. Otherwise he acts simply as the tenant's immediate landlord, collecting any rent due and enforcing the provisions of the lease.

More than one tenant

A lease can be granted to two or more persons to hold as joint tenants, but **2–14** it cannot be vested in more than four persons. On the death of one of them, the others become entitled by survivorship to the whole of the interest remaining in the lease. If the lease is to a partnership of four or fewer partners, then the partners are the parties to the lease, but if there are more than four partners, then the first four named partners will hold as joint tenants in trust.

In England, an agent with sufficient authority can grant a lease on behalf of his principal. An agent cannot sign a lease as agent for an undisclosed principal, so as to make that principal the tenant.

The lease of a floor of the building extends at least as far as the joists of the underside of the floor above it. The outside walls are deemed to be part of the premises in a multi-storey building, unless the outside wall is excluded or reserved or there is an inference to the contrary.

Registration of leases

2–15 Every lease for more than seven years must be registered in the Land Registry, as must a lease of any duration where possession is not to be given for at least three months. The transfer of unregistered leases with more than seven years remaining must be registered.

Concurrent (over-riding) leases

2–16 A concurrent or overriding lease is one granted subject to and with the benefit of a lease that is already in existence.

CHAPTER 3

COMMON LAW AND IMPLIED TERMS

Introduction

When entering into a lease, it is tempting to believe that the whole landlord and **3–01** tenant relationship and all obligations are contained in the actual lease document. The lease will only contain the whole information if it has contracted out of the very significant terms that are implied at common law. The common law fills in any gaps so as to provide a set of rules that will apply, but it should be remembered that the courts will not write or rewrite a lease so as to make it work. In addition, there are some terms implied by statute that will affect the lease. It is of the utmost importance that these common law and statutory provisions are understood.

The specific clauses in commercial leases that deal with the various aspects of common law, and their interaction with common law, and a summary of the corresponding English law provisions are addressed in the relevant chapters in this book.

A—SCOTLAND—IMPLIED TERMS

At common law, there are obligations and certain rules that automatically apply unless the lease document says otherwise.

Tenant's obligations

   (a) To enter into possession, and initially to occupy and use the premises. **3–02**
   (b) To pay rent when due.
   (c) To plenish. The tenant is required to stock the premises with moveable items to provide security for the rent, so as to enable the landlord to exercise his right of hypothec, which gives him the right to sell off moveable property on the premises in order to recover the rent.
   (d) To take reasonable care of the premises. The tenant is liable for any damage to the property caused by his non-occupancy. In *Smith v Henderson*[1] the tenant left a house unoccupied without telling the landlord. A water pipe burst and ran for days, and the windows were broken because the house looked dirty and deserted. The court held that the tenant was liable to the landlord in damages for breach of his obligation to take reasonable care of the premises.

---

[1] *Smith v Henderson*, 1897 24 R. 1102; (1897) 5 S.L.T. 96.

In *Mickel v McCoard*[2] the tenant left a house empty during the winter without turning off the water or notifying the landlord. The house was damaged due to the bursting of water pipes through frost. The court held that the duty of a tenant is to keep the premises aired and heated to preserve the property from damp. The judgment quotes Erskine who said that a tenant must use a reasonable degree of diligence in preserving the property from injury. Here the pipes were likely to freeze in the depth of winter, and the tenant had taken no precautions to prevent the damage.

In *Fry's Metals Ltd v Durastic Ltd*[3] the tenant of a factory and office offered the keys back to the landlord at the end of a lease, but the landlord refused to accept them because the electricity and gas meters needed to be read before handover was complete. There were two separate alarm systems in the premises. The tenant had notified the security company that cover would not be required. The premises were then vandalised, and both alarm systems failed to operate. The court held that the tenant knew and accepted that the landlord relied on him to maintain the alarm system in operation after termination of the lease, and that the non-operation caused loss and damage to the landlord. The tenant was liable to the landlord for failing to protect the premises during his period of occupation after expiry of the lease.

In *Glebe Sugar Refining Co v Paterson*[4] the tenant overloaded the premises, causing damage. It was held that the tenant had failed to check whether the premises were suitable for his business, and he was held liable to the landlord in damages. This was a case of the tenant failing in his implied obligations to take reasonable care of the property.

    (e) To use the property only for the purpose let. If the tenant uses the premises for a different purpose to that for which they were let, he is "inverting possession" and the landlord can seek a court order to stop this. In *Leck v Merryflats Patent Brick Co*[5] a tenant who had leased a property for making bricks was stopped from using part of it as a private railway that had nothing to do with the brick works. In *Bayley v Addison*[6] the tenant of a meal mill was stopped from using it as a mill for grinding sawdust.

    (f) Various statutory obligations on the tenant. There are a number of obligations imposed on the tenant as occupier and as the person having control of the premises, such as to pay rates, to be responsible for compliance with asbestos regulations, to be responsible for occupier's liability, etc.

Landlord's obligations

3–03   (a) To give the tenant exclusive possession of the whole of the premises leased at the agreed commencement of the lease, for the whole of the duration of the lease. If the landlord fails to comply with this

[2] *Mickel v McCoard*, 1913 S.C. 896; (1913) 1 S.L.T. 463.
[3] *Fry's Metals Ltd v Durastic Ltd*, 1991 S.L.T. 689.
[4] *Glebe Sugar Refining Co v Paterson* (1900) 2 F. 615; (1900) 7 S.L.T. 374.
[5] *Leck v Merryflats Patent Brick Co* (1868) 5 S.L.R. 619.
[6] *Bayley v Addison* (1901) 8 S.L.T. 379.

obligation to a material extent, then the tenant can terminate the lease, or alternatively he can seek damages in the form of rent abatement.

(b) Not to derogate from the grant. Once the tenant is in the property, the landlord must not do anything to prejudice the tenant's full possession. In *Huber v Ross*[7], the landlord carried out operations to the remainder of the building, and these physically affected the premises, even though they were conducted with reasonable regard to the tenant's interests. The court held that the landlord was not only to repair the structural as well as other damage caused, but was also to compensate the tenant for loss of business due to the effect of his operations. If the landlord derogates from the grant, he is liable for the loss suffered by the tenant; deprivation of use to full advantage for the purposes for which they are let is a loss to the tenant.

In *Lomond Roads Cycling Club v Dumbarton County Council*[8] the landlord, without terminating the club's lease of a wooden hut, instructed contractors to build a school on the site. The contractors started destroying the hut, and vandals completed the destruction. The court held the destruction was at least started by landlord's contractors, and that the landlord has the obligation to put and maintain the tenant in possession of the premises. The general rule is that once possession is taken, the landlord must not do, nor allow to be done, anything to remove the tenant from the premises. If a landlord carries out building operations on neighbouring premises, then his duty is higher than if the work were done by a neighbour. The neighbour's duty is only to take reasonable care, but the landlord is liable for any structural or material physical injury to the premises because of his obligation to not derogate from the grant.

However, the landlord is not liable for acts of God or for the acts of third parties. In *Chevron Petroleum UK Ltd v Post Office*[9] a sub-tenant sought damages from his immediate landlord, who was the main tenant of the building, due to flooding of the premises. The court held there can only be a derogation of grant giving rise to a claim for damages where there is deliberate or voluntary behaviour on the landlord's part, and that there is no implied obligation on a landlord to ensure that nothing will happen on the premises that causes loss to a tenant.

In *Owlcastle Ltd v Karmik Ltd*[10] the tenant argued that the landlord had derogated from the grant by allowing the local authority to use the landlord's adjoining site for keeping building materials, and because road works were carried out outside the premises and barriers were put up on the pavement nearby, it made it difficult for the tenant's customers to enter the premises. Both of these factors reduced the tenant's profitability. The lease did not allow deductions from rent, but the tenant refused to pay rent, saying that he was postponing payment. The court held this was not derogation of grant, as there was in this case no physical and tangible damage suffered by the tenant.

---

[7] *Huber v Ross* (1912) 1 S.L.T. 399.
[8] *Lomond Roads Cycling Club v Dumbarton County Council*, 1967 S.L.T. (Sh. Ct) 35.
[9] *Chevron Petroleum UK Ltd v Post Office*, 1987 S.L.T. 588.
[10] *Owlcastle Ltd v Karmik Ltd*, 1993 G.W.D. 33–2157.

(c) To provide subjects reasonably fit for the purpose let. The premises must be wind and watertight, and in a reasonably habitable and tenantable condition. Breach of this will justify a tenant refusing to take entry, and will allow him to claim a reduction of rent.

The property is to be in reasonable condition, but not necessarily fit for a particular kind of business—the tenant is to satisfy himself on the latter. In *Glebe Sugar Refining Co v Paterson*[11] a warehouse was let to a sugar refinery company to store sugar. A month after the tenant took entry, the warehouse collapsed, and he sued the landlord, claiming that because of insecure foundations the building was unsuitable for purpose. It was held that the tenant had, according to his own trade practice, overloaded the warehouse and had failed to check whether the premises were suitable for their business, and so he was found liable to the landlord in damages.

The common law rule is that if the condition of the property makes it substantially unsuitable, this is a material breach allowing the tenant to rescind. In *McArdle v City of Glasgow District Council*[12] the landlord failed to rectify damp in the premises despite requests from the tenant. It was held that there is an implied obligation on the landlord to keep the premises tenantable and habitable, and that they had failed to do so, and were therefore liable in damages.

(d) To carry out repairs. This includes "extraordinary repairs", such as making good damage caused by any latent or inherent defect, and renewing or replacing anything that has become worn out due to the passing of time. Note that the landlord's common law repairing obligation is not a warranty; the landlord does not guarantee that the property will never fall into disrepair. The landlord's obligation switches on only when the tenant draws to his attention the need for the repair. Once the requirement for repair has been notified to the landlord, he will be in breach if he fails to carry out the repair within a reasonable time. In *Scottish Heritable Security Co Ltd v Granger*[13] the landlord took a little over two months to repair drains after being called on to do so. In the meantime the tenant had moved out and it was held that the landlord was in material breach, thus allowing the tenant to terminate.

Once the tenant has moved into premises that are reasonably fit for the purpose of let, the landlord is required to keep the premises in a tenantable and habitable condition throughout the lease. This includes the obligation to keep the premises wind and watertight.

In *Gunn v National Coal Board*[14] a ground-floor flat that was let to an employee was affected by rising damp that caused dampness and mould. The court held that the dampness was a breach of general obligation on the landlord's part to keep the premises in a habitable condition.

---

[11] *Glebe Sugar Refining Co v Paterson* (1900) 2 F. 615; (1900) 7 S.L.T. 374.
[12] *McArdle v City of Glasgow District Council*, 1989 S.C.L.R. 19.
[13] *Scottish Heritable Security Co Ltd v Granger* (1881) 8 R. 459; (1881) 18 S.L.R. 280.
[14] *Gunn v National Coal Board*, 1982 S.L.T. 526.

However, in *Whitelaw v Fulton*[15] the tenant of shop premises threatened to terminate the lease unless the landlord fixed the damp. The court held that the tenant had taken entry into the premises, had made alterations and had not complained until long after he must have known of the problem, and the tenant could therefore not terminate the lease. The court also held that the tenant has obligations at common law to furnish the premises and to fire and air the premises.

In *Wolfson v Forrester's Trustees*[16] a drain choked due to the bad workmanship of plumbers; this caused flooding of the premises, and the tenant argued that the landlord was in breach of his duty to keep the premises wind and watertight. The court held that, unless a lease provides to the contrary, the landlord is to provide and keep the premises wind and watertight, but this is not a warranty, and accordingly there is no breach by the landlord until the problem is brought to his notice and he fails to remedy it. The court also stated that "wind and water tight" means wind and watertight against the ordinary attacks of the elements, not against exceptional encroachments of water due to other causes. It was held that in this case, the landlord was not in breach, as there was no specific duty on the landlord to keep the pipe unchoked.

In *McGonigal v Pickard*[17] a tenant's bed fell through the floor due to damp and rot in the premises, and the tenant claimed that the landlord was in breach of his common law duty to keep the premises wind and watertight. The court held that keeping the premises wind and watertight means that the roof and outer walls of the structure must be kept in a condition in which they are protected against the ordinary attacks of the elements, i.e. wind, rain and snow in the ordinary course of the climate, and that in this case, the landlord was not liable.

It should be noted that there are two major exceptions to the landlord's repairing obligations:

(1) Damage caused by acts of God such as a flood or a hurricane— *Sandeman v Duncan's Trustees*[18]; and
(2) Damage caused by the action of a third party—in *Allan v James Robertson's Trustees*[19] subsidence was caused by mineral operations where someone encroached on the landlord's minerals. The court held that the landlord was not liable to make good, because the damage was caused by third parties. There was no breach of contract by the landlord, and no wrong was done by him.

It has also been held that the landlord is not liable for damage due to a defect in nearby premises owned by him. In *Golden Casket (Greenock) Ltd v BRS Pickfords Ltd*[20] the premises were flooded, causing damage to the tenant's property due to a blocked drain on the landlord's adjoining premises. It was held that, apart from the common law duty to keep premises in tenantable repair and wind and watertight against the ordinary attacks of the elements, a

---

[15] *Whitelaw v Fulton* (1871) 10 M. 27.
[16] *Wolfson v Forrester's Trustees* (1910) 1 S.L.T. 318.
[17] *McGonigal v Pickard*, 1954 S.L.T. 62.
[18] *Sandeman v Duncan's Trustees* (1897) 4 S.L.T. 336; (1897) 5 S.L.T. 21.
[19] *Allan v James Robertson's Trustees*, 18 R. 932.
[20] *Golden Casket (Greenock) Ltd v BRS Pickfords Ltd*, 1972 S.L.T. 146.

landlord is only liable in damages if the insufficiency of the premises arises from his inconsiderate or culpable act.

Personal bar against the tenant in respect of landlord's repairing obligation

3-04   If the tenant remains in occupancy knowing there is a defect that makes the premises less than wind and watertight, or not in reasonable habitable or tenantable repair, then any injury sustained is his own responsibility. In other words he is personally barred (or prevented) from enforcing the common law repairs obligation against the landlord. In *Proctor v Cowlairs Co-operative Society Ltd*[21] a tenant died due to an injury from losing his footing on a broken step. The court held that the tenant had remained in occupancy after becoming aware of the defect without complaining about it, and therefore the landlord was not liable.

However, in *Dickie v Amicable Property Investment Building Society*[22] injury was suffered due to an insecure railing on the ground floor at the top of a stair leading to the basement. The tenant had complained about this problem, and the landlord had promised to repair it, but had failed to do so. The court held that there was no personal bar against the tenant because he had complained about the defect and had received an assurance from the landlord that it would be repaired.

Neither party responsible for repair

3-05   It does not follow that, if the landlord is not liable to the tenant, the tenant is liable instead; there can be a black hole. In the case of total destruction of the premises or damage severe enough to render them unable to be used or occupied, nobody is liable, and in the case of third party damage, the third party may be liable under the law of negligence to the landlord or tenant or both.

The common law rule of rei interitus

3-06   In the absence of an express or strongly implied provision to the contrary, a lease will be terminated if the premises are destroyed or become so seriously damaged that they cannot be used and occupied, due to something that was not caused by the tenant. This is also the case where possession is lost due to supervening legislation or where the premises are unable to be used and occupied.

In *Duff v Fleming*[23] the lease contained an obligation on the tenant to keep the premises in repair. There was a fire. The court held that an obligation on a tenant to keep in repair does not include making good total destruction. The true test is whether, without rebuilding, the tenant is able to use the premises. There was no obligation on the landlord to rebuild, and therefore the lease terminated, and the tenant had no liability.

In *Mackeson v Boyd*[24] a lease was granted of a house with ground, outbuildings and sporting rights. Following the start of the Second World War, the house and some of the outbuildings and ground were requisitioned by the

---

[21] *Proctor v Cowlairs Co-operative Society Ltd*, 1961 S.L.T. 434.
[22] *Dickie v Amicable Property Investment Building Society*, 1911 S.C. 1079.
[23] *Duff v Fleming* (1870) 8 M. 769.
[24] *Mackeson v Boyd*, 1942 S.C. 56.

military. The tenant abandoned the lease. The court held that the action of the military had made it impossible for the tenant to occupy the premises; this amounted to constructive and total destruction of the premises, and therefore the tenant was entitled to abandon the lease.

In *Robert Purvis Plant Hire v Brewster*,[25] the court considered a lease where the permitted use was recycling and storing bulk road materials. The planning authority served an enforcement notice to stop using the site for the recycling of construction and demolition materials. The tenant asked the court to declare that the lease was frustrated, and was void due to illegality, as there was no planning permission for the proposed use. The court held that there was no supervening event that caused the lease to be frustrated, as the lack of planning permission pre-dated the grant of the lease. The court also decided that the tenant's case of the lease being void due to illegality was irrelevant, as the lease did provide for the tenant to be able to use the site legally by applying to the landlord for consent to a use that was authorised under planning permission and planning legislation.

Contracting out of the rule of rei interitus

Some leases fully contract out of the rule, while others only partially contract **3–07** out, so as to allow for termination if insured risk damage or destruction is not made good within a specified period of time. It has become fashionable for some leases to have an opt-out for the landlord when it comes to making good uninsured risk damage.[26]

In *Cantors Properties (Scotland) Ltd v Swears & Wells Ltd*[27] a lease imposed on the tenant the obligation to repair and, when necessary, to renew and replace the premises, except where they are damaged or destroyed by fire, and for the tenant to insure the premises and 12 months' loss of rent all in the landlord's name. There was no clause imposing any liability on the landlord for making good damage or destruction by fire. The premises were in turn sublet, and the sub-lease replicated the terms of the head lease. Due to transfers of the various parties' interests, one person became entitled to the head-landlord's and the sub-tenant's interest. The premises subsequently suffered a fire; the sub-tenant had insured loss of rent, and he continued to pay rent. The building was rebuilt within three years. The court held that destruction of the property terminated the contract, and that the relationship of landlord and tenant could only be re-established by a new lease. The court also held that it is competent to contract out of the common law rule of *rei interitus*.

It is always a matter of degree as to whether damage is serious enough to bring the lease to an end. In *Allan v Markland*[28] a shoemaker was the tenant of premises that were partially destroyed by fire approximately two-thirds of the way through a seven-and-a-half-year lease. The tenant abandoned the premises and argued that the lease was terminated. The court held that, on the evidence, the damage had not been bad enough for the tenant to have to leave the premises for even a single day. Although the tenant suffered inconvenience, he could have carried on business, and therefore the lease was not terminated.

---

[25] *Robert Purvis Plant Hire v Brewster* [2009] CSOH 28; 2009 Hous L.R. 34
[26] See Ch.13.
[27] *Cantors Properties (Scotland) Ltd v Swears & Wells Ltd*, 1980 S.L.T. 165.
[28] *Allan v Markland* (1882) 10 R. 383.

Irritancy

3–08 If the lease does not contain an irritancy clause, there is a right at common law for the landlord to seek a court order to terminate the lease and to recover possession if the tenant fails to pay rent for two successive years; this is called a "legal irritancy". The tenant can save his lease by paying the arrears before the court issues its extract decree.

Most commercial leases do contain an irritancy clause that allows the landlord to terminate the lease for non-payment of rent or other sums, for any other breach of tenant's obligations, if the tenant goes into liquidation or if there is any other insolvency event. A landlord can never evict a tenant and recover possession of the premises, unless a court decree has been issued allowing him to do so, although the decree will often backdate the termination to the date of the landlord's notice to the tenant informing him the lease is terminated on the grounds of the tenant's breach.

The Law Reform (Miscellaneous Provisions) (Scotland) Act 1985 imports into every commercial lease statutory protections in favour of the tenant, and these apply to leases granted before the Act came into force, as well as to subsequent leases. These protections, which can not be contracted out of, are:

(a) that the landlord must give the tenant notice allowing him a minimum of 14 days within which to pay any outstanding amounts due under the lease, specifying the amount, and threatening to terminate the lease if the tenant fails to pay in time. If the lease stipulates a longer period of notice, then the longer period will apply; and

(b) for non-monetary breaches, the court will only grant a decree of irritancy if in the circumstances a fair and reasonable landlord would seek to terminate the lease.

A landlord cannot irritate a lease on the grounds of the appointment of an administrator of the tenant, except with the leave of the court or with permission of the administrator, even if the lease states that the landlord is allowed to irritate in the event of the tenant going into administration.[29]

Rescission for material breach

3–09 Either party is entitled to terminate the lease if the other is in material breach of its obligations under the lease. However, the statutory protections for tenants on irritancy apply to any proposed rescission by the landlord.

Tacit relocation

3–10 The expiry of the agreed term of a lease does not bring the lease to an end. There is implied agreement that whatever the stipulated period of the lease may be, such period can be extended by the silent consent of the parties. If neither party gives the required minimum period of notice of intention to terminate at the contractual expiry date, then the parties are deemed by their silence to have agreed that the lease should be prolonged.

---

[29] Insolvency Act 1986 s.8 and para.43(5) of Sch.B1.

Where tacit relocation operates, the lease continues on the same terms except in respect of duration. If the lease was for one year or longer, then tacit relocation operates to continue the lease for a further year and so on from year-to-year until and unless notice is given by either party. If the lease was for less than one year, it is continued for the shorter period, again until notice is given. The liability of a guarantor is not extended by the operation of tacit relocation.

It is not entirely clear whether it is possible to contract out of the operation of tacit relocation, and so it is safer to assume that it cannot be contracted out of. However, it is possible to vary the actual operation of tacit relocation by saying that the lease runs for a specific period of time and thereafter for a shorter or longer period than tacit relocation would imply. Note that a provision in a lease stipulating that it terminates and that the tenant is to remove without warning or process of law is not sufficient to exclude tacit relocation.

The subject of tacit relocation is treated fully in Ch.19.

Tenant's right of renewal of lease

In Scotland there is no statutory or common law right of renewal of a lease, **3–11** apart from a limited right under the Tenancy of Shops (Scotland) Acts 1949 and 1964. In terms of these Acts, the tenant of a shop can apply to the court within 21 days of receiving the landlord's notice of termination (of expiry of the lease) for a period of continued occupancy. The court can grant such continuation for up to one year at a rent determined by the court. The remedy can be applied for and granted on more than one occasion. This remedy is not often used by tenants. It is thought that the longer the period of notice given by the landlord, the less likely the court will be to grant an extension

Leases sometimes contain an option in favour of the tenant to extend the term or to renew the lease. This topic is dealt with in some detail in Ch.22.

No compensation for tenant's works

At common law, the tenant is not entitled to any compensation at any time for **3–12** works and improvements that he has carried out to the premises.

Condictio indebiti (unjustified enrichment)

If a tenant carries out work in error when he is under no obligation to do so (by, **3–13** for example, misinterpreting the repairs clause) and such work benefits the landlord, the common law principle of unjustified enrichment entitles the tenant to reimbursement of the cost of such work.[30]

B—ENGLAND

Tenant's obligations

- There is no implied term to pay rent. **3–14**
- There is an implied term to pay rates and other taxes.
- The tenant is liable for "waste", which includes any act, such as improvements or omission, that changes the premises; "voluntary waste" is a

---

[30] *Morgan Guaranty Trust Co of New York v Lothian Regional Council*, 1995 S.L.T. 299.

positive action, such as knocking down an internal wall, whereas "permissive waste" is failing to do something, such as breach of repairing obligations.

In weekly, monthly and quarterly tenancies, the tenant is liable for voluntary waste but not permissive waste. In yearly tenancies, the tenant is required to keep the premises wind and watertight, but the tenant is not liable for fair wear and tear, and so is not liable for gradual deterioration caused by normal use or by the normal action of the elements. He therefore does not have to replace tiles blown off the roof by the wind.

For leases for a fixed term of years, the tenant is liable for voluntary waste and most probably for permissive waste, therefore there is an implied term that the tenant should maintain the premises in the condition that he received them at the start of the term.

The "usual covenants"

3–15 Although an agreement for lease will usually have attached to it the agreed form of lease, there is sometimes reference in an agreement for lease to the "usual covenants". It is an implied term that if there is an agreement for lease then the lease will, when granted, contain the "usual covenants". The class of usual covenants is not totally fixed, and this will vary depending on where the property is located or due to the nature of a trade carried on at the premises. The following are always regarded as usual:

- the tenant is to pay rent, rates and tax other than those that must statutorily be paid by the landlord;
- the tenant is to keep the premises in repair (if the landlord has expressly undertaken to repair, he is to be allowed reasonable access to view and repair the premises);
- the landlord will allow the tenant quiet enjoyment and will not derogate from his grant; and
- the landlord has the right to terminate the lease if the tenant fails to pay rent.

Landlord's implied and statutory obligations

3–16 To allow quiet enjoyment, i.e. uninterrupted possession of the premises. The landlord is not responsible for the actions of unrelated third parties. A mid-landlord is not liable for the actions of the owner of the freehold (although the Court of Appeal held in *Pennell v Payne*[31] that a sub-tenant can claim damages against his immediate landlord if the sub-lease perishes because his immediate landlord has given notice to quit to the head landlord or exercises a break clause in the head lease).

Not to derogate from the grant. If the landlord does something to make use impossible or to interfere with use, then he is derogating from the grant. However, the landlord can do something that makes use less convenient or more expensive, without incurring any liability to the tenant.

---

[31] *Pennell v Payne* [1995] Q.B. 192.

To ensure no injury or damage is caused to the tenant and his invitees, etc. due to any defect in the premises. This arises from statutory liability, but only where the landlord is responsible for repairs under the terms of the lease.

Note that there is no implied term that the premises will be fit for any particular purpose—the rule caveat emptor applies—the tenant is to examine the property and decide whether it is fit for its purpose. There is an exception in respect of furnished houses, and there are some statutory provisions that imply terms on the condition of the property or the landlord's obligation to repair, such as property let at a low rent and leases that are granted for less than seven years.

There is no implied obligation on the landlord to make any repairs, unless he himself has built the premises, or unless he retains common items such as a stairway, lift, etc.

Holding over

At common law, a lease for a fixed term expires at the end of that term, at **3–17** which time the tenant must give up possession; tacit relocation does not apply in England.

The common law position has been altered by statute for many residential, agricultural and business leases. In these cases, the tenant may be able to stay in the property following the end of the contractual term. In the case of business tenancies, holding over describes the statutory continuation of the lease following the end of the contractual term. This continues indefinitely until the lease is brought to an end by notice following the statutory procedure. If a tenant remains in the premises when he has no right to do so, he will potentially be liable for "mesne profits", which is a payment of damages for trespass by a former tenant. The Scottish equivalent is "violent profits".

A lease of business premises under Pt 2 of the Landlord and Tenant Act 1954 does not end at expiry of the term, unless it is terminated in accordance with the provisions of the Act.

Business tenant's right of renewal of lease (security of tenure)

"Security of tenure" is the name given to the right of a tenant who leases **3–18** premises for professional or business purposes to renew their lease. Security of tenure is not absolute; the landlord can oppose the grant of a new lease on a number of grounds. It is possible to contract out of the security of tenure regime in the first place by following the statutory procedure, and this is done before the elase is entered into. Such leases are called "contracted out".

Permitted uses

In the absence of restriction, the tenant is free to use the premises for any **3–19** purpose. Therefore, as in Scotland, it is normal for leases of business premises to set out the use the tenant can make of the property. If the lease states that landlord's consent is required for a change of use, he can not mormally charge a premium for agreeing to the change of use. This is a statutory restriction provided by the Landlord and Tenant Act 1927.

There is no implied warranty by the landlord that the premises can be used for any purpose specified in the lease.

Frustration

3–20 In *National Carriers Ltd v Panalpina (Northern) Ltd*[32] it was held that where premises let as a warehouse for 10 years were unable to be accessed for a period of 20 months because the street was closed by the local authority due to a dangerous building, the lease had not been frustrated because the actual interruption did not destroy the entire contract. However, the principle was accepted that in exceptional circumstances the doctrine of frustration could apply to a lease despite the fact that a lease in England is more than a contract as it creates an estate in land.

Forfeiture

3–21 There is, in some cases, statutory relief from forfeiture available for tenants in England. This is treated more fully in Ch.17.

---

[32] *National Carriers Ltd v Panalpina (Northern) Ltd* [1981] A.C. 675.

Chapter 4

STATUTORY PROVISIONS

Introduction

In Scotland, there are relatively few statutory provisions that regulate commer- **4–01** cial leases, compared to the wide range of statutes that govern commercial leases in England. In this chapter, we consider the main statutes that affect Scottish leases, although the matter of conversion of ultra long leases to ownership is dealt with in Ch.5.

Leases Act 1449

The oldest Scottish statute that affects commercial leases is the Leases Act 1449, **4–02** which introduced statutory protection for tenants against anyone who buys the property after the lease has been granted. In terms of the Act a lease is enforceable against successors of the landlord if the following conditions are fulfilled:

- the tenant has entered into possession of the premises;
- the premises must be land and/or buildings;
- if the lease is for more than a year, it must be in writing; if it is for a year or shorter, it does not have to be in writing;
- it must have a definite, or ascertainable, termination date;
- it must specify a rent, even if only £1 per annum; and
- the tenant must take possession;
- the landlord must have been the recorded or registered owner of the property (or of the landlord's interest) at the time of granting the lease, or have acquired this subsequently.

Although the lease needs to have a termination date, it does need to be a fixed date—the lease is able to come to an end when something in the future happens, so long as it is something that *must* happen. Possession is achieved by physical actual possession, or by recording the lease in the Register of Sasines, or registering it in the Land Register of Scotland. The tenant will *not* have the protection under the 1449 Act if the landlord sells his interest after granting the lease but before the tenant has taken possession. Possession by a sub-tenant is considered sufficient to constitute possession by the tenant.

Registration of Leases (Scotland) Act 1857[1]

This allows a lease that is for longer than 20 years (the minimum period is **4–03** therefore 20 years plus one day) to be recorded in the General Register of

---

[1] As amended.

Sasines, or registered in the Land Register of Scotland. The lease must be for longer than 20 years, or must contain an obligation on the granter to renew it from time to time for fixed periods so that it will endure for more than 20 years. Note that under the Land Registration (Scotland) Act 1979 as amended, a lease that runs for over 20 years *must* be registered in the Land Register of Scotland, in order for the tenant to obtain a good leasehold title that is valid against successors of the original landlord.

Law Reform (Miscellaneous) Provisions (Scotland) Act 1985

4–04 Section 3 of the Act enables real conditions (i.e. obligations and provisions that continue in the event of assignation of the tenant's interest or disposal of the landlord's interest of a recorded or registered lease) to be inserted in an assignation document, provided the assignation itself is recorded or registered.

Land Tenure Reform (Scotland) Act 1974

4–05 Sections 8 to 10 of this Act limit to a maximum of 20 years the residential use of property that is let under leases of over 20 years duration granted after the Act was passed — this affects any lease signed after September 1, 1974. Use as the site of a caravan does not constitute a dwellinghouse[2]. However, the Act does not prevent a tenancy from being or becoming a protected or statutory tenancy (i.e. giving the tenant permanent security of tenure). Breach of the statutory prohibition against use as a dwellinghouse of property let for more than 20 years does *not* render the lease void or unenforceable, but does allow the landlord to terminate the prohibited use within 28 days by notice to the tenant, and if the tenant fails to comply the landlord can seek a court order terminating the lease.

Section 17 of the Act allows an interposed lease to be granted at any time in respect of any lease that was granted before or after the Act came into force. The interposed lease can be of all or part of the premises let by the existing lease and can be for a term that is the same, shorter or longer than the existing lease. The effect of the interposed lease is that (a) the landlord remains the same; (b) the tenant in the original lease now becomes the sub-tenant; and (c) the tenant in the interposed lease now becomes the landlord of the tenant in the original lease, as if the original lease had been assigned to the grantee of the interposed lease, and a sub-lease had then been granted. If for any reason the interposed lease terminates by irritancy or otherwise, then there is statutory protection[3] for the sub-tenant, as his lease continues as if the interposed lease has never been granted.

Leasehold Casualties (Scotland) Act 2001

4–06 This Act makes it incompetent to provide for a periodical payment apart from rent, service charge or insurance (called a "casualty") in a lease signed after September 1, 1974. Casualty payments in leases and sub-leases of at least 175 years duration that were granted before September 1, 1974 are, since May 10, 2000, no longer enforceable.

---

[2] Land Tenure Reform (Scotland) Act 1974 s.8(2).
[3] Land Tenure Reform (Scotland) Act 1974 s.17(2).

The Act also prohibits irritancy at common law or in terms of an irritancy clause in a lease where the lease was granted before August 10, 1914 and the rent is £150 or lower per annum.

Sheriff Courts (Scotland) Act 1907

This Act provides for different periods of notice to be given for leases of **4–07** different properties to stop tacit relocation (automatic continuation of the lease) operating (see Ch.19). The Act provides different forms of notice for different purposes. For leases of commercial premises the notice can be oral or in writing. For non-agricultural leases, the forms of notice provided by the Act are optional. However, the notice needs to be a definite and unconditional notification that allows the addressee to know exactly his position, and it must specify the date of removal, which is of course the termination date specified in the lease. If notice is given in terms of the provisions of the lease, it must comply exactly with the requirements of the lease. In the case of *Ben Cleuch Estates Ltd v Scottish Enterprise*,[4] a notice sent by the tenant to the landlord which was sent to the correct registered address, but addressed to the wrong company was found not valid, but at appeal the tenant won on the basis of personal bar.

Removal Terms (Scotland) Act 1886

Where a lease specifies the expiry date (or term of removal) as Whitsunday or **4–08** Martinmas, then unless specified to the contrary, the tenant must remove by noon on May 28 or November 28, or on the following day if that term day falls on a Sunday. However, the notice of termination must be given forty days before the old term days of May 15 or November 11 as the case may be.

Term and Quarter Days (Scotland) Act 1990

For all leases granted after July 13, 1991 if the quarter days or any of them are **4–09** mentioned as being rent payment dates (Candlemas, Whitsunday, Lamas and Martinmas respectively) then unless specified otherwise, these dates are February 28, May 28, August 28 and November 28 each year. However, for a lease that was entered into on or before or on July 13, 1991 if the quarter days are named and the dates are specified as any of the previously used dates of February 2, May 15, August 1 and November 11, then these specified dates will prevail.

Prescription and Limitation (Scotland) Act 1973

Any claim for payment of rent or other periodical payments, such as service **4–10** charge, under a lease or sub-lease prescribes (i.e. is no longer enforceable) after five years from the date on which the payment became due.

The period of positive prescription for leases that are recorded in the Sasine Register or are registered in The Land Register of Scotland is 10 years from the date of recording/registration. Therefore, unless the deed does not appear to be invalid, or unless it is forged, a tenant's title is not able to be challenged, after the tenant has been in possession for 10 years without challenge during that time.

---

[4] *Ben Cleuch Estates Ltd v Scottish Enterprise*, 2008 S.C. 252.

Insolvency Act 1986[5]

4–11 If the tenant goes into administration, there is a statutory moratorium that prevents the landlord from irritating the lease, enforcing irritancy, and from raising any other proceedings against the tenant. The court's permission is needed in order to raise any court proceedings, including actions of irritancy.

Law Reform (Miscellaneous Provisions) (Scotland) Act 1985

4–12 This Act gives protection to tenants in respect of irritancy (refer to Ch.17: Irritancy) for an in depth treatment of this topic.

The Act also allows a party to a contract (which of course includes leases) to seek a court order to rectify any errors in that contract, but the court will not grant such an order where the other party to the contract would be adversely affected.

Tenancy of Shops (Scotland) Acts 1949 and 1964

4–13 These Acts give a limited right to the tenant of a shop to apply to the court to extend the term of the lease for up to a year, at such rent and on such terms as the court considers appropriate. This topic is dealt with in more detail in Ch. 19.

Requirements of Writing (Scotland) Act 1995

4–14 A lease that has a duration of one year or less does not require to be in writing; all leases that last for over one year must be in writing.

Bankruptcy and Diligence etc. (Scotland) Act 2007

4–15 This regulates court actions for removal of a tenant, and also reforms the law relating to landlord's hypothec by abolishing his right to sequestrate for rent (i.e. to sell items belonging to the tenant) where the landlord exercises his hypothec. The remedy of hypothec is still available, but it now only gives the landlord a preferred status as creditor in some instances.

---

[5] As amended by the Enterprise Act 2002.

CHAPTER 5

CONVERSION OF ULTRA LONG LEASES TO OWNERSHIP: THE LONG LEASES (SCOTLAND) ACT 2012

Introduction

The Long Leases (Scotland) Act 2012[1] was passed in June 2012, but the main **5–01** operative provisions will only come into force on a date that is still to be specified by order of the Scottish Ministers. The Act provides for conversion of the tenant's interest in an "ultra long" lease to outright ownership, and for the landlord to lose his right of ownership, and for him to receive compensation for this loss. The Act also deals with the consequences of these changes by providing for conversion of certain lease obligations to title conditions affecting the newly acquired ownership right of the tenant.

"Appointed Day"

The Appointed Day, when most of the Act will take effect, will be the first 28th **5–02** November to occur two years after the main part of the Act comes into force. This date is still to be set by the Scottish Ministers

The lease ladder

It is helpful to introduce the concept of a *"lease ladder"*—in any property, **5–03** there can be a hierarchy of occupancy rights, with the owner at the top. If he grants a lease and his tenant then grants a sub-lease, and the sub-tenant in turn grants a sub-sub-lease or an occupancy licence, and so on, then a ladder is established, as seen by the following example:

```
          owner
            I              head lease
          tenant               I
            I              sub lease
        sub-tenant             I
            I              sub-sub-lease
      sub-sub-tenant           I
            I              occupancy licence
         licensee
```

We will use this example to explain some of the statutory provisions.

---

[1] Long Leases (Scotland) Act 2012 (asp 9).

Conversion of tenant's interest to outright ownership

5–04   The Act converts the interest of the tenant in an existing lease to ownership[2] and deprives the landlord of his ownership right, if all the following conditions are met in respect of that lease:

- It was originally granted for a term of more than 175 years.
- It has been registered in the Register of Sasines or in the Land Register of Scotland.
- If it is a lease of commercial premises it has more than 175 years left to run at the Appointed Day; or if it is a lease of residential premises, it has more than 100 years left to run at the Appointed Day.
- The annual rent is £100 or less.
- It does not include all or any part of a harbour, where there is a harbour authority.
- It was not granted for the sole purpose to allow the tenant to install and maintain pipes or cables.
- It is not a lease of minerals, or relating to extraction of minerals.

Length of lease

5–05   In determining the duration of a lease, break options are to be disregarded, but obligations on the landlord to renew the lease are to be taken into account. There are specific provisions in s.71 for calculating the term, if this is geared to a person's life. Leases that are continuing by tacit relocation are included in the Act.

Rent covering more than one lease; variable rent

5–06   Section 2 provides that, if a total rental is payable in respect of two or more leases, then the rent for all of them is deemed to be zero. However, the landlord can allocate rent among the leases in terms of ss.38 to 41. If the rent is variable from year to year, then the variable element of the rent is to be ignored.

Other points regarding qualification of leases

5–07   If a lease would otherwise qualify, but is not presently recorded in the Sasine Register or registered in the Land Register of Scotland, then the tenant can register the lease in the Land Register of Scotland, and thus make it eligible for conversion.

Section 3 provides that, if there are two or more leases in a "lease ladder"[3] that satisfy the requirements for conversion, then only one will qualify for each part of the premises. The intention is that the lowest lease on the ladder should qualify for conversion, so that if, for example, a property is let in terms of a head lease and the tenant has granted a sub-lease of the whole premises, and both would qualify for conversion to ownership, then the sub-lease will qualify and the head tenant and the owner will both lose their rights. If only part of the premises have been sub-let, conversion would apply to the sub-lease in respect of that part, and the head lease would qualify for conversion for the remainder.

---

[2] s.1.
[3] See para.5–03.

Effect of conversion

All "real" rights and obligations in the qualifying lease and any superior **5–08**
lease are extinguished[4] but personal rights and obligations continue, and the
obligation to pay rent for the period up to the appointed day remains
enforceable.

Sub-leases and other subordinate rights remain in place following conversion[5]; any standard security affecting the landlord's title is extinguished on
conversion.

Lease obligations may be able to be created as title conditions

Section 7 provides that rights of access and other reservations can be created **5–09**
as servitudes against the new title.

Section 8 allows the landlord to issue a notice reserving sporting rights such
as game and fishing. Such a notice must be recorded in the Register of Sasines
or registered in the Land Register of Scotland, before the appointed day, against
the tenant's interest in the lease that is about to be converted.

Sections 10 and 11 provide for certain lease obligations to be converted into
real burdens affecting the new title, but they must be capable of being constituted as real burdens under the Title Conditions (Scotland) Act 2003, and must
be binding on successors.

Obligations to pay rent and restrictions on assignation and sub-letting are
based on the relationship of landlord and tenant, and therefore cannot be
converted into title conditions.

Irritancy and penalty clauses are excluded but rights of pre-emption or to
retake possession may be capable of conversion.

Sections 14 to 20 provide for the landlord and tenant to be able to agree on
converting many lease obligations (which must be enforceable immediately
before the Appointed Day, in order to be eligible for conversion) into title
conditions (real burdens). The landlord is able to seek an order from the Lands
Tribunal for Scotland in certain circumstances.

The landlord can nominate a benefitted property, whose proprietor will be
entitled to enforce the condition. In order to achieve conversion to a title condition, the landlord must register a notice before the appointed day against the
tenant's leasehold title and also against the benefited property title, to convert
lease obligations into title conditions (real burdens).

Section 23 provides for creation of personal pre-emption burdens or personal
redemption burden, provided that immediately before the Appointed Day, the
conditions were still enforceable, and the requirements of the sections are
complied with. Sections 23 to 30 of the Act contain provisions for conversion
of lease obligations to facility or service burdens, economic development
burdens, climate change burdens, health care burdens, conservation burdens,
and manager burdens (where the obligation gives a power of management over
a group of related properties).

If the landlord does not satisfy the conditions for converting a lease obligation to a real burden, the landlord can seek an order from the Lands Tribunal
for Scotland within one year after s.21 comes into force, provided the landlord

---

[4] s.5.
[5] s.6.

has tried to obtain the tenant's agreement to convert the condition to a real burden.

Section 34 provides that if a lease obligation becomes a real burden, then any counter-obligations contained in the lease will be enforceable by the proprietor of the new title against the proprietor of the title entitled to enforce the lease obligation.

Prescription of new real burdens

5–10 At present the period of negative prescription for a leasehold condition is 20 years, but after conversion to a real burden, the period is reduced to five years.[6]

Allocation of rents and renewal premiums

5–11 There is provision in s.39 for the landlord to be able to allocate cumulo rents and renewal premiums, where a single payment is made in relation to two or more leases. The landlord has to give notice before the Appointed Day, and the allocation must be reasonable. However, if at least one of the leases is extinguished by conversion to ownership, then the landlord is given until two years after the Appointed Day to allocate the amounts.

Compensation for loss of landlord's rights to fixed rent

5–12 The compensation payment to the landlord is based on the capitalised value of the rent. In some cases a landlord can claim a further payment, which is called an "*additional payment*". Sections 47 to 55 contain detailed provisions on the calculation of the amount payable. Section 56 provides for the landlord to serve a preliminary notice where the claim is likely to be more than £500. The tenant can pay by instalments if the amount due is £50 or more.[7] There is a time limit of two years after the appointed day for the landlord to serve on the tenant a notice in prescribed form—a copy of the explanatory note that is provided by the Act must also be issued.

If the amount claimed is £50 or more, an instalment document must be served along with a notice allowing the tenant the right to pay by instalments. If the instalment document is not served, then the notice is invalid. If a preliminary notice has not been served, the amount of compensatory payment is limited to a maximum of £50. If the notice is served correctly, the former tenant (unless paying by instalments) must pay the compensatory payment within eight weeks after the date on which the notice was served. Section 47 sets out how the payment is calculated; the scheme is designed to give the same economic benefit to the landlord as the ongoing income from rent. Renewal of premium payments are also taken into account.

Additional payment for loss of other rights

5–13 Sections 50 and 51 give detail about the landlord's right to demand an additional payment for loss of a right; a notice in prescribed form must be served within two years of the appointed Day, and the amount is calculated as detailed

---

[6] s.35; s.18 of the Title Conditions (Scotland) Act 2003.
[7] s.57.

in s.52. The rights that are lost on conversion of the lease, and that that are eligible for additional payment are as follows:

- Non-monetary.
- The right to have the rent reviewed or increased (the lease may provide for a fixed formula).
- Annually variable rent, for example, based on turnover of a business.
- Right to receive a renewal premium of more than £100.
- Landlord's right of reversion (i.e. to get the Premises back at the end of the lease), provided the lease would expire no later than 200 years after the appointed day;
- The right to terminate the lease early (apart from by exercising a right of pre-emption) – such termination right must be within the full control of the landlord, and exercisable within 200 years of the Appointed Day;
- Right to development value, provided the right has not been converted into a real burden.

The lost right is to be valued as at the appointed day, in accordance with the provisions on s.52.

There is provision in ss.53 to 55 for the parties to agree the additional payment or for it to be determined by the Lands Tribunal for Scotland. Where there is a claim of more than £500 in respect of compensatory or additional payment, the landlord must serve a notice, no later than six months before the appointed day, on the person who is registered at that time as the tenant.[8] A separate notice has to be served in respect of each type of payment and if the compensatory or additional payment is £50 or more an instalment document must be served along with the relevant notice (s.57). If the tenant wants to take advantage of the instalment arrangement he has to sign, date and return the document along with a 10% surcharge payment. If the tenant (the owner) sells all or part of the property that he now owns, the option of paying by instalments is then lost. If any instalment is not paid for six weeks after the due date then the whole balance becomes payable immediately. The obligation to pay the compensatory or additional payment prescribes after five years, and it starts to run from the date the obligation arises.

Exemption from conversion

A tenant is able to opt out of his lease being converted to outright ownership. **5–14** If the tenant wants to exempt his lease from conversion, he must register a notice at least 2 months before the Appointed Day[9].

The tenant can recall an exemption, thus making his lease eligible for conversion, but not where agreement has been reached to exempt the lease, or where the landlord has obtained a Lands Tribunal order exempting it. If the tenant does issue a recall of exemption notice, the landlord has six months from then to register a notice converting leasehold conditions into real burdens.

The landlord can only claim an exemption from conversion in respect of a lease where the annual rent at any time during the five years before the Act was

---

[8] s.56.
[9] s.63.

passed, was over £100,[10] but he must either register an agreement with the
tenant about this, or register an order made by the Lands Tribunal confirming
this, no later than two months before the appointed day.[11]

Restriction on irritancy of a lease

5–15 Once s.73 of the Act comes into force, a lease will no longer be able to be
terminated by irritancy if the lease was granted for more than 175 years, and
if on the date when the section comes into force it has an unexpired term
of more than 175 years for commercial premises, or more than 100 years for
residential, and is not exempt from conversion due to agreement between the
parties or due to an order from the Lands Tribunal.

Proceedings already commenced for irritancy will be deemed to have been
abandoned, but any final decree that has been granted is not affected.

---

[10] s.64.
[11] s.66.

CHAPTER 6

MISSIVES OF LEASE

Introductory

It is not necessary to have missives in order to enter into a lease; it is possible **6–01** to proceed straight to a lease document. Nor is it essential to have a lease document that is separate from the missives, provided the missives contain all the essentials that are required for a valid lease to exist. However, there are usually ancillary matters that are addressed when agreeing to enter into a lease, and these are best provided for by having missives. In Scotland, the missives (in England this is called an "agreement for lease") are treated as being the same as a lease itself, and therefore the lease can merely be missives signed by the solicitors as agents for the parties.

The usual situation is to have a short missive with a draft lease attached. Often the draft that is attached is a pro forma style with blanks to be filled in, although sometimes the issuing solicitor will attach a bespoke draft, in which case the missive could be very brief, as the main terms will be contained in the draft lease.

In this Chapter, we consider the main points to be covered in missives of lease not only for existing properties, but also (in paras 6–19 onwards), in the case of new or refurbished property, where there are additional points to consider.

Where the lease is for only up to five years, it is quite common to have a short form missive of lease, and this is dealt with in Ch.32.

In this Chapter we are not addressing how agreements for lease are entered into in England, as the main purpose of this Chapter is to explain the issues regarding entering into leases in Scotland.

A—MISSIVES OF LEASE OF EXISTING PROPERTY

The parties and the premises

The landlord's solicitor will usually issue the offer to grant a lease, and will **6–02** attach a draft lease that will then be adjusted between the parties, before entering into the missives. If the tenant's solicitor merely issues an acceptance without revising the draft lease and importing the revised draft into a qualified acceptance, then the tenant will be bound by the terms of the landlord's draft lease, and it will then be too late to suggest amendments.

The offer will name the parties and describe the premises to be leased. There should ideally be a plan annexed to the offer to show the extent of the premises, and a copy of that plan will be annexed and signed as relative to the actual lease. The plan should meet the requirements of the Registers of Scotland if the lease is to be registered in the Land Register of Scotland.

Registration is necessary from the tenant's point of view if the lease is to run for longer than 20 years, in order for the tenant to obtain a real right (good leasehold title). If the plan is said to be indicative only (or if it is said to not be taxative), then the plan will not be sufficient for registration of the tenant's leasehold title.

Conditionality

6–03   The transaction may be conditional on various things, such as:

- the landlord obtaining vacant possession from the existing tenant or occupier;
- the grant of planning permission, and if the property is or is in a listed building, also on the grant of listed building consent;
- satisfactory survey;
- satisfactory environmental audit;
- landlord's lender's consent; and
- the landlord being satisfied with accounts and references in respect of the tenant.

The well-drafted conditionality clause should provide for:

- who is to do what, so as to enable the condition to be satisfied: whether one party can do whatever is needed, if the other fails to do so, and/or whether that party can terminate the missives;
- whether it is possible for the conditionality to be waived and, if so, how this can be done and by whom;
- who is to say if the item is satisfactory, and whether they have to act reasonably or have complete discretion;
- how the conditionality is to be purified (satisfied);
- a deadline for dealing with the conditionality; and
- what is to happen if the item of conditionality is not purified or waived in time, and the right to purify or waive late.

The duration and options to terminate and extend

6–04   The date of entry (commencement) of the lease and the termination date should be specified. It is good practice, and avoids ambiguity, if the offer says the lease is to run from and including a specific date until and including a specific date.

An option to terminate early and/or to extend the duration the lease is sometimes granted, and this should be clearly expressed so as to say who has the right to exercise the option, to set out any conditions attached to the exercise of the option, to provide for the period of notice to be given and to specify the procedure for giving notice. It is of the utmost importance that the option is carried into the lease. Many offers and leases contain options that specifically provide that the option cannot be exercised if the tenant is or has been in breach of his obligations, or if he is in breach at the date of exercise of the option. In *Trygort (Number 2) Ltd v UK Home Finance Ltd*[1] the lease provided that the

---

[1] *Trygort (Number 2) Ltd v UK Home Finance Ltd*, 2008 G.W.D. 35–529.

tenant was not entitled to exercise his break option if he had been in breach of his obligations under the lease. The court held that the commercially sensible interpretation was that the tenant is entitled to exercise the option if, at the date on which notice was given, there was no subsisting breach.

It is thought that, if at the time the tenant serves notice there is an expired schedule of dilapidations with which the tenant has not complied, he would not be entitled to terminate the lease at that time. However, the landlord would not, it is suggested, be able to prevent the tenant from exercising his break option by serving a schedule of dilapidations shortly before the tenant's deadline for serving the break option notice.

Note that missives usually contain a clause that limits their life to one or two years after the date of entry but, even if the missives are silent about this, they will prescribe (cease to be enforceable) after five, or in some cases 20, years. Therefore it is essential that any options to terminate early or to extend, and any other ongoing matters, be carried into the lease document itself.

Notices in missives (and in leases)

The notice provision is worthy of attention—there is case law that, if a contract **6–05** or lease states that three months' notice is to be given, then exactly three months' notice must be given, and that if needs be notice must be personally given by sheriff officer, etc. The safer method is to say that not less than three months' notice is to be given, which means the notifying party can serve notice well in advance. Thought also needs to be given as to how and where notice should be served—is it only to the registered office or last known address of the addressee and/or, in the case of the tenant, to the premises?

If the clause says that notice is sufficiently given if sent by recorded delivery, this does not mean that other forms of giving notice are invalid—all it is saying is that notice is deemed given if by the specified method. However, if the notice clause says that notice shall be given by a particular method, then that is mandatory and precludes other methods.

If a party has its registered office outside the UK, then the missives should provide a UK-based agent who is authorised to receive notices on its behalf.

Notices are dealt with more fully in Ch.21.

Rent, rent review and VAT

The amount of rent payable and the rent payment dates should be specified. If **6–06** there is a rent-free or concessionary period, this should be stated. Many land-lords will insist on receiving a quarter's rent at commencement of the lease, with any rent-free period being given at the end of that quarter, while some will spread the rent-free concession throughout the first year of the lease so as to provide for a smaller rent in the first year which is paid constantly throughout the first year. Many landlords will prefer to keep any rent-free concession in the missives and for that provision to over-ride the lease (which will provide for the full rent to be payable from day one). However, most tenants may want additional protection if the rent-free period is longer than, say, two months, because there could be a change in landlord, leaving a tenant only with a contractual right against the initial landlord, whilst the new landlord is knocking on his door looking for payment of rent. This protection is obtained by having a minute of agreement confirming the rent-free arrangements which varies the lease and is thus binding on future owners, but the minute of agreement will contain a clause that the document is to be treated as never having existed once the rent-free or concessionary period has expired.

The clause should say how often the rent reviews are and when the first review date is.

If the landlord has waived VAT on the rents, or if VAT is mandatorily chargeable, then unless the lease specifically provides for the tenant to pay any VAT in addition to rent, the rents will be deemed to be VAT inclusive. VAT is more fully dealt with in Ch.23.

Use and fitting-out works

6–07   The initial permitted use can be specified, or it can instead be provided for in the draft lease.

The landlord might require the tenant to fit out the premises and to produce details of fitting out proposals for the landlord to consider. The tenant should not enter into missives unless either: (a) he has already obtained approval for the specific fit-out; or (b) there is provision that the landlord's consent will not be unreasonably withheld to his proposals. The offer may provide for landlord's consent to be given in a licence for works in the landlord's standard form, which should be annexed to the offer so that, when the tenant receives the offer, the tenant can see the document that will be entered into.

Draft lease to be binding

6–08   The missives should state that if the lease itself has not been signed and delivered by the date of entry, then the draft lease that is annexed to the offer (or to the last qualified acceptance) is binding on the parties from the date of entry until the actual engrossed lease has been fully signed and delivered. A timetable should be set out for signature and delivery of the documents.

Damage or destruction

6–09   The missives should state what is to happen if, between entering into the missives and the date of entry, the property is seriously damaged or destroyed. Many missives will provide for either party to be able to terminate the contract without liability in this event.

No assignation or dealings

6–10   The missives should prohibit the tenant from assigning his interest under the missives or dealing with his interest except with the landlord's prior written consent. This is quite different to the restrictions on assignation and sub-letting, etc. contained in the lease itself, and this is merely to protect the landlord up to the period when the lease actually commences.

Guarantees

6–11   If there is to be a guarantee provided in respect of tenant's performance, the missives should provide for it to be given either within the body of the lease document itself or in a separate document. The guarantor needs to be bound in to the missives so as to make sure that he will sign the lease as guarantor, or that he will sign and deliver the separate guarantee document. The landlord will therefore provide that the missives are entered into between the landlord, the tenant and the guarantor. If the guarantor is a company, there should be a commercial benefit to the guarantor in agreeing to provide the guarantee. The guarantor should always receive separate legal advice, from a different law firm. Guarantees are more fully dealt with in Ch.20.

Other matters

The missives should require the landlord to exhibit the title deeds and searches, **6–12** and should deal with Coal Authority Reports and the Property Enquiry Report. Statutory Notices issued prior to the date of entry should be stated to be the landlord's responsibility, and there should be a statement that the landlord is not aware of any existing or proposed planning applications relating to the property or to other property nearby, which could adversely affect the tenant's proposed use. An Energy Performance Certificate is needed for all new leases granted after January 4, 2009. The EPC lasts for 10 years from its date of issue

Expenses

It is normal for each party to pay their own respective legal fees, but for the **6–13** tenant to pay the search dues, stamp duty land tax and registration costs.

Stamp duty land tax certificate

The missives need to impose on the tenant the obligation to complete and **6–14** lodge the stamp duty land tax return SDLT-1 if the transaction is notifiable.

Stamp duty land tax is a tax imposed on the tenant, and if the lease is notifiable to HM Revenue & Customs it is the tenant's responsibility to fill in and submit to HM Revenue & Customs a stamp duty land tax return and to pay any tax due. The landlord cannot do summary diligence (fast track enforcement) unless the lease has been registered for execution in the Books of Council and Session. The landlord cannot register the lease unless and until a stamp duty land tax certificate has been produced by the tenant, if the lease is notifiable. Stamp duty land tax and its proposed replacement, land and buildings transaction tax, are more fully considered in Ch.23.

Local authority consents

The tenant should provide for planning permission for the proposed use and for **6–15** previous works, building warrants and completion certificates for all works carried out on the premises. This can be very important because enforcement action could be taken if all consents have not been obtained. The landlord may be able to pass on to the tenant in terms of the lease the obligation for carrying out remedial work or for curing any problems which have arisen prior to the lease starting, and so the tenant needs to ensure all permissions are in place.

The missives are only enforceable against the first landlord personally, and they cannot be enforced against any party to whom the landlord sells the property.

Checklist for tenants

- Is the extent of the premises correctly stated in the landlord's offer? **6–16**
- Do the premises coincide with the extent of the landlord's title? Does he own everything he is letting out?

- Is there a standard security in respect of the landlord's interest? If so, then consent from the secured lender is needed.
- Has the landlord granted any floating charges or debentures? If so, the consent of the charge holder may well be needed.
- Check the landlord's title to ensure he has a good title. Examine prescriptive progress and burdens writs.
- Examine searches in Property/Land, Personal and Charges Registers.
- Examine a Property Enquiry Report—are there any orders, notices or proposals?
- Check that the tenant is aware of the rateable value and rates liability.
- Check the tenant has had the property surveyed and that he is satisfied with the report.
- If the premises form part of a larger building, find out information about the factor or managing agent, and ask for written confirmation as to whether any common repairs or improvement scheme is current or anticipated.
- Check that alterations carried out to the property in the past have received planning permission (if within the past 10 years) and have received a building warrant and completion certificate (no time bar involved).

Schedule of Condition

6–17 The tenant may want certain items of repair to be excluded from his responsibility under the lease. It is quite usual for the parties to agree as to which items should be excluded, and for these to be listed in a Schedule of Condition, which is a factual report of the state of repair of the premises as at the start of the lease. Schedules of Condition are fully considered in Ch.13.

The Schedule of Condition should be annexed and signed as relative to the missives and to any relevant back letter or to the lease itself.

Back letters

6–18 A back letter does not vary a lease—it is merely a direct contractual document between the granter and the grantee that sets out arrangements between them. It can be used for different matters, such as a rent-free period or a stepped or concessionary rent arrangement, to limit the service charge liability, to water down the repairs clause, to allow additional or different uses, etc.

From the tenant's point of view, it is important to be aware that the back letter is likely to cease to be effective on any assignation of the tenant's interest in the lease. Depending on the actual wording of the back letter, it may only be available if the tenant is actually occupying the premises, and so it would no longer apply if the premises were sub-let. The back letter should include an obligation on the granter to take any future owner as landlord bound to grant a back letter in identical terms to the tenant, including the obligation to make the next in turn landlord bound to grant one in the same terms. If the tenant does not have this protection, then when the landlord sells the property with the benefit of the existing lease, the tenant would have no recourse against the new landlord, as the back letter would only be personal as between the original landlord and the tenant, and the original landlord may have disappeared.

From the landlord's point of view, it is important that the back letter contains a statement that the concessions are given for as long as the granter is the landlord under the lease; otherwise, the granter could have continuing liability after he sells or conveys the property.

B—MISSIVES—DEVELOPMENT OR REFURBISHMENT—NEW LEASE

Some initial points

If the premises are to be, are being, or have just been, constructed or refur- **6–19** bished, it is necessary from the point of view of both the landlord and the tenant that there is adequate planning permission, any necessary listed building consent, building warrants, road construction consent, services consents, servitudes and wayleaves, so that the premises can be accessed and used. It may be necessary to make the missives conditional on these being obtained by the landlord, within a reasonably strict timetable, with the right in favour of each party to terminate the missives if the consents, etc. are not obtained by a certain time.

The landlord may want to have the right to terminate the missives if planning permission is not obtained for a specific amount of minimum development, as he will not want to be required to develop something that is not particularly viable from a financial point of view. If the missives envisage a minimum amount of permitted development, the tenant needs to be satisfied he will be able to trade or operate viably. If the tenant is a retailer, he is likely to want the strength of other retailers around him so as to attract more people into the locality.

Section 75 agreements

A planning agreement under s.75 of the Town and Country Planning (Scotland) **6–20** Act 1997 may be required in order to obtain planning permission. If so, the landlord will want to ensure that the tenant accepts the agreement as being a burden on the title, and the tenant must insist in the missives that the terms of the s.75 Agreement do not restrict the tenant's proposed use and/or trading hours.

The Planning etc. (Scotland) Act 2006[2] replaces planning agreements with planning obligations, and there is the ability for unilateral undertakings to be granted by the landowner.

Avoiding tenant loneliness

For new shopping centres, retail parks, business parks, etc. tenants will gener- **6–21** ally want to have a minimum amount of total development, and they may require their transaction to be conditional on a major tenant or other tenants proceeding with a lease that is to last for a minimum specified period of years. If so, the parties should consider whether the standard is to be set as a minimum number of other tenants, a certain number of units or a minimum amount of square feet taken up. Any such lettings should be required to be "at arm's length" so as to avoid the problem of the landlord granting leases to new companies set up by the landlord for the purpose of getting the numbers up.

---

[2] Planning etc. (Scotland) Act 2006 (asp 17).

Construction obligations

6–22   The landlord should be required to commence works within a specific period after obtaining the necessary consents, and thereafter to proceed with the works with all due diligence and to complete the works by a specific time. The landlord will want to provide for extensions of time to match extensions of time allowed to the contractor under the building contract. These will include things like force majeure or acts of God, strikes, lockouts, bad weather, non-availability of materials, etc. Both parties should consider how long they want to be bound for; there should be an absolute end stop date so that, come what may, if practical completion has not taken place by that date, then the tenant (and possibly the landlord) can walk away. There should be a right for the tenant to walk away if the landlord has not actually commenced works by a specific date.

    The landlord will want to reserve the right to alter the location and layout of the premises. The tenant will be disappointed if he is intending leasing a roughly square area in a good strategic position in the mall or estate, to find that he ends up with a long and narrow, or other odd shape of, premises tucked away at the back. The tenant should therefore stipulate that his premises are to be within an agreed location, and that the shape and size of the premises should not be changed (as this could be adverse to the tenant's standard way of operating), and that the premises should be no less (or not materially less) convenient for access and parking.

    It is important to understand and agree the specification, i.e. the detail of what is to be built. If the landlord is providing a "shell", it should be clear as to exactly what the landlord is providing—are the services being introduced into the premises and, if so, is this merely a connection that the tenant will arrange to be made live with the utility providers? What about floor covering? Is it screeding or is the landlord providing polished wooden flooring or something else? What about toilets, heating and air conditioning, etc.? What about lifts, escalators and the like? Are these being provided by the landlord where the premises comprise more than one storey? Is the landlord even providing stairs, lifts and escalators within the premises?

6–23   Who is providing the shop front? If it is the tenant, then what state will the landlord leave the premises in? What about the tenant carrying out works for its own fitting out? Can he start these prior to practical completion, and if so is there to be some procedure for certifying when the premises have reached a state that the tenant can take access for fitting out? How is the relationship between tenant's and landlord's workmen regulated for them to be working at the same time (if at all)?

    The landlord will want the right to vary the specification, and it is usual to allow for some variation so as to enable the landlord to substitute materials with others and to accommodate the requirements of planning and building control departments. The tenant should stipulate that any substitution does not involve any materials of inferior quality, and he may want to limit the circumstances in which substitution can be made, such as non-availability of the relevant materials or where planners or building control insist on a substitution. The tenant may want to have a substitution of materials or a variation of the specification, and if so then it is only right that the tenant should pay for this. The landlord will not want to suffer delay because of a change of mind on the tenant's part, and he is likely only to agree to some variation in the specification if such is readily achievable without causing him difficulties with the remainder of his works.

Tolerances and right to resile

The missives should impose on the landlord the obligation to construct in **6–24** accordance with the planning permission, building warrants and the specification and drawings. Accordingly, the size of what is to be built will be defined. The initial rent may be a fixed amount or it may be an amount per square foot of gross internal area or of net internal area, possibly subject to a minimum and/or maximum amount. Either way, many landlords will be quite happy for the property to be built slightly larger than the anticipated area, as this will most likely involve a better result at rent review, as there will be more area let to the tenant, and this therefore enhances the capital value of the whole entity. The landlord will usually reserve the right to make variations (which may be minor), and these would need to be defined such as substituting materials with others of no less quality, or doing something that does not require an amendment to the planning permission or the building warrant. Any non-minor variations should require the tenant's consent, and it is a matter for negotiation as to whether the withholding of such consent should or should not be subject to a reasonableness test.

It is reasonable to allow for a certain amount of tolerance so that the tenant must take the premises if they are built slightly larger or smaller than intended; many tenants and landlords will accept a tolerance of anything up to five per cent either way. Some missives will provide that the tenant must proceed with the lease provided the landlord builds within the tolerance, and that if the landlord builds outwith the tolerance, then the tenant alone has the right to resile without penalty. The parties should be aware that the premises may not be able to be measured until near to the date of practical completion, by which time the tenant has incurred considerable cost in professional fees, and may have recruited staff and ordered stock, and engaged contractors to do his shop fitting.

Some agreements for lease (missives) will provide that if the landlord "over builds", then the tenant is only required to pay rent for the amount of square feet that the landlord was supposed to build, and that if the landlord under builds then the tenant only pays for what has been built. The tenant may require the lease to contain an assumption in the rent-review clause that the gross or net internal area, as the case may be, is deemed to be the target area, so that the parties are not prejudiced by the fact that there has been a difference between target and actual area. Another variant on this is to provide in the agreement for lease for two different tolerances, so that if the area falls within the smaller tolerance (for example two per cent either way) the rent is the anticipated amount as if it had been built exactly on target, but if what is built is outwith this smaller tolerance, but within the larger tolerance (for example four per cent either way), then the tenant pays for what has actually been built if smaller, but does not pay extra if the landlord over builds at all.

The missives should specify how and by whom the unit is to be measured (gross or net internal area) and which basis or standard of measurement is to be used. There should be a procedure for the parties to try to agree on the measurement, and for the actual measurement to be done by a third party in the absence of agreement.

Date of entry—prior access for fitting-out

6–25 Many missives provide for the lease to commence on the date when the tenant is given access for fitting-out, which is often before the date of practical completion. One of the reasons for this is that any rent-free concession would then possibly run from the early access date. The tenant should try to negotiate that the lease starts on the day of or after practical completion, as the contractor will be responsible for the property until the certificate of practical completion is issued. Any early access should be on licence, so that the lease obligations that are imposed on the tenant do not start until the property has been handed over by the contractor to the landlord, i.e. until practical completion.

There is a complication, in that the building contractor is usually responsible for the property until the date of practical completion. Therefore it is necessary to provide that any pre-practical completion occupancy by the tenant is at the tenant's own risk. However, that only goes some of the way towards resolving the problem. It is worthwhile checking whether the contractor is happy for the tenant to take early entry to do his own shopfitting and whether such early entry could in any way prejudice the contractor's all risks insurance.

Practical completion issues and snaggings

6–26 The lease is likely to impose full repairing obligations on the tenant, and so the landlord could look to the tenant to sort out the inevitable snagging problems that arise in new or refurbished buildings. The tenant has no contractual relationship with the contractors or indeed with the architect and other professionals who were involved in the design of the works; although the tenant does have a very limited right of recourse at common law, very few tenants would be comfortable with relying on that right. The Contracts (Rights of Third Parties) Act 1999 does not apply in Scotland.

Some issues arise—first, the missives should provide for the landlord to have all snaggings and defects that arise during the period of 12 months after practical completion rectified without any cost to the tenant. Many building contracts have a defects liability period of one year following practical completion, therefore any snagging issues, i.e. items that remain to be finally completed, and any defects arising during that period will be the contractor's responsibility provided notification is given to the contractor. The landlord may want to limit his obligations to items that are properly the contractor's responsibility in terms of the building contract, so that the landlord is not caught for latent defects or any other "black holes". The tenant will want to ensure that, if the landlord disposes of the property before the end of the 12 month defects liability period (which starts on the date of practical completion), the landlord's successors in title are bound until all snaggings notified within the period have been made good.

6–27 The original landlord may of course sell the property before snaggings and defects are made good, and this would leave the tenant with only a personal right against the original landlord, who would by that time not have any right to go in and make good any defects. It is therefore important for the tenant to make sure that rights in respect of snaggings and making good of defects are enforceable, by having the original contracting party bound to produce an undertaking from any successor to have any snaggings and defects arising during the defects liability period made good. This undertaking should contain the same "perpetuation" provision that successors will grant and continue the obligation.

Secondly, the landlord has the contractual relationship with the professionals and the contractor, and can look to them to make good any defect due to negligence in design or workmanship in construction. The landlord therefore has two choices if and when something goes wrong: he can look to his tenant under the full repairing obligation, or he may possibly be able to look to his design team and contractor. If the problem occurs after the defects liability period has expired, he would need to show negligence on the part of the contractor or design team.

Collateral warranties

The missives should provide for the landlord to deliver to the tenant at prac- **6–28** tical completion duty of care undertakings (sometimes these are called collateral warranties) from the professionals and the contractor and from specialist sub-contractors.

These duty of care undertakings acknowledge that the granter owes a duty of care to the tenant, and warrants that reasonable care has been taken in carrying out the duties, and that any defect that becomes apparent within, usually 10, but sometimes 12, years will be made good. It is important for the tenant to have the right to assign the benefit of the duty of care undertakings once and for his assignee to be able to onwardly assign them once; otherwise the marketability of his lease will be adversely affected. Of course, the duty of care undertakings are not a total guarantee against any repairs or maintenance being needed; they merely guarantee that the work has been done with reasonable care and in accordance with the professionals' appointment or the building contract respectively. The tenant should see the appointment of professionals, the building contract and all variations of these. A full treatment of development obligations and collateral warranties is beyond the scope of this book.

CHAPTER 7

PREMISES, RIGHTS AND RESERVATIONS

Introduction

7–01 It is essential that in handling commercial lease work, we fully understand exactly what is included in the premises that are exclusively leased to the tenant, and what rights are given to him, as well as the rights that are reserved to the landlord. Every property is different, but the tenant needs to know what he is getting and what he is not getting. This Chapter considers the description of the premises and the package of rights and reservations not only in ground leases but also in single occupancy and multi-occupancy leases, as well as addressing what happens to improvements made to the premises by the tenant.

Premises–ground leases

7–02 The landlord owns the ground and everything beneath it and above it, subject to over-flying rights, reservations of oil in favour of the Crown, of coal and associated minerals in favour of the Coal Authority and of other minerals, mines, metals and stone in the ground in favour of any third parties. If the lease is of a vacant area of ground, and the tenant subsequently builds, or if the landlord leases the ground together with any buildings on it, and the tenant subsequently makes improvements that are heritable in nature such as installing a central heating system, air conditioning, etc. then the works that are carried out by the tenant will belong to the landlord. The tenant will not be entitled to remove these at any time during, or at termination of, the lease.

Premises—single occupancy leases

7–03 If the landlord is letting out everything that he owns at a certain location to the tenant, then the description of the premises will be straightforward, as it will mirror the landlord's title. If the premises owned by the landlord form part of a larger building that is in different ownerships, then the title deeds will usually provide for certain items of structure, etc. to be owned or used in common by the various owners, and rights to use these common items should be granted in the lease.

Premises—multi-occupancy leases

7–04 If the landlord lets out less than he owns at a specific location and he owns the whole of the larger entity, then care needs to be taken to describe clearly what is exclusively leased to each tenant, and to ensure that the remainder of the whole entity (i.e. everything that is not leased, or is able to be leased, to an individual tenant for exclusive occupancy) is defined as "common parts".

The premises exclusively let to the tenant are likely to be an envelope of airspace, together with the inner surfaces of the walls, floor and ceiling enclosing the airspace. In this case the landlord retains the remainder of the larger entity, and the lease will define which items are to be used in common.

If the premises are in a shopping centre, the landlord will retain the external walls, roofs, the foundations, the solum (ground on which the building is constructed), the malls, lifts, escalators, stairs, service area and parking areas, etc. The landlord may want to grant rights to various tenants to extend their shop fronts into the mall, and to grant concessions or occupancy licences for moveable sales units or sales structures in the mall and he should reserve the right to do so. In defining the premises it should be clarified that the shop front, windows and the plate glass all form part of the premises; the shop front may require to be constructed by the tenant with merely the space of the shop front being left by the landlord at handover of the unit. The lease should define that the windows and doors form part of the premises; window frames may be part of the common parts.

In multi-occupancy leases there will be a full repairing, replacing and rebuilding obligation imposed on the tenant in respect of the premises, but the tenant should remember that this is merely airspace and the inner faces of its surround. The landlord will usually undertake to repair, maintain, insure, replace, renew, rebuild and reinstate the common parts (which invariably includes the structure) with full recovery of the cost of so doing through the service charge.

Common parts

If the landlord is letting out everything that he owns within a larger entity, the **7–05** title deeds should contain a description of "common parts", i.e. items that are available for use in common by the owners and occupiers of that entity.

If the premises form part of larger property owned by the landlord, the lease should contain a definition of common parts. These will vary depending on the type of property involved. A typical list for a retail shopping centre or retail park could include: means of support; all structure including foundations, roof and external walls; fire escape and service corridors and stairs; lift shafts; toilets; stores and all other utilities provided for public or common service; car park; service roads; loading areas; pedestrian walkways; landscaped areas; plant and equipment; security and fire alarm systems; CCTV system; channels, ducts, drains, sewers, pipes, including sprinkler systems, pumps, valves, meters and connections in and passing through the centre, except so far as exclusively serving premises let to a single tenant.

Often, the lease will provide for the landlord to be allowed to decide what is, and is not, a common part. This is generally acceptable, provided the tenant revises the clause so as to ensure that nothing will detract from his beneficial use and occupancy of the premises, and that if items are being added to the common parts, these have to be appropriate for the type of property and within the principles of good estate management.

Tenant's fitting out works

If the tenant installs fixtures and fittings for his trade or manufacture then he is **7–06** allowed to remove these provided he has performed his obligations under the lease, and so long as the lease does not provide otherwise. In *Smith v Harrison*

& Co's Trustee[1] it was held that, although the lease allowed the tenant to remove at termination of the lease the items he had provided, he was prevented from so doing because he was in breach of his obligations under the lease.

An item will not be a fixture if it can easily be removed without injuring the property and if it was inserted for a temporary purpose rather than as a permanent improvement to the building.

In *Cliffplant Ltd v Kinnaird; Mabey Bridge Co Ltd v Kinnaird*[2] a tenant hired from a third party a large expandable building and a Bailey bridge which he installed on the premises. The tenant subsequently went into receivership and the lease was terminated. The owners of the expandable building and of the Bailey bridge asked the court to declare that they were the rightful owners of these items and for these to be handed back to them. The court held that once these items had been placed on the site they became heritable in nature and that they then belonged to the landlord.

Rights granted

7–07   If the premises are a self-contained building, then it should not be necessary to have specific rights of access and egress, unless the building is not immediately accessible from a public road. Otherwise it will be necessary for rights of pedestrian and vehicle access to be granted.

If the landlord is leasing all that he owns in a larger entity, then the tenant needs to check that all rights that he requires are contained in the landlord's title.

If the premises form part of a larger entity owned by the landlord, there will be a definition of "common parts" and the lease should give the tenant a right in common to use these.

The tenant should insist on rights of support, shelter and protection where the premises form part of a larger building, and also a right to use specific toilets where none are included in the premises. He should insist on rights of access and egress for vehicles and pedestrians to and from the premises, from and to the nearest public road and across service yards and internal estate roads, and for pedestrians by way of entranceways, malls, passages, stairs, etc. He will also typically need rights to use service roads, loading bays and docks, service stairs and goods lifts. In addition he will need the right of free passage of ventilation, coolant, gas, heating, water, waste and electricity and any other services from time-to-time serving the premises.

7–08   The tenant should also have the right to have his name on the directory board at the entrance of the estate or shopping centre, and the right to go onto the common parts to carry out repairs and renewals to the premises.

If the lease is of premises that are in a larger building, centre or estate, the tenant should try to ensure that access is available so he can get into the premises to use them when he wants, rather than only being able to do so during core or trading hours. He will need access to the premises for carrying out repairs, fitting out works, overtime working, shift working, etc.

The tenant should check that there are sufficient emergency escape rights and that the premises comply with all statutory requirements, such as disabled

---

[1] *Smith v Harrison & Co's Trustee* (1893) 21 R. 330.
[2] *Cliffplant Ltd v Kinnaird; Mabey Bridge Co Ltd v Kinnaird*, 1982 S.L.T. 2.

access laws. Additional rights may be needed to enable the tenant to comply with these obligations.

If the tenant needs or wants satellite dishes, TV aerials, telecoms or specialised electrical equipment on the premises, he will usually need to obtain landlord's consent and in some cases planning permission and, if it is a listed building, listed building consent. If the premises form part of a larger building in different ownerships, then the tenant will usually need the consent of all the other owners, as he is likely to need to use, or to carry out works to, the common parts. The tenant may have to ask the landlord to grant a wayleave (right across his property) to a utility or service provider in order for the tenant to obtain the required service.

Reservations

As absolute warrandice is implied in a lease unless contracted out of, the tenant **7–09** is entitled to possession of the entire premises without any encroachment or interference by the landlord throughout the period of the lease.

It is important for the landlord to reserve certain rights over the property and these reservations will vary depending on the actual property and its surroundings, but would typically include:

- the right to enter the premises for inspection and to compile a list of wants of repair;
- the right to enter the premises to carry out repairs to the premises in the event of the tenant's default;
- the right of access to the premises to carry out repairs to other premises or to the common parts;
- the right to lead existing pipes, cables, transmitters, etc. for electricity, gas, phone and other services, and to pass utilities and services through these;
- the right to replace and renew these pipes, cables, etc.;
- the right to install additional pipes, cables, etc. (the tenant should revise this so that any additional cables, etc. are installed in the same location as the existing ones and that they will not reduce the tenant's usable area);
- the right to attach to or place items on the common parts (including walls), advertising panels and signs, kiosks, TV aerials, lighting brackets with lamps, seats, vending machines, waste bins, etc;
- the right of support shelter and protection for adjoining and adjacent properties;
- the right to regulate and control use of the common parts including closing public entrances and varying and changing use of all or part of the common parts;
- the right to use the common parts for displays, exhibitions, entertainment and promotion;
- the right to put up scaffolding for carrying out works (the landlord may also want to consider reserving the right to attach an advertising hoarding to the scaffolding and to let out and receive the income from advertising space on it); and
- the right to vary, extend or reduce the common parts.

7–10 The tenant should revise the reservations clause so that the tenant's beneficial use and occupancy is not significantly affected, that the convenience of access to and from the premises is not significantly diminished, and if the access ways are to be obstructed, that the landlord must provide at all times suitable alternative access. A landlord should not accept a tenant's revisal that use and access will not be affected at all, as it would surely be impossible for a landlord to go into the premises without affecting these!

The tenant will also want to say that light and air to the premises are not to be diminished; this does not sit well with the landlord's reservation of right to put up scaffolding! In any event, the tenant will want to provide in the lease that scaffolding should be put up only if and for as long as necessary and there should be a banner saying the premises are open as usual for business

The tenant should also provide for the landlord to not be allowed entry to the premises for carrying out the reserved rights unless these cannot be practicably done from outwith the premises, for the landlord to cause the minimum of inconvenience to the tenant and his business, and to make good all damage to the premises and to the tenant's fixtures, fittings, stock and property. The tenant should stipulate that any change in the larger entity, whether by varying the common parts or otherwise, does not make any less advantageous any access arrangements or the strategic location of the premises.

Reservations will be interpreted according to the ascertainable intention of the parties at the time the lease was entered into. In *Possfund Custodial Trustees Ltd v Kwik-Fit Properties Ltd*[3] the lease allowed the landlord to enter to inspect and to examine the state of repair of the premises, and to serve a schedule of dilapidations on the tenant. The landlord asked the court to grant an order to allow him to drill boreholes in order to check for any contamination from underground fuel tanks. The court held that the meaning of the clause depended on the parties' intention at the time of entering into the lease, which would be ascertained from the language used, and that when it was construed in the light of other provisions of the lease, it was not wide enough to cover investigation of the kind proposed. The court commented that the meaning of the clause could not be altered retrospectively to take account of new legislation that requires the tenant to carry out all works required by law or by a local authority, and in the circumstances, the tenant's compliance with this legislation could only be determined by carrying out investigations that would go beyond the scope of the reservations clause.

---

[3] *Possfund Custodial Trustees Ltd v Kwik-Fit Properties Ltd*, 2009 G.W.D. 1–16.

CHAPTER 8

USE CLAUSE AND KEEP-OPEN OBLIGATIONS

Introduction

Landlords used to severely restrict the use that the tenant was allowed to make **8–01**
of the premises, so as to keep very strict control. This worked against the landlord at rent review as too restrictive a use clause was seen as onerous against
the tenant. The trend over the past 25 years has been to insert more lenient use
clauses in commercial leases. In this Chapter, we examine the main aspects of
use clauses, the degree of landlord's control, change of use and solus trading
undertakings. We also consider keep-open, or continuous occupancy and
trading, clauses and their enforceability.

A—USE CLAUSE

Common law

The lease will normally specify the permitted use either as a statement that the **8–02**
tenant will use the premises only for a specific purpose or alternatively as a
statement that the tenant is prohibited from using the premises except for the
stated purpose. Most leases will provide a degree of flexibility, by stating that
landlord's consent to a change of use will not be unreasonably withheld. This
is not done as an act of kindness; it is because a strict use clause is harmful to
the landlord when it comes to rent review.

At common law, if the tenant uses the premises other than for the purpose it
was let, he is deemed to be "inverting the possession", and the landlord can
stop this by a court action of interdict.

The landlord warrants at common law that planning permission exists for
the use permitted from time-to-time in terms of the lease. It is usual to exclude
this warranty. The tenant should check that planning permission does exist for
the proposed use.

The landlord also warrants at common law that the premises are reasonably
fit and suitable for the permitted use. Once again, this warranty is usually
specifically excluded.

Use classes order (planning)

Planning legislation provides a use classes order for the purpose of grouping **8–03**
together certain uses within a use class, so that planning permission that is
granted for one use within a particular use class is valid for any other use
within the same class. Other planning legislation from time to time allows
change of use from certain use classes to others (but not necessarily vice versa),
without needing planning permission. The planning regime is entirely different
to the landlord and tenant regime in a lease, but commercial leases often

include reference to the current use classes order[1] so as to provide convenient definitions. For example offices can be either Class 2 (offices generally supplied to visiting members of the public for professional banking, etc.) which are appropriate to be provided in a shopping area; or Class 4 (administrative offices) which are usually found in office blocks or business parks. The use clause in the lease may provide for use only as, for example, Class 4 offices.

An additional reference in the lease to the use classes order can be inserted to allow for a limited change of use by the tenant so that, for example, the premises may be let as a retail shop for the sale of men's and women's clothes, and for no other purpose except with the landlord's prior written consent, which will not be unreasonably withheld in the case of a proposed use within Class 1 of the current use classes order. It is good practice to state in the lease that a reference to a specific use classes order remains good despite revocation or replacement of that order, so that it remains a good point of reference for the remainder of the period of the lease.

Permitted use and ancillary uses

8–04 If the premises are leased as a supermarket, then the presumption is that items normally sold in supermarkets from time-to-time can be sold, and this would include alcohol. However, it is thought here that if the permitted use is as a "food store" or a grocery, then separate permission would be needed to sell alcohol.

The message to the tenant is therefore to widen the permitted use as far as possible, and to specify particular items or uses if such are required. This is not only to allow for flexibility in favour of the tenant, but also to help make the lease attractive to a prospective assignee or sub-tenant.

The tenant's use of the premises may be restricted in terms of the obligation to comply with the terms of planning permissions, licences, other provisions of the lease and the obligations in the title deeds. The tenant should revise in to the lease a statement that the use of the premises for purposes from time-to-time permitted in the lease will not be deemed to be a breach of any of the provisions of the lease.

Landlord's consent to change of use

8–05 A statement that landlord's consent for a change of use will not be unreasonably withheld is much wider in favour of the tenant than one that states that consent will not be unreasonably withheld to a change of use within a specific use class. A lender to the landlord or the tenant will want to see a workable use clause that is not too restrictive, so that the marketability of the tenant's interest is not adversely affected. Too harsh a use clause would detract from the value of the security, as a prospective assignee would be reluctant to sign up, and lenders would dislike the adverse effect it would cause at rent review and the adverse effect on marketability of the tenant's interest.

Too restrictive a use clause will be prejudicial to the tenant as it will limit the scope for marketability of the lease, and it will be prejudicial to the landlord as

---

[1] The current use classes order is Town & Country Planning (Use Classes) (Scotland) Order 1997 (SI 1997/3061).

it will reduce any uplift otherwise achievable at rent review as being an onerous term against the tenant. See Ch.11 (Rent Review—Valuation).

It is usual to provide for a specific use and then to insert various prohibitions of uses.

The landlord of a shopping centre or retail park may want to limit the uses of the units so as to obtain a beneficial mix of tenants, and in such event the landlord will usually reserve the right to refuse consent to a change of use where it conflicts with the good estate management/user mix within the larger entity.

Prohibition against residential use

Sections 8 to 10 of the Land Tenure Reform (Scotland) Act 1974[2] prohibit the **8–06** grant of a lease of residential property for longer than 20 years. Commercial leases usually contain an absolute prohibition against using the premises for residential purposes. The landlord will also want to exclude residential use so that the tenant does not acquire any rights to have the rent controlled under the various Rent Acts.

Residential use as ancillary to a commercial main use is not prohibited by the 1974 Act.

Other restrictions on use

It should be borne in mind that a restriction on use may be contained not only **8–07** in the use clause itself, but also in the obligations to comply with all planning legislation and planning permissions. The obligation to comply with the title deeds and planning permissions may restrict the range of items that can be sold, or the hours of operation, and title conditions may contain restrictions on use and hours of trading.

If a use clause contains reference to the business carried on by the tenant then it is important to check whether the definition of "the tenant" includes successors of the original tenant, in which case it will be the business of the tenant at the particular time, rather than being the business of the original tenant. However it is preferable to avoid reference to "the tenant's business" in the use clause, and instead to specify the actual types of use permitted.

Tenant cannot prevent competitive use of other premises

There is no obligation on the landlord to refrain from using, or to prohibit use **8–08** by others of, any adjoining property owned by the landlord where such use competes with that of the tenant. In *Geoffrey (Tailor) Highland Crafts Ltd v G.L. Attractions Ltd*[3] a landlord reserved an area "the landlord's administrative office" within the leased premises with a right of access for him to get to and from that area. The landlord then used that area for a use that competed with the tenant's use of the premises. The tenant sought a court order to stop this happening. The court held that, although at common law there is nothing preventing a landlord from competing with his tenant, it was unlikely the parties intended the landlord would actually compete with the tenant from

---

[2] Land Tenure Reform (Scotland) Act 1974 (c.38).
[3] *Geoffrey (Tailor) Highland Crafts Ltd v G.L. Attractions Ltd*, 2010 G.W.D. 08–142.

within the leased area and, in the circumstances, the reserved area was only to be used as an office.

If the tenant wants protection against the landlord competing or allowing others to compete with him, then he will need to obtain an undertaking from the landlord. This may be by way of a back letter, in which case the tenant should include provision for the landlord to procure that successors will grant a back letter in the same terms, or it maybe an actual obligation on the landlord within the lease. Such obligations will restrict the landlord's marketability in respect of the adjoining premises, and should not be given lightly.

Informal consent by landlord to change of use

8–09 In *BP Oil Ltd v Caledonian Heritable Estates Ltd*[4] a lease provided for the tenant to occupy and use the premises for erecting a petrol filling station and for no other purpose whatsoever. The irritancy clause provided for irritancy if there was a breach. In the first year of the term, the tenant obtained planning permission for use of part of the property as a car display and sales area. Consent from the landlord was not obtained until several years later, when a letter was issued indicating his acquiescence to the change of use, subject to the car sales and display area continuing to be part of the arrangement between the tenant and their filling station operator. The property was sold two years after the letter was issued, and then the new landlord objected to the change of use, and threatened to irritate the lease. The court held that in appropriate circumstances a provision in a lease could be varied by informal agreement, followed by the actings of the parties. In this case, the letter from the original landlord could not be seen as an arrangement to vary the use clause, but was merely a personal arrangement between that particular landlord and the tenant allowing the changed use subject to the conditionality being satisfied. The letter was held to be a personal arrangement, and was thus not binding on future owners of the property.

Solus undertaking

8–10 In *Optical Express (Gyle) Ltd v Marks & Spencer Plc*[5] the original landlord gave a "solus undertaking" back letter to the tenant, saying the tenant's premises would be the only unit, the principal use of which is an optician's in the shopping centre as originally built, and if the centre were extended in the future there would be no more than one additional optician. The back letter did not provide for the granter to obtain a letter in the same terms from any future landlord. The centre was sold, and the new landlord granted a lease of another unit to one of the tenant's competitors. The tenant sought interdict against the new landlord and the competitor to prevent it from trading as an optician in the centre and to have the lease to the competitor cancelled. The court held that the fact that the exclusivity provision was in a back letter meant it was collateral to the lease, and was not a variation of the lease as such, and was therefore not binding on anyone to whom the landlord conveyed the property. The tenant therefore lost, and was not granted interdict.

---

[4] *BP Oil Ltd v Caledonian Heritable Estates Ltd*, 1990 S.L.T. 114.
[5] *Optical Express (Gyle) Ltd v Marks & Spencer Plc*, 2000 S.L.T. 644.

In *Warren James (Jewellers) Limited v Overgate J.P. Ltd*,[6] an exclusivity clause contained in the lease itself was held to bind successor landlords. However, in that case, there was no argument about the point as such, and the court may not have followed the correct test for identifying real conditions. The case was concerned with which rules of interpretation should apply—the normal contract rules, or the real conditions rules. There was an implicit acceptance by the parties involved in the case that an exclusivity clause was a real condition, and therefore transmitted to singular successors. But the decision was reached without the benefit of argument, as the point was conceded. So it is safer to rely on the *Optical Express* position at this stage, i.e. that exclusivity clauses do not bind singular successors of the original landlord to the lease.

In *Ralph Lauren London Ltd v the Mayor and Burgesses of the London Borough of Southwark as Trustee of the London Burgh of Southwark Pension Fund*,[7] the court considered a back letter granted by the original landlord to the tenant saying that the landlord would not grant any first lettings to retailers, other than such high quality fashion retailers as are approved by the tenant (such approval not to be unreasonably withheld or delayed). The landlord intended granting a lease of another unit to a hairdressing salon. The tenant tried to prevent this, but the court held that a hairdressers is not a retailer and, as the back letter did not say that leases could *only* be granted to retailers, there was nothing to stop him from letting out for a non-retail use.

Competition law

The Competition Act 1998 (Land Agreements Exclusion Revocation) Order **8–11** 2010 came into force on April 6, 2011, and it applies to all existing contracts signed before, on and after that date. Before the Order was brought into force, "land agreements" enjoyed a presumption that they do not contravene Competition Law, unless proved to be to the contrary.

The sort of clauses in leases that are most likely to be affected by the Order are:

- Exclusivity agreements that limit the type of commercial activity the tenant can undertake, especially if this is intended to protect the landlord or other tenants from competition.
- Restrictions that limit the freedom of the landlord to let out other premises to competitors of the tenant, for example in a shopping centre.
- Restrictions on competition affecting retail outlets, restaurants or refreshment kiosks at sporting venues, conference centres and event sites etc.

If a lease contains a provision that is in breach of the competition law, then that provision will automatically be unenforceable in the courts. In addition, a third party who is adversely affected by the clause could seek an interdict and/ or damages for any losses it sustains as a result. The Office of Fair Trading can

---

[6] *Warren James (Jewellers) Limited v Overgate J.P. Ltd* [2010] CSOH 57.
[7] *Ralph Lauren London Limited v the Mayor and Burgesses of the London Borough of Southwark as Trustee of the London Burgh of Southwark Pension Fund* [2011] CSOH 103.

investigate alleged breaches and can impose fines on the parties to the relevant contract. A clause will only be in breach of competition law if it has an appreciable effect on competition in relevant markets, for example if there is a shopping centre that only allows one supermarket unit, to the exclusion of competitors, then the question of whether or not that has a restrictive effect on competition may depend on whether that supermarket faces competition from other supermarkets outside the centre and within a reasonable radius. Additionally, where parties are below certain market share thresholds (10 to 15 per cent), this will generally be seen as of being only of minimal consequence and will not be caught by the competition law prohibition.

Even if a clause is on the surface in breach of competition law, it can be treated as "exempt" if the parties can show that it brings economic and consumer benefits, that the restriction is no wider than necessary to achieve these benefits and that it does not effectively rule out competition. An example of this would be where a shopping centre developer restricts competition so as to protect a department store that is the "anchor tenant". The justification would be that the shopping centre brings economic and consumer benefits and that the restriction is needed to attract enough tenants or rent to justify the substantial investment that is made, i.e. no other tenants would find the centre attractive to trade from unless the anchor tenant was there. The OFT has issued a helpful guidance note which can be found at *http://www.oft.gov.uk/OFTwork/policy/land-agreements/* [accessed April 2, 2013].

B—KEEP-OPEN CLAUSES

Background

8–12 If a property is unoccupied, it is more difficult to market, and its condition is likely to deteriorate quicker that if it were occupied. Neighbouring properties will also be less attractive to customers and prospective tenants and purchasers. This applies even more in a shopping centre or a retail park, where landlords are likely to find it more difficult to rent out properties and to obtain satisfactory increases at rent review if tenants of some of the other units have decided to cease trading, albeit they are still paying their rents. The negative effect of a shop or office tenant stopping trading is all the more noticeable if that tenant is a major or anchor tenant in the centre or building.

The fashion therefore grew for landlords to insert a "keep-open" clause in their leases, requiring the tenant to continuously occupy and trade from the premises throughout the duration of the lease. This is very different to an obligation to take possession of and commence occupying the premises, which the tenant can perform at the start of the lease, following which he is free to move out.

Effect on rent review and marketability

8–13 A keep-open clause might have the effect of reducing any increase in the rent otherwise achievable at rent review, as being an onerous clause on the tenant. If there is a keep-open clause inserted in the lease, the tenant should try to revise this so as to allow the premises to be closed during repair, refurbishment, staff training, and while trying to find an assignee or sub-tenant, and also until the date of entry of the assignee or the sub-tenant. The landlord should remember that the wording of the use clause and keep-open clause should be sufficiently clear so that an application for specific implement would have a reasonable chance of success. If the landlord is unable to obtain an order of specific implement then his only remedy will be damages and he would need to clearly show the loss suffered.

Enforcement of keep-open clause

There is a general principle that it is not competent to enforce a positive obliga- **8–14** tion on the tenant by way of interdict. In *Co-operative Insurance Society Ltd v Argyll Stores (Holdings) Ltd*[8] the lease contained an obligation on the tenant to keep the supermarket premises open for retail trade during the normal business hours in the locality. The tenant notified the landlord of his intention to stop trading before the expiry of the lease. The landlord sought injunction against the tenant from stopping continued occupation and usage of the supermarket premises for the purposes of trading as a supermarket. The House of Lords held that it would be impossible to enforce an injunction, and that instead an order for specific performance would normally be appropriate, but not in this particular case because the obligation in the lease was too imprecise to be readily enforceable.

In *Britel Fund Trustees Ltd v Scottish & Southern Energy Plc*[9] a lease provided for the tenant to keep open the premises for normal trading between 08.30 and 18.00 every day except Sundays and public holidays, or during such other hours as the landlords specify to meet any change in shopping patterns. The lease also provided for landlords' consent not to be unreasonably withheld in the case of a proposed sub-lease, and for the tenants to enforce performance by any permitted sub-tenant of all obligations binding on the sub-tenant under the sub-lease. The tenant was agreeable to an order being made requiring him to keep the premises open during the trading hours on condition that the order would cease to apply to the premises or a part thereof lawfully sub-let, on the grant of any such sub-lease. The court held that a final order in terms that compelled the tenant himself to comply with the use clause and to keep open during the running of a lawful sub-lease, would demand more of the tenant than was required in terms of the lease, and that it would be inappropriate to grant an order in these terms.

In *Highland & Universal Properties Ltd v Safeway Properties Ltd*[10] the lease provided for the landlord to perform the services and others between 08.30 and 18.30 Mondays to Saturdays inclusive, with the right to the landlord to vary these hours each day if he considers this necessary or desirable. The lease imposed on the tenant the obligation to keep the premises open for trade throughout normal hours of business, and prohibited the tenant from using or allowing to be used the premises other than for the retail sale of goods sold in a high class retail store. The tenant publicly announced his intention to close the store, and the landlord asked the court to order the tenant to keep the store open for retail trade during the normal hours of business. The court held that specific implement was competent, and that in Scottish law a party to a contractual obligation was generally entitled to enforce that obligation as a matter of right subject to the court's discretion to refuse it. The discretion would be exercisable only in exceptional circumstances where there were good reasons to

---

[8] *Co-operative Insurance Society Ltd v Argyll Stores (Holdings) Ltd* [1998] A.C. 1.

[9] *Britel Fund Trustees Ltd v Scottish & Southern Energy Plc*, 2002 S.L.T. 223.

[10] *Highland & Universal Properties Ltd v Safeway Properties Ltd*, 2000 S.C. 297.

refuse it, and in particular if it would be inconvenient and unjust or if it would cause exceptional hardship to grant it. The terms "high class retail store" and "normal hours of business" did not make the obligation void from uncertainty.

8–15 In *Retail Parks Investments Ltd v The Royal Bank of Scotland Plc (No.2)*[11] the lease provided for the premises to be used as bank offices and for no other purposes except with the landlord's written consent, and for the tenant to use and occupy the premises and to continue to use and occupy them during all normal business hours and to keep the premises open for business throughout the whole period of the lease. The court held that the order sought by the landlord merely required the tenant to continue to honour his obligation for the remainder of the term, and that it was sufficiently precise and specific.

In *Douglas Shelf Seven Ltd v Co-operative Wholesale Society Ltd*[12] a lease of a supermarket in a shopping centre contained an obligation on the tenant to take possession of, and to use and occupy, the premises from commencement of the term and within three months after that to start trading and to continue to use and occupy the premises throughout the whole term. The lease also imposed on the tenant obligations to repair the premises to FRI standards and to contribute to service charge. The tenant closed the premises. The original case[13] awarded the landlord damages for the tenant's breach of the keep-open clause due to the reduction in the capital value of the shopping centre and the loss of income in the form of rent and service charge from other units within the centre, as a result of the tenant having closed the premises. The subsequent case was a separate matter in that the landlord sought an order that the tenant should carry out repairs needed to the premises. The court held that the fact that the landlord had already been awarded, and had received, damages for breach of the keep-open clause, did not prevent the landlord from enforcing the obligation on the tenant to repair and maintain the premises, and that all other obligations (apart from the keep-open clause which had been dealt with) remained fully enforceable.

ENGLAND

Use clause

8–16 In England there is no restriction on the duration of a residential lease.

It may be considered a breach of the landlord's covenant of quiet enjoyment if the landlord allows a use to be made of adjoining land he owns so as to compete with the use made of the premises by the tenant.

Keep-open clause

8–17 In England, the courts will not grant an order for specific performance to force a tenant to remain open and trading. The appropriate remedies available to the landlord are forfeiture and/or damages.

---

[11] *Retail Parks Investments Ltd v The Royal Bank of Scotland Plc (No.2)*, 1996 S.C. 227.
[12] *Douglas Shelf Seven Ltd v Co-operative Wholesale Society Ltd* [2009] CSOH 3.
[13] *Douglas Shelf Seven Ltd v Co-operative Wholesale Society Ltd* [2007] CSOH 53.

CHAPTER 9

RENT AND OTHER PAYMENTS

Introduction

In this Chapter we look at the common law and the main provisions in a lease **9–01**
in respect of payments by the tenant to the landlord. We consider rent, turnover
rent, interest, liability for the cost of applications for consent or approval,
dilapidations and the cost enforcement of the lease. We also consider performance deposits (although these are more fully dealt with in Ch.24) and joint and
several liability. Finally we look briefly at the position in England.

A—SCOTLAND

Rent

In order for a valid lease to exist, there must be a rent payable, even if it is only **9–02**
£1 per annum. Traditionally, ground leases have provided for rent to be payable
half-yearly in arrear, but in recent times there has been a trend towards having
rent payable quarterly or half-yearly in advance.

Many other leases provide for rent to be payable quarterly in advance, while
others provide for rent to be payable monthly in advance.

The old quarter days for payment were:

- Candlemas, February 2;
- Whitsunday, May 15;
- Lammas, August 1; and
- Martinmas, November 11.

The Term and Quarter Days (Scotland) Act 1990[1] has redefined the quarter
days as:

- Candlemas, February 28;
- Whitsunday, May 28;
- Lammas, August 28; and
- Martinmas, November 28.

If a lease that was granted before the Act came into force provided for
payment of rent on Lammas, Candlemas, Whitsunday and Martinmas respectively then the payment dates for these were automatically changed to February
28, May 28, August 28 and November 28 respectively, but if the lease provided

---

[1] Term and Quarter Days (Scotland) Act 1990 (c.22).

for rent to be paid on the named term day and this was defined as a specific calendar date or in fact on any other specific date, then that specific date will prevail.

VAT on rent

9–03   Most leases provide for the tenant to pay VAT on the rent and on all other sums from time-to-time payable. If the landlord has waived VAT exemption before entering into the lease itself (or before entering into an obligation to grant a lease), and if the lease is silent about VAT being payable, the rent and other sums are deemed to be inclusive of VAT, and the landlord has to account to HMRC for the VAT element.

If the landlord has not waived VAT exemption before entering into the lease, and then proceeds to waive it some time after the lease starts, and if the lease is silent about VAT, then the landlord is not prejudiced. The act of waiving VAT exemption is considered by HMRC to be a change in the law taking place after the start of the contracts, and so the tenant then has to pay all VAT on the rents after the date of the landlord's waiver of VAT exemption.

Turnover rents

9–04   It is common for leases of premises in shopping centres to provide for rent to consist of two separate elements: a basic rent which is a specified amount, and which is reviewed every five years, and an amount based on the tenant's turnover (volume of business done), which may or may not be reviewed. Some leases will have only a turnover rent. The basic rent will usually be payable quarterly in advance, and the turnover rent is usually payable annually in arrear.

It is important to define "turnover", to specify the period of time to be used for calculating turnover, and to provide a procedure for determining the amount of turnover in the event of dispute. For the purpose of calculating turnover, "the tenant" should include any permitted occupant.

The first turnover period should start on the date of entry, or if later on the date on which the basic rent starts to be payable, and run from then to the end of the turnover year, which will be a date chosen by the landlord. The final turnover period will be the proportion of the turnover year from the anniversary until the date of termination of the lease.

9–05   Some shopping centres have a facility for electronic point of sale information to be fed directly to the landlord, but even if this is available there will need to be adjustments to take account of returns, discounts, etc. The definition of "turnover" varies from lease to lease, and can usually be negotiated to a certain extent, depending on market conditions. The landlord will usually try to include all of the following:

- the total amount of money received or receivable for all goods sold and services supplied from the premises even if payment is made to a third party;
- all amounts payable from orders taken at the premises even if delivery or performance is made elsewhere;
- all amounts payable from orders taken elsewhere by people operating from or reporting to the premises;
- all amounts payable from vending machines or devices at the premises;

- all amounts payable in respect of the tenant's business at the premises;
- all grants, subsidies and other income paid to the tenant by any public or national authority or government to assist with the cost of supply of goods or services at the premises (the tenant will usually try to resist inclusion of grants and subsidies);
- all delivery, insurance and post charges relating to any transaction;
- all sales on credit or instalment terms are deemed to be sales for full price at the date entered into even though the tenant will receive payment later;
- all hire purchase transactions are deemed a sale of goods for full price at the date of entering into the contract; and
- deposits paid by customers are included at the time of receipt but will be deducted if and when repaid.

Usually, no allowance is given for bad or doubtful debts, or commissions payable to credit card companies or credit providers.

The following deductions are often allowed from turnover:

- VAT and similar tax imposed directly on the tenant;
- staff discounts for goods or services supplied by the tenant;
- reasonable amounts on trade-ins from customers;
- refunds given for return of goods provided this is not more than the sale price that had been charged; there is a problem for the landlord if he allows the tenant to deduct from turnover refunds at the store for goods bought on the internet or from another of the tenant's outlets, as these distort the turnover figure;
- capital sums received from the disposal of assets apart from normal stock in trade;
- rents and contribution to service charge received from sub-tenants and other occupants;
- allowances for defective or unsatisfactory goods or services; and
- interest charges and credit account service charges.

The growth of internet shopping and service presents an interesting **9–06** situation for the landlord who is dependent on the tenant's turnover at the premises. If a member of the public visits the shop and sees and even tries out an item, and does not buy it at the shop, but instead goes home and buys the item on the internet, is that a sale from or attributable to the premises? How can anyone prove that the customer went into that particular branch, or that he went into any actual shop, as opposed to buying on the internet? One possible way to deal with this problem could be to provide for the definition of turnover to be actual sales made and orders taken at the shop plus a proportion of the tenant's total internet sales. This could be as crude as dividing the turnover from internet sales by the number of shops the tenant operates from time to time.

The lease could also contain a prohibition against directly or indirectly (such as by way of a nominee or a related company) selling goods or services cheaper at other outlets or over the internet than they are sold from time to time in the shop. This is a matter for detailed negotiation at the time of entering into the lease. However, the practical difficulty is how to actually monitor this.

The lease should provide for the tenant to supply within a specified period of time after the turnover period, a statement from external auditors, certifying the days on which the property was not open for trade and the amount of turnover for the turnover period. The landlord usually insists on the right to have its own accountant carry out an audit, and if this shows higher turnover than the tenant's audit, the cost will be borne by the tenant, and the landlord's figures will prevail. The tenant may want the landlord to keep confidential the amount of turnover of the tenant except to the extent the landlord has to disclose to comply with any legal requirement.

The lease should say that the turnover rent provisions continue to apply after termination of the lease, but only in respect of the period up to termination of the lease.

The landlord has a strong interest in the business success of the tenant. Turnover rent leases usually prohibit sub-letting throughout the whole term, and many prohibit assignation within three years after the premises first open for trade, and within one year after the date of a permitted assignation. Concessionaires up to a certain amount of floor area may be permitted provided that the concessionaires' turnover is taken into account.

Turnover rent leases are likely to provide for no turnover rent to be payable during the period of one year after date of entry of the assignee and for the basic rent to increase by a given percentage during that period.

Interest

9–07   There is, probably at common law, no right to payment of interest in respect of sums payable in commercial leases (the position not having been tested in Scotland). Nor does the Late Payment of Commercial Debts (Interest) Act 1998[2] help the landlord. Therefore, unless interest is specifically contracted for, the landlord is unlikely to be entitled to interest on late rent or other sums in terms of the lease. If the landlord raises a court action against the tenant for payment of late rent or other sums, then he can ask the court to award interest on the sum due, but this will usually be from the date of commencement of the court action, as opposed to being from the date when the rent or other sum was actually payable.

Similarly, there is no right for the landlord to receive interest on any increased amount of rent payable from a rent review date if the rent review is not agreed or determined until after the review date. This is why leases usually provide for interest to be payable, often at lower than the penalty rate, on this uplift in rent following review. Apart from being beneficial to the landlord, this encourages the tenant to try to reach agreement sooner rather than later in respect of an outstanding rent review.

Most leases provide for interest to be payable at or around four per cent above base rate of one of the clearing banks from the due date until paid (in the case of rent), and from the due date or if later from the date of demand (in respect of all other sums). There is no period of grace implied at law, and therefore if the tenant wants a period of grace during which no interest will apply, then this needs to be revised into the lease. Landlords are not enthusiastic about granting periods of grace as this puts them in the position of being the tenant's

---

[2] Late Payment of Commercial Debts (Interest) Act 1998 (c.20).

banker. However, if any concession is to be given, it should be that there will be no interest payable if the amount is paid within 14 days of the due date, but if it is not paid within that time then interest is payable as from the due date.

In England it has been held in *Trusthouse Forte Albany Hotels Ltd v Daejan Investments Ltd*[3] that an arbitrator has power to award interest.

Rates

The tenant or other occupier has the obligation to pay local rates for the prop- **9–08** erty. If a short-term lease is granted, the rent is sometimes stated to be inclusive of rates and other sums, such as insurance premia.

Applications for consent

Most leases provide for the tenant to be responsible for all costs incurred by the **9–09** landlord in connection with any application for consent or approval in the lease. The landlord will usually provide for his legal, surveyor's and lender's costs to be met by the tenant. The tenant should try to revise this so that he is responsible for "reasonable" costs. The landlord will not want an argument every time he looks for reimbursement of costs, and the parties may ultimately compromise on the tenant being liable for costs "properly and reasonably incurred".

Schedules of dilapidations

The landlord will want the lease to provide for the tenant to pay for his survey- **9–10** or's costs of inspection, preparation of schedules of dilapidations and monitoring of the works. The tenant will not want to pay for frequent and, in his view, unnecessary schedules, and he may seek to limit the frequency of schedules of dilapidations and to provide that he is only responsible for reasonable costs that are properly and reasonably incurred. The landlord will want to recoup his whole costs, and he will usually argue that if there is no breach of repairing and maintenance obligations, then there will be no schedule of dilapidations. Of course, the landlord cannot know whether there are any dilapidations until and unless he has an inspection carried out. Market conditions and the relative strength of the parties will determine the outcome of the expenses tug of war.

Enforcement

The lease should provide for the tenant to pay the landlord's costs in enforcing **9–11** the tenant's obligations in the lease. Once again the tenant will want to qualify this with reasonableness, but if he is in default, then he should pay the landlord's costs. A usually acceptable compromise is that the tenant pays "costs properly incurred".

Management charge

Many commercial landlords will appoint managing agents to invoice and **9–12** collect the rent, deal with insurance and, in multi-occupancy properties, to deal

---

[3] *Trusthouse Forte Albany Hotels Ltd v Daejan Investments Ltd* [1980] 256 E.G. 915.

with repairs, maintenance and all other matters relating to the larger entity. The managing agents charge for this and the landlords seek to pass on this charge to the tenant. Sometimes landlords will self-manage a property or will set up a sister company to perform the management function. These landlords consider the management charge to be a "bonus rent".

There is no right in favour of the landlord to charge for management unless the lease specifically provides for this. If the property is stand-alone and self-contained, or does not form part of a larger entity owned by the landlord, the tenant may be successful in arguing that there is no management involved, and that there should thus be no management charge.

Landlords usually invoice the management charge at the same time as the rent, and the management charge is usually expressed as a specified percentage of the rent. Sometimes, in multi-occupancy situations, it is a percentage of the total service charge costs. In cases where there is a strong tenant, a cap on management charge, and indeed on service charge itself, is often negotiated.

Other sums

9–13   The landlord will look to the tenant for reimbursement of the cost of insurance valuations; the tenant should seek to limit his exposure to paying for this to only once every three years or less frequently. The lease will usually provide for the tenant to pay the insurance premia and any sums payable in terms of the title deeds or by statute or at common law, including sums necessary to carry out works to comply with statute and subsidiary legislation, such as provision of disabled access, obtaining asbestos reports, etc.

For multi occupancy premises the landlord will set up a service charge regime, and this is more fully dealt with in Ch.29.

Performance deposit agreement

9–14   If the landlord is not satisfied with the financial strength of the tenant, then the parties may agree that a performance deposit should be put in place. Note that it should be a "performance deposit" as opposed to a "rent deposit", in order that the fund can be used not only for rent but also for other sums payable by the tenant. Whatever the parties choose to call the money or the agreement that regulates its use, what matters is what the agreement actually says. It is normal to enter into a performance deposit agreement stating the amount of deposit paid, what is to happen to the money if the tenant pays his rent, etc. on time, what is to happen to the interest earned on the money and how and when the rent deposit is to be paid back to the tenant with interest thereon. This topic is fully discussed in Ch.24.

Joint and several liability

9–15   If the lease imposes joint and several liability on the tenant and his successors and assignees, the landlord can look to any previous tenant for full payment, leaving his "target" to seek recovery of the sum from the current tenant. If the current tenant assigns the lease, then he, and every previous and future tenant for the duration of the lease, is liable for payments for the remainder of the term. Some leases impose joint and several liability for rent only, while others will impose it for all payments and for performance of all other obligations imposed on the tenant. It is considered to be very prejudicial for a lease to impose joint and several liability, and this will usually justify a significant reduction of any increase in rent otherwise available at rent review. Most leases do not impose joint and several liability on tenants and assignees.

However, it is normal, and is not deemed prejudicial, for a lease to impose joint and several liability on all individuals who are the tenant at any one time, as there are often joint tenants.

B—ENGLAND

Rent payment dates

In England the rent payment dates are: **9–16**

- Ladyday, March 25;
- Midsummer, June 24;
- Michaelmas, September 29; and
- Christmas, December 25.

Privity of contract

Leases that were granted before January 1, 1996 of premises in England **9–17** imposed on the first tenant continuing liability throughout the entire term, even after assignment of the lease. This continuing liability was abolished for leases granted after January 1, 1996 by the Landlord and Tenant (Covenants) Act 1995,[4] which introduced Authorised Guarantee Agreements. However, the continuing liability remains in place for leases that were granted before January 1, 1996. This is discussed in more detail in Ch.15.

Recovery of rent and other sums from former tenant or a guarantor

In terms of s.17 of the 1995 Act, a landlord cannot recover from a former **9–18** tenant, or from a former guarantor, arrears of rent or other fixed payments, such as service charge, unless within six months of the money becoming due, the landlord has notified the former tenant or the guarantor, as the case may be, of the amount due and that he intends to seek payment.

A former tenant or guarantor can demand an over-riding lease. This is discussed in more detail in Ch.15.

In terms of s.19 of the 1995 Act, the former tenant (or guarantor) has the right, in certain circumstances, to receive an overriding lease where he has paid a fixed sum for arrears of rent or some other amount reserved as rent, such as insurance premia or service charge, following demand by the landlord. He must notify the landlord within 12 months of making the payment; otherwise he loses his right to be granted the over-riding lease. The overriding lease is to be for slightly longer than the current lease (usually three days) and should contain the same obligations and terms.

---

[4] Landlord and Tenant (Covenants) Act 1995 (c.30).

CHAPTER 10

RENT REVIEW—PROCEDURE

Introduction

10–01 In many jurisdictions, leases of commercial premises last for only one or two years, and accordingly there is no need for a rent review clause, as the parties will simply renegotiate if the lease is to be renewed. In the UK, the traditional 25-year term has given way to a trend towards shorter term leases of 10 or 15 years, often with early termination options.

If the lease does not provide for any rent reviews then the specified rent remains payable throughout the whole term of the lease. There are various types of rent review, which include review to open market value; inflation linked to the general Retail Prices Index or some other index; and a stepped rent where the actual rent payable throughout the whole term of the lease is specified or is subject to increase by way of a formula such as a specified percentage compounded annually. Some leases provide for minimum and/or maximum increases with reference to inflation.

In order to allow the landlord to receive rent payments from his tenant at a level that remains realistic during the whole period of the lease, it became necessary to provide for the amount of rent payable to be reviewed from time to time, so as to take account of the effects of inflation. In recent years, the pattern has been for five-yearly rent reviews (sometimes three-yearly) on an "upwards only" basis, meaning the rent can never go down. There is a fundamental difficulty with rent reviews, as it is necessary to value the rent that should be payable for the premises, at a time when the premises remain leased to the tenant. Therefore it is necessary to provide what is to happen in a "hypothetical lease" by saying that the rent payable is the amount that would be payable if the premises were, at that time, available for let to a willing tenant. This has created a rent review "industry" and a raft of litigation. Valuation in rent review is dealt with in Ch.11.

The modern day rent review clause should contain various guidelines, in the form of assumptions and disregards, as to how to value the rent and what procedure should be adopted. If there is some, but not enough, guidance in the rent review clause, the courts will step in to give commercial business sense to the clause, but the courts will not rewrite a clause that is so uncertain as to be unworkable.

10–02 In addition to saying when the rent is to be reviewed, and the basis of valuation of the new rent, most rent review clauses contain a method for resolving disputes as to the amount of rent payable. If this is arbitration, then an award will be made at the end of the rent review process. Arbitrations do not produce reported case law, unless a point of law has been referred to the courts for determination. There is a large amount of case law on rent review from the English courts, and as usual, this is not binding on the Scottish courts unless it takes the form of a judgment issued by the House of Lords, (now known as the Supreme Court). However, surveyors and solicitors regularly rely on case law from England and elsewhere in considering rent review clauses in leases.

When investment purchasers, lenders and their professional advisers look at an existing lease of a property, the main provisions they will examine are the rent review clause, the repairing obligations and the assignation and sub-letting clauses, in order to determine whether the lease is acceptable for a purchase or loan transaction.

Once a lease has been granted, the parties might never have to look at the other clauses, but they will definitely have to consider and implement the rent review clause. If the clause has not been drafted properly, the disadvantaged party will have regular opportunities and much time in which to contemplate the effects of the poor draftsmanship.

Different types of rent review

The usual position is that rent is reviewed to Market Rent (the basis of review **10–03** laid down in the surveyors' "red book") at specified intervals, and these reviews are "upwards only", which means that the rent can never be reduced at rent review, even if a lower rent would be justified at that time. Some leases do not provide for upwards only rent review, and so the rent could decrease at review; such leases are not attractive to a prospective purchaser of the property as an investment, i.e. buying with the benefit of that lease.

Some leases provide for stepped rents, so that the rent increases to specific amounts at periodic intervals; this is often found in leases of nursing homes. Some rent review clauses will link the rent review to inflation, and in some cases there will be minimum possible increases so as to protect the landlord against low or zero inflation and from deflation, and maximum possible increases so as to protect the tenant from high inflationary increases.

Rent reviews in sub-leases may be tied to the rent review in the head lease, so that the sub-tenant pays the rent from time to time payable under the head lease.

Rent reviews to Market Rent involve negotiation and in some cases delay, and they carry a cost implication, as the parties usually consult surveyors to collate evidence of rent payable for comparable premises. Reviews on the basis of fixed and known uplifts have the benefit of certainty, but involve a gamble by the parties, as the rent that would be payable in the market at each review will almost always be different to the prescribed amount in the lease, and so one party is likely to lose out by having increases pre-determined. Linking rent reviews to inflation may sound like the purist's answer to the problem, but much will depend on which inflation index is chosen, and this choice may not prove to be appropriate, in light of actual rental growth in the market within the vicinity of the premises. There is also an inherent danger of using an arithmetical formula, and it is essential that the formula is checked to see that it actually works.

Rent review clause void from uncertainty

A tenant will try, if at all possible, to argue that the rent review clause is so **10–04** unclear in its terms that it should be declared to be void from uncertainty. It is therefore important from the landlord's point of view that the lease be clearly drafted.

In *Crawford v Bruce*[1] the court had to consider a lease for 10 years with the possibility of an extension for a further five years. The lease merely provided for the rent to be reviewed every three years. The court held that the rent review provision was void from uncertainty because the review clause lacked the elements that would be necessary before a reviewed rent could be determined, and the terms of the lease were such that it could be read as meaning that in the absence of review, the original rent would continue to be payable.

In *McCalls Entertainments (Ayr) Ltd v South Ayrshire Council (No.1)*[2] it was held that if a contract provides for a price (or rent) to be agreed, or to be determined by a valuer, then it is implied that the price (or rent) to be determined is one that is fair and reasonable.

10–05 In *City of Aberdeen Council v Clark*[3] the court considered a 99-year ground lease, which provided for either the landlord or the tenant to require the rent to be renegotiated at the end of each period of 21 years, and failing agreement for the rent to be determined by an arbiter. The tenant argued that the rent review clause lacked the elements necessary for a reviewed rent to be able to be determined, and if the lease could continue without reference to the review provision on the basis of the original rent, then it would be inappropriate to imply terms so as to give effect to the rent review.

The court held that:

- there was a clear intention of the parties that there should be a rent review;
- it would be extraordinary if the landlord had been willing to commit itself to a fixed rent for 99 years; and
- as there was a specific clause dealing with rent review, the tenant must have understood that the rent would be subject to review.

The court also held that as the contract expressly laid down the process for settling the new rent including the nomination of an arbiter who was to be a surveyor skilled in valuation of property, it was reasonable to suppose that the parties intended that the arbiter would fix the rent on the basis of what was fair and reasonable. In addition, the arbiter should proceed to determine the rent on the basis of the terms of the existing lease, and this would give effect to what the parties had contemplated, rather than introducing a wholly artificial result that would be inconsistent with the original intentions.

Rent review dates

10–06 The lease should specify the rent review dates. It is preferable to say the rent will be reviewed on an actual date and on every fifth (or whatever) anniversary of that date during the lease, and during any extension and continuation thereof.

---

[1] *Crawford v Bruce*, 1992 S.L.T. 524.
[2] *McCalls Entertainments (Ayr) Ltd v South Ayrshire Council (No.1)*, 1998 S.L.T. 1403.
[3] *City of Aberdeen Council v Clark*, 1999 S.L.T. 613.

Interim rents

Some old fashioned leases (and indeed some new leases!) contain provisions **10–07** that not only allow the landlord to serve a trigger notice to start the rent review process, stating the amount of rent that he seeks at rent review, but also for an interim rent to be payable from the review date until the actual rent review is agreed or determined. These clauses usually provide for an accounting to take place between the parties in respect of any over- or under-payment taking place following agreement or determination. The amount of interim rent payable may be sky-high, and this could in fact lead to an irritancy (termination) of the lease on the grounds of breach by the tenant if he cannot afford to pay the interim rent.

Carrying out the rent review

It is important that any notice starting the rent review procedure should be **10–08** correctly prepared, and correctly and timeously served.

In *Durham City Estates v Felicitti*[4] the landlord issued a rent review notice in which the amount in figures differed from the amount in words. The amount in words was lower than the amount in figures. The court held that the tenant would be correct in assuming that the words are right and that the numbers had a typographical error.

If the lease does not provide for upwards only rent review, but only provides for the landlord to be able to initiate the review, then the courts have stepped in to protect the tenant. In *Sudbrook Trading Estate v Eggleton*[5] the court held that it can appoint a valuer where one party to the lease has failed to comply with the requirement in the lease that he should appoint a valuer.

In *The Royal Bank of Scotland Plc v Jennings*[6] the rent review was not upwards only, and the lease said that the initial yearly rent was payable only until the first review date and after that the rent should be a market rent calculated in accordance with the review clause. The review clause said that only the landlord was entitled to have an expert appointed. The court held this was a contractual term for the new rent to be determined in accordance with the rent review clause and for the new rent to be substituted from the first review date for the initial rent, and that this was mere machinery, and as the landlord had failed or refused to do so, the court could appoint an expert. The landlord could not frustrate the operation of the contract by failing to operate the review clause.

In *Barclays Bank v Savile Estates*[7] the court commented that it could be **10–09** appropriate to imply a term requiring a landlord to apply for the appointment of a third party to determine the rent review even in the case of an upwards only review. This case was different to *The Royal Bank of Scotland v Jennings* case, as in that case there was no upwards only provision, but the lease did require the rent to be reviewed.

---

[4] *Durham City Estates v Felicitti* [1990] 03 E.G. 71; [1991] 1 E.G.L.R. 143.
[5] *Sudbrook Trading Estate v Eggleton* [1983] 1 A.C. 444; [1983] 265 E.G. 215; [1983] 1 E.G.L.R. 147.
[6] *The Royal Bank of Scotland Plc v Jennings* [1997] 19 E.G. 152; [1997] 1 E.G.L.R. 101.
[7] *Barclays Bank v Savile Estates* [2002] EWCA Civ 589; [2002] 24 E.G. 152; [2002] 2 E.G.L.R. 16.

However in *Standard Life Assurance Co Ltd v Unipath*[8] the rent review provision in a lease was upwards only and the court said that it would be pointless for a tenant to seek to initiate a review.

There are cases where the rent review can be upwards or downwards (as in *The Royal Bank of Scotland Plc v Jennings* case) and the landlord alone has the right to decide whether to review. If he does so, he takes the risk that the rent may go down, however the courts have held that the landlord should not be forced to take that risk.

There is no presumption that a rent review clause should be able to be exercised by both parties; it will always depend on the type of the review and on the wording of the clause.

In *Hemingway Realty Ltd v Clothworkers Co*[9] the review clause said that the landlord had the right to review the yearly rent; the rent review was upwards or downwards. The court held that where the lease provides clearly for the landlord alone to be able to initiate the review, the absence of an upwards only review formula is not enough to require or allow the court to take a view that the review clause is exercisable by landlord or tenant.

Time of the essence

10–10　Most leases that are currently granted do not contain any timetable for the parties to start a rent review, although these leases provide for the rent to be reviewed on certain dates, and for the rent review to be determined by a third party surveyor if the parties do not agree on the new rent by a stipulated time. However, some landlords still provide, and many leases that are still running contain, a timetable to start and then conduct the rent review. There is a general presumption in both Scotland and England that time is not of the essence (i.e. dates are not crucial), and there has been much case law on the subject. It is suggested here that the case law, whether Scottish or English, should be assumed to apply in Scotland.

In *United Scientific Holdings Ltd v Burnley Borough Council*[10] the House of Lords held that, if a timetable is specified in a rent review clause in a lease, then time is not of the essence, unless there is something in the lease to make it of the essence.

The parties can expressly state that time is, or is not, of the essence if they so wish. In *Panavia Air Cargo Ltd v Southend-on-Sea Borough Council*[11] the rent review clause provided for an increase of 25 per cent in the rent if the review had not been completed by a particular date but it also said that time was not to be of the essence. The court held that time not being of the essence prevailed, and the landlord could have the rent review determined by an independent surveyor.

In *Robert Prow and others as Trustees of the RM Prow (Motors) Limited Directors' Pension Fund v Argyll & Bute Council*,[12] the landlord's surveyor

---

[8] *Standard Life Assurance Co Ltd v Unipath* [1997] 38 E.G. 152; [1997] 2 E.G.L.R. 121.
[9] *Hemingway Realty Ltd v Clothworkers Co* [2005] E.H.W.C. 299 [Ch.]; [2005] All E.R. [D.] 121.
[10] *United Scientific Holdings Ltd v Burnley Borough Council*, 1978 A.C. 904.
[11] *Panavia Air Cargo Ltd v Southend-on-Sea Borough Council* [1988] 22 E.G. 82; [1988] 1 E.G.L.R. 124.
[12] *Robert Prow and others as Trustees of the RM Prow (Motors) Limited Directors' Pension Fund v Argyll & Bute Council* [2013] CSIH 13.

had issued a notice to start the rent review. The notice contained various errors, and his surveyor issued an amended notice five weeks later. The tenant took no steps to give a counter notice specifying an alternative rent. The lease provided for the rent to be reviewed every five years, with the landlord giving three months' written notice before the review date of his intention to exercise the rent review, and specifying the amount of rent sought. The lease went on to state that, if the landlord failed to give the required notice, or if the rent was not reviewed for any other reason, he could call for the rent to be reviewed on the 28th day of any month following the review date, by giving three months' notice. The court held that the clause in the lease contains six clear requirements: the notice must be in writing; it must be given by the landlord; it must be given to the tenant; it must be given three months before the relevant term; it must specify the rent that the landlord proposes as the fair market rent; and it must specify the term at which that is to be assessed and payable. Each of these is a fundamental requirement for a valid notice, as the clause is mandatory in its language. The parties have stipulated the conditions for a valid rent review notice and if the landlord want to have the rent reviewed they must comply strictly with these.

The original rent review notice was given by the wrong party as landlord, it contained the wrong rent review date and was therefore invalid. The court held that the reasonable recipient test in *Mannai*[13] does not help here. It omitted the landlord's name and designation, and named an entirely different company as the landlord, and gave the wrong review date. The court held that the second notice corrected all of the defects of the first notice, but was issued by the surveyor as opposed to being issued by the landlord. However, the court held that rent reviews are routinely conducted, and rent review notices are routinely served, by surveyors on behalf of landlords, and although the Lease said that notices are to be issued by the landlord, it goes against commercial common sense to insist it be signed by the landlord, as opposed to being issued by a surveyor on his behalf. The second notice was held valid.

The *Prow* case also dealt with the question of whether time is of the essence in the lease in question. The court said that the rent review clause provided that the rent will be the sum specified in the landlord's notice, unless a different sum is agreed or the tenant serves a counter notice within three months of the tenant's receipt of the landlord's trigger notice. There is no requirement for a further notice or ultimatum by the landlord to enable him to rely on the provision, and he is entitled to rely on his notice, unless one of the two specified events occurs. The parties have already set out what will happen if the tenant does nothing; namely the rent specified in the landlord's rent review notice will be payable. This is a deeming provision.

The court went on to say that, although time is of the essence for the tenant's counter notice, it does not follow that time is of the essence for issue of the initiating notice. The rent review clause required the landlord to give the tenant three months' written notice before the relevant term and, if the rent was not reviewed at that term, the landlord could review at a subsequent date by giving three months' written notice before that term. The court held that the natural construction of these provisions is that notice must be given *not less* than three months before the relevant term, as opposed to having to give exactly three

---

[13] *Mannai Investment Co Ltd v Eagle Star Life Assurance Co Ltd* [1997] A.C. 749.

months notice. This is because the purpose of the three month period is to give the tenant adequate warning, and to allow him to consider the notice, obtain professional advice, and if so advised, serve a counter notice. Therefore, provided that at least three months' notice is given, that purpose is served. The second review notice was served three months and three days before the relevant date and this does not invalidate the notice.

In *Rey v Ordnance Estates Ltd*[14] a lease provided for the landlord to initiate a rent review by issuing a notice "proposing a rent". The landlord duly issued his notice, and the tenant failed to send a counter-notice in time. The tenant argued that the landlord's figure was excessive because it took tenant's improvements into account, and was not representative of market value. The court held that the evidence did not support the tenant's arguments. It said that the lease only required the landlord to propose a rent but did not say that it had to be the landlord's estimate of the market rent, and that the rent review notice was valid. The tenant was therefore bound by the rent quoted as he had not issued a counter-notice in time.

10–11   In *Wilderbrook v Oluwu*[15] the rent review clause said that time was of the essence, but then went on to say that either party could require a surveyor to determine the revised rent despite any delay. The court held that this proviso cancelled the effect of the time of the essence statement.

In *Visionhire Ltd v Britel Fund Trustees Ltd*[16] the landlord had proposed the amount of rent to be payable at review; the lease provided that if the tenant served a counter-notice saying the amount of rent it considers should be payable, the landlord then had three months within which to apply for the appointment of an arbiter, failing which the rent payable would become fixed at the amount stated in the tenant's notice. The court held that the general rule in Scottish law, as in English law, is that time is not of the essence in rent review clauses in commercial long leases, unless the wording of the contract indicates expressly, or shows by necessary implication, that this is intended by the parties. The court also said that the use of an ultimatum is appropriate where one party wants to make time of the essence, but in this case it would have been wrong for the tenant to have to put a further ultimatum on the landlord, because serving his notice of proposed rent was in itself an ultimatum procedure to which the parties had agreed by contract. The court contrasted the landlord's position where time was not of the essence with the tenant's position which made time of the essence as the lease had provided for the tenant to serve a counter-notice specifying the tenant's proposed rent figure and that such figure was to apply unless the landlord went to arbitration.

The presence of a break clause (option to terminate early) will not make time of the essence if the review clause provides for an automatic review and does not contain a timetable. In *Metrolands Investments Ltd v J.H. Dewhurst Ltd*[17] it was held that the inter-relationship between a break clause and the review procedure will not make time of the essence if the tenant has the right

---

[14] *Rey v Ordnance Estates Limited* Unreported June 11, 2001, Chancery.

[15] *Wilderbrook v Oluwu* [2005] EWCA Civ 1361.

[16] *Visionhire Ltd v Britel Fund Trustees Ltd*, 1991 S.L.T. 883.

[17] *Metrolands Investments Ltd v J.H. Dewhurst Ltd* [1986] 3 All E.R. 659; (1986) 52 P. & C.R. 232.

to initiate the review himself so as to get the rent review determined before he has to decide whether to break the lease.

In *Al Saloom v Shirley James Travel Services Ltd* [18] the deadline for the **10–12** tenant to exercise an early termination option in a lease was the same day as the last day on which the landlord could initiate a rent review. The landlord served his rent review notice two weeks late; the court held that in this lease there was a co-relation between the rent review and the early termination option that made time of the essence, and so the landlord lost his right to have the rent review because he was late serving his notice.

A clause that says a party is deemed to accept a situation unless something is done has been held to be enough to make time of the essence. By contrast, if a clause only says that if something is not done, then the rent will be a specific amount, this does not make time of the essence, because this latter situation is only seen as procedural machinery.

In *Scottish Life Assurance Co Ltd v Agfa-Gevaert Ltd* [19] the rent review clause said that the tenant is deemed to have accepted the figure specified in the landlord's notice if the tenant fails to serve a counter-notice within a speci-fied period of time giving his version of the amount of open market rent. The tenant wrote to the landlord on time, saying he rejects the amount stated by the landlord, and saying he has instructed a surveyor who would be in contact with the landlord. It was held that since no counter-figure was proposed in the tenant's notice, the notice was not valid, and that the tenant was bound by the landlord's figure.

In *Starmark Enterprises Ltd v CPL Distribution Ltd* [20] the court held that **10–13** time was of the essence in a deeming provision concerning service of a tenant's counter-notice. In that case, the lease provided for the tenant to serve any counter-notice within one month calling on the landlord to negotiate, failing which the tenant is deemed to have approved the amount shown in the land-lord's notice. The tenant served his counter-notice six weeks late, and the tenant was bound by the landlord's notice.

Time can be deemed to be of the essence due to the inter-relation of other clauses, such as a break clause. In *C. Richards & Son Ltd v Karenita Ltd* [21] the last day for exercising a break clause was six months after the deadline for the landlord to serve a rent review notice. The landlord served his review notice after the deadline for exercising the break option. The court held that time was of the essence for serving the review notice, and decided against the landlord.

In *Drebbond v Horsham District Council* [22] the court considered a lease that provided for the landlord's trigger notice to be served within six months before the rent review date and that, if no agreement is reached within three months after the trigger notice is served, then the rent review is to be referred to arbitra-tion if the landlord gives notice to the tenant within three months, but not otherwise. In this case the landlord did not serve the arbitration notice until one

---

[18] *Al Saloom v Shirley James Travel Services Ltd* (1981) 42 P. & C.R.181; (1981) 259 E.G. 420; (1981) 2 E.G.L.R. 96.

[19] *Scottish Life Assurance Co Ltd v Agfa-Gevaert Ltd,* 1997 S.L.T. 1200.

[20] *Starmark Enterprises Ltd v CPL Distribution Ltd* [2001] 1 EWCA Civ 1252; [2002] 4 All E.R. 264.

[21] *C. Richards & Son Ltd v Karenita Ltd* (1972) 221 E.G. 25.

[22] *Drebbond v Horsham District Council* (1978) 37 P. & C.R. 237; (1978) 245 E.G. 1013; [1978] 1 E.G.L.R. 96.

year after the review date. The court held that the words "but not otherwise" made time of the essence for the service of the notice. All that is needed to make time of the essence in a rent review clause is an expression that shows a time limit is intended to be obligatory and not merely indicative.

10–14   In *Charterhouse Square Finance Co Ltd v A & J Menswear*[23] the lease provided for a landlord's trigger notice to initiate the rent review and for that notice to specify the rent the landlord wanted to charge from the review date. It also provided for the tenant to serve counter-notice within 21 days of the landlord's notice and that, if the tenant does not serve counter-notice, then the rent payable from the review date will be that stated in the landlord's notice. The court held that time is of the essence if the clause made it clear that the parties intended strict application of the timetable, and that if the clause sets out the consequences of failure to adhere to the timetable, this generally demonstrates the parties intended the timing to be strict.

In *Patel v Earlspring Properties Ltd*[24] a lease provided for a rent review to be started by a landlord's notice specifying an increased rent. The tenant had 28 days after receiving that notice to serve counter-notice specifying the rent the tenant was willing to pay and calling on the landlord to negotiate the amount of rent. If the tenant failed to serve counter-notice on time he was deemed to have agreed to pay the increased rent shown in the landlord's rent notice. If the tenant did serve counter-notice, the parties were to use best endeavours to reach agreement and, failing agreement being reached within 56 days after service of the counter notice, the rent review was to be determined by arbitration. The review clause provided that time was of the essence for all periods of time.

The landlord served a notice specifying an increased rent, and the tenant issued a notice in time saying that his turnover was not substantial enough to meet the proposed rent and asking the landlord to reconsider. The landlord acknowledged receipt of the letter. The court held that the provisions regarding the tenant's counter-notice specifying the rent sought were not mandatory, that the counter-notice was valid, and that although the clause anticipated that negotiations would be carried on between the parties, there was no need for such negotiations, and therefore the parties could then refer the matter to arbitration. The court commented that it is always dangerous to try to apply rent review case law in different circumstances to a different situation, and it is more appropriate to deal with each case on its own particular facts, and to apply these facts to the particular rent review clause under consideration.

Upward only

10–15 If a rent review is "upward only", it really means that the rent can never be reviewed downwards. The rent review clause should therefore provide for the rent at each review date to be the higher of (a) the rent then payable and (b) the open market rental value. In order for a lease to be acceptable to an investment purchaser or a lender, it needs to have an upward only review clause.

---

[23] *Charterhouse Square Finance Co Ltd v A & J Menswear*, 1998 S.L.T. 720.
[24] *Patel v Earlspring Properties Ltd*, 1991 46 E.G. 153; 1991 2 E.G.L.R. 131.

Some leases have a qualified upward only clause that provides for the rent at each review date to be the higher of the amount of rent payable at commencement of the term or the open market rental value as at the review date. This means that rent could be reviewed downwards at the second or any subsequent review, but not to less than the original rent payable under the lease.

In *Harben Style Ltd v The Roads Trust*[25] the rent review clause did not contain any upward only provision; the reviewed rent was to be determined by a surveyor appointed by the President of RICS (surveyors' professional body) on the landlord's written request. The clause went on to say that rent would remain payable at the previous rate if the revised rent was not ascertained at all or was not ascertained until after the review date. The court held that there was no reason to imply an obligation on the landlord to seek the appointment of a surveyor to determine the rent, as the clause expressly contemplated the possibility that the revised rent for the review period might not be ascertained at all.

In *Flower Services Ltd v Unisys New Zealand Ltd*[26] a lease had been varied so as to delete the upwards only provision. The parties waived an upwards only provision in respect of the first rent review only; meanwhile rents on the open market had reduced between the date of the lease and the first review date. The lease did not contain any mechanism for the tenant to trigger the first review, as the clause clearly stated that it would only be activated if the landlord serves a rent review notice. The landlord refused to serve the notice and the court held that there was no obligation on the landlord to trigger the rent review. The court held that the landlord could only safely trigger that rent review if it were sure that a higher rent would result.

As we have seen above, there is a difference between the landlord having the right to trigger a rent review on the one hand, and there being machinery for operating a rent review on the other.

Late review—abandonment—saving provision

Some leases provide for the landlord to have the right to initiate a rent review, albeit late. Such clauses usually provide for the rent to still be reviewed on the basis of valuation as at the review date, and to be payable from the review date, or alternatively for the rent to be valued as at and payable from the quarter day following the date when the landlord gets round to starting off the rent review. **10–16**

The right in favour of the landlord to start the review late may not be contained in a positive clause as such, but may instead be contained in a clause stating that demand for and acceptance of rent at the current rate does not constitute a waiver by the landlord of his right to have a rent review, and preserving the landlord's right to start the review late. If the lease does not have such a "saving provision" then the landlord will be held to have abandoned his right to have the rent review if he demands and/or accepts rent at the current rate for a period of time following the review date. In *Banks v Mecca Bookmakers (Scotland) Ltd*[27] there were two leases where the landlord allowed at least three quarterly rent payment dates to come and go, accepting rent at the

---

[25] *Harben Style Ltd v The Roads Trust* [1995] 17 E.G. 125; [1995] 1 E.G.L.R. 118.
[26] *Flower Services Ltd v Unisys New Zealand Ltd* (1997) 74 P. & C.R. 112.
[27] *Banks v Mecca Bookmakers (Scotland) Ltd*, 1982 S.L.T. 150.

then current rate before waking up to the fact that there was a rent review. It may seem extraordinary that a landlord would be so sleepy, but it can happen, especially if rent is being paid in by standing order or direct debit, and if the landlord is not management-intensive in his style.

However, even if the lease does contain a clause allowing the landlord to review late, and saying that he does not waive or abandon the review even if he asks for and receives rent at the current rate, it is not certain by any means that he will be able to rely safely on such a clause! The point has not as yet been judicially tested.

In *Waydale Ltd v MRM Engineering Ltd*[28] the landlord did not seek a review on the review date, and the tenant continued to pay rent at the current rate, which the landlord accepted for 18 months after the review date. The landlord then tried to review the rent with effect from the missed review date. It was held that the proper inference to be drawn from the facts was that the landlord had waived its right to a rent review at the review date.

Third party determination

10–17   Very often, the new rent has not been agreed or determined by the review date, and so the lease should provide for what is to happen in such event. The matters that need to be covered are:

- to set a deadline for agreeing the review;
- to provide for referral to a third party to determine the amount of rent payable from the review date;
- to say what qualification the third party should have;
- to say who can appoint him or her;
- to say who can initiate the third party referral; and
- whether the third party is to act as expert or arbiter.

It is usual for the third party to be an independent surveyor, but there may be provision that he or she must have a minimum amount of experience or must have been qualified for a certain period of time. Some leases will provide for the rent review to be determined by arbitration rather than by an expert. In arbitration, both parties put forward their views and they argue their case; the arbiter then determines the rent review on the basis of the evidence put to him. An arbiter is allowed to use his own personal knowledge to a certain extent. Arbitration involves a proper judicial and fair process, and both parties must be allowed the opportunity to put their case forward. With an expert, there is an instruction given to someone to actually determine the rent review himself using his own knowledge. If there is provision for an expert then it is quite common for the lease to provide for the parties to be able to put forward representations on what the rent should be and indeed for a hearing to be held if so required, so that effectively a similar judicial process is gone through. The difference, however, is that the expert can use his own personal knowledge and come up with his own decision on rent, regardless of what the parties' submissions contain. If the expert is negligent then he can be sued for damages, whereas an arbiter cannot generally be sued, provided he sticks to the subject matter and to the scope of his remit.

---

[28] *Waydale Ltd v MRM Engineering Ltd*, 1996 S.L.T. (Sh. Ct) 6.

Current rent payable until review is agreed or determined—accounting

If there is no provision for an interim rent to be payable, the lease should **10–18** provide for the current rent to be payable until the rent review is agreed or determined. The lease should also provide for an accounting once the rent review has been agreed or determined. Usually any increase from current rent to reviewed rent will be payable on the next occurring rent payment date or within a specific period of time after agreement or determination of the review.

If there is no provision for the tenant to pay interest on the difference between old and new rents for the period from the review date until the rent payment date, then the landlord is not entitled to charge interest on this amount. Therefore there is not much incentive on the tenant to agree to the new rent as he is using the landlord as his banker, by paying at the old rate and deferring having to pay the higher rent that will be determined or agreed. It is usual to provide for interest at, say, base lending rate, from the review date or from each rent payment date as appropriate until the date on which the tenant is to account for any increase that is agreed or determined. If this balancing payment is not paid on time, then interest at the full penalty rate on late rent should apply from the date the balancing payment was due until it is paid.

Backdating the review

In *Sahota v R.R. Leisureways (UK) Ltd*,[29] the court held that if the lease is **10–19** silent regarding backdating the increased rent to the rent review date then it is to be so backdated.

Calderbank offers

A Calderbank offer is a method of trying to settle an outstanding rent review; **10–20** it is an unconditional offer to settle, expressly reserving the right to submit the offer to the arbiter after he has issued his award on all aspects apart from costs. If the offer is not accepted, then it can have the effect of protecting the offering party against being found liable for post-offer expenses in respect of having the rent review determined. A Calderbank offer needs to have several elements:

- it must specify the amount of rent offered;
- it must deal with the costs of arbitration or determination. The issuer should say that each pays their own costs up to the deadline for acceptance of the offer, and if the offer is not accepted then the recipient is to pay the costs from that date forward until accepted or adjudicated;
- it must give enough time for the recipient to consider and respond; and
- it must deal with any other issues that need to be addressed, such as interest on the uplift in rent as provided for in the lease.

---

[29] *Sahota v R.R. Leisureways (UK) Ltd* [2010] EWHC3114 (CH).

CHAPTER 11

RENT REVIEW—VALUATION

Introduction

11–01 The rent review surveyor has to live in a pretend world of looking at something that exists in reality, and value it as something quite different. This is because the default position is that the lease and the premises are valued as they exist at the rent review date, but neither the landlord nor the tenant actually want it to work that way!

In the absence of clear wording to the contrary, the courts will interpret the review clause as referring to a hypothetical lease starting on the rent-review date, lasting for the remainder of the term that was granted in the actual lease, with the same provisions as the actual lease. Therefore any clauses that are more adverse to the tenant than those usually found in commercial leases will justify a reduction in any increase in rent otherwise obtainable. Conversely, any clauses that are significantly softer than the usual to the tenant may justify a greater increase. The clauses that would most justify such adjustment are repairs, use, keep-open obligations, assignation and sub-letting.

The rent-review clause should, and usually does, contain directions on how to value the rent at the review date. This is done by providing for rent to be reviewed to open market value, with various assumptions and disregards. There are certain items that are inserted as more or less standard, such as the premises being available with vacant possession on the open market and there being a willing landlord and a willing tenant. There are other matters that are frequently inserted, and the assumptions and disregards have been fertile ground for a large amount of litigation.

If the parties intend that the rent should be reviewed on an artificial basis (i.e. not on the usual hypothetical lease basis, but instead on the basis that the premises are something or somewhere that is fictional), and the wording falls short of being operable, the court will not rewrite the contract for the parties.

A—ASSUMPTIONS

Assume willing parties

11–02 In England it has been held, in *Dennis & Robinson Ltd v Kiossos Establishment*[1], that the existence of a willing tenant is implied as being necessary in order to achieve an open market letting. This, however, is based on English statute law, which has no application north of the border. It is thought that in Scotland, if a tenant has tried hard to find an assignee, and has failed to do so, and if he can

---

[1] *Dennis & Robinson Ltd v Kiossos Establishment* (1987) 1 EGLR 133.

satisfy an arbitrator or expert that nobody would take on a hypothetical lease of the property, then a Scottish court would be unlikely to assume that a willing tenant is available. Therefore it is not safe to rely on this English case, and so it is important that the lease should contain an assumption that there is a willing landlord and a willing tenant.

Assume no premium

The lease should contain an assumption that a letting would be entered into **11–03** without payment of a premium or capital sum to or by either party. This is because any such payments can distort the amount of rent payable.

Assume vacant possession

Most rent review clauses will stipulate that the rent is to be valued on the basis **11–04** of vacant possession of the premises. If there is no such statement in the lease, then the actual clause needs to be examined to ascertain whether the parties intended that valuation be on the basis of vacant possession. If the lease being reviewed is an interposed lease (i.e. there was already a sub-lease in place at the start of the lease) or, if partial sub-letting is contemplated, then it would follow that the parties may not have intended that at rent review the premises should be valued on the basis of vacant possession. Apart from these two scenarios, it is thought here that in most cases vacant possession would be intended, as the principle of the rent review exercise is to look at the premises without the existing lease being in place and to say they are available to let. Therefore how can one let out premises to a tenant without him having the right to occupy and use them?

In *Bishopsgate (99) Ltd v Prudential Assurance Co Ltd*[2] the court considered the rent review clause in a lease of a large office block. The clause provided for valuation on the basis of vacant possession, and the tenant argued that someone taking a lease of the whole building would seek a substantial rent-free period in order for him to be able to sub-let parts of it. The court held that the clause required valuation on the basis of vacant possession of the whole, with one tenant leasing the whole from the landlord, and that the discount applied by the arbiter so as to allow for a rent-free period was justified.

If the premises let in a lease are a very large building, the tenant may be entitled to a discount in any increase otherwise applicable at rent review, due to the large size of the premises.

Assumptions regarding term

The lease in respect of which the rent is being reviewed has a fixed duration. It **11–05** is normal for rent review clauses to say that at rent review there is to be a "notional term", i.e. a period of time that the hypothetical lease is to last. It used to be considered beneficial to a landlord at rent review if, for leases of certain premises, the duration of the hypothetical lease was the full original duration of the actual lease. It is fashionable now for office, industrial and non-prime retail tenants to have shorter leases with break options, and therefore it

---

[2] *Bishopsgate (99) Ltd v Prudential Assurance Co Ltd* (1985) 273 E.G. 984; [1985] 1 E.G.L.R. 72.

is now the case that if the rent-review clause provides for the hypothetical lease to be for the entire duration of the lease being reviewed, then this is adverse to the landlord. Conversely, the tenant of a prime licensed or retail property might prefer a longer term in order to protect their interest in the particular location. Some odd results can arise if, for example, in a multi-occupancy entity most of the leases that are granted are for 10 years, and the lease that is being reviewed has a notional term at rent review of 25 years. Would a tenant be quick to sign up for that particular lease, when he can theoretically take a lease for a much shorter term in the same development? Similarly, in the same situation, would a prospective purchaser want to buy the investment if one of the leases has a duration that is very different to the rest of the leases? Such a scenario would make redevelopment unattractive.

The parties to a lease are free to provide for any duration or notional term to be taken into account when valuing the rent. If the length of notional term is not clearly expressed or is left unstated, the courts will assume that it is the remaining term under the actual lease. If the parties want to say that it is the remaining term, then wording such as "for a term of years equal to the residue of the term originally granted by this lease subsisting at the relevant review date" should be used. If, however, the parties want the notional term to be the full original term of the lease then the clause should state that valuation is "for a term of years equal to the entire term of this lease commencing on the relevant review date".

In *Norwich Union Life Insurance Society v Trustee Savings Bank Central Board*[3] a lease was granted for 22 years with rent reviews as at the seventh year and every five years after that. The review clause provided for rent to be on the basis of an open market letting between willing parties and otherwise on the terms of the actual lease. The court held that the notional term for review purposes was the then remaining period of the actual lease.

In *The Ritz Hotel (London) Ltd v Ritz Casino Ltd*[4] a 21-year lease provided for rent review every five years, and the clause said that the notional letting was for "a term equivalent to the term hereby granted". It was held that the natural construction of these words was a term of 21 years from the start of the lease, of which 10 years had expired at the relevant review date, and that if a constant 21 years on each review were to be assumed, then this would depart from the general principle that a notional letting should reflect as closely as possible the actual terms of the lease.

In *British Gas Plc v Dollar Land Holdings Plc*[5] the rent-review clause in a 35-year lease required valuation to be on the basis of what value of rent could reasonably be expected on the open market between willing parties on the same terms as the lease, ignoring the amount of rent initially payable in the lease, but with provision for rent reviews. The court held that the hypothetical term should be the remainder of the original term unexpired.

In *Worcester City Council v A S Clarke (Worcester) Ltd*[6] a lease was granted for 99 years with a rent review every 35 years. Valuation was to be on the basis

---

[3] *Norwich Union Life Insurance Society v Trustee Savings Bank Central Board* (1986) 278 E.G. 162; (1986) 1 E.G.L.R. 136.

[4] *The Ritz Hotel (London) Ltd v Ritz Casino Ltd* (1989) 46 E.G. 95; (1989) 2 E.G.L.R. 135.

[5] *British Gas Plc v Dollar Land Holdings Plc* (1992) 12 E.G. 141; (1992) 1 E.G.L.R. 135.

[6] *Worcester City Council v A.S. Clarke (Worcester) Ltd* (1995) 69 P. & C.R. 562.

of a term of 99 years from "the date hereof". The court held that this required valuation on the basis of the then remaining term.

In *Monkspath Industrial Estate (No.1) Ltd and Monkspath Industrial Estate (No.2) Ltd v Lucas Industries Ltd*[7] the court considered a rent-review clause that said "the hypothetical lease be for a term of years commencing on the review date equivalent in length to the term hereby granted". The court held the wording was ambiguous, and it was therefore open to the court to interpret the wording so as to give effect to commercial reality and common sense, and that the hypothetical term would therefore be the remaining five years of the original term.

However, in *Canary Wharf Investments (Three) v Telegraph Group Ltd*[8] the court considered a lease that had been granted for 25 years, in which the rent-review clause defined the open-market rent as that expected for the grant of a term of 25 years at the relevant review date, and otherwise on the same terms and conditions of the lease other than rent. The court held that the hypothetical lease was for a term of 25 years commencing on the review date.

In *Prudential Assurance Co v Salisbury Handbags Ltd*[9] a lease for a 97-year term provided for seven yearly rent reviews to the best rent that might reasonably be expected on the open market between willing parties and subject to similar conditions other than the amount of rent and provisions of the lease for reviewing the rent to those contained in the under-lease. The court held that the notional lease, unlike the lease itself, would not contain any provisions for rent review, and so it was necessary to depart from the normal assumption that the notional term would be the unexpired residue, and that instead it should be the term that the landlord might reasonably be expected to grant and the tenant might reasonably be expected to take in respect of a letting of the premises in the open market at the best rent.

If the lease contains an option to terminate, the option will be included in the hypothetical lease, unless otherwise stated. Of course if the option contained in the actual lease has now expired and there are no further options exercisable after the rent review date, then the hypothetical lease will be unlikely to include such an option. However if the actual lease provides for a right to terminate early after, for example, the first five years of the term, then that is likely to be included in the hypothetical lease unless otherwise stated.

Assumption regarding location of premises

In *Dukeminster (Ebbgate House) Ltd v Somerfield Properties Ltd*[10] a rent-review clause allowed the landlord to choose to review the premises (which were located in Ross-on-Wye) to the rental value of a warehouse unit within 35 miles of Ross-on-Wye with a total gross internal area of 50,000 square feet. The reason for this was because there were not many similar comparables near **11–06**

---

[7] *Monkspath Industrial Estate (No.1)Ltd and Monkspath Industrial Estate (No.2) Ltd v Lucas Industries Ltd* Unreported February 27, 2006.

[8] *Canary Wharf Investments (Three) v Telegraph Group Ltd* (2003) EWHC 1575; [2003] 46 E.G. 132 and [2003] 3 E.G.L.R. 31.

[9] *Prudential Assurance Co v Salisbury Handbags Ltd* (1992) 23 E.G. 117 and (1992) 1 E.G.L.R. 153.

[10] *Dukeminster (Ebbgate House) Ltd v Somerfield Properties Ltd* [1997] 40 E.G. 157; [1997] 2 E.G.L.R. 125.

to the actual premises. The landlord wanted to choose where within the 35-mile radius the notional unit would be situated. The tenant wanted the unit to be deemed to be in Ross-on-Wye and for the 35-mile radius to apply to allow account to be taken of comparables actually within the radius. The court held that the landlord can only choose to review on the basis of where the premises were actually situated or within a comparable location within the 35-mile radius. The court said that it is important to be realistic, and that it can only be reasonable for the notional premises to be in a location comparable to the site of the premises in Ross-on-Wye.

In *HMV UK Limited v Propinvest Friar Limited Partnership*[11] a lease provided for the rent to be reviewed to the highest of the then current rent, open market value or "comparable rental value" in respect of premises in Reading. Comparable rental value was defined as "prime units" in a prime retail location in the main shopping street of the same town. A "prime unit" was defined as a shop constructed in proper and workmanlike manner, and enjoying the same facilities as the actual premises. The actual premises had no secondary means of escape. The arbitrator held that the comparable value premises should also be deemed not to have a secondary means of escape, but he decided that in any event there is no adverse effect on value due to the lack of the secondary means of escape. The court held that the arbitrator was not obviously wrong in his decision.

Assume there are rent reviews

11–07 If the hypothetical lease excludes rent reviews then the landlord is likely to achieve a much higher figure at rent review as the hypothetical lease will be for a rent that is payable throughout the whole term without being reviewed. It is therefore important from the tenant's point of view, and indeed most leases do now provide for this, that the hypothetical lease disregards the amount of rent actually payable but does provide for the rent to be reviewed every five years.

In *Amax International Ltd v Custodian Holdings Ltd*[12] a sub-lease provided for periodical upwards only rent reviews on the basis of the fair yearly rent for the premises at the review date, having regard to rental values then current for a property let without a premium, with vacant possession and on the provisions of the lease (other than the rent reserved). The court held that, in accordance with general principles, the expectation was that the parties intended a hypothetical lease to contain the same provisions as an actual lease, and the hypothetical lease should therefore contain provisions for rent review in the same way as the actual lease did.

Assume parties have performed their obligations

11–08 It is recommended that the rent review clause lease contain an assumption that all of the obligations of the landlord and the tenant have been performed. Some tenants will try to amend this by saying that it is assumed that the tenant has complied with his obligations. The effect of this is that there is no assumption that the landlord has complied with the landlord's obligations, and therefore, if

---

[11] *HMV UK Limited v Propinvest Friar Limited Partnership* [2011] EWCA Civ 1708.
[12] *Amax International Ltd v Custodian Holdings Ltd* (1986) 279 E.G. 762.

there is damage or destruction by any insured risk before the review date, the premises will be reviewed in their damaged state. It is therefore necessary for the landlord to include an assumption that the landlord's obligations have been performed, or at the very least, that any damage or destruction has been made good.

Assume the premises can be sub-divided to form separate units (if appropriate)

Generally, premises will be reviewed as a single entity, without taking into **11–09** account that they can be sub-divided to create separate units (and thus command a higher rent).

In *Iceland Frozen Foods Plc v Starlight Investments Ltd*[13] the lease contained an assumption that the premises remained in existence and were ready for immediate use and occupancy. The lease included a qualified right to grant sub-leases, and in fact at the rent-review date the property comprised two separate parts. The landlord argued that the premises could physically be divided into several units, which would command a higher rent, and even though this had not happened, the rent should be valued on the basis that it could happen. The court held that it is unrealistic to assume the tenant would do such sub-division without the effect on rental value being disregarded, and that the premises must be valued in their existing state, and valued on the basis of being available for immediate occupation. The court went on to say that the phrase "ready for immediate occupancy and use" means that if the premises were destroyed or damaged, there is an assumption that they remain able to be occupied, rather than (for example) being a gutted shell.

Assume the premises are a shell

Ask ten different surveyors to define a "shell" and they are likely to come up **11–10** with ten different meanings! It is therefore important to say what is deemed to have been provided, if the lease says the premises are to be reviewed as "a shell". The main aspects that come to mind are: floor screeded, walls and ceiling plastered, gas, electricity and water connections led into the premises and working, with one point for connection for each, working toilets (how many?) and wash hand basis (how many?), and very importantly, if retail premises, a shopfront. This list is not by any means comprehensive, but it is a start point.

In *Webber v Halifax Building Society*[14] the lease provided for valuation on the basis of the premises being a "developer's shell", but the tenant was to provide his own shop front and interior fixtures and fittings. The court held that it would be open to the tenant to argue that a deduction should be made to reflect the cost and time of fitting-out.

Assume the premises can be used for the permitted use

This is not the same as an assumption that the premises are ready for use and **11–11** occupancy (which is dealt with at para.11–12 below). Premises may be fully

---

[13] *Iceland Frozen Foods Plc v Starlight Investments Ltd* (1992) 7 E.G. 117; (1992) 1 E.G.L.R. 126.
[14] *Webber v Halifax Building Society* (1985) 273 E.G. 297; (1985) 1 E.G.L.R. 58.

fitted out, with all services and utilities connected and working, but cannot be used for the permitted use because some licence or consent does not exist or has expired or been recalled or cancelled. The most obvious example is a licence to sell alcohol. However, a rent review of a bookies' will not end happily for the landlord, if there is no assumption that there is a valid current bookmaker's licence in force. The point is no less relevant for leases of restaurants, pharmacies, lap dancing clubs, etc.

Tenants will be very reluctant to see this assumption included, and the fair compromise is that the existence of a licence or consent is assumed, but that there be disregarded the terms of the actual licence or consent, without prejudice to the assumption mentioned. Therefore in the case of a pub, it will be assumed it can sell alcohol during normal licensing hours, but any regular extension, etc. would be disregarded. This then raises the question of pubs with gaming machines—these would be disregarded because it is not essential to have such machines in a pub—they are add-ons that the tenant has obtained at his own cost.

Assume the premises are ready for use and occupancy

11–12 This means that the premises are ready to receive the tenant's fit out—it does not mean the premises have been fitted out. Therefore the tenant can argue for a reduction in any increase otherwise achievable so as to compensate him for the time and cost of fitting out.

The landlord wants to avoid any deduction due to the hypothetical tenant having to spend time and money fitting-out the premises before he can trade. At rent review, the actual tenant remains in place and there is no disruption to his business, as he has already moved in and is trading. However, the tenant will want to ensure that if he has fitted out the premises, the rent is not increased due to the added value of that fit out, otherwise he would be paying twice for his fit-out works.

If there is an assumption that the premises have been fitted out, this does not imply that the tenant's actual fit out works will be taken into account, and indeed these will not be taken into account if his fit-out works are disregarded. An assumption that the premises have been fitted out means that they are ready to trade, but it only needs to be the most basic of fit out. There are various compromises available to satisfy the concerns of both parties—the tenant does not want to have to pay twice for his fit out works i.e. to pay for actually doing the works and then to pay rent on them but similarly the landlord does not want to be penalised by having the premises reviewed as a "shell" at a review date when they have in fact been fitted out and are trading on a continuous basis. A suggested form of wording, which is quite often found, is that at rent review it is assumed that the premises are ready for use and occupancy and that it is assumed that the tenant has before the review date received the benefit of a rent free period or other concession in order to compensate him for the time and cost of fitting out.

In *Pontsarn Investments Ltd v Kansallis-Osake-Pankki*[15] the review clause contained an assumption that the premises were vacant, but fit for immediate

---

[15] *Pontsarn Investments Ltd v Kansallis-Osake-Pankki* (1992) 22 E.G. 103; (1992) 1 E.G.L.R. 148.

occupation and use. It was held that the expression "vacant, but fit for immediate occupation and use" does not mean that the premises have been fitted out by anyone, but only means the premises are assumed to be free of defects and are fit to be occupied. The premises were to be treated as being in the state they were in when they were handed over by the landlord, and this could mean occupation for the purpose of fitting-out. In this situation, the tenant could argue for a reduction in any increase otherwise payable, to reflect the time involved in fitting-out at the tenant's cost, because he would have to fit out the premises for his use after the rent-review date.

Assumption leading to headline rents

A lease will often state an artificially (but not ludicrously) high rent as being **11–13** payable from the start of the lease, so as to set a high "base rent", when in actual fact a lengthy rent free period, or a lump sum payment, may have been given by the landlord as a "bribe" to take on the lease. For example, a property that is worth rent of only £15,000 per annum may be let out at £20,000 per annum, because a sweetener has been given, so that the net effect is that during the period until the first rent review the tenant is only paying £15,000 per annum. When it comes to rent review the base rent that will be used as a reference point will be £20,000 per annum and if the rent review is 'upwards only', then the minimum rent after the first rent review date would be £20,000 per annum. The rent that is stated in the lease is evidence that can be used in rent reviews of comparable properties. The investment value of a commercial property is partly calculated by multiplying the amount of annual rent by a percentage.

A lease is, of course, a contract and there is therefore nothing preventing the parties from agreeing that the headline rents should operate at rent review. The courts will only be likely to confirm that the headline rent figure should prevail if the wording of the rent review clause cannot be construed in any other way. Therefore, in the majority of cases any ambiguity in the wording is more likely to be interpreted as justifying a market rent, rather than headline rent valuation.

The compromise that seems to be fair to all is to disregard any rent free or other inducement that is equivalent in value to the time and cost likely to be taken by an incoming tenant to fit out the premises. Therefore the grant of a two or three month rent-free period would not generally have an adverse affect on the market rent obtainable for the property, and the tenant can rest assured that he will not be paying extra rent to reflect the value of bribes given to other tenants but which they have not received for entering into the lease.

The leading case in Scotland is *Church Commissioners for England v Etam Plc*.[16] At rent review, the headline rent figure obtainable from other lettings was more than the market rent for the shop in question. Normally surveyors would consider the sweeteners given and discount these back, to arrive at the true market rent figure. However, the rent review clause in this lease said that the surveyor was to disregard any rent free period or other inducements given on the open market to tenants of comparable properties. At the start of the lease in question the actual tenant had not received any sweetener. The tenant argued

---

[16] *Church Commissioners for England v Etam Plc*, 1997 S.L.T. 8.

that the existence of rent concessions or inducements should be disregarded so that none would have been granted to anyone and therefore the headline rent evidence from other units would have to be discounted back so as to take account of the sweeteners given to these other tenants. The Court agreed with this argument and said that rent reviews should be based on the reality of what has been paid in true economic terms and not the fiction of what may be stated in a lease.

In *City Offices Plc v Bryanston Insurance Co Ltd*[17] the review clause provided for the rent to be valued on the basis of the rent payable after expiry of any rent-free or fitting-out period, and on the assumption that the premises were suitable and available for immediate occupation and use, and were fully carpeted. There was a disregard of any notional rent-free concession or fitting-out period for which allowance may be made if the premises were let on the open market with vacant possession at the review date. The court held that at the review date the position in the market was that a 12-month rent-free period would have been allowed, including three months for fitting-out, and that the "headline rent" payable after expiry of that 12 months should be averaged out over the whole of the five years until the next review date, so that four years' worth of full headline rent would be deemed to be payable evenly over the five-year period.

The landlord succeeded in the case of *Broadgate Square Plc v Lehman Brothers Ltd*[18] where the lease provided for the rent to be reviewed to the best yearly rent reasonably to be expected after expiry of a rent-free period of such length as would be negotiated in the open market on a letting of the whole of the premises, between willing parties, with vacant possession without fine or premium. At arbitration, the headline rent for the premises was determined, and was then adjusted downwards to reflect an incentive rent-free period of 24 months, amortised over the 10-year notional term. The tenant argued that the arbiter should have discounted the headline rent to reflect not only inducement rent-free periods then being offered on the market, but also rent-free periods offered to new tenants for fitting-out. The court held that the wording of the clause left no escape from the conclusion that the open market rent was to be the headline rent. In this case, the rent to be applied for the whole term was the rent that would be payable after expiry of a rent-free period that would be negotiated on the review date. The reference to the rent-free period being of "such length as would be negotiated in the open market" made it impossible to restrict the words to only rent-free periods for a tenant having to move in.

The courts will try to construe headline rent clauses so as to favour the tenant wherever possible. This happened in *Co-operative Wholesale Society Ltd v National Westminster Bank Plc*[19] where the lease provided for the rent to be reviewed to open market rental value for a notional term equal to the remaining term, starting on the relevant review date, between willing parties with vacant possession and without fine or premium, assuming that any rent-free period or concessionary rent or other inducement that may be offered in

---

[17] *City Offices Plc v Bryanston Insurance Co Ltd* (1993) 11 E.G. 129; (1993) 1 E.G.L.R. 126.

[18] *Broadgate Square Plc v Lehman Brothers Ltd* [1995] 1 E.G. 111; [1995] 1 E.G.L.R. 97.

[19] *Co-operative Wholesale Society Ltd v National Westminster Bank Plc* [1995] 1 E.G. 111; [1995] 1 E.G.L.R. 97 (this case has the same reporting date as *Broadgate Square Plc v Lehman Brothers Ltd*, because that case, along with this case and two others, were all heard together by the Court of Appeal in England).

the case of a new letting in the open market at the relevant date of review had expired, or had been given immediately before the relevant review date. The Court of Appeal in England held that the wording of the clause meant that it was necessary to assume that any rent-free or concessionary rent period or other inducement had already been given, i.e. before the hypothetical lease was agreed. Therefore the valuer would not be comparing like with like if he simply took the headline rent from a comparable property that provided for a rent-free period after commencement of the term. The court said that the effect of the provision was that the hypothetical tenant was to be treated as already being in occupation, so he could not argue for the equivalent of a rent-free period for fitting-out. Therefore the clause only succeeded in denying the tenant the right to claim discount for the time and cost of fitting-out; it failed to remove the discount for other inducements.

Assume no work done to reduce rental value

As works are done to suit the requirements of the tenant, then it is reasonable **11–14** for the tenant to accept this revisal. Just as any works that increase the value are to be disregarded so should there be disregarded any works that reduce the rental value.

Assume all damage and destruction has been made good.

There should be an assumption that all damage or destruction, not only to **11–15** the premises themselves, but also the common parts, has been made good. Otherwise the landlord could find himself in the unfortunate position of five years of no increased income if there is a storm or fire shortly before the review date, and the insurance proceeds have not yet been released or spent.

B—Disregards

Disregard goodwill and occupancy

It is standard practice to include in a rent review clause that any effect of rent **11–16** value arising from goodwill or occupancy of the tenant will be disregarded. The tenant should make sure the disregard includes goodwill and occupancy by any permitted sub-tenant and occupant as well. This may be catered for in the definition of "the tenant", but it is worth checking.

Disregard licences consents and permissions obtained by the tenant

The specific and actual benefit of any licences, consents or permissions **11–17** obtained by the tenant should be disregarded. This is because the tenant has added value himself. However, the landlord should ensure that although the specific terms of the actual licences etc obtained by the tenant are disregarded, there is specific wording contained in the rent review clause that a licence, permission or consent to use the premises for the permitted use are assumed to be in existence.

Disregard works carried out by tenant

A disregard of improvements and works carried out by the tenant may not **11–18** achieve the desired result for the tenant. It all depends on the definitions in the lease; if the definition of the tenant is the named original tenant and successors and assignees then any works that have been carried out before the lease started may not in fact be disregarded. Clarification should be provided in the drafting as to what is required.

A disregard of improvements or works carried out by the tenant with the consent of the landlord may, on the surface, appear satisfactory. However, many tenants will not accept it, unless wording is added in "if such consent is required". The reason for this is that certain works will be permitted in terms of the lease. If these are permitted but are not the subject of an actual consent from the landlord, then it is reasonable to expect that these works will be taken into account at rent review.

In *London & Leeds Estates Ltd v Paribas Ltd*[20] the lease stated that the premises were fit for immediate occupation and use, and that all fitting-out and other tenants' works required by the willing tenant had already been completed. The court held that this assumption prevented the tenant from arguing that the hypothetical tenant would require other or different works to those carried out, but these works fell within the usual disregard of tenants' improvements so that the end effect was that the tenant was not penalised by having the rent increased by the value of his fitting-out works.

In *Church Commissioners for England v Etam Plc*,[21] a Scottish case, the lease provided for the rent to be reviewed assuming the property is fully constructed, fitted out and equipped, fit, ready and available for and capable of immediate occupancy and use. The clause went on to say that the rent would not be discounted or reduced to reflect the absence of any rent-free period or other concession or consideration that might be granted. It was assumed that the willing tenant had been entitled before the review date to the benefit of the property for a period reflecting the value of the rent-free period or other concession. Any increase due to any alteration or improvement to the property by and at the tenant's cost other than in an obligation to the landlord was to be disregarded, as was the fact that the tenant may have fitted out the property and paid for toilets, staircases, escalators, lifts, etc. At the first review there was an argument about an internal staircase that had been installed by the tenant as part of his fitting-out. The tenant argued that the provision of internal staircases should be disregarded as well as the fact that it was the tenant who paid for these. The court held that it was appropriate to disregard the effect on rental value of the fact that it was the tenant who paid for the internal staircases.

There is usually a disregard in respect of works carried out by the tenant (the definition of "tenant" being the tenant from time to time under the lease) other than works carried out under an obligation to the landlord. The obligation to the landlord may not just be contained in the lease; it may be in a separate document or in the missives for lease.

The original tenant in the lease may have previously been a tenant under an older lease, or there may have been a sale and leaseback transaction, in which case extensive fitting-out works could have been done prior to commencement of the lease.

---

[20] *London & Leeds Estates Ltd v Paribas Ltd* (1993) 30 E.G. 89; (1992) 2 E.G.L.R. 149.
[21] *Church Commissioners for England v Etam Plc*, 1997 S.L.T. 8.

Tenants sometimes try to include a disregard of works done to comply with statutory obligations. The landlord should not accept such a provision, as the premises may well not be able to be used if these works are not done. Therefore if the works have been done but are to be disregarded, the tenant could argue for a reduction in any uplift otherwise achievable, because these works are deemed not to have been carried out.

Disregard of works carried out off-site

In *Cordoba Holdings Limited v Ballymore Properties Ltd*,[22] the court consid- **11–19** ered a lease of a data centre, which benefitted from an enhanced power supply from two electricity sub-stations which were off-site. At arbitration in respect of the rent review the arbitrator decided that he should assume that there is sufficient power to use the premises as a data centre, and so the upgraded supply should *not* be disregarded. The lease contained a disregard in respect of any increase in value due to improvements carried out by the tenant and any predecessor in title. As the enhanced power supply was due to works having been carried out off site, they did not fall within the disregard. Therefore if it is intended that any increased value due to works having been carried out off site should be disregarded, this needs to be specifically provided for, otherwise the tenant could lose out. The same point arises in respect of works done to the common parts, as these do not form part of the premises.

Valuation—Rent review in sub-leases

If a sub-lease is granted then the probability is that rent reviews will be at the **11–20** same date as in the head lease. They may also require to be conducted in accordance with the same procedures as stated in the head lease. On the surface this leads to there being two separate rent review exercises—one between the head landlord and tenant and the other between the tenant and sub-tenant. In some instances the sub-lease will provide for the rent to be reviewed to the amount payable from time to time under the head lease, but the trouble there is that the sub-tenant may not be satisfied that his landlord will put in much effort to keep to a minimum the increase payable under the head lease as the tenant has the sub-tenant to whom he passes on the rent increase. The sub-tenant therefore seeks control by restricting his landlord from agreeing the rent payable under the head lease except with the sub-tenant's prior written consent (not to be unreasonably withheld) and restrict his landlord from going to third party to determine the head lease review except with his consent (not to be unreasonably withheld). This fetters the freedom of the tenant under the head lease and can lead to difficulties.

Repairs and rent review

The valuer's initial stance is that the premises are valued as they exist at the **11–21** review date. Many leases provide an assumption that the tenant has complied with his obligations. If the lease does not contain such a statement, the tenant cannot say the rent should not increase (as much) just because, for example,

---

[22] *Cordoba Holdings Ltd v Ballymore Properties Ltd* [2011] EWHC1636 (CH).

the premises are not in good repair, if the tenant is, at such time, in breach of his repairing obligation.

If repairing, etc. obligations on the tenant are particularly harsh, the impact on the rent at review can be significant. In *Norwich Union Life Assurance Society v British Railways Board*[23] a lease for 150 years contained obligations on a tenant not only to repair the premises, but also when necessary to rebuild, reconstruct or replace them. At arbitration the arbiter made a reduction of 27.5 per cent to take account of these obligations, because in a 150-year period of time a building is very likely to need to be rebuilt or replaced.

Inflation–linked rent reviews

11–22 Some leases provide for the rent to be reviewed on the basis of inflation. There are various indices that are used to measure inflation, and it is important to specify the correct one. It is also important to be clear as to what is to happen. Does the rent payable increase by the same percentage as the increase in the index? Does one look at the latest available index figure as at the review date in question, and the figure at commencement of the lease, or at the last review date as the case may be? It is worthwhile to provide a worked example and to say this is to clarify the intention of the parties.

There can be problems if the index is rebased or if the index ceases to exist. If it becomes impossible to carry out the rent review because the procedure or the machinery is no longer available, the courts will not rewrite the rent review clause to make it workable. It is therefore always helpful to have a fall-back to arbitration or expert determination of which index should be used and how this is to work, or to determine a fair open-market rent.

Review of limits on turnover rent increase

11–23 In *Manchester Associated Mills Ltd v Mitchells & Butler Retail Ltd*[24] the court considered a 99-year ground lease of premises in Aberdeen. A pub had been constructed on the ground. The rent payable throughout the term was to be equivalent to seven per cent of gross annual turnover of the pub, subject to a minimum amount and a maximum amount, which were 15 per cent above and below the initial anticipated turnover. The ground lease provided for the minimum and maximum amount to be reviewed periodically, but for the rent to remain at seven per cent of gross annual turnover. The 2009 rent review went to arbitration at which the arbitrator decided that the minimum and maximum levels should be referable to five per cent of turnover, which he considered as being a fair market rent for the ground lease, and he ignored the seven per cent figure stated in the ground lease itself. The arbitrator considered he was entitled to determine the maximum and minimum levels of rent by reference to market conditions—he took an average of turnover for the immediately preceding two years and applied five per cent of that as a fair market rent and then fixed the maximum and minimum levels with reference to the plus or minus 15 per cent calculation. The court held that the commercial purpose of the rent review clause was to maintain a link between the rental

[23] *Norwich Union Life Assurance Society v British Railways Board* (1987) 283 E.G. 846; (1987) 2 E.G.L.R. 137.
[24] *Manchester Associated Mills Ltd v Mitchells & Butler Retail Ltd* [2013] CSOH 2.

payments and seven per cent of gross annual turnover of the pub. Although there may have been evidence that the current market rent payable in the market for pubs held under ground leases was five per cent of turnover, the lease was clear in its terms and the arbitrator's award was overturned.

Artificial gearing clauses

Unfortunate situations can arise where formulae are used in a rent review **11–24** clause. In *British Railways Board v Ringbest*[25] the tenant paid for development of the premises and it was agreed that he would recover this cost by way of having a discount of 16 per cent from the open market rent for the first five years of the term and then at each rent review. This discount would be continued, so that at all times the rent payable would be 84 per cent of the open market value of the premises. Following the grant of the lease, the property was sold, and at the first review the landlord successfully argued at arbitration that the tenant under the hypothetical lease would be enjoying a benefit of paying only 84 per cent instead of 100 per cent of the then open market rent, and therefore the open market rent should be notionally adjusted upward to compensate for this. The court upheld the arbiter's award. Better drafting of the rent review clause would have been more likely to achieve the result that the tenant intended.

Effect of restrictive use clauses

If the actual lease has a very restrictive use clause, then the tenant can argue for **11–25** a reduction in any increase that would otherwise apply at rent review. This is because a lease with a restrictive use clause is less attractive to a prospective tenant.

In *Plinth Property Investments Ltd v Mott, Hay & Anderson*[26] the court held that the arbiter was correct in deciding that a restrictive use clause would reduce any increase otherwise achievable at rent review. In this case, the use clause provided for the premises to be used only as offices in connection with the tenant's business as consulting engineers.

In *The Law Land Co Ltd v The Consumers' Association Ltd*[27] the lease provided for the rent to be reviewed to open market value, subject to the terms of the lease, which contained an obligation on the tenant to use the premises only as offices of the Consumer's Association and its associated organisations. The tenant argued that at review this restriction should be taken into account, so that the only tenant who could occupy the premises would be the Consumer's Association. The court held that in the hypothetical lease it would be reasonable to suppose that the name of the tenant would not be actually stated, as the assumption is that the tenant has not yet been identified. The clause envisages the existence of an open market, a willing landlord and, by implication, a willing tenant, and that there would be no market if the premises could not be used by anyone other than one specified occupant.

---

[25] *British Railways Board v Ringbest* [1996] 30 E.G. 94; [1996] 2 E.G.L.R. 82.

[26] *Plinth Property Investments Ltd v Mott, Hay & Anderson* [1979] 38 P. & C.R. 361; [1978] 249 E.G. 1167; [1978] 1 E.G.L.R. 17.

[27] *The Law Land Co Ltd v The Consumers' Association Ltd* [1980] 255 E.G. 617; [1980] 2 E.G.L.R. 109.

In *James v British Crafts Centre*[28] the lease allowed use only as high class offices, or in respect of the part from time to time occupied and used by British Crafts Centre, for storage, sale and display of craftsmen's work and ancillary offices, and the first floor whilst not occupied or used by British Crafts Centre as office and studio for the trade or business of designers, advertising agents and press agents. The court held that there was an alternative user (high class business, commercial or professional offices) that was available to the world at large, and that the reference to the British Crafts Centre was to be treated as being a reference to only the British Crafts Centre and not to a hypothetical lessee.

If the lease allows use for a purpose for which a licence is needed the landlord should include an assumption that all necessary licences are available to the notional tenant.

In *Homebase Ltd v Scottish Provident Institution*[29] the court considered a rent review clause that provided for valuation to be on the basis of the uses permitted in the lease. The use clause was for a non-food retail warehouse within class 1 (retail), together with car parking, servicing and landscaping. Any change of use was subject to the landlord's prior approval, which was not to be unreasonably withheld. However, the lease included a clause that the tenant must comply at all times with the Planning Acts and with all planning permissions granted. An agreement was entered into with the planning authority that restricted the use of the retail warehouse premises so as to exclude food, other than an in-store café, and for specific consent to be needed from the council for the sale of any other category of goods. The definition of the range of goods permitted to be sold in the premises was completed by a letter from the council, which referred to the agreement, and the letter consented to the sale of the range of goods normally retailed in DIY outlets, including a garden centre with sales related thereto.

The court held that the lease had to be considered as a whole, and because of the innocuous looking planning compliance clause, the use that was to be taken into account at the rent review was the more restrictive non-food retail use limited to the sale of range of goods normally retailed in DIY outlets including garden centres. This more restrictive use was laid down in the planning clause in the lease, as qualified by the letter from the council.

In *C & A Pensions Trustees v British Vita Investments Ltd*[30] the court considered a strict use clause that provided for a specific use or any other use from time to time authorised by the landlord. Just before the rent-review date the landlord wrote to the tenant allowing use of the premises within various use classes without having been asked to issue this. The court held that the parties must have intended that:

- the landlord's authorisation in the use clause was to be as a result of a request by the tenant;
- the rent review was to be on the assumption that the permitted use was for any trade or business that was requested by the tenant and authorised in writing by the landlord; and

---

[28] *James v British Crafts Centre* [1987] 282 E.G. 1251; [1987] 1 E.G.L.R. 139.

[29] *Homebase Ltd v Scottish Provident Institution*, 2004 S.L.T. 296.

[30] *C & A Pensions Trustees v British Vita Investments Ltd* (1984) 272 E.G. 63; [1984] 2 E.G.L.R. 75.

- the landlord's unilateral authorisation of an extended use was to be disregarded for the purpose of rent review.

In *Pacific West System Supply Ltd v British Columbia Rail Partnership*,[31] a Canadian case, the rent review clause was silent regarding the use permitted in the notional lease. The court held that the rent was to be valued on the basis of the restrictions on use contained in the actual lease.

In *McDonalds Real Estate LLP v Arundel Corporation*[32] the rent review clause contained an assumption that the building (which was originally a factory) is

> "a modern single storey warehouse with a net usable area of 20,000 square feet, of which 15 per cent is usable as ancillary offices, and that the building is of a high standard in accordance with all statutory and other relevant consents with all usual amenities including parking and loading facilities."

The court held that the notional warehouse should be assumed to be an industrial warehouse used for storage as opposed to any other type of warehouse such as a retail warehouse. However, the court went on to say that it is inappropriate to say that the rent should be valued on the assumption that the premises are only able to be used as an industrial warehouse, as the rent review clause said that any restriction on permitted use is to be disregarded, and it is possible that in the future the premises could be used for retail. Therefore the prospect of obtaining planning permission for use for retail purposes could be taken into account.

Ground lease rent reviews

In a ground lease, the rent payable is usually in respect of a vacant and cleared **11–26** site, and any value attributable to any buildings is usually disregarded. The existence of any planning permission for construction of the buildings that are in fact standing on the site is usually taken into account in valuing the rent. The disadvantages of a ground lease rent review are that there are unlikely to be many comparables and that any change in planning policies is unlikely to be catered for. The lease may not include any obligation to build, and the review clause may fail to adequately deal with hope value (in respect of future planning permissions). The provision to value a cleared site can produce difficulties if the parties fail to provide an obligation on the tenant to construct anything on the site. However, on the other hand, a tenant could argue that an obligation to build is onerous and that allowance should be made for cost and time in building. It is necessary to distinguish in the rent-review clause between:

- planning permission that has been granted before the grant of the lease itself;
- planning permission granted at any time before the relevant review date; and

---

[31] *Pacific West System Supply Ltd v British Columbia Rail Partnership* (2004) 238 D.L.R. (4th) 724.

[32] *McDonalds Real Estate LLP v Arundel Corporation* [2008] 30 E.G. 84.

- hope value of any planning permission that might be granted in the future.

In some cases, the ground lease rent is calculated as a percentage of the open market rental value of the building, which solves the problem of the lack of comparables.

In *Hahota v R.R. Leisureways (UK) Ltd*[33] a lease had been granted of ground, following the construction by the tenant at its own cost of commercial buildings. The lease provided for rent reviews to open market value of the premises, disregarding any increase in value due to tenants' improvements, fixtures and fittings. At first rent review the rent was increased on the basis of it being a ground lease by mutual agreement. Before the second review occurred the property was sold, and the new landlord wanted to take the value of the buildings into account. The tenant argued that all improvements including the buildings should be disregarded. The court held that the premises were to be valued as the ground only, due to the direction in the rent review clause to disregard tenant's improvements.

End note

11–27 Rent review is a legal minefield, and it is easy for the parties who are drafting and revising the lease to get it very wrong when it comes to the review clause. The courts will not rewrite a clause to make it work, and will not be over-sympathetic to the party who wants to change a review clause because it says something different to what he wanted it to say. Creativity in drafting in a rent-review clause is not recommended. If there is any room for ambiguity, the provision should be redrafted and, where appropriate, such as in an inflation linked clause, there should be a worked example to clarify the intention of the parties.

---

[33] *Hahota v R.R. Leisureways (UK) Ltd* [2010] EWHC3114 (CH).

CHAPTER 12

INSURANCE

Introduction

The owner of a property has an obvious interest and incentive to insure **12–01** adequately, but the tenant under a lease should also be keen to have sufficient insurance cover in place, as most leases will exclude from the tenant's responsibility all damage caused by risks that are insured. The tenant will want to have the premises put back in good repair quickly, so that he can continue using them. In this Chapter, we consider various aspects of, and the obligations of the parties in respect of, insurance of commercial properties. Insurance should be in place, not only for the bricks and mortar, but also to cover occupier's and third-party liability and loss of rent and, if applicable, service charge.

At the end of the Chapter, we very briefly consider some differences in English lease law.

A—SCOTLAND

Who insures and who pays?

Whether the premises are single or multi-occupancy, the landlord will want to **12–02** retain control over the insurance and over the reinstatement of insured damage or destruction. If the premises are single occupancy (i.e. the landlord lets out all that he owns at a certain location to one tenant), then the landlord will usually undertake to insure entirely at the tenant's expense. If the premises are multi-occupancy (i.e. the landlord owns an entire building or larger entity and lets out separate parts to different tenants and grants rights to use common parts), the landlord will insure the whole entity and will recover the cost of the premiums from the various tenants.

The landlord may receive commission from the insurance company; the tenant has no right to this commission unless the lease specifically provides for that.

If the premises are held on a very long lease or a ground lease and there are occupational sub-leases, then the landlord in these sub-leases will want to control the insurance. Many ground leases or very long leases provide for the tenant to insure. These leases quite often impose development obligations on the tenant and provide for the tenant to insure in joint names of the landlord and the tenant. This enables the tenant, who is the landlord of the occupational sub-tenant, to insure and to control the reinstatement works.

In *Victor Harris (Gentswear) Ltd v Wool Warehouse (Perth) Ltd*[1] the lease imposed the obligation on the tenant to pay to the landlord the insurance

---

[1] *Victor Harris (Gentswear) Ltd v Wool Warehouse (Perth) Ltd*, 1995 S.C.L.R. 577.

premiums at such rate as the landlords from time to time consider appropriate. The landlord sued the tenant for payment of an insurance premium; the tenant considered the level of the premium to be unreasonable and wanted the matter to be determined by arbitration. The court held that there is no implied term that insurance premia have to be reasonable and therefore there was no dispute.

Excess (self insured amount)

12–03   In order to keep premiums lower, insurance companies make the insured party pay the first slice of any claim, and this is called the "excess" or self-insured amount. Usually this is a low amount for fire and most other damage to buildings, but it will often be a higher amount for subsidence. Because leases tend to excuse the tenant from liability for making good insured damage or destruction, the landlord will usually impose on the tenant the obligation to pay the excess, as the tenant is benefitting by paying a lower premium. However, the tenant should revise the lease so that any excess is a "normal commercial" excess, so that the tenant is not exposed to a very high payment in the event of a claim.

The insured risks

12–04   Many leases contain a definition of "insured risks", with the right for the landlord to insure for additional risks (either as he desires or with some qualification that such additional risks are "normal commercial" or that the landlord is to act reasonably). The risks that are often insured include: loss or damage by fire, in peace time aircraft (and aerial devices or articles dropped from these), explosion, malicious damage, riot and civil commotion, storm, lightning, earthquake or tempest, bursting or overflowing of water tanks, apparatus or pipes, flood and impact. Many landlords prefer to have the right, but not the obligation, to insure against terrorism, subsidence and landslip, although the tenant may require these to be included. The landlord will usually require the right to insure for additional risks. The tenant will usually qualify this so as only "normal commercial risks" are added. This is because the tenant, who is paying for the insurance cover, does not want to pay very high premiums for "obscure" risks. The tenant will usually want the right to add to the list of risks so as to reduce his repairs liability, and this is generally acceptable to landlords, provided these additional risks are "normal" risks, and are able to be insured.

The landlord's obligation to insure—property and common parts

12–05   At common law, the rule of *rei interitus* provides that, if premises are destroyed or are so damaged that they are unable to be used or occupied, the lease terminates, with neither party having any further liability, unless the tenant has wilfully caused the damage or destruction.

The landlord has no obligation at common law to insure the premises. Therefore, the parties to the lease should be aware of the extent of the landlord's obligation within the lease document to insure. If the lease defines the "insured risks" as a specific list of risks and imposes on the landlord the obligation to insure these, then the position is clear.

An obligation on the landlord to lay out insurance proceeds in making good the damage does not imply that the landlord has to pick up any shortfall, unless either the lease requires the landlord to insure for full reinstatement cost and he has failed to do so, or the lease excludes tenant's liability for insured risk damage or destruction. In fact, some leases specifically exclude landlord's liability for any shortfall; some leases go further and impose liability for any shortfall on the tenant.

The landlord should not undertake to insure for anything on an absolute and **12–06** unqualified basis; it may be that insurance for certain risks is simply not available from time to time, or that the policy provisions may not be met for continuous cover (such as the premises being vacant for more than 30 days), even though the tenant is not in breach of his obligations. The landlord should therefore insure only to the extent that cover is available from time to time.

The landlord needs to protect himself against the situation in which insurance for any one or more of the risks is not from time to time available. The landlord should also cover the situation in which insurance ceases to apply due to the tenant or any authorised occupant vacating the premises, as insurance companies tend to restrict cover for empty premises. The landlord will want control over the amount of cover. The landlord is likely to pick up shortfall in the event that he is under-insured, and so he should have the right to increase the amount of cover. The tenant however will want him to act reasonably so that the tenant is not paying way over the odds for premium.

The lease should contain an obligation on the landlord to notify the tenant if he cannot get cover at any time in respect of any of the risks that are to be insured. This is because the liability for uninsured risks will usually fall on the tenant, if the definition of "insured risks" is "the risks to the extent cover is available from time to time".

If any of the risks ceases to be insurable, then the landlord should monitor whether that risk becomes insurable again, as he will usually have an obligation to insure it again if it does.

The lease may prohibit the tenant from insuring but, if so, the tenant should revise the draft so as to allow him to insure for any risks that are from to time to time not insured by the landlord, but only for as long as the landlord himself cannot obtain cover.

The landlord will sometimes add in that he has no obligation to insure if **12–07** insurance is not available at economic or reasonable rates. If the tenant accepts this, he should impose on the landlord an obligation to disclose to the tenant if, and to the extent that, any of the insured risks are not insured against. If the landlord is covering himself by saying that he does not have to insure for risks that are not insurable at reasonable rates then he needs to make sure that he is not caught out by the definition of the insured risks. He may have achieved not having to insure against something, but he may be stuck with paying for repair, reinstatement, etc. because a risk is still within the definition of the insured risks, and therefore the tenant can avoid liability.

If the definition of the insured risks is "such of the following risks, namely ..." or "the following risks namely ... to the extent such risks are insured / included in the policy of insurance", then the tenant does not know whether all or indeed any of the risks are insured against. This has an impact on the tenant's repair obligation, as he will then become liable for making good damage that he had believed was insured.

Inter-relationship of landlord's lease and loan obligations

In many cases the landlord will have borrowed using the property as security, **12–08** and the loan documentation will impose certain insurance and reinstatement obligations on the landlord as borrower. To take account of this, the landlord needs to have flexibility within the lease provisions, so that he can add to the insured risks and can increase the amount insured (and payable by the tenant).

The landlord should not accept a revisal or a provision that insurance is to be in joint names of the landlord and the tenant, as the lender may require that insurance be in joint names of lender and borrower. The landlord must be free to arrange insurance without needing to ask the tenant for consent. However, many landlords accept that the tenant's interest should be noted (or endorsed) on the policy.

Any property owner who borrows against the security of the property should not accept a provision in the loan documents that the lender is entitled to take the proceeds of any insurance claim so as to reduce the amount owed to it. This is because the borrower will have to undertake in the lease document that he will make good damage or destruction caused by any of the insured risks, therefore if the lender takes the insurance proceeds, the landlord will most likely have to borrow to fund the reinstatement or rebuilding, and many lenders will not look favourably on lending against a damaged building.

Making good insured damage or destruction

12–09   The tenant should revise the lease so that he is excused from making good any damage or destruction caused by any of the risks that the landlord has insured or should, in terms of the lease, have insured.

If the lease is silent as to who is to make good severe insured risk damage or destruction, then neither party is required to make good. If the property is destroyed or is so damaged as to be unfit for use and occupancy, then the lease is terminated by the rule of *rei interitus*. If the damage is not severe enough to prevent use and occupancy, the lease continues in force and, at common law, the landlord would have to make good in terms of the repairing obligations provided by common law.

If insurance is in the joint names of landlord and tenant then the insurance proceeds will be paid to them jointly, and this gives the tenant control over spending it.

From the tenant's point of view, the landlord should be required to seek whatever consents are necessary without any delay and, on receipt of these consents, to proceed with reinstatement as soon as possible.

The lease should provide that if the premises suffer damage or destruction due to any of the insured risks, then the landlord should be required to make good. The landlord should draft the lease to contain the right in his favour to make variations to the property if rebuilding or reinstating, so as to change the layout, and for the materials used to reflect current practice at the time, without being held back by the tenant. The tenant should revise the lease so that any variation does not make any significant change to the size, configuration of or access to and from the property. The tenant will want a comparable area and reasonably comparable layout, and may only agree to the landlord's ability to vary materials and layout so as to reflect changes in building regulations, etc.

Termination if reinstatement is not completed—insured risk damage

12–10   The lease will usually provide for a termination option if the premises are not fit for use and occupancy again within a specific period of time, following damage or destruction by any of the insured risks. This should include the common parts, at least to the extent these are necessary for actual use and enjoyment of the premises.

If any "insured damage/destruction" to the premises and common parts has not been made good by the landlord within a specified time, which is usually three years, then the lease will normally provide for either party, or in some cases only one of the parties, to be able to terminate the lease on, say, one month's written notice. In that event the insurance proceeds will usually be stated to belong to the landlord.

If the deadline is the same as the end of the loss of rent insurance period, then if there is a time between giving notice of termination and actual termination, there may be a short period when the landlord does not receive rent, or during which the tenant has to start paying rent again, depending on the wording of the clause. Many tenants will insist the lease be revised to allow them to serve one month's notice of termination if the premises have not been reinstated within 2 years and 11 months after the damage occurs, so they do not have to pay rent as form the end of the rent abatement period.

The parties should consider the position whereby the reinstatement works are ongoing but have not been completed by the deadline. There could be a situation where the landlord continues to completion and the tenant then turns round and terminates the lease because the works were not completed on time. The lease should therefore provide for notice to be served at any time after the deadline, but not after completion of the works.

Landlord's redevelopment option

Some leases provide for the landlord to be entitled to terminate the lease if the **12–11** premises are destroyed or are severely damaged by any of the insured risks, so as to allow him to redevelop. If so, the tenant should be aware that he will not be able to go back into the premises, and he will have to relocate. The tenant should revise the lease so that the landlord is only entitled to exercise his option to terminate if he gives notice of this within a short period of time, so as to reduce the period of uncertainty for the tenant.

Tenant's fixtures and fittings and stock

There is scope for confusion about the tenant's fixtures and fittings. Anything **12–12** that becomes heritable property, i.e. that is affixed with a degree of permanence and that would cause damage if removed, should properly be insured along with the property itself. The lease should make it clear that the landlord only has an obligation to insure tenants' items if and when the tenant gives the landlord full details of these items and their replacement value. The tenant should separately insure his stock.

Loss of rent and service charge—insured risk damage

At common law, the tenant is entitled to abatement (excusal) of rent and of **12–13** service charge if and for as long as the premises cannot be fully used and occupied by any cause whatsoever. The lease will usually contract out of this right in the case of damage or destruction due to any non-insured risk, and will specifically allow rent and service charge abatement for a limited period of time, or if sooner, until the premises can again be used and occupied if damaged or destroyed by any of the insured risks. If rent abatement is provided for, the tenant should try to make sure it will apply if the premises or common parts are destroyed or seriously damaged by any of the risks the landlord was to insure against. If the landlord only has to insure to the extent cover is available at reasonable rates, and one of the risks is not insured because of this exception, the question arises as to whether the landlord or the tenant is responsible for making good. It will usually fall on the tenant in a lease that has been well-drafted by the landlord. The wording of the lease needs to be carefully checked at revisal stage and the position understood, negotiated or accepted.

In order to maintain an income stream during this period, the landlord will insure, at the cost of the tenant, against loss of rent and, if applicable, service charge for the period the landlord estimates it would take to obtain all necessary permissions and to rebuild or reinstate the property.

This period is usually three years, but it could be up to five years if the property is a listed building or is of unusual construction. Loss of rent insurance should take into account increases at rent review; the increase may be "potential" (in which case the sky is the limit) or probable/likely.

Uninsured Risks

12–14 Many commercial leases now include provision for "*uninsured risks*". The devil is in the detail, and in particular in the definition of "uninsured risks". The tenant's concern is that the landlord does not insure for all the risks that he should, because he does not bother or forgets to insure, or because insurance cover may simply not be available, or it ceases to be available. *The clause will usually deal with what happens if the property is damaged or destroyed by an "uninsured risk".* The compromise often found is that the tenant has to notify the landlord of the damage or destruction, and the landlord then has to decide, within quite a short period of time, whether he is, or is not, going to make good at his own cost. If he says that he will make good, then he must do so, and the lease will provide for rent abatement to continue until the property is made good again. The provision for rent abatement is, of course, only required if the lease elsewhere contract out of the tenant's common law right to withhold rent if the premises are unable to be fully used and occupied.

If the landlord says he is not going to make good, or if he says nothing, then the clause will usually provide for the lease to end immediately. The clause will usually also provide for automatic termination of the lease if the premises are not able to be used or occupied within three years of occurrence of the uninsured risk damage. The topic of uninsured risks is dealt with fully in Ch.13.

Noting of interest and subrogation waiver

12–15 In *Fehilly v General Accident Fire and Life Assurance Corp Ltd*[2] a lease imposed on the tenant the obligation to maintain the premises throughout the term of the lease in the same good and reasonable repair and condition they were in at the start of the lease. The tenant insured the premises, which subsequently went on fire. The court held the tenant was not required, in such an instance, to repair or rebuild the premises, unless he had been responsible for the fire, and therefore the tenant had no insurable interest. In order for a tenant

---

[2] *Fehilly v General Accident Fire and Life Assurance Corp. Ltd*, 1983 S.L.T. 141.

to have had an insurable interest, the obligations imposed on the tenant would have had to be stronger, such as an obligation to insure the building, or to repair or rebuild it if damaged or destroyed.

The tenant will want to have his interest noted on the policy, and he will sometimes ask for a letter to be obtained from the insurers waiving their rights of subrogation. It may be that the landlord has a block policy covering a large number of properties or that there is a common policy in force, and in either of these instances it may not be possible to have the tenant's interest noted. Alternatively there may be a generic noting of interest for the generality of tenants.

The point of the tenant asking for a waiver of subrogation rights is that if insurance is in the landlord's name and damage or destruction is due to negligence on the part of the tenant, then under general insurance law the insurer would be entitled to claim from the tenant the amount that it has had to pay out to the landlord under the insurance policy. Some insurance companies will agree to grant a waiver of subrogation rights, but others will not.

In *Eurocrest Ventures Ltd v Zurich Insurance Plc*[3], the High Court in England decided that the noting of the tenant's interest on the landlord's insurance policy does not give the tenant benefit of cover under the public liability section of the policy. The court said that the noting of an interest merely records the existence of that interest, and to notify the insurer that the beneficial owner of the policy proceeds may be someone other than the insured. It said that in order to confer a benefit, the policy must go further than mentioning the third party by name—it has to give specific rights to the third party.

In *Barras v Hamilton*[4], the landlord insured four industrial units, and each **12–16** tenant paid the proportion due for his unit. A fire broke out in one unit and spread into the other units, completely destroying all four of the units. The landlord sued the tenant of the unit in which the fire originated for uninsured losses in respect of all four units. The court held that as the landlord was to insure the unit against fire at the tenant's cost, the intention of the parties must have been that the landlord was to recover his loss only from the insurance policy without any further claim against the tenant. However, the landlord was not precluded from seeking to recover from the tenant his loss in respect of the other three units. The court held that the landlord's implied obligation to insure was restricted to insuring only the tenant's single unit, and the tenant was only responsible for the cost of insurance of that unit.

The principle of "average"

Property insurance is a contract of indemnity, by which the insurer makes good **12–17** the loss suffered. Therefore, if one over-insures only the amount of the loss will be payable. However, the principle of "average" also applies so that if one under-insures, the insurance company will reduce the payout by the same proportion by which the insured party has under-insured. For example, if a building would cost £1 million to rebuild but the owner has only insured for £750,000, and there is damage of £750,000, the insurer will only pay out 75 per cent of the £750,000. This principle of average also applies to defective title insurance policies.

---

[3] *Eurocrest Ventures Ltd v Zurich Insurance Plc* Unreported April 25, 2012, Chancery.
[4] *Barras v Hamilton*, 1994 S.L.T. 949.

Non-invalidation clause

12–18   A non-invalidation clause will keep the insurance cover in place even if the tenant does something that would otherwise render the policy invalid. The landlord's lenders will invariably insist that the insurance policy has a non-invalidation clause.

B—ENGLAND

Differences in common law and implied terms

12–19   The rule of *rei interitus* does not apply in England, and so a lease will remain in force if the premises are destroyed or are severely damaged.

There is no right in favour of a tenant to rent abatement in England; the rent continues to be payable if the premises cannot be used due to any cause whatsoever, unless there is specific provision to the contrary. Such provision might include loss of rent insurance being obtained and for rent to be excused following insured risk damage.

Subrogation

12–20   In *Mark Rowlands Ltd v Berni Inns Ltd*[5] the owner of a building leased the basement to a tenant, whose negligence caused a fire that destroyed the whole building. The landlord insured the building and the tenant paid a due proportion of the premium. The lease said that the tenant does not have to make good any damage caused by the insured risks. The court held that the landlord was to be seen as having insured the whole building for joint benefit of landlord and the basement tenant, even though the tenant was not co-insured with the landlord. The tenant was considered to have an insurable interest in the continued existence of the building, and therefore the insurance company had no claim against the tenant.

---

[5] *Mark Rowlands Ltd v Berni Inns Ltd* [1986] Q.B. 211; [1985] 3 W.L.R. 964.

CHAPTER 13

REPAIRS

Introduction

This Chapter should be read along with Ch.14 (Dilapidations).   **13–01**

In Ch.3 we examined the various rules provided for by common law, which apply to every lease of commercial property unless and to the extent they are contracted out of.

An FRI (full repairing and insuring) lease is one that imposes on the tenant full repairing, renewing and rebuilding obligations and the liability to pay for insurance premiums. An FRI lease is sometimes referred to as a "clear lease" or an "institutionally acceptable lease". If a lease is not fully FRI, then the property may be down-valued, and it may be more difficult to borrow against the property or to sell it as a property investment. It is therefore necessary, when dealing with the repair clause, to be fully aware of the common law position.

An IRI (internal repairing and insuring) lease is much more tenant-friendly than the FRI lease. An IRI lease is often used for leases to government departments. It imposes on the tenant the obligation to maintain and repair the interior parts of the premises, leaving the landlord responsible at common law, or in terms of specific provisions contained in the lease, for the exterior and the structure. IRI leases impose on the tenant the obligation to insure the property or, alternatively, for them to pay the premia incurred by the landlord in insuring. Typically, if there are two identical buildings, one of which will have an FRI lease and the other an IRI lease, the tenant who takes an IRI lease should pay a higher rent than if he takes an FRI lease, because the obligations imposed in the IRI lease are less onerous on him.

In this Chapter, we briefly revisit these common law rules, and then we examine how these can be contracted out of. We also look at the relevant case law on repairs in commercial leases. We then briefly address how repairs are dealt with in English law.

A—SCOTLAND

Summary of common law on repairs

- The landlord must provide the tenant with premises that are reasonably **13–02** fit for their purpose, and he warrants that they will throughout the lease be fit for their purpose. If the premises are not fit for their purpose the landlord can be found liable to the tenant in damages and, in serious cases, the tenant can terminate the lease.
- The landlord must keep the premises wind and watertight, and must carry out repairs. This includes renewing any constituent part of the

premises, even if this is because the part in question has become worn out due to the passage of time. The landlord's repairing obligation is not a warranty, but it is an obligation to be performed by the landlord as and when required, and the tenant can call on the landlord to carry out works of repair. In *John Menzies Plc v Ravenseft Properties Ltd*[1] it was held that where the terms of the lease make the landlord responsible for repairs, this is not an absolute obligation unless the lease expressly states it to be; otherwise the landlord's duty is merely to take reasonable care in his maintenance obligations.

- The landlord is responsible for any damage caused by a defect in the design or construction of the premises, but he is not required to make good damage caused by a third party, by an act of God or by an accident such as a fire. In *Bayne v Walker*[2] it was held that if there is accidental destruction or damage for which nobody is at fault, then neither the landlord nor the tenant has any obligation to repair or rebuild, even though each might have an interest to do so.

- If the premises are destroyed, or are so damaged as to be unfit for use or occupancy, then the rule of rei interitus provides that the lease comes to an end at the date of that destruction or damage, and neither party has any liability to the other.

- If the lease imposes an obligation on the tenant "to repair", this does not include an obligation to carry out extraordinary repairs. These include any replacement or renewal of something that has become worn out through the passing of time. Therefore lifts, boilers and central heating systems, flat roofs and other parts of the premises may well be the subject of extraordinary repairs. Latent and inherent defects in the design and/or the construction of a building also come within the definition of "extraordinary repairs", and are thus not the tenant's obligation, unless the repair clause specifically or by very strong implication requires the tenant to be responsible for these.

In *Co-Operative Insurance Society Ltd v Fife Council*[3] Lord Glennie provided helpful guidance on determining whether a particular item of repair is an ordinary or an extraordinary repair. Extraordinary repairs are not comprehensively judicially defined anywhere, but they include latent and inherent defects, and inevitable deterioration over a period of time, such as floor joists becoming so worn out they can no longer support the premises. He said there are three matters to be considered in deciding whether work to be done is an ordinary or an extra-ordinary repair: (i) the cause of the damage, (ii) the nature and extent of the damage, and (iii) the extent to work that needs to be done.

In this case, the court held that on the wording of the lease, the tenant was not required to carry out extraordinary repairs—the clause states the tenant had to "repair and keep in good and substantial repair and maintained, renewed, and cleansed in very respect . . . the leased subjects, and to repair, maintain, and renewal vertical and horizontal structures separating the leased subjects from the landlord's adjoining premises on any side or below". Lord Glennie

---

[1] *John Menzies Plc v Ravenseft Properties Ltd*, 1987 S.L.T. 64.

[2] *Bayne v Walker* (1815) 3 D. 233.

[3] *Co-Operative Insurance Society v Fife Council* [2011] CSOH 76

held that the clause did not displace on to the tenant the liability for extraordinary repairs.

Contracting out of the common law

The common law provisions are usually contracted out of to a large extent, but **13–03** it is important if acting for a landlord to check the actual extent to which these are contracted out of, and if acting for the tenant to check whether there is any window of opportunity for successfully denying liability for some repairs, etc. under the lease.

The FRI lease will normally displace on to the tenant the common law obligations, although many tenants will try to negotiate to soften their repairing obligations. It is surprising how often the landlord unwittingly gives away his position of strength due to bad drafting of the repair clause, or due to not fully understanding the effect of the tenant's revisals to the draft lease. This can be very adverse for the landlord, as it not only leaves him with liability, but it also reduces the marketability and value of his property, as a weak lease will be less attractive to purchasers and lenders.

In order to contract out of the common law obligations and warranties in respect of repairs that are imposed on the landlord, the landlord will want the clause to read something like the following:

> "The Tenant accepts the premises (and the common parts) as at the date of entry as being in good and tenantable repair and condition, notwithstanding any latent or patent defect therein, and undertakes throughout the period of this Lease to put and keep the premises in good repair and to maintain, repair, clean, and to keep the premises wind and water tight, and when necessary to replace, reinstate, renew and rebuild the premises, and that irrespective of the cause of damage or destruction, (but excepting from the Tenant's obligations the making good, rebuilding, renewing or reinstating or replacing where the cause of damage or destruction is any of the insured risks, except to the extent that the Tenant or anyone for whom the Tenant is legally responsible, or any subtenant or other occupant of the premises is responsible for the insurers refusing or withholding payment under the insurance policy). The rent payable under this Lease will continue to be payable, (except to the extent provided for in the rent abatement clause), and this Lease will continue notwithstanding any actual, notional or constructive damage to or destruction of the premises (and/or of the common parts)."

It is not necessary for the lease to specifically impose on the tenant the obli- **13–04** gation to carry out extraordinary repairs or to make good latent or inherent defects in the design or construction of the building; the words "irrespective of the cause of damage or destruction" achieve this.

The tenant should try to water down the repairing obligations. He should try to delete any obligation to "put into" good repair; he should also try to resist any obligation "to repair", because this is the same as to put into good repair. The tenant should try for an obligation to keep in the same state of repair as at commencement of the lease, although few commercially-minded landlords will accept that. The tenant should also try to provide for repairs to be to the landlord's reasonable satisfaction. Ideally, from the tenant's point of view, there should be a schedule of condition that sets out the state of the premises at the start of the term, with no obligation on the tenant to make good wants of repair shown in the Schedule. Paragraphs 13–07 to 13–11 contain further material about drafting aspects of the repairing clause.

The meaning of "to repair"

13–05 In order for something to need to be repaired, it must have fallen into a state of disrepair.

"To repair" includes renewal or rebuilding of a constituent part (as opposed to the whole) of the premises. An external structural wall is merely a subsidiary part of the premises leased. Many repairs involve replacing part of the entity with something new. In *Proudfoot v Hart*[4] it was held that, where a tenant has an obligation to repair a building and it is not possible to patch up a floor, he needs to replace what has become no longer a floor with something that is a floor.

In *Lurcott v Wakely & Wheeler*[5] the court held that an external structural wall is merely a subsidiary part of the premises that were leased, and its restoration would leave the remainder of the premises untouched and would not change the character or nature of the building. The court also held that the age and type of structure of the premises do not relieve the tenant of his obligation to maintain or repair, and that many repairs involve replacing part of the entity with something new.

In *House of Fraser Plc v Prudential Assurance Co Ltd*[6] the court considered a lease that required the tenant to repair the premises exclusively let to him, and the landlord was to keep in good and substantial repair the foundations, roof, main walls and main structural parts of a three-storey building, with the tenant being required to reimburse the landlord for the cost of all repairs. A retaining wall needed repair and the landlord proposed to take down the wall and rebuild it. The tenant argued that in terms of the lease he was not required to reimburse the cost of the work, because it was an extraordinary repair for which the landlord had responsibility at common law, as opposed to the tenant having responsibility in terms of the lease.

The court held that the landlord has the right and the responsibility to preserve and maintain the structural integrity of the whole building, which was likely to include ordinary repairs and extraordinary repairs. The natural reading of the clause was that the landlord has the same responsibility for extraordinary repairs that the common law would have imposed upon him, and although the lease merely states that the landlord is to repair and keep in good condition, given the common law background, these words are entirely appropriate to put on to the landlord the responsibility for extraordinary repairs. The tenant was therefore liable to pay his contribution.

In *Taylor Woodrow Property Co Ltd v Strathclyde Regional Council*[7] the lease required the tenant to repair and keep the premises in good and substantial condition to the satisfaction of the landlord. The court held that as the test of "satisfaction" of a landlord is indefinite, some qualifying language has to be

---

[4] *Proudfoot v Hart* [1890] 25 Q.B.D. 42.
[5] *Lurcott v Wakely & Wheeler* [1911] 1 K.B. 905.
[6] *House of Fraser Plc v Prudential Assurance Co Ltd*, 1994 S.L.T. 416.
[7] *Taylor Woodrow Property Co Ltd v Strathclyde Regional Council*, 1996 G.W.D. 7–397.

imported to give it practical business sense. It was therefore appropriate for each party to assume that the other would act reasonably and that the tenant's obligation to repair includes partial renewal if such is necessary.

In *Ravenseft Property Ltd v Davstone (Holdings) Ltd*[8] the tenant had to insert expansion joints when repairing, which effectively involved replacing the brick cladding which had bulged dangerously because the original design had not included these joints. The court held that the insertion of the joints did not amount to changing the character of the building and that the cost was trivial compared to the value of the premises, and it was accordingly within the tenant's repairing obligation.

Extraordinary repairs

A useful summary of the difference between ordinary and extraordinary repairs **13–06** is given in *Co-operative Insurance Society Ltd v Fife Council*,[9] where the tenant was to repair and keep in good and substantial repair, maintained, renewed the premises, and was, at joint cost and expense of landlord and tenant, to repair, maintain and renewal all vertical or horizontal structures separating the premises from the landlord's adjoining premises on any side or below. The court held that the terms of the repairing clause in this lease were not sufficient to make the tenant liable for extraordinary repairs at common law.

Although the decided cases do not give any very precise method of distinguishing between ordinary and extraordinary repairs, they do identify the main things to be taken into account, which are: the origin of the damage, its extent and its nature. If the damage is caused by an event that is unanticipated and outwith either party's control, it is likely to be an extraordinary repair (to be contrasted with the ordinary effects of bad weather). Decay through passage of time falls into this extraordinary repair category, but the landlord would not be required to make good if the decay has occurred because it got into that state through neglect on the part of the tenant. If a wall or a roof were to collapse, it may suggest the repair is an extraordinary repair, for which the landlord is liable unless it happens due to the tenants neglect and nature of damage and necessary repair—does it amount to total reconstruction? The word "renewed" is not sufficient to put the responsibility of extraordinary repairs onto the tenant.

Drafting points—landlord's viewpoint

If the premises are a self-contained and stand-alone building, then there is no **13–07** need to provide any definition or obligations in respect of common parts; however, if the premises are part of a larger building, shopping centre, industrial estate or business park, it is necessary for the lease to contain a definition of "common parts". It is essential that the lease contains a statement that the tenant accepts the premises and the common parts as being in good condition and fit for their purpose, or else there could be a claim against the landlord that the premises are not fit for the purpose let because of some problem with the common parts.

---

[8] *Ravenseft Property Ltd v Davstone (Holdings) Ltd* [1980] Q.B. 12; [1979] 1 All E.R. 929.
[9] *Co-operative Insurance Society Ltd v Fife Council*, 2011 CSOH 76.

A typical definition of "common parts" could include the roof, foundations, lift, heating system, stairs and entranceway and passages, the outer walls and other parts of the structure as well as services pipes, cables, etc. If the premises comprise a building on an estate, the common parts may include roads and pavements, boundary walls, a communal heating system, estate signboards, etc. The landlord will be responsible for these common parts, whereas the tenant will usually be responsible for the premises themselves.

Landlords should beware of "circular repair clauses". If the lease requires the tenant "to maintain and repair, and for the purposes of maintenance and repair, to renew, replace and rebuild", then the landlord could possibly be exposed, unless the clause also imposes on the tenant the obligation to carry out extraordinary repairs. If it does not include these, the words "for the purposes of maintenance and repair" will be considered by some people to mean that the tenant is only liable for renewing or rebuilding a constituent part of the premises, as opposed to the whole. A safer concession that is often given to the tenant is in the wording: "to repair and maintain, and if beyond economic or viable repair or maintenance, to reinstate, renew, replace and rebuild".

13–08   From the landlord's point of view, in a well-drafted lease, the tenant should be stated as accepting the premises and the common parts as being in good condition, even if the reality is quite different! In *Blackwell v Farmfoods (Aberdeen) Ltd*[10] the lease contained a statement that the tenant accepted the premises as being in their present condition, but there was no such statement in respect of common parts. The court held that the common law warranty by the landlord that the common parts were reasonably fit for the purpose for which they were let remains in place, and that the work to the common parts could not be related to the tenant's liability for the premises.

It is also important, from the landlord's point of view, for the lease to impose on the tenant the obligation to make good any defects that may not be evident from inspection, i.e. latent or inherent defects. An obligation on the tenant "to repair" does not go far enough. In *Thorn EMI Ltd v Taylor Woodrow Industrial Estates Ltd*[11] the court held that a clause imposing on the tenant the obligation "to repair, rebuild, reinstate or replace the premises in the event of damage however the same shall arise", is sufficient to impose on the tenant the obligation to make good latent and inherent defects. Many leases nowadays provide the wording "irrespective of the cause of damage or destruction".

There is a difference between having to keep the premises in "good repair" and having to keep them in "good condition". In *Quick v Taff-Ely Borough Council*[12] it was held that a property can be in good repair but in bad condition; it could be damp and suffer from condensation and thus suffer from being inefficient and having less than ideal amenity. This would not be something requiring repair (as there is no disrepair), but it would have to be treated by the tenant if the lease requires the tenant to keep the premises in good condition.

13–09   In *Napier v Ferrier*[13] the court considered the difference between an obligation to put premises into repair on the one hand and to keep premises in repair on the other. The court held that an obligation to keep premises in repair

---

[10] *Blackwell v Farmfoods (Aberdeen) Ltd*, 1991 G.W.D. 4–219.

[11] *Thorn EMI Ltd v Taylor Woodrow Industrial Estates Ltd* Unreported October 29, 1982.

[12] *Quick v Taff-Ely Borough Council* [1986] Q.B. 809.

[13] *Napier v Ferrier*, 1847 S.C. 1354.

throughout the lease implies an understanding of the parties that the premises were in repair when the lease commenced, which is in accordance with the usual obligations of a landlord. If the tenant is to put the premises into repair, this is contrary to the usual understanding, and would require the clearest expression of intention to support it.

From the landlord's point of view, the only exception to the repair obligation imposed on the tenant should be any damage or destruction from any risk insured against, except to the extent the tenant renders void the insurance policy. If the premises are destroyed or damaged by any of the risks insured against, and the tenant has not rendered void the insurance, then the landlord should be required (subject to getting the necessary consents) to use the insurance money to make good. The landlord should also be responsible for any shortfall in insurance, due to under-insuring. This will apply if, in terms of the lease, the tenant is excused from making good insured damage and the landlord is liable for making good insured damage.

From the landlord's point of view, a lease should ideally include a statement that the landlord does not have to carry out any repairs or other works, whether in terms of the lease or at common law or otherwise, except where such is expressly imposed on the landlord in terms of the lease (which is usually only in respect of making good insured damage).

Tenant's revisals of repairs clause and Schedule of Condition

The tenant should always make sure that his liability for damage by any **13–10** insured risks is excluded. If the property is not in perfect condition at the time of negotiating the lease, he should try to provide for a schedule of condition to be annexed to the lease. A surveyor should prepare the Schedule of Condition, which is a report in text and/or photographs showing the condition of the property. This can be used to identify defects that are to be made good by the landlord by a stipulated time, or defects that the tenant does not require to make good at any time. Alternatively, it can be used to record the state of the premises as at the date of entry, with a statement in the lease itself that the tenant does not require to put the premises into any better condition (or must keep them in no worse condition) than that shown in the Schedule of Condition.

If the concessions in respect of the repair clause are contained in a back letter, this should, from the tenant's point of view, be stated to be for the benefit of the original tenant and all permitted assignees (so that future tenants get the benefit of the back letter), but the landlord will probably insist that only the first tenant gets the benefit. This would not be a problem for the tenant if he grants a sub-lease, because the tenant remains in place and so he could allow the same benefit to his sub-tenant for as long as he remains the tenant.

From the tenant's viewpoint, the back letter should be expressed as being binding on the landlord and his successors as landlord; this is likely to be unacceptable to the landlord. The fall-back is for the landlord to undertake that he will take any future landlord as bound to grant a back letter in identical terms, including the obligation to take the next in turn landlord as bound by it. If the tenant does not have this protection, then when the landlord sells the property, the tenant would have no recourse against the new landlord, as the back letter would only be personal as between the original landlord and the tenant, and the original landlord may have disappeared.

13–11   The tenant should also try to revise the repairs clause so as to exclude any obligation to make good wants of repair that exist at the time of commencement of the lease and also any deterioration that arises due to such wants of repair not being made good. He should also try to exclude liability for any defects in design or construction (latent defects) of the premises or of any building of which they form part. The landlord should not accept either of these revisals, but perhaps some comfort can be given to the tenant in the form of latent defects insurance cover for a new or refurbished building and/or collateral warranties (duty of care undertakings) being provided to the tenant by the design team and the contractors. If neither of these is available, then the landlord could undertake to enforce all rights he has against the professional team involved in design of the property and the building contractor.

The tenant should also try to provide for his obligation to renew, replace or rebuild to only apply if the item in question is beyond economic or viable repair. This provision should not be objectionable to the landlord.

Any damage caused by any of the risks against which the landlord is to insure should also be excluded from the tenant's responsibility.

In multi-occupancy properties, such as shopping centres, office buildings, etc. the tenant could not realistically expect to exclude or water-down liability for common parts, but he can try to limit his expense by agreeing that his payment of service charge be fixed at a specific amount or capped (i.e. will not be more than a specified amount) for a period of time, and that increases in his liability will not be greater than a specific percentage. Such tinkering with service charge liability is not wildly popular with landlords, but concessions are available depending on the market forces and the relative negotiating strength of the parties at drafting stage.

Uninsured Risks

13–12 Many commercial leases now include provision for "*uninsured risks*". The devil is in the detail, and in particular on the definition of "uninsured risks".

The main concern is that the landlord does not insure for all the risks that he should. This can happen for one of two reasons: first, the landlord simply does not bother, or he forgets, or does not realise that he has to get the insurance cover. This could easily happen where a property owner has various properties and he buys another one, which he insures under his block insurance policy, but the lease of which provides for specific risks to be insured, and these are not covered by his policy. Secondly, insurance cover may simply not be available, or it ceases to be available.

Some tenants' solicitors will try to expand the definition of "uninsured risk" to mean any risk that is not insured against. This effectively renders useless the whole repairing obligation, as it transfers all repair liability and more (because of the drafting of the lease) back on to the landlord, and will make the landlord's interest unmarketable, as few property investors will want to buy into such an onerous liability!

Perhaps the fairest compromise for both parties is to define uninsured risks as "any risks expressly specified in the definition of the insured risks which (i) are not insured because insurance is not available at all, or are not available in the UK insurance market (at economic rates); or (ii) are not insured or fully insured by reason of a policy exclusion, such that the full cost of reinstatement is not recoverable by the landlord under the insurance policy".

It is important to exclude any act of the tenant that renders invalid the policy (unless the tenant promptly pays to the landlord the amount of insurance monies rendered irrecoverable).

However, what if the list of insured risks is quite narrow? The landlord may give himself the *right* but not the obligation, to insure against certain risks. In such a case, the "optional risks" would not be insured risks, and would thus not fall within "uninsured risks" if these are not insured, in which case the tenant is left with liability for these. So it is really better for there to be an open and honest discussion between the solicitors for the landlord and the tenant to ensure complete understanding on all sides.

The clause will usually deal with what happens if the property is damaged or destroyed by an "uninsured risk". The landlord is unlikely to accept an absolute obligation to make good and to do without payment of rent in the meantime. After all, he will not be getting any money from the insurers, as the damage will have been caused by a non insured risk. The compromise often found is that the tenant has to notify the landlord of the damage or destruction, as the landlord is unlikely to know of the problem. This starts a clock ticking for the landlord to decide whether he is or is not going to make good at his own cost, and for rent abatement to apply. A period of, usually, anything from 1 month up to 12 months is allowed for the landlord to decide whether or not he wants to make good at his own cost. If he says that he will make good, then he must do so, and rent abatement continues until the property is made good again. If the landlord says he is not going to make good, or if he says nothing, then the clause will usually provide for the lease to end immediately.

The clause will usually also provide for automatic termination of the lease if the premises are not able to be used or occupied within three years of occurrence of the uninsured risk damage.

More case law on repairs

Although common law fills any gaps left by a lack of specific or strongly **13–13** implied contractual terms, there can occasionally be a "black hole", where a lease continues in existence and neither party is liable for carrying out repairs or rebuilding works. If the damage is not serious enough to render the premises unable to be used or occupied, and if the landlord has contracted out of its common law obligations but has not passed these on to the tenant, then there can be a situation where neither party is required to carry out repairs or other works. The tenant would, or would not, have to continue paying rent, depending on whether the common law right of rent abatement has been contracted out of, as is seen in the case of *Bayne v Walker* referred to in para.13–02 above.

Another case that deals with this situation is *Little Cumbrae Estate Ltd v Island of Little Cumbrae Ltd*,[14] which concerned rural premises, for which (contrary to the position in urban premises, which of course includes commercial lease premises) the tenant is liable for repairs at common law. The lease imposed on the tenant the obligation to carry out repairs and maintenance, except for repairs necessitated by any of the insured risks, including storm damage. An insurance claim was lodged after damage was caused by a storm, and there was a shortfall in insurance money received. The lease provided for

---

[14] *Little Cumbrae Estate Ltd v Island of Little Cumbrae Ltd*, 2007 S.C. 525.

the landlord to use all money received from the insurance policy (apart from proceeds of loss of rent insurance) in reinstating the premises. The court held that the common law states that neither party is required to repair if damage or destruction is caused by accident, but this can be contracted out of. This lease did not provide for what is to happen if there is a shortfall, so the common law provisions would therefore operate. There was no express obligation on the landlord to carry out storm damage repairs. The common law obligation lay with the tenant because this was rural property, but the tenant had been excused from making these repairs in terms of the lease.

In *Proudfoot v Hart*[15] it was held that the obligation to keep and to leave the premises in good tenantable repair must take into account their age, character and locality, so they would be reasonably fit for occupation by a reasonably-minded tenant. The premises need not be put into the same condition as when the tenant took entry, nor be put into perfect repair.

13–14 In *William Collins & Sons Ltd v CGU Insurance Plc*[16] the tenant, who had repairing obligations under a head lease of an office building, notified his sub-tenant, CGU, of his intention to carry out extensive works of repair and renewal to the building some 13 months before termination of the lease. The sub-lease to CGU reserved in favour of their landlord the right to enter the premises as often as necessary to carry out the landlord's repairing, maintaining and other obligations, whether in the sub-lease or in the head lease. The cost of the repairs was recoverable by way of service charge under the sublease.

CGU refused to allow access to the premises to carry out these works and disputed the extent of deterioration alleged by their landlord. They also raised issues of the cost of the consequent disruption of their business. The sub-lease contained a declaration that the landlord is the judge as to the necessity of all expenditure and will carry out the works, services and others. The court decided on the evidence that:

- it would not be workable for CGU to remain in occupancy of the premises while the proposed works were being carried out, notwithstanding that William Collins were anxious to carry out the works;
- it has not been suggested that there was an incoming sub-tenant entitled to take entry on expiry of the sub-lease; and
- while William Collins may have lost the opportunity of recovering the cost of the work by way of a service charge if the work is not done before the sub-lease ends, they would be entitled to recover the cost in the form of damages for breach of contract. The sub-tenant had an obligation to accept the premises as being in good and substantial repair at the date of entry and to repair, maintain, renew and keep, and in certain events to rebuild, reinstate and replace the premises and all additions, so that they are in good and substantial condition and repair during the whole period of the lease, all to the landlord's satisfaction.

In *McCall's Entertainments (Ayr) Ltd v South Ayrshire Council (No.2)*[17] the lease required the tenant to accept the premises in the condition they were in at

[15] *Proudfoot v Hart* [1890] 25 Q.B.D. 42.

[16] *William Collins & Sons Ltd v CGU Insurance Plc*, 2006 S.C. 674.

[17] *McCall's Entertainments (Ayr) Ltd v South Ayrshire Council (No.2)*, 1998 S.L.T. 1421; 1998 G.W.D. 19–988.

the start of the lease and to keep them in good condition and to return them at the end of the lease in no worse condition than at the start. The court held: (i) that the tenant had no obligation to improve the premises; (ii) that on the evidence led, the condition of the premises at commencement of the lease was such that if more than normal maintenance were to have been required, there would have to be an express provision included in the lease; and (iii) that the condition of the premises now could not be attributed to any failure on the tenant's part to carry out normal repairs.

In *Marfield Properties Ltd v Secretary of State for the Environment*[18] the **13–15** lease provided for the tenant to contribute to the cost of maintenance of common parts, which were defined as including a car park, common service yard, internal access roads and pedestrian access-way, fixtures and fittings used in common, services in the building development and "all other parts of the said development which are common to the premises and other parts of the said building development". The landlord carried out maintenance works to the roof and external walls and then demanded payment of the relevant proportion from the tenant, on the basis that the roof and walls formed part of the common parts. It was held that there is no common law definition of "common parts" and so the ordinary rules for interpretation of contracts should apply, and if there is ambiguity, the court should if possible try to resolve it using the language of the contract. The court held that the phrase "all other parts" was wide enough to include anything that was common to the premises and other parts of the building development, and was thus wide enough to include the roof and external walls by implication. It was also held that the *contra preferentem* rule of construction (to favour the tenant as the underdog) would not apply here, as leases of this kind are assumed to have been entered into by parties negotiating on an equal footing, having arrived at the terms of the lease by mutual adjustment.

In *Lowe v Quayle Munro Ltd*[19] the lease provided for the tenant to accept the premises in their present condition and to repair and keep in good repair, maintain, replace or renew or rebuild whenever necessary, all to the satisfaction of the landlord, irrespective of the age or state of dilapidation or any latent or inherent defects. The court held that the landlord must act reasonably in considering whether works were carried out to his satisfaction, that it could not have been the intention that the landlord would be entitled to act arbitrarily or unreasonably and that the clause does not provide the landlord with a blank cheque to recover the cost of any works that might conceivably be brought within the scope of one of the heads of the tenant's obligation. The court also held that as the lease imposed the obligation of renewal along with replacement and rebuilding, proof of necessity is needed if the landlord is to enforce this or if he is to be able to recover the cost. Furthermore, the court held that the ability to recover is conditional on the works that fall within the tenant's obligations having been carried out to the reasonable satisfaction of the landlord.

In *Douglas Shelf 7 Ltd v Co-operative Wholesale Society Ltd*[20] the court considered two points; first, that although the landlord had previously sued the tenant for damages for breach of the keep open clause in the lease, he is not

---

[18] *Marfield Properties Ltd v Secretary of State for the Environment*, 1999 S.L.T. 1244.
[19] *Lowe v Quayle Munro Ltd*, 1997 S.L.T. 1168.
[20] *Douglas Shelf 7 Ltd v Co-operative Wholesale Society Ltd* [2009] CSOH 3.

prevented from enforcing the repairing obligation in the lease. Secondly, that the tenant had no obligation to contribute towards the cost of provision of security services as this was not covered by the catch-all phrase "costs in connection with management and administration of the shopping centre".

B—ENGLAND

Terms implied by law

13–16
- In England there is no implied warranty or covenant by the landlord that commercial premises are reasonably fit for habitation or occupancy or for any purpose for which they are let. There is no obligation automatically implied on the landlord to make any repairs whatsoever during the lease. In certain circumstances, a repair obligation may be implied in order to give the lease business efficacy. Unless the lease says otherwise, it is implied that a landlord is not liable for defects rendering the premises dangerous or unfit for occupancy.
- A landlord has a duty to the tenant under the Defective Premises Act 1972, but only if the landlord is responsible for repairs under the lease, which is very rare.
- If the landlord grants leases of various parts of a building to separate tenants and he retains, for example, the entranceway, passages, lifts, etc. he must use reasonable care to keep these reasonably safe. If he retains control over the roof, he must use reasonable care to prevent the roof from falling into disrepair. These provisions are, however, usually contracted out of.
- The lease does not come to an end if the premises are severely damaged or destroyed, unless specific wording to this effect is included in the lease itself.
- There must be disrepair for an obligation to repair to arise, and this cannot happen unless the premises are in a worse condition than at an earlier time. Preventative measures can be included as repair, as can work not only to remedy damage, but also to prevent a recurrence.
- If the property is not in good repair at the date of entry, and the tenant undertakes to keep the property in repair, it follows that he must first put the property into repair.
- An inherent defect is not necessarily outside the scope of repair; if the defect does not cause damage to the property, then there is no repairing obligation. If it does damage the property, then it is a question of degree. Is the tenant is being asked to merely repair, or is he being asked to give back to the landlord a wholly different thing from that which he leased? If it is the latter, this would not come within the definition of "to repair" (*Ravenseft Properties Ltd v Davstone Holdings Ltd*[21]).
- The matters that need to be considered in determining whether something is "repair" include: whether works are needed to (substantially) the whole of the structure or only a part, whether the works would result in a building of a wholly different character, the cost of the

---

[21] *Ravenseft Properties Ltd v Davstone Holdings Ltd*, 1980 K.B. 12.

works in relation to the previous value of the building and their effect on the value and life expectancy of the building.

- A covenant to repair does not include a duty to improve by introducing something different in kind to what was let, even if this is necessary by modern standards.
- Repair does not include rebuilding the whole, but it does include renewal of subordinate parts (*Lurcott v Wakeley*[22]).
- There is no right for the tenant to stop paying rent if the premises are damaged or destroyed, and so it is necessary for the tenant to specifically provide for this in the lease. Such rent excusal is normally accepted by landlords, but only in the case of damage caused by one of the insured risks.

Landlord's repairs notices

Forfeiture for breach of the tenant's repair covenant is not enforceable unless **13–17** the landlord proves that a s.146 Notice had been served on the tenant and that a reasonable time to enable repairs to be carried out has elapsed.

If a landlord serves notice on the tenant to carry out repairs, then unless the lease allows the landlord to enter the premises and carry out the works at the tenant's expense, the landlord's notice must say that the tenant can serve a counter-notice within 28 days claiming the benefit of the Leasehold Property (Repairs) Act 1938. The landlord's notice must also state the circumstances in which such notice can be served. The effect of the tenant serving counter-notice is that the landlord cannot render forfeit (irritate) the lease except with permission of the court. The counter-notice procedure only applies where the lease in question was granted for a term of at least seven years and if proceedings begin more than three years before expiry of the term. If the tenant does not serve counter-notice, then the court's leave is not required for forfeiture.

Defective Premises Act 1972

If the lease imposes on the landlord the obligation of repair, then in terms of the **13–18** Defective Premises Act 1972, he owes a duty to take reasonable care that the premises are reasonably safe from damage or personal injury. In practice, the obligations are only really relevant if persons are injured or their property is damaged due to defects in the premises.

---

[22] *Lurcott v Wakeley* [1911] 1 K.B. 905.

CHAPTER 14

DILAPIDATIONS

Introduction

14–01 This Chapter should be read together with Chs 3 (Common Law, etc.) and 13 (Repairs), because dilapidations occur at any time where the tenant is in breach of his repairing obligation or, when at the end of the lease, the tenant is to remove alterations and effect reinstatement. The repairs, decorating, maintenance and waygoing (things the tenant is to do at the end of the term) obligations and the terms of all licences for works and consents from the landlord need to be examined. It is essential to understand the rules implied by common law and also the meaning of the repairs and other clauses in the lease, so as to identify whether the tenant is indeed in breach.

The lease does not have to contain any right for the landlord to serve a schedule of dilapidations (notice of repairs needed) on the tenant, as it is implied that the landlord can draw to the tenant's attention a breach of the obligations imposed on the tenant and require the tenant to make good that breach. However, most leases will provide for the landlord to have the right to inspect (which is not implied) and to serve notice on the tenant requiring repairs and other works to be carried out within a specified time period.

It is normal for leases to impose on the tenant the obligation (in varying degrees) to put and keep the premises in good repair, and to renew, reinstate, rebuild and replace as necessary, and to leave the premises in good repair and condition at the end of the lease. Depending on the landlord's degree of active management, he may serve a schedule of dilapidations periodically during the lease, but he is very likely to serve one shortly before the end of the lease. This is sometimes called a "terminal schedule of dilapidations". The schedule is ostensibly a list of what the landlord requires to be done, but the landlord often intends it to be a basis for negotiation, so as to try to obtain a cash payment instead of having the works carried out.

In this Chapter, we briefly revisit the common law on repairs, and then we address the case law on dilapidations in Scotland. Finally, we take a brief look at the position on dilapidations in English leases.

A—SCOTLAND

Common law summary

14–02 In Scotland, unless the lease provides to the contrary (which it often does, to a greater or lesser extent):

- the landlord is responsible for providing premises that are reasonably able to be used and occupied, and for making and keeping the premises wind and water tight;
- the landlord must carry out repairs throughout the lease, and this includes renewing any constituent part of the premises, even if this is because the part in question has become worn out due to the passage of time. The landlord's repairing obligation at common law is different to the usually-found contractual obligation on the tenant to put and keep in good repair;
- the landlord is responsible for any damage caused by a defect in the design or construction of the premises, but he is not required to make good damage caused by a third party, by an act of God or by an accident such as a fire; and
- there is no right at common law or statute in favour of a tenant in Scotland to receive compensation for any works or improvements he has made.

Preparing the schedule of dilapidations

The landlord will usually instruct a building surveyor to inspect the premises **14–03** and prepare a schedule of dilapidations. The schedule should of course only relate to the premises that are exclusively leased to the tenant, and it should therefore not deal with common parts or any other parts of a multi-occupancy building or estate. If works need to be done to common or other parts, then the lease should contain provisions that enable the landlord himself to carry out these works and to recover the cost of them from the tenant, otherwise these costs are unlikely to be recoverable.

The schedule of dilapidations will often contain technical terms that are not easily understood by people who are not surveyors, and therefore a solicitor looking at the schedule is unlikely to be able to say whether specific items are indeed the tenant's responsibility in terms of the lease in question. It is important that the surveyor who is to prepare the schedule of dilapidations is given a copy of the lease and any amending documentation, and that he understands the full impact of the common law of commercial leases. In an ideal world, there would be dialogue between the surveyor and the solicitor before the schedule is finalised and issued to the tenant. The landlord can easily score an own goal by including things in a schedule of dilapidations that are not truly the tenant's responsibility, because the lease has not fully passed on to the tenant all of the landlord's common law obligations. This can rebound uncomfortably on the landlord so as to form the basis for a quid pro quo negotiation in which the tenant has the upper hand.

Case law on tenant's liability

In *Westbury Estates Ltd v The Royal Bank of Scotland Plc*[1] the landlord served **14–04** a schedule of dilapidations before the expiry of the lease, requiring the tenant to replace some electrical or mechanical items because they had reached the end of their economic life according to guidelines issued by the Chartered Institution of Building Services Engineers. The landlord argued that, as these

---

[1] *Westbury Estates Ltd v The Royal Bank of Scotland Plc*, 2006 S.L.T. 1143.

items had reached the end of their economic life, the premises could not be in good and substantial repair and condition. The court held that the fact that something was at the end of its economic life did not mean that the tenant was required to replace it, and if the current guidelines indicate an item is at or near the end of its economic life, that does not mean that the premises were other than in good and substantial repair and condition.

In *West Castle Properties Ltd v Scottish Ministers*[2] the lease required the tenant to keep the premises in good condition and decorative order to the land-lord's reasonable satisfaction and to keep them in "like good tenantable condi-tion and repair" as when the lease began. The landlord issued a schedule of dilapidations. The court held that the tenant was required to carry out any works that a prudent owner would have carried out to maintain the premises so they could be expected to last for their normal life, but the fact these items were not in such a good state at the end of the 25-year lease did not automati-cally mean the tenant had failed to keep them in "like good tenantable condi-tion and repair". The tenant was entitled to take account of the increasing age of the premises.

In *Pacitti v Manganiello*[3] the lease required the tenant to leave the premises in good condition and repair at expiry of the lease. The court held that the tenant's obligation was to leave the premises in the condition that they ought to be in, if the tenant had fulfilled his duties of repair and maintenance, as opposed to leaving the premises in the same condition as at commencement of the lease. It was also held that the tenant had agreed in the lease that the premises had been in good tenantable condition at commencement of the lease, and he could not now argue that it was for the landlord to prove this.

In *Allied Dunbar Assurance Plc v Superglass Sections Ltd*[4] a lease contained an early termination option in favour of the tenant, which was not conditional on anything. In terms of the lease the tenant had certain repairs obligations and was, at the end of the lease, to hand back the premises in the condition required in terms of the repairing obligation. The tenant served notice to terminate early; the landlord then served a schedule of dilapidations, but this was not fully complied with by the early termination date. The landlord argued that the tenant should not be entitled to terminate the lease early because he was in breach of his lease obligations—the tenant could not found on his own breach. The court held that there is no specific provision in the lease suggesting that termination could only take place if neither party was in breach of his obliga-tions, and therefore the lease had terminated. In this situation, of course, the landlord would have a claim of damages against the tenant for breach of contract in that the tenant left the premises without having fully complied with his repairing obligation.

Specific implement and damages

14–05 As with any other positive obligation that is imposed on the tenant in a lease, the landlord can seek from the court an order of specific implement to force the tenant to perform. The court will only grant such an order if the obligation is in terms that are very clear and leave no doubt as to what is required of the

[2] *West Castle Properties Ltd v Scottish Ministers*, 2004 S.C.L.R. 899; 2004 G.W.D. 20–444.
[3] *Pacitti v Manganiello*, 1995 S.C.L.R. 557.
[4] *Allied Dunbar Assurance Plc v Superglass Sections Ltd*, 2003 S.L.T. 1420.

defaulting party. The tenant's obligations in the repair clause should be stated clearly, and the schedule of dilapidations that is served on the tenant should be relevant and clear as to what is required of the tenant. The landlord will, when asking for an order of specific implement, usually seek the right to enter the premises and carry out the works himself, at the tenant's expense. Sometimes landlords ask for an award of damages to compensate them for the tenant's breach if the tenant fails to comply.

In Scotland, the measure of damages is the loss that is suffered by the landlord arising from the tenant's breach of obligations in the lease. This may simply be the cost of carrying out the works necessary to achieve compliance with the obligations. However, there can be a significant increase or reduction in this amount, depending on the circumstances. If a sale or new lease transaction that is beneficial to the landlord aborts because the premises have been left in a state of disrepair in breach of the lease obligations, then the landlord will suffer more of a loss than just the cost of making good. If the landlord has a sale transaction arranged and the purchaser is going to demolish and rebuild, or is going to carry out a major refurbishment, then the state of the premises at handover will be largely irrelevant, and thus the landlord may suffer no loss whatever.

In the case of *Prudential Assurance Company Ltd v James Grant and Co. (West) Ltd*[5] the landlord sought recovery of the costs he expected to incur in carrying out repairs which should have been carried out by the tenant. The court accepted that method of quantifying loss. The court noted that it was appropriate to consider the various possible measures of loss and cross check them against one another. The court also held, however, that, if the tenant could prove that the true losses recovered by the landlord was materially less, it was open to the tenant to prove this.

This opens up the possibility of the tenant arguing that the landlord has no intention of carrying out the works and therefore has suffered no loss. An example of this may be if the tenant is aware that the landlord has obtained planning permission for demolition or redevelopment of the building.

If, as must invariably be the case, the landlord has to spend time as well as money in making good the premises after the lease has ended so that they will be attractive to a prospective tenant or purchaser, then he can include in his claim for damages an amount equivalent to rent for the reasonable period of time needed to make good the tenant's breach. Many landlords include in their leases an obligation on the tenant to pay the equivalent of rent for such a period. Such a provision is usually objectionable to tenants and is revised out. The mere fact that it was in a draft and has been revised out does not remove the right in favour of the landlord, at common law, to seek such payment. If the tenant wants to avoid having to pay this amount, he should have a specific exclusion of this in the lease but, of course, few landlords would accept this. The usual compromise is to limit the period of payment to a specific time, say, four weeks.

It is not competent for a decree of specific implement to be granted to a **14–06** landlord to force a tenant to carry out works at the premises once the lease has ended, unless the tenant remains in place by tacit relocation. In such a

---

[5] *Prudential Assurance Co. Ltd v James Grant and Co. (West) Ltd*, 1982 S.L.T. 423.

situation, the proper remedy available to the landlord is damages for the tenant's breach of contract.

In *Sinclair v Caithness Flagstone Co.*[6] it was held that after the lease had expired, the tenant cannot be called upon to go back to the property to carry out works that he ought to have done during the lease, and that the landlord's remedy is damages as opposed to specific implement.

In *PIK Facilities Ltd v Shell UK Ltd*[7] the lease required the tenant to keep storage tanks and plant in the premises in good repair and to hand them over to the landlord at the end of the lease in good repair. When the lease ended the landlord sought specific implement to have the tenant carry out repairs and replacement of the infrastructure, or to pay damages of over £10 million to cover the cost of these works, and to compensate the landlord for the consequent disruption to his business. The court held that specific implement was not a competent remedy as a party cannot be required to do something that he was to do under a lease once that lease has ended, as there is then no contractual relationship remaining between the parties. In this case the landlord's claim would have required the tenant to do something he was no longer contracted to do and the landlord's remedy is only in damages.

In *Coventry v British Gas Corp*[8] there was a specific provision imposing on the tenant the obligation to do works at the expiry of the lease in order to restore the property to its original condition. The court held this was an independent provision that could not arise before the end of the lease, and in terms of the lease in question the tenant had the right to operate on the premises until the day of departure, but he then had an obligation to restore the premises. Specific implement was held to be competent in this case. This is quite different to an obligation to leave the premises in good repair and condition, which was the case in PIK Facilities, in which *Sinclair* was followed.

Tenant's fixtures and fittings

14–07   Certain items in the premises will be landlord's fixtures, while others will belong to the tenant. It is important to know who owns what in order that the schedule of dilapidations is correct and justifiable. If the tenant previously leased the premises and installed items during that lease, and then entered into a new lease of the premises, the items that he installed might possibly be part of "the premises" as defined in the current lease.

In Scotland, there is no right at common law for a tenant to receive compensation for any improvements he has made to the premises or for things that he leaves in the premises.

Landlord's fixtures will generally include items that were fixed to the premises by a previous occupant or by the landlord which were let along with the premises, or items that were affixed by the landlord during the lease itself. If the tenant is allowed to remove something at the end of the lease, that thing will generally be part of the tenant's fixtures. If the tenant attaches something then it is deemed a tenant's fixture unless the lease prohibits removal, or if the removal of the item would cause irreparable injury or damage to the premises.

---

[6] *Sinclair v Caithness Flagstone Co.* (1898) 25 R. 703; 5 S.L.T. 364.
[7] *PIK Facilities Ltd v Shell UK Ltd*, 2003 S.L.T. 155.
[8] *Coventry v British Gas Corp.* Unreported August 15, 1984 (OH).

In *Scottish Discount Company Ltd v Blin*[9] the court held that the proper tests to determine whether an item is a landlord's (heritable) fixture or a tenant's fixture include:

- the degree of its attachment to the premises;
- whether it can be removed without destroying the item itself or the building;
- to what degree enjoyment of the building, etc. would be affected by its removal; and
- the intention of the party attaching it (which is to be discovered from the nature of the article itself, the building and how it was attached, as opposed to being ascertained from other evidence as to the intention of the parties).

Irritancy for failure to comply with a schedule of dilapidations

In terms of the Law Reform (Miscellaneous Provisions) (Scotland) Act 1985, **14–08** a landlord can only obtain a court decree of irritancy (termination of the lease due to breach by the tenant) if in all the circumstances a fair and reasonable landlord would seek irritancy.

In *Euro Properties Scotland Ltd v Alam*[10] the local authority had served a statutory repairs notice, which the landlord copied to the tenant, and told the tenant to do the works. The landlord served a pre-irritancy notice 18 months later saying that the tenant was in breach of his repairing obligations (as the works referred to in the statutory notice had not been done) and that the landlord would irritate the lease unless the tenant carried out and completed the repair works in the notice within 60 days. The court held that the notice and the original letter did not amount to a schedule of dilapidations, especially since there had been subsequent discussion between the parties and a report was then commissioned, and the time given in the pre-irritancy notice is what counts, as opposed to the date of the statutory notice. The court went on to say that on the evidence led, it would take between 9 and 12 months to do the works, and therefore the tenant had not been given reasonable opportunity to remedy the breach. The court said that it is generally unfair for landlords to opt for irritancy where there is an alternative remedy that adequately protects the landlord, although there might be cases where a landlord could be able to show that it is fair and reasonable to choose the irritancy route.

In *Crieff Highland Gathering Ltd v Perth & Kinross District Council,*[11] a landlord sought decree of irritancy against its local authority tenant in respect of failure to comply with a schedule of dilapidations. The landlord had served the schedule on the tenant in late 2007 and had stated in its notice that failure to comply with the schedule within three months might result in the lease being terminated. 14 months later, the landlord inspected the premises and found that the repairs had not been done. The court held that the tenant had indeed not carried out the works, but that a period of three months to carry out the repairs was in the circumstances not reasonable, that none of the repairs was material,

[9] *Scottish Discount Company Ltd v Blin*, 1985 S.C. 216.
[10] *Euro Properties Scotland Ltd v Alam*, 2000 G.W.D. 23–896.
[11] *Crieff Highland Gathering Ltd v Perth & Kinross District Council*, 2011 S.L.T. 992; 2011 G.W.D. 20–474

that the breach was not material, and that in the circumstances a fair and reasonable landlord would not have sought to terminate the lease.

The court also said that, in the situation of a long lease, a landlord should only be allowed to rescind a lease where the tenant has committed a material breach, a fair and reasonable opportunity has been given to make good, and the tenant has shown he is unwilling or unable to perform.

B—ENGLAND

Yielding up

14–09 In England, it is implied in all commercial leases that the tenant will give vacant possession of the premises to the landlord at expiry of the term, but the tenant is entitled to remove his fixtures before expiry of the term. It is unusual to contract out of this implied term.

Dilapidations and reinstatement

14–10 There is no obligation implied on the tenant to remove his fixtures, etc. although he is entitled to remove these at any time before expiry of the lease. However, the lease will often provide for the tenant to remove fixtures and alterations and to make good any damage caused in reinstatement.

There is sometimes a right in favour of the landlord to payment for the cost of making good any dilapidations and compensation for loss of rent during the period required for making good.

It is necessary to examine not only the repairs and reinstatement clauses, but also the decorating and signage provisions and the conditions contained in any licence of consent to works.

Damages for breach

14–11 If the tenant is in breach of his repairing covenant, the primary measure of damages available to the landlord is the reasonable cost of repair plus loss of rent for the period until the works have been completed, where appropriate. However, it may now be the case that for damages to be awarded to the landlord, the carrying out the works must be a reasonable course of action to take. The amount that can be recovered as damages for breach of repairing covenants is capped by s.18(1) of the Landlord and Tenant Act 1927, which states that the damages must not be more than the amount (if any) by which the value of the reversion (landlord's interest) is diminished by the breach. This is a very important statutory limitation, which has no Scottish equivalent.

CHAPTER 15

ASSIGNATION, SUB-LETTING AND OTHER DEALINGS IN THE TENANT'S INTEREST

Introduction

In Scotland, a tenant of commercial premises is free to assign or sub-let, unless **15–01**
this is restricted in the lease. It is normal for leases to contain some restriction
of these freedoms. This Chapter examines the common law, the different
degrees of control that are usually imposed and the case law on reasonable
withholding of consent. We then consider the relevant law in England.

A—SCOTLAND

Common law position

A tenant of commercial premises is totally free: **15–02**

- to assign (or transfer) the lease;
- to grant sub-leases of all or part of the premises;
- to allow occupancy by others; and
- provided the lease was granted for a period of more than 20 years, to
  grant a standard security over his leasehold interest;

unless and to the extent these freedoms are specifically restricted in terms of
the lease.

Difference between assignation and sub-lease

If the tenant wants to give up trading at the premises he can try to assign, i.e. **15–03**
transfer his interest in the lease, or he can try to sub-let the premises. If the
tenant assigns the lease, then unless the lease imposes joint and several liability
on the original tenant and every assignee (which is unusual in modern-day
leases), he will be free from all liability in respect of the lease from the date of
assignation onwards, provided he has obtained landlord's consent to the assignation going ahead. However if he grants a sub-lease, he stays on as tenant and
remains totally responsible to the landlord for paying rent and performing all
other obligations; all he is doing is doing is creating a lower layer so as to
impose obligations on his sub-tenant, while he himself remains liable to his
landlord in terms of the lease.

Joint and several liability

If a lease imposes joint and several liability on the tenant and its assignees, **15–04**
then the first tenant and each successor tenant remains fully liable for payment

of rent and performance of tenant's obligations in the lease, despite having assigned his interest in the lease. The landlord can look to the original tenant, the present tenant or any tenant in between for payment or performance, leaving that party to seek to recover from the current tenant. An example of joint and several liability being imposed in a lease is "the tenant binds itself and its successors and assignees all jointly and severally, without discussing them in their order". However, the same liability could possibly be imposed using less explicit wording, such as "the tenant binding itself and its successors", if the definition of "the tenant" includes assignees.

This joint and several liability is highly onerous on the tenant, and it will have the effect of significantly reducing any increase that would be achievable at rent review. Therefore such joint and several liability is unusual in modern-day leases.

It is, however, very common and acceptable to provide in leases for joint and several liability to be imposed on the tenant or guarantor if there is more than one person as tenant or guarantor at any one time. The normal way for the tenant to deal with such a provision at drafting stage is to insert a statement that there will be no continuing liability on an outgoing tenant following a permitted assignation. The landlord should not find this objectionable.

Protecting the different interests

15–05 If there is an assignation transaction, then the landlord, the outgoing tenant (assignor) and the incoming tenant (assignee) all have different interests to protect.

The landlord will want to make sure that the proposed incoming tenant has sufficient financial strength (or "covenant") to be able to pay the rent and to perform the other obligations imposed on the tenant. The assignation document should impose obligations on the incoming tenant to pay rent and perform all obligations under the lease irrespective of whether they refer to any period before as well as after the incoming tenant becomes the actual tenant under the lease. The reason for this is that the outgoing tenant is responsible for matters referable up to the date of the assignation; however, he may disappear and prove difficult to enforce against. The landlord does not want to be faced with arguments from the new tenant about repairs, etc. if the premises were dilapidated before he took entry, or complaints that rent was not paid up to date. Therefore the landlord is protected by making the incoming tenant liable for all past as well as future performance.

The landlord should never accept wording in a draft assignation to the effect that the landlord confirms or warrants that the tenant has performed all obligations to date under the lease. The acceptance of such wording could lead to the landlord encountering difficulties in enforcing repairing and other obligations in the future, as the current tenant could argue that the premises were in the same state when he took over. If the landlord accepts the wording in the draft assignation, the landlord is on record as having been satisfied with the state of repair of the premises.

15–06 The outgoing tenant (assignor) needs to make sure that the landlord has consented to the grant of the assignation. If the outgoing tenant has accepted an unduly onerous lease, then he may find that he is saddled with an unmarketable lease or one that is less attractive to a prospective assignee. The outgoing tenant will usually have to pay the landlord's surveyors' and legal expenses for considering the application for consent.

The incoming tenant (assignee) has to make sure that:

- there are no ongoing disputes or proceedings under the lease;
- planning permission exists for all works that have been carried out and for the current use;
- all tenant's alterations to date have received landlord's consent;
- rent and other obligations are up to date (so that he is not inheriting an arrears situation);
- the landlord had a good title to grant the lease in the first place;
- there are no secured lenders whose consent has not been obtained; and
- the outgoing tenant is solvent, has a good leasehold title and is able to grant a valid assignation.

If the lease was granted before the premises became operational for land registration purposes and if the lease was for an original term of longer than 20 years, or has been extended to provide for a term that is more than 20 years, then the assignation must be registered in the Land Register of Scotland in order for the assignee to get a "real right" or a good leasehold interest, even if at that particular time the lease has shorter than 20 years to run.

If the lease was originally granted to an entity that is exempt from having to pay stamp duty land tax (such as a charity) or if stamp duty land tax was otherwise not payable, for example as a result of group relief, or because the original tenant was a charity, then stamp duty land tax may be payable if the lease is assigned to a non-exempt entity or if something else changes at or before assignation so as to trigger a charge to stamp duty land tax upon assignation.

Intimation of assignation

At completion of the assignation transaction, the assignation needs to be inti-   **15–07**
mated, i.e. notified to the landlord. It is in the interest of both the outgoing and the incoming tenant that the assignation be notified to the landlord as soon as possible, as the incoming tenant's right as tenant is not complete against the landlord until that notification has been given.

Restricting the tenant's right to assign and sub-let, etc.

In considering matters relating to assignation and sub-letting, it should always   **15–08**
be remembered that it is not only the landlord or investor client and the tenant, but also their lenders, who have to be satisfied with the wording of the clause. If the lease is to totally exclude assignation or sub-letting, then this must be very clearly stated. The more severe the restriction, the more adverse the impact on the tenant's marketability, and there will also be an adverse effect on the landlord's interest, because there will be a reduction of any uplift otherwise achievable at rent review, due to the lack of marketability.

Some landlords want to protect the quality of their investment by saying that consent to assignation will not be granted unless the prospective assignee is of a strength of covenant at least as good as that of the tenant. The problem with this wording is that there is no guidance as to whether the comparison is related to the current tenant's strength of covenant at commencement of the lease (or his date of entry) or at the time of application, as the tenant may have weakened or strengthened considerably in that time.

There are various other degrees of control that the landlord can impose when negotiating the lease at the outset, ranging from the rather extreme total prohibition against assignation and sub-letting to a very soft level of control, including the following examples:

- prohibition against partial assignations;
- prohibition against partial sub-letting;
- restriction on the number of sub-leases and /or restricting these to an entire storey, etc;
- consent not to be unreasonably withheld in the case of assignation to an FTSE 100 company;
- consent not to be unreasonably withheld in the case of a respectable and responsible assignee of sound financial standing, clearly able to perform all obligations on the tenant under the lease;
- consent not to be unreasonably withheld to an assignation of the whole;
- prohibition against sub-letting at a rent that is lower than the greater of:

    (a) the then passing rent; and
    (b) the then open market rent.

It should be noted that at rent review, a prohibition in the lease against sub-letting at lower than the then passing rent could be prejudicial to the landlord as being seen to be onerous against the tenant, as rents could be falling at the time of an application for consent. If a landlord, in negotiating his lease, wants to avoid such prejudice, he could allow sub-letting at open market rent but insert a statement into the rent-review clause that the existence of sub-leases and the rents payable under any sub-leases will be disregarded;

- prohibition against assignation unless the outgoing tenant, or someone else who is proposed by the tenant, who the landlord finds suitable, provides a guarantee in respect of the incoming tenant's performance; and
- prohibition against assignation within the first, say, three years of the term.

15–09 Many corporate tenants want the freedom to have any member of their group of companies occupy and trade from all or part of the premises. Landlords generally allow this concession, but only on the basis that such occupancy does not give the occupant any security of tenure or other tenancy rights against the landlord, and that the occupancy right ceases if and when the occupant stops being a member of the tenant's group of companies.

A prohibition against assignation or sub-letting does not prevent the tenant from parting with or sharing possession with a member of the same group of companies, nor from allowing licensees, franchisees or concessionaires to occupy and trade from the premises. To achieve such a prohibition, the lease needs to prohibit sharing or parting with possession.

It should be noted that a prohibition against assignation, etc. does not prevent the shares of a corporate tenant from being sold, and so a landlord could find he still has the same company as tenant, but the quality of that company's covenant (financial strength) has changed beyond recognition. A landlord could seek to prevent such a change of control of a corporate tenant by making such an event a trigger for a landlord's option to terminate the lease. This is a contractual option to terminate, as opposed to being a trigger of irritancy. It would be highly unlikely that such an event could be seen as a breach by the tenant, as the activity involved is not done by the tenant itself, but by its shareholders.

It is important for the landlord to prohibit the sharing or giving up of possession of the premises, so as to prevent the tenant effecting a virtual assignation: see para.15–23 below. However, this would not prevent a tenant from having someone who claims to be his "manager" occupying the premises, which happens where a tenant gives up possession to someone else who trades at the premises without assigning the lease, but the tenant remains liable under the lease.

Consent not to be unreasonably withheld—case law

There has been a wealth of litigation on the meaning of "consent not to be **15–10** unreasonably withheld".

In *Muir v Wilson*[1] it was held that the words "without the consent of the landlord" mean what they say–the landlord is entitled to give consent or not as he so chooses. In Scotland, there is no implied term of reasonableness when it comes to assignation or sub-letting.

The main case on assignation is *International Drilling Fluids Ltd v Louisville Investments (Uxbridge) Ltd*,[2] in which the Court of Appeal (in England) considered the meaning of "consent not to be unreasonably withheld", in the context of lease assignation. The principles set out in this decision have been applied in Scotland, and can be summarised as follows:

- the purpose of a prohibition of assignation for which the landlord's consent is not to be unreasonably withheld, is to protect the landlord from having the premises used or occupied in an undesirable way or by an undesirable tenant or assignee;
- the landlord is not entitled to refuse consent to an assignation on grounds that have nothing to do with the relationship of landlord and tenant in regard to the subject-matter of the lease;
- the tenant has to prove that consent has been unreasonably withheld (as opposed to the landlord having to show that he has acted reasonably);
- it is not necessary for the landlord to prove that the conclusions that led him to refuse consent are justified, so long as they were conclusions that might be reached by a reasonable person in the circumstances;
- it may be reasonable for the landlord to refuse consent to an assignation because of the proposed use of the premises by the prospective assignee, even if such use is not prohibited in terms of the lease; and
- although a landlord usually only needs to consider his own interest, there may be instances where the benefit to the landlord in refusing consent is so vastly outweighed by the harm to the tenant as to make the refusal of consent unreasonable.

---

[1] *Muir v Wilson* Unreported January 20, 1820.
[2] *International Drilling Fluids Ltd v Louisville Investments (Uxbridge) Ltd*, 1986 1 Ch. 513.

15–11 In view of principles (b) and (f), it is questionable whether a landlord is entitled to withhold consent to an assignation or sub-lease merely because the incoming occupant is of significantly weaker financial strength than the existing tenant (but where the prospective tenant is strong enough to perform the tenant's obligations). Landlords are reluctant to allow an assignation or sub-lease to such a tenant as this is likely to result in a reduction in the landlord's investment value.

In *Lousada & Co v J.E. Lesser (Properties) Ltd*[3] the court held that a landlord was not acting unreasonably in making consent to assignation conditional on a long outstanding rent review being settled.

Some landlords will try to use an application for consent from a tenant as an opportunity to serve a schedule of dilapidations and to insist that consent will only be effective when the works have been completed. It is suggested here that it is unreasonable for a landlord to serve a schedule of dilapidations when he receives an application for consent so that he can insist as a condition of that consent that the schedule be complied with in full prior to the assignation going ahead. However, if one continues the line of thought from Lousada, if there had been a very long outstanding schedule of dilapidations that had not been complied with, then the landlord might well be held to be acting reasonably if he insisted that the schedule be complied with in full before the assignation went ahead. This is, however, different to a long outstanding rent review, where there could be a question of sufficiency of tenant covenant depending on the outcome of the rent review.

15–12 The landlord cannot refuse consent in order to gain a collateral benefit. In *A.B. Leisure Ltd v Renfrew District Council*[4] the court considered a lease where the tenant had gone into liquidation and the liquidator had found a prospective assignee and had applied for landlord's consent which, in terms of the lease, was not to be unreasonably withheld. The landlord granted consent subject to four conditions:

(1) all arrears of money were to be paid;
(2) there was to be an immediate additional rent review;
(3) the repairing obligations in the lease were to be tightened up; and
(4) the rent-review cycle was to be increased from every five years to every three years.

The court held that the condition relating to payment of arrears was reasonable and fair, but the other three conditions were unreasonable, as they sought to give to the landlord a commercial benefit.

The landlord is not allowed to insist on a payment as a condition of granting consent. In *Scottish Tourist Board v Dean Park Ltd*[5] the lease provided for consent to not be unreasonably withheld to a proposed sub-lease. The landlord was only willing to consent to the sub-lease if the tenant paid a premium to the landlord for granting consent. The court held this was an unreasonable condition.

15–13 In *Sears Properties Netherlands BV v Coal Pension Properties Ltd*[6] it was held that a head landlord had no contractual right to enforce a clause contained

---

[3] *Lousada & Co v J.E. Lesser (Properties) Ltd*, 1990 S.L.T. 823.
[4] *A.B. Leisure Ltd v Renfrew District Council*, 1988 S.L.T. 635.
[5] *Scottish Tourist Board v Dean Park Ltd*, 1997 S.L.T. (Sh. Ct) 1121.
[6] *Sears Properties Netherlands BV v Coal Pension Properties Ltd*, 2001 S.L.T. 761.

in a sub-lease prohibiting assignation without the head landlord's consent, because the head landlord was not a party to the sub-lease itself, and all he could do was enforce contractual provisions in the head-lease. The effect of this case is that if a head landlord wants to control the assignation of a sub-lease he must either be a party to the sub-lease, and be given rights to enforce its terms, or alternatively he must make assignation of a sub-lease without his consent an event of irritancy of the head-lease.

It has been held that a landlord is acting reasonably in refusing consent to assignation if there is clear evidence to show that the proposed assignee is unable to pay the rent (and perform the other obligations of the tenant): *Continvest Ltd v Dean Property Partnership*.[7]

In *Scotmore Developments Ltd v Anderton*[8] the court considered a lease where consent to assignation was not to be unreasonably withheld. The tenant comprised two individuals who were in partnership, and they wanted to assign the lease to one of the individuals as the other had left the business. The landlord initially refused consent, but offered to reconsider in two years, to allow time for the remaining individual to establish a track record on her own. Four years later, she asked for consent to assign in her own favour, but in the meantime the rent had increased substantially at rent review. The landlord said this had changed the whole circumstances, and the court held that following the rent increase, the landlord was entitled to reconsider his whole position, and that although there may well be evidence that the assignee could pay the old rent, there was no evidence that she could pay the new rent. The court held that a prudent landlord would not ordinarily accept a single tenant in place of two tenants unless there was a separate guarantor or some other independent financial support, and that such a landlord would not agree to the assignation if the assignee were unable to pay all sums including rent increases following review, and to perform all other obligations.

The court also stated that a refusal of the landlord to consent, where he would otherwise be required to grant consent, amounts to a material breach that goes to the root of the contract; therefore one could argue that in such a case, the tenant's remedy may not only be damages but also the right to terminate the lease.

In *Ashworth Frazer Ltd v Gloucester City Council*[9] the House of Lords had **15–14** to consider whether it was reasonable for a landlord to refuse consent to an assignation because the proposed use of the assignee would be in breach of the user clause of the lease. It was held in that case that there is no rule of law that it will always be reasonable for a landlord to withhold consent, solely on the ground that the intended use would be in breach of the user clause. While it will usually be reasonable to refuse consent on such grounds, there may be specific situations where it would be unreasonable to do so.

The inter-relationship of use clauses and assignation was further considered in *Scottish Property Investment Ltd v Scottish Provident Ltd*.[10] In this case, the court had to consider whether a landlord had unreasonably withheld consent to a sub-lease where the lease: (a) provided for landlord's consent to

---

[7] *Continvest Ltd v Dean Property Partnership*, 1993 G.W.D. 40–2675.
[8] *Scotmore Developments Ltd v Anderton*, 1996 S.L.T. 1304.
[9] *Ashworth Frazer Ltd v Gloucester City Council* [2001] 1 W.L.R. 2180.
[10] *Scottish Property Investment Ltd v Scottish Provident Ltd*, 2004 G.W.D. 6–120.

not be unreasonably withheld to a proposed partial sub-lease; and (b) contained a totally strict user clause, and the draft sub-lease shown to the landlord provided for a different use. The court referred to the *Ashworth Frazer* decision and pointed out that the House of Lords did not hold that it would always be reasonable for a landlord to refuse consent solely by having regard to the proposed assignee's or sub-tenant's use, nor did it hold that it would always be reasonable for a landlord to withhold consent because of the proposed use being in breach of the user clause. Essentially, each case has to be decided on its own facts.

Sub-leases

15–15 Often, the rent payable under the sub-lease will be expressed to be the same as the rent from time to time payable under the head-lease, the intention being that the rent as reviewed from time to time simply washes through to the sub-tenant. Other sub-leases provide for a separate rent review exercise to be undertaken.

If the tenant is confident that the sub-tenant is of substantial enough covenant to be likely to remain in business, then he will not be too worried about what rent is agreed or determined at rent review, as he is merely a middle man passing on the obligations. However, in most cases the tenant will want to make sure that the rent review is agreed or settled at a reasonable amount, in case the sub-tenant becomes insolvent, or if the sub-lease terminates before the head-lease, thus leaving him with the full liability.

The sub-tenant will be worried that the tenant does not try hard to keep any rent review to a minimum increase, and the sub-tenant should therefore demand input in the head-lease rent review. He can achieve this by having a clause in the sub-lease prohibiting the tenant from agreeing to a rent review in the head-lease or appointing a third party to determine the rent review except with his prior consent, and by providing for the him to be allowed to feed into representations and submissions made by the tenant to the third party.

15–16 The tenant may have an FRI lease, or alternatively it is possible that the repairing (and indeed other) obligations are watered down either in terms of the lease or in terms of a back letter that may be personal to the tenant. The sub-tenant should enquire whether there are any such concessions available to the tenant, and if so then he should benefit likewise (albeit probably only for as long as the tenant has such benefit). In any event, the sub-tenant may want to limit his repairing obligations, and he may require a schedule of condition to be prepared and attached to the sub-lease, so as to qualify the repairing obligation in the sub-lease.

The sub-tenant may be paying less rent than is payable under the head-lease or may be getting some other concessions from the tenant. These may be taken care of by way of back letter, if the head-lease contains (as is very likely) restrictions against sub-letting at less than either full market rent or then passing rent, and restrictions against sub-letting at less onerous terms than in the head-lease. It is important to not be in breach of the lease or of the terms of the landlord's consent to sub-letting, either of which may prohibit back letters.

A sub-lease depends for its existence on there being and remaining in place a head-lease. There are two exceptions: first, where what was originally a head-lease becomes a sub-lease because an interposed lease is granted by the owner there is statutory protection of security of tenure for the sub-tenant.[11] The other exception is where the head lease is renounced, or where the interest of the head landlord and mid-landlord become owned by the one entity, the sub-lease will remain in place.[12] Many sub-leases will be drafted so as to incorporate and repeat obligations and provisions of the head-lease, and this is all well and good except if the head-lease is being renounced or amended. If the head-lease is irritated, the sub-lease perishes. Therefore a solicitor acting for a prospective sub-tenant will usually want some sort of irritancy protection, whereby the landlord at least provides to the sub-tenant a copy of any pre-irritancy notice served on the tenant, and allows the sub-tenant to save the head-lease, and/or that the landlord is bound in the event of irritancy of the head-lease to grant to the sub-tenant a direct lease on the same terms as the sub-lease, if so requested by the sub-tenant. This is usually framed as a right in favour of the sub-tenant rather than being a mutual right as between landlord and sub-tenant, so that the sub-tenant can choose to walk away.

In *The Howgate Shopping Centre Ltd v Catercraft Services Ltd*[13] it was held **15–17** that where there is a head-lease and a sub-lease, and the same party acquires the right to the landlord's and the tenant's interests in the head-lease, there is no effect on the continued existence of the sub-lease. This was because the sub-tenant remains in a contractual relationship with the party who has succeeded to the tenant's interest in the head-lease, so that the assignation of the tenant's interest in the head-lease can not affect the sub-tenant's position as sub-tenant.

Many leases contain a prohibition against sub-letting at less than the amount of rent payable at that time in respect of the lease itself, or paying a capital sum to the sub-tenant to compensate him for the amount of rent that he has to pay to comply with the terms of the lease.

The problem with restrictions in the lease against sub-letting is that the tenant may only be able to find an occupant who is willing to pay at a lower rate than he is paying and/or wants to soften the obligations affecting his occupancy. The landlord does not want to see sub-letting go ahead at a discounted rate because this would be adverse for him at rent review. A disregard of the existence of any sub-leases or rents payable in sub-leases only goes so far, especially if the landlord owns nearby premises that are also leased out, where any disregards in one particular lease will not help him at all at rent review in the lease of a nearby property. Some tenants have got round the restriction against sub-letting at less than then passing rent or less than open market value, as the case may be, by granting a sub-lease that is ostensibly at an appropriate rent, and its other terms appear to comply with the restrictions imposed in the head-lease, but have granted a back letter allowing rent reduction and/or other softening that is not disclosed to the landlord.

This device was struck at in the case of *Allied Dunbar Assurance Plc v* **15–18** *Homebase Ltd*,[14] where the court decided that a separate agreement between Homebase Ltd and its proposed sub-tenant, which softened the terms of the sub-lease, was to be looked at as being part of the sub-lease documentation

---

[11] Land Tenure Reform (Scotland) Act 1974 s.17.

[12] *The Howgate Shopping Centre Ltd v Catercraft Services Ltd*, 2004 S.L.T. 231.

[13] *The Howgate Shopping Centre Ltd v Catercraft Services Ltd*, 2004 S.L.T. 231.

[14] *Allied Dunbar Assurance Plc v Homebase Ltd* [2002] 27 E.G. 144.

(even though the separate agreement would not be binding on the landlord) and thus was in breach of the restrictions in the head-lease, and so the landlord did not have to grant consent to the sub-lease.

An interesting approach to the problem was the device used in *Crestfort Ltd v Tesco Stores Ltd*,[15] where Tesco arranged for one of its associated companies to grant to the sub-tenant an indemnity in respect of some of the sub-lease obligations so that the sub-lease complied fully with the restrictions laid down in the lease, and the indemnity (or softening) was by a third party, as opposed to being by the tenant. The court held that the sub-tenant was fully liable to his landlord in terms of the sub-lease, and he can merely look to the indemnifying third party to help him.

It is not clear whether the payment of a reverse premium needs to be disclosed to the landlord. In *Kened v Connie Investments Ltd*[16] the Court of Appeal held that a landlord was not entitled to be given information in respect of the amount of premium or reverse premium on assignation of a lease, and it would seem the same logic would apply to payment of a reverse premium on the grant of a sub-lease. It is thought here that if the lease prohibits payment of a capital sum between tenant and assignee or sub-tenant, the landlord is entitled to insist on full disclosure.

B—ENGLAND

Assignment

15–19 The law changed on January 1, 1996, and there are different rules relating to assignments of leases depending on whether the lease was entered into before January 1, 1996 (or as a result of an agreement for lease, a court order entered into or an option granted before that date) or on or after January 1, 1996. We will call these "old leases" and "new leases" respectively.

In old leases, the original tenant remains liable throughout the whole term of the lease. Although the original tenant remains liable at common law, each successive tenant is released from liability on a permitted assignment by that tenant. It was customary for landlords to insist that as a condition of granting consent to an assignment of an old lease, the incoming tenant would contractually agree to privity of contract so that he would remain liable throughout the remainder of the term, following subsequent assignments.

The Landlord and Tenant (Covenants) Act 1995,[17] which does not apply to Scotland, changed the rules to a certain extent for old leases and imposed new rules for new leases.

15–20 The 1995 Act provides that all the landlord and tenant covenants run with the respective interests.

In new leases, privity of contract does not apply. However, leases can, and often do, give the landlord the right to include in new leases the right to require an authorised guarantee agreement ("AGA") to be given on an assignment. Even if the lease does not include such a provision, the landlord can insist on an AGA being given as a condition of consenting to an assignment if it is reasonable in the circumstances to require this. In terms of the AGA, the tenant

---

[15] *Crestfort Ltd v Tesco Stores Ltd* [2005] 37 E.G. 148.
[16] *Kened v Connie Investments Ltd* [1997] 1 E.G.L.R. 21.
[17] Landlord and Tenant (Covenants) Act 1995 (c.30).

guarantees performance under the lease by the immediate assignee only. An authorised guarantee agreement can require the tenant, if the lease is disclaimed by a liquidator, to enter into a new lease for the remainder of the term or shorter and on no more onerous obligations.

The landlord can agree with the tenant in any new lease to specify the circumstances where he will withhold his consent to a future assignation of the lease and the conditions on which he will give his consent.

Similar considerations apply to the liability of an assigning tenant's guarantor. There is a technical issue about how to draft this type of AGA. This is still being debated. At the time of writing, it looks like it should be a guarantee of the assigning tenant's AGA obligations, but further clarification will no doubt be given by the courts.

Section 17 of the 1995 Act provides that a former tenant or a guarantor of a **15–21** former tenant's obligations does not have to pay rent or other fixed payments, such as service charge, unless within six months of the money becoming due, the landlord has notified the former tenant or guarantor of the amount due and that he intends to seek payment. If the former tenant or the guarantor makes payment, then he can require the landlord to grant an overriding lease so that the person making the payment becomes the landlord's tenant, and therefore the original tenant becomes the immediate landlord of the defaulting current tenant and can then take steps to avoid becoming liable for any further breaches by that party. The overriding lease is to be for slightly longer than the current lease (at least three days) and should contain the same obligations and terms.

The effect of a permitted assignment of a new lease is to free the original tenant from continuing liability (apart from liability under an AGA).

A former tenant or guarantor is not liable for any amount referable to any relevant variation of the obligations after the assignment of an old lease, unless (unusually) they are actually a party to the variation document.

If the lease provides that the tenant is not allowed to assign except with the landlord's consent, there is an implied term that the landlord's consent is not to be unreasonably withheld. This is different to the position in Scotland where there is no such implied term.

It is not possible to contract out of (i.e. to disapply) the Act.

Under-letting

An under-lease is a letting (or "demise") by a tenant for a term that is for a **15–22** shorter term than his lease. A purported under-lease for the whole term of the tenant's own lease, or for a period beyond that term, amounts to an assignment.

At common law, the head landlord cannot sue the under-lessee for performance of any of the covenants, but the general practice is to include in a licence to under-let the right for the landlord to proceed against the under-lessee in relation to any restrictive covenants in the lease. See Chapter 20 (Enforcement) for information on enforcing financial obligations in leases and under-leases.

If the lease provides that the tenant is not allowed to under-let except with the landlord's consent, there is an implied term that the landlord's consent is not to be unreasonably withheld. This is different to the position in Scotland where there is no such implied term.

Virtual assignment

15–23   A virtual assignment transfers all the tenant's economic benefits and obligations of a lease, but it does not transfer the leasehold interest itself and does not
give the grantee any right of occupancy.

In *Clarence House Ltd v National Westminster Bank Plc*[18] the court considered a "virtual assignment". The lease in question prohibited assignment and
under-letting and sharing or parting with possession or occupation, except
wioth landlrod's consent The tenant assigned the economic benefits and obligations under its lease to a third party, by granting the third party power of
attorney and appointing it as its agent in respect of all dealings with the
premises (including paying rent to the head landlord and receiving rent from
the sub-tenant). The landlord was not told about the arrangements and was not
asked to consent to the virtual assignment. However, the grantee was not given
any right to occupy the property. There was a sub-lease in place with the sub-
tenant occupying the premises. In addition, under the terms of the master
agreement, if forfeiture were threatened, the relevant property could be withdrawn from the arrangements without the whole transaction unravelling, and
so the arrangement was not irrevocable.At first instance the court held that, by
entering into a virtual assignment (which transferred all the economic benefits
and burdens of the lease, but not the leasehold interest itself, and involved no
change of occupant), the tenant was in breach of a prohibition against parting
with or sharing possession of the premises. However, the Court of Appeal held
that "possession" in this context meant having the right to occupy premises to
the exclusion of others, and did not include the receipt of rent or the right to
receive rent. Even if it had included the receipt of rent, there would have been
no breach, because the virtual assignee received rent as agent for NatWest.
However, even if it had included the right to receive and keep rent payable by
the sub-tenant, there would still be no breach because the virtual assignee still
had no proprietary interest in the lease.

Landlords should consider including in their leases a prohibition against
transferring the economic benefits and obligations of the lease and any sub-
lease by way of a virtual assignment or any similar concept or arrangement.

---

[18] *Clarence House Ltd v National Westminster Bank Plc* [2009] EWHC 77 (Ch.).

CHAPTER 16

TENANT'S WORKS AND ALTERATIONS

Introduction

At common law, a tenant is free to carry out fitting out and other works to the **16–01** premises, provided he does not cause damage, and that he gives back to the landlord at the end of the lease the premises in the same condition as when they were leased to him.

Most leases contain some restriction against the tenant making any alterations or additions to the premises. These range from total prohibition to blanket permission for non-structural works. The degree of control of the landlord for different types of works varies from lease to lease. If the tenant carries out works to the premises, this may have an effect at rent review, depending on the wording of the tenant's works clause, and the wording of the rent-review clause. In this Chapter, we consider different types of tenant's works, the various degrees of control found in commercial leases and the effect of tenant's works in respect of repair, rent review and the tenant's obligations at the end of the lease.

A—SCOTLAND

What is exclusively leased?

The lease will describe the premises that are let to the tenant. They will be all **16–02** or part of the heritable property owned by the landlord, together with landlord's heritable fixtures and fittings. There may be floor coverings, false ceiling, lighting, etc. which may or may not be specifically referred to. If the lease has been granted so as to allow continuous occupancy by the tenant following the end of a previous lease, then any alteration works that were carried out during the previous lease, and which were not specifically referred to in the description of the premises in the current lease, may be deemed to form part of the premises. Some works that the tenant carries out will become part of the landlord's heritable property: see para.16–08 below. If the premises are a new shop, it is important to check whether the shopfront in being provided by the landlord or whether it is to form part of the tenant's fit out works. It is also of significance in relation to the repairing obligation.

Different types of tenant's works

The list of potential works that can be carried out by a tenant is endless. The **16–03** most common works are the installation or change of a shop front, installation of shelving, racking, demountable partitions, IT and phone cabling, air conditioning, heating, new floor coverings and lighting. However, high cost and permanent works might also be carried out, such as the installation of lifts, escalators, etc.

Many retail tenants have standard footprints that dictate the size of their operation, and it may well be that the premises are not quite the right shape or are slightly too big for their needs. Tenants will therefore often install a partition or wall so as to reduce the premises to their ideal size for their operation.

Degrees of landlord's control

16–04 If the lease does not prohibit or restrict the tenant's freedom to alter or add to the premises, then the tenant is free to do so, provided he is not changing the permitted use or damaging the premises. Most leases will contain some restriction against the tenant's freedom. The most basic restriction is a total prohibition against carrying out any alterations, additions or other works to the premises. This is an absolute prohibition, and the landlord's specific consent would be needed for any works to be carried out by the tenant, and the landlord can withhold consent at will. If the lease says that the landlord's consent is needed for tenant's works/alterations, but there is no further wording or qualification of this, then once again the landlord has absolute discretion whether or not to grant consent. There is no implied term that the landlord has to act reasonably.

If the landlord's consent is not to be unreasonably withheld, then the landlord must of course act reasonably, but his consent is needed for every single alteration or addition. While the position of "consent not to be unreasonably withheld" may appear to be acceptable from a tenant's point of view, he will often try to have the freedom, without needing landlord's consent, to carry out internal non-structural works such as shelving, racking and internal demountable partitions. Some landlords will insist on having absolute discretion as to whether or not to permit any structural or external works, but will give the concession that their consent, while still needed, is not to be unreasonably withheld for internal non-structural works. The shop front needs to be considered—is landlord's consent required for change of the shop front, or is consent not to be unreasonably withheld? This is a matter for negotiation between the parties.

If the lease is in fact a sub-lease, then head-landlord's consent may well also be required.

If the landlord has granted a standard security over his interest, the consent of his lender should be obtained so that the landlord is not placed in breach of his loan obligations.

Tax implications

16–05 There may be SDLT and other tax implications if the tenant carries out works to the premises that are not solely for his own benefit, but that (also) benefit the landlord, especially if the landlord is paying a reverse premium to the tenant for taking the lease. The landlord and tenant should obtain detailed tax advice at the time, as tax legislation changes frequently.

Rent review implications

16–06 The basic position at rent review is that the premises are valued as existing at the rent-review date. Most leases that contain a rent-review clause also contain detailed instructions to the valuer as to how to value the premises. There is usually a list of items that are to be assumed and taken into account and also a list of items that are to be disregarded. A commonly found provision is that any works that are carried out by the tenant are disregarded at rent review, but this is usually qualified so as to exclude from that disregard, and thus to take into account at rent review, any works that are carried out by the tenant to satisfy an obligation that he has to the landlord. The wording of the disregard of tenant's works is of significant importance. The following have to be considered.

(a) What is the definition of "the tenant"? In many cases, the lease will define "the tenant" as the original tenant and his successors, and therefore works carried out by the original tenant and every assignee will be disregarded. Depending on the definition, it is possible that works carried out by a tenant under a previous lease will not be disregarded. It is therefore important if a tenant is an assignee, as opposed to being the first tenant in the lease, to know exactly what works have been carried out during the period of the lease and by whom, so that he will have an idea of what is to be taken into account and what is to be disregarded at rent review. It is equally important for the landlord, especially if he was not the original landlord under the lease but has bought the property as an investment, to understand which works are to be taken into account and which are to be disregarded.

(b) If the tenant under the lease was also the tenant under a previous lease of the premises, then any works that were carried out by him during the previous lease might be disregarded. This is not certain, as it depends on the definition of "the premises" in the lease that is being reviewed; it may be the premises as originally existing at the start of the previous lease or it may be, and more usually is, the premises as at the start of the lease under review.

(c) The landlord will usually want to rentalise (i.e. take into account the value of) works carried out by the tenant in compliance with any obligation to the landlord. The obligation may not be contained in the lease itself, but may have been contained in a separate development agreement or in the missives. When negotiating the lease, if the tenant is agreeing to carry out specific works, he should resist having to pay rent on the value of these works, and he can only achieve this if these works are to be specifically disregarded at rent review. However, once the lease has started, if works are subsequently needed in order to comply with statute, then such works would normally be taken into account. The importance of understanding and negotiation of the drafting cannot be over-emphasised.

(d) The lease is likely to impose on the tenant the obligation to carry out any works to comply with statute. It may well be that the landlord has not specifically called on the tenant to carry out any works that are needed to comply with statutory requirements, but that the tenant has done these works because of his legal duty. Such works will therefore not be disregarded at rent review.

(e) If the lease provided that landlord's consent is not required for certain types of tenant's works, then the tenant could argue that all such works have automatically received landlord's consent, and should be disregarded at review. However, the landlord could argue that if such works have been carried out, there has been no landlord's consent asked for or given, and therefore the works should be taken into account at rent review. The tenant's argument would probably prevail, but the ambiguity and the scope for argument can be seen.

16–07   The principle behind disregarding any value of tenant's works is that the tenant is paying the actual cost of the works, and it is therefore unfair that he should be have to pay twice, by also paying rent on the value of the works. Some leases are drafted so as to attempt to rentalise the tenant's fitting-out works by saying that tenant's works are disregarded, "other than works carried out under an obligation to the landlord and other than fitting-out works". This has the effect of rentalising the fitting-out works, but some tenants miss the point because of the double negative in the drafting.

There can be instances where tenant's works may be rentalised, as the landlord may specifically want to take into account the value increase due to certain works carried out by the tenant. For example, if the premises are on more than one floor of a building and the tenant replaces an awkward staircase which is difficult to use and which would not comply with current standards, with a better staircase so as to be able to trade from and fully use that other storey of the premises, or if the tenant installs an escalator or a lift, then this will increase his ability to trade from the premises. The landlord may want to try to have the whole of the increase in value attributable to these works to be taken into account at rent review, or there may be a compromise situation of an assumption at rent review that both floors are fully available for full use, and that the public, the tenant and his staff can easily move between floors. This would disregard the bespoke staircase, lift or escalator as the case may be.

Tenant's works becoming heritable property

16–08   If the tenant carries out infrastructure engineering works or construction, extension or alteration of a building, then these works will be considered to be heritable in nature and will belong to the landlord, without any compensation being payable to the tenant at the end of the lease or at any other time. Similarly, if the tenant carries out works that would cause damage to the property if removed, or that have a degree of permanence, these also will belong to the landlord. This is more fully discussed in Ch.33. Normal tenant's trade fixtures and fittings remain the property of the tenant.

Carrying out the works

16–09   Leases usually provide for the tenant to have to obtain any planning permission, building warrants and any other necessary consent in order to carry out any authorised works, and then to do the works in a good and workmanlike manner, and to comply with all statutory requirements in carrying out the works. Some leases restrict the tenant from applying for, or implementing, planning permission except with the landlord's prior written consent. They also usually provide for the tenant to take on all responsibility for compliance with the current version of the Construction (Design and Management) Regulations.

Licence for works

The parties should both want a licence for works in order to record the works **16–10** that the tenant wants to carry out. The licence for works should be prepared by the landlord's solicitor, narrating that the tenant wants to carry out the works, that the landlord grants consent to these works being carried out and, if the tenant does go ahead with the works, that the obligations set out in the document are to be performed by the tenant. The document should specify the works that are to be carried out and may also include a method statement as to how this is to be done. The tenant will want the document to be signed so as to show clearly the works that are being carried out by the tenant, especially if these works are to be disregarded at rent review.

There are various points the landlord should consider.

(a) Will the works have any harmful effect on the stability of the building?

(b) Will the works reduce the net internal or net lettable area? If so, the landlord could suffer at rent review if the works are to be taken into account at rent review, unless the works are disregarded. If the works are to be disregarded at rent review, the extent of the area prior to the works being carried out should be recorded for use in future rent reviews. If the works increase the sales or useable area, then the tenant will want to disregard the works.

(c) If the landlord has granted a standard security over his interest, then the consent of the secured lender will be required for the works. The landlord should seek this consent and make it a condition of any consent that the tenant pays the expenses incurred by the secured lender and by the landlord.

(d) The landlord may want to have his own surveyors examine the tenant's plans and specification, and he may also want to attend at site and inspect the works while they are being carried out and after they have been completed. The costs of these surveyors should be met by the tenant.

(e) The tenant should be made liable for complying with the Construction (Design and Management) Regulations and should indemnify the landlord in respect of these.

(f) The landlord will want to make sure that the tenant has obtained all local authority consents which may be required and that the tenant gets an acceptance of completion certificate from the building control department.

(g) The landlord will want to make sure that the works do not prejudice or indeed invalidate the landlord's insurance policies, and so the proposed works should be notified to the insurers and their approval should be obtained.

(h) There should be an indemnity obligation on the tenant to be liable for any expense, claims or losses suffered by the landlord as a result of the works being, or having been, carried out.

(i) The lease may or may not include an obligation on the tenant to remove any works and reinstate on termination of the lease, but in any event the licence for works should contain such an obligation or should contain the right in favour of the landlord to call on the tenant to remove all or part of the works and to reinstate.

Removal and reinstatement

16–11 The tenant is allowed to remove and replace his trade fittings and fixtures throughout the term and can remove them at termination of the lease, unless restricted or prohibited by the actual wording of the lease. If the landlord does not impose on the tenant, either in the lease or in the licence for works, an obligation to remove the works and to reinstate the premises, then the landlord will not be entitled to insist on this.

Landlords quite often provide for the right to have all or some of the works left in place, without compensation being payable to the tenant. Some leases or licences for works provide that the tenant must remove all his works and reinstate the premises at or prior to termination of the lease.

B—ENGLAND

Various provisions in England

16–12 If a lease does not say anything about alterations or works, the tenant can carry out any works he wants, subject to the rules on "waste" (relevant to the repairs clause). Therefore, the lease will normally set out restrictions.

If the lease provides that the tenant is not allowed to carry out alterations or works except with the landlord's consent, there is an implied term that the landlord's consent is not to be unreasonably withheld. This is different to the position in Scotland where there is no such implied term.

For commercial leases, the tenant has in certain cases a statutory entitlement to compensation for improvements made if these add to the letting value of the premises at the termination of the lease. There is no compensation payable for tenant's and trade fixtures that the tenant is entitled to remove under the general law or where the tenant received valuable consideration for the improvements. In order to be entitled to compensation, the tenant needs to have complied with procedural requirements when carrying out the works and must adhere to the procedures necessary for claiming compensation.

CHAPTER 17

IRRITANCY

Introduction

Irritancy is termination by the landlord of a lease due to breach by the tenant. **17–01**
Most leases do contain an irritancy clause, setting out circumstances in which
the landlord can terminate the lease due to breach by the tenant. If the lease
does not contain an irritancy clause, there is a limited right in favour of the
landlord to terminate the lease at common law, but this is only in respect of
non-payment of two years' rent and is qualified.

A tenant can never unilaterally terminate a lease by founding on his own
breach.

In this Chapter, we will examine the common law right of irritancy, the type
of irritancy clause found in many leases, the case law on irritancy and the
limited statutory protection for tenants. We will then look briefly at the English
law on forfeiture of leases.

A—SCOTLAND

Common law right of irritancy

This is implied by law, is called "legal irritancy" and will apply whether or not **17–02**
the lease has any irritancy clause. If the tenant has failed to pay rent for two
years, the landlord can seek a court order terminating the lease. The limited
statutory protection in favour of the tenant detailed in para.17–04 below applies
to this remedy. In addition, the tenant has the right to save his lease by paying
the amount due at any time before the extract decree is issued by the court,
even if judgment has already been granted in favour of the landlord.

Irritancy clauses in leases

It is usual for modern-day leases to contain an irritancy clause that sets out the **17–03**
various circumstances in which a landlord can seek termination of the lease,
and this is called a "conventional irritancy". The irritancy clause should
provide for exactly which events entitle the landlord to irritate the lease.

Examples of conventional irritancies are an instalment of rent being 14 days
late, whether or not demanded, any other payment being 14 days late after
demand, the tenant becoming insolvent (bankrupt/sequestrated or a receiver,
administrator or liquidator being appointed) or any other breach of the tenant's
obligations.

A tenant will normally revise the clause so as to provide for a period of at
least 14 days' notice to be given by the landlord specifying the failure to pay
and threatening to terminate unless payment is made by the time the notice
expires, and for a reasonable period of time to be allowed for making good any

other breach. The tenant will usually also require the landlord to allow a period of anything from six months to a year for a receiver, administrator or liquidator to be allowed to dispose of the lease. If the landlord agrees to this concession, he will invariably insist that this will only apply if the receiver, etc. undertakes personal liability for all payments including arrears and for performing all other obligations during this period. The tenant's lenders will expect these amendments to be allowed.

Statutory protection

17–04 It has always been a principle of law that irritancy can never be used oppressively, but this principle has now been to a large extent superseded by a limited measure of statutory protection, introduced by the Law Reform (Miscellaneous Provisions) (Scotland) Act 1985.[1] Section 4 of the Act states that in the case of irritancy for non-payment of money, the landlord must give the tenant at least 14 days' written notice to pay the sum due (if the lease itself specifies a longer period of notice, then the longer period applies), saying that the lease may be (or will be) terminated unless the sum is paid within the specified time. This notice is called a "pre-irritancy notice". If the tenant has not paid within the specified period, the landlord can then ask the court to grant an order irritating (terminating) the lease.

The landlord's pre-irritancy notice has to be sent by recorded delivery.

For non-monetary breaches the court will only grant an order terminating the lease if in all the circumstances a fair and reasonable landlord would seek to terminate the lease. If the breach is one that is able to be remedied within a reasonable time, such as failure to carry out repairs, the court will take into account when exercising its discretion whether the tenant has been given a reasonable opportunity to make good. It is prohibited to contract out of the 1985 Act, and the Act applies to leases that were already in existence when the Act came into force, as well as to new leases.

In *Scott v Muir*[2] the landlord had sent a pre-irritancy which required the tenant to pay rent and other monies totalling £7,800 with interest as provided for in the lease. The notice stated that, if the tenant failed to comply with these requirements, the lease might be terminated on a specified date. The court held the pre-irritancy notice failed to comply with the 1985 Act as it did not require the tenant to make payment within any specified period; there was no mention of a deadline or time limit, and s.4(3) of the 1985 Act was prescriptive in this regard. For the notice to be effective it had to specify the periods from which the rent arrears arose. In any event, proper specification was required, as it was imperative that the tenant should be able to calculate the interest, and so he needed to know the date from which interest should be calculated, and therefore the month of arrears and the prescribed rate.

In *Edinburgh Tours Ltd v Singh*[3] the landlord issued a pre-irritancy notice by recorded delivery in respect of unpaid rent. As the rent was not paid by the time the notice expired, the landlord terminated the lease. In terms of the lease, notices were deemed to be sufficiently served if sent by recorded delivery, and were deemed served two business days after posting, unless the contrary could

---

[1] Law Reform (Miscellaneous Provisions) (Scotland) Act 1985 (c.40).
[2] *Scott v Muir*, 2012 S.L.T. (Sh. Ct) 179; 2012 Hous. L.R. 20; 2012 G.W.D. 5–94.
[3] *Edinburgh Tours Ltd v Singh*, 2012 Hous. L.R. 15; 2012 G.W.D. 4–75.

be proved. The tenant claimed that as the irritancy notice had not been served upon him, the sublease had not been validly terminated.

The court held that the notice procedure set out in s.4 of the 1985 Act was designed to protect the tenant against the harshness of irritancy, and that it was neither logical nor reasonable to suggest that the statutory requirement (i.e. that the pre irritancy notice be sent by recorded delivery) should over-ride the parties' own wishes contained in the lease, where it provided both parties with an opportunity of challenging what might be regarded as "deemed service" of the notice. It was inconceivable that the statutory notice provisions should be construed in a way which operated to the disadvantage of the recipient of the notice when set against the parties' contractual remedies.

In *Crieff Highland Gathering Ltd v Perth and Kinross Council*[4] it was held that where the tenant was in breach of its repairing obligation, but the breach Is not a material breach, the landlord is not entitled to irritate the lease. In this case, the landlord had drawn to the tenant's notice various wants of repair to be reme-died within three months, under threat of irritancy. The tenant failed to do the works, and the landlord served a notice of irritancy. The court held that the clear purpose of the "pre-irritancy" notice and accompanying schedule of dilapidations were to notify the tenant of wants of repair; on the evidence, none of the local authority's breaches could properly be said to have been material, whether viewed singly or cumulatively: The total cost of the wants of repair had amounted to just over £9,000 and the wants of repair did not detract from the value and utility of the property as a facility for public recreation. Although the landlord's notice had set out the wants of repair in sufficient detail, it was unfair and unreasonable to expect the tenant to address them within a period of three months where it was inadvisable to carry out the particular repairs because of the difficulties in doing so during winter. The court said that a fair and reason-able landlord would not have sought to terminate the lease in the circumstances of the case, in particular where there were alternative remedies available.

Enforcing the irritancy (removing the tenant)

If the landlord serves a pre-irritancy notice, he does not actually have to go **17–05** ahead and seek a court order to terminate the lease. He can threaten without seeing the threat through, and sometimes the actual threat is enough to bring the tenant into line.

A tenant can never be lawfully removed from premises except with a court order. In particular, in Scotland a landlord is not entitled to change the locks. The court order is then given to court officers who will then lawfully evict the tenant.

If the landlord does obtain a court order of irritancy, he cannot sue the tenant for damages for early termination of the lease or for breach of contract and he is not entitled to any rent in respect of the period after which the lease is irritated.

The position of charge-holders

A tenant can only grant a standard security over his interest in the lease if **17–06** the original duration of the lease is longer, or is capable of lasting longer, than

---

[4] *Crieff Highland Gathering Ltd v Perth and Kinross Council* [2011] CSOH 78; 2011 S.L.T. 992; 2011 G.W.D. 20–474.

20 years. Therefore, a lease from January 14, 2009 to January 14, 2029 is sufficient in length, but if the lease expires on January 13, 2029 it would not be eligible.

If the lease restricts the grant of any charge over the tenant's interest, then the landlord's consent will be needed not only for the grant of any standard security by the tenant, but also for the grant of a floating charge or debenture that a corporate tenant wants to grant after commencement of the lease.

The statutory protection on irritancy given to tenants does not extend to charge-holders. If the tenant wants to use the lease as a security for borrowing, then the irritancy clause should provide for a copy of the pre-irritancy notice to be given to charge-holders, liquidators, receivers and administrators, granting them the right to pay any outstanding sums so as to save the lease, and for the charge-holder, etc. to be entitled to carry on with the lease and dispose of it within a certain period of time, say up to a year, provided that they accept personal liability.

The position of sub-tenants–irritancy protection agreements

17–07   If the lease is irritated then, unless the landlord has given security of tenure to the sub-tenants, all sub-leases immediately terminate, leaving the sub-tenant with only a personal claim against the tenant and no recourse against the landlord.

The statutory protection on irritancy given to tenants does not extend to sub-tenants, and so the tenant granting a sub-lease should provide for a copy of any pre-irritancy notice to be issued by the landlord to the sub-tenants with the right for the sub-tenants to pay any outstanding sums so as to save the lease.

It is quite common for an irritancy protection agreement to be granted by the landlord in favour of the sub-tenant, in which the landlord undertakes that if the lease is irritated, then the sub-tenant has the right to have a new lease granted directly in his favour for the then remaining term of the sub-lease at the same rent payable as under the head-lease. Some of these agreements provide for the sub-tenant to be required to enter into such a new lease, while others merely give the sub-tenant a right to call for the new lease.

Rescission

17–08   The landlord can rescind (terminate) the lease if the tenant is severely in breach of his obligations. This remedy is hardly ever used as the more common remedy of irritancy will usually be available. Generally, if the tenant has committed a material breach of his lease obligations, and if the landlord has drawn this to the tenant's attention and has asked him to put it right, and the tenant fails or refuses to do so, then the landlord will be justified in rescinding the lease. The statutory protections in favour of the tenant in respect of irritancy apply equally to rescission.

Case law on irritancy

17–09   In *CIN Properties Ltd v Dollar Land (Cumbernauld) Ltd*[5] the landlord had served a pre-irritancy notice on the tenant allowing 14 days for payment. The

---

[5] *CIN Properties Ltd v Dollar Land (Cumbernauld) Ltd*, 1992 S.L.T. 669.

tenant failed to pay on time. The court held that although the loss to the tenant would be extreme if the lease was irritated, the Act was clear and there was no leeway for refusal of irritancy.

In *Blythswood Investments (Scotland) Ltd v Clydesdale Electrical Stores Ltd (in receivership)*[6] the landlord sought decree of irritancy on the grounds of the tenant having gone into receivership. The court held that a fair and reasonable landlord was entitled to take into account not only the interests of the tenant, but also the interest of other tenants in the vicinity, and would, in addition, be allowed to also take into account the fact that proceeding with the irritancy would confer considerable advantages to the landlord.

In *HMV Fields Properties Ltd v Skirt'n'Slack Centre of London Ltd*[7] the tenant in a lease incurred an irritancy due to failure to pay rent, and the land-lord terminated the lease by notice, but the tenant did not remove. The landlord obtained a declarator of irritancy and removing, and the tenant appealed and his appeal was eventually refused. The landlord sought payment from the tenant in respect of his occupancy after the date of the irritancy notice. The court held that the terms of the lease showed an intention of the parties that there should be complete termination of the contractual relationship after the irritancy, and therefore there could be no claim available for a continuing breach of contract. The court also decided that a reasonable rent for the continued occupation was not the rent that would have been achieved under a new lease in normal terms entered into at the date of the irritancy, but was the rent payable at the time of the irritancy.

In *What Every Woman Wants (1971) Ltd v Wholesale Paint & Wallpaper Co Ltd*[8] the current landlord, who had purchased the property with the benefit of the lease, had irritated the lease due to failure on the tenant's part to pay rent. The tenant argued that since the start of the lease the original landlord had repeatedly allowed late payment, and so the landlord from time to time had waived the right to irritate the lease for late payment of rent where no notice was timeously sent to the tenant to pay. The court held that: (a) the lease had been irritated; (b) the tenant knew that the property had been sold and the new landlord was in place; (c) the tenant knew if he failed to pay on time then the landlord was entitled to exercise his irritancy right; and (d) the tenant had no reason to suppose that the new landlord would allow the same indulgence in respect of rent payment as the old landlord had.

17–10

In *Life Association of Scotland v Blacks Leisure Group Plc*[9] it was held that if an owner issues to the tenant a pre-irritancy notice and then sells the property, he is entitled to assign the pre-irritancy notice to the new landlord, but the new landlord must be infeft (i.e. he must register his ownership title) before he can rely on the notice. It is safer to bring the action at the instance of both parties.

The Insolvency Act 1986 provides[10] that while an administration order is in force, no other steps can be taken to enforce any security over the company's

[6] *Blythswood Investments (Scotland) Ltd v Clydesdale Electrical Stores Ltd (in receivership)*, 1995 S.L.T. 150.

[7] *HMV Fields Properties Ltd v Skirt'n'Slack Centre of London Ltd*, 1987 S.L.T. 2.

[8] *What Every Woman Wants (1971) Ltd v Wholesale Paint & Wallpaper Co Ltd*, 1984 S.L.T. 133.

[9] *Life Association of Scotland v Blacks Leisure Group Plc*, 1989 S.L.T. 674.

[10] Insolvency Act 1986 s.8 and Sch.B1, para.43(5) (as added by Enterprise Act 2002 s.248 and Sch.16).

property or to repossess goods under any hire purchase agreement, and no other proceedings or other legal process can take place except with the administrator's or the court's consent. In *Scottish Exhibition Centre Ltd v Mirestop Ltd (in administration) (No.2)*[11] the lease contained an irritancy clause that if a receiver or other administrator or manager for creditors were appointed to the tenant, the landlord could irritate the lease. The court held that the wording in the Act "other legal process" did not include the taking of a non-judicial step such as service of a notice under the contract of the lease, and that the appointment of the administrators on an interim basis was enough to allow the landlord to give notice under the irritancy clause. Interestingly in this case, the court said that a hearing would have to take place to decide whether a fair and reasonable landlord would, in the circumstances, seek to terminate the lease.

It would appear that if the irritancy clause states that the appointment of an administrator is an event justifying irritancy of the lease, the landlord is entitled to serve notice of irritancy to terminate the lease. However, the seeking of a decree of irritancy and removal would be something that would require the permission of the court.

17–11   In *HMV Fields Properties Ltd v Bracken Self Selection Fabrics Ltd*[12] the landlord discovered that the premises had been sub-let without his consent and that the sub-tenant was using the premises in breach of the user clause. The landlord served an irritancy notice; the tenant maintained he was not in breach, and the matter was referred to arbitration. After the irritancy notice was served the tenants remained in possession and made payments of rent on various dates for the next 18 months. Only the first two payments were initially accepted by the landlord, but these were subsequently returned. The court held that where a tenant remains in occupation of premises and tenders payment of rent when it fell due and the rent was accepted by the landlord, it appeared objectively that the landlord was indicating he was willing for the contract to remain in force. However, it is always a question of evidence as to whether or not a subsequent acceptance of rent is a clear waiver of an irritancy notice, and in this particular instance, the arbiter was entitled to hold that the acceptance of rent did not amount to a waiver of a notice of irritancy.

In *Whitbread Group Plc v Goldapple Ltd*[13] there had been a business transfer arrangement between the party who paid the rent and the tenant, but this specifically recognised that the tenant still had to pay the rent. Rent was subsequently paid by the third party, but was clearly meant to be in respect of the tenant's obligation to pay rent. The landlord refused to accept payment because it had not been received from the tenant. The lease contained an irritancy clause entitling the landlord to serve a pre-irritancy notice saying that he intends to irritate the lease. In this case the landlord said in his pre-irritancy notice that he would be entitled to irritate. The court held that the pre-irritancy notice was effective, even though it referred to the landlord being entitled to irritate the lease rather than referring to the landlord intending to irritate, as it was the entitlement to irritate that created the risk, and the landlord's intention is an essentially subjective matter that could change during the period specified in the notice. The court also held that the cheque from the third party was

[11] *Scottish Exhibition Centre Ltd v Mirestop Ltd (in administration) (No.2)*, 1996 S.L.T. 8.
[12] *HMV Fields Properties Ltd v Bracken Self Selection Fabrics Ltd*, 1991 S.L.T. 31.
[13] *Whitbread Group Plc v Goldapple Ltd*, 2005 S.L.T. 281.

valid payment of rent, as the payer was acting as the ad hoc agent of the tenant for the purpose of making the payment, and no assignation of the tenant's interest had taken place.

In *Maris v Banchory Squash Racquets Club Ltd*[14] a lease imposed on the tenant the obligation to construct squash courts and then to keep them in good repair and to renew them if destroyed. The irritancy clause entitled the landlord to irritate the lease if the tenant was in breach of his obligations under the lease. The landlord served a schedule of dilapidations on the tenant and at the same time served on the tenant a pre-irritancy notice requiring the tenant to carry out repairs within three months, failing which the lease would be forfeited. The tenant did not respond to the notice and carried out only two very minor repairs, leaving most of the schedule of dilapidations outstanding. The landlord then issued his notice terminating the lease on the grounds of the tenant's breach. Subsequently, the tenant did carry out most of the necessary repairs. The court held that as at the date of the landlord's irritancy notice, a fair and reasonable landlord would have relied on the tenant's breach to terminate the lease.

In *Dollar Land (Cumbernauld) Ltd v CIN Properties Ltd*[15] the court considered a situation where a development corporation had granted a head lease to a developer who was to develop the town centre and then grant a sub-lease back to the development corporation. The development corporation sold the ownership interest and assigned their interest under the sub-lease to Dollar Land (Cumbernauld) Limited. CIN Properties Limited irritated the sub-lease on the grounds of failure to pay the rent. The effect of this was to extinguish the leases that had existed. CIN Properties Limited raised a court action to claim unjustified enrichment arising from the irritancy. The House of Lords held that, in order to succeed with the court action, the sub-tenant had to show that CIN Properties Limited had been enriched at their expense without any legal justification and that it would be fair to compel them to redress the enrichment, that CIN Properties Limited had contracted to observe the irritancy clause which made it clear that if the lease were irritated they would lose all right under the lease, and that there was no room for the operation of law of unjustified enrichment. Dollar Land had argued that the irritancy clause was unreasonable on the grounds that the relationship between the parties was more like a joint venture rather than just landlord and tenant.

In *Glasgow City Council v Morrison Developments Ltd*[16] the court considered a lease which provided for payment of a capital amount of £340,000 which was to be paid on the earliest of one of three days relating to the construction of a shopping centre. The lease contained an irritancy provision allowing the landlord to seek a Decree of Irritancy if the capital amount were not paid within 21 days of its due date, and failing to carry out construction of the shopping centre itself. The tenant argued that the obligation to pay the capital amount and to carry out the construction work fell within the five-year prescriptive period laid down by s.6 of the Prescription and Limitation (Scotland) Act 1973, whereas the landlord argued that these were both obligations relating to the land and were therefore subject to the long negative 20 year prescription. The court held that as the capital amount was not a periodical payment, it did

---

[14] *Maris v Banchory Squash Racquets Club Ltd*, 2007 S.C. 501.
[15] *Dollar Land (Cumbernauld) Ltd v CIN Properties Ltd*, 1998 S.C. (H.L.) 90.
[16] *Glasgow City Council v Morrison Developments Ltd*, 2003 S.L.T. 263.

not fall within the same class of obligation as payment of rent etc. and that the tenant's obligation had not been cancelled by the 5 year short prescription period. The lease was therefore held irritated.

B—ENGLAND

Forfeiture and taking back possession

17–12　In leases of commercial property the position in England is the same as in Scotland; the lease will normally provide that forfeiture will be available to the landlord as a remedy for non-payment of rent, breach of covenant (positive or negative) and for tenant insolvency. The restriction against forfeiting a lease following the appointment of an administrator of the tenant is the same as in Scotland.

In the case of long leases of, say, 99 years and longer (on which the tenants hold in effect enough years for it to be valued as freehold property), tenant insolvency should not be a ground of forfeiture, as the landlord is then recovering the capital value of the property simply because his tenant is insolvent. Such a provision is unlikely to be at all acceptable to tenants and their lenders.

On forfeiture of a lease, physical entry (more commonly known as peaceable re-entry) is usually done by changing the locks outside working hours. In the case of re-entry following a court order for possession, re-entry takes place by virtue of the court order, which would normally be during working hours.

Forfeiture (or re-entry)

17–13　In practice, forfeiture is mainly for breach of positive covenants (obligations) as opposed to breach of restrictions (negative obligations). A tenant cannot found on his own breach to terminate the lease. Forfeiture can only be implemented by physical re-entry or by court judgment. Physical re-entry is usually completed by changing the locks. Basically, commercial premises can only be re-entered outside working hours. Court authority is needed in certain cases where there is tenant insolvency or where forfeiture is for breach of the repairing obligation and the tenant has claimed benefit under the Leasehold Property (Repairs) Act 1938.[17]

The landlord cannot forfeit for non-payment of rent unless the reservation amounts to a condition or there is an express clause allowing the landlord to forfeit and terminate the lease for non-payment.

Section 146 notice

17–14　Section 146 of the Law of Property Act 1925[18] is relevant for everything other than non-payment of rent. The landlord must serve a formal written notice on the tenant before forfeiture, specifying the breach, requiring the tenant to remedy the breach if it is capable of remedy and, in any other case, requiring the tenant to pay compensation for the breach. If the tenant fails within a reasonable time to remedy the breach or to pay reasonable compensation to the landlord's satisfaction, then the landlord is entitled to forfeiture. There are

---

[17] Leasehold Property (Repairs) Act 1938.
[18] Law of Property Act 1925.

additional requirements in the case of claims involving service charges and dilapidations. There is no actual time limit laid down for remedy, but a reasonable time must be allowed.

Relief from forfeiture following a s.146 notice

The tenant, a sub-tenant of all or part of the premises, or a mortgagee can apply **17–15** to the courts for relief against forfeiture of the lease. Relief is at the court's discretion, but the party seeking relief must normally, as far as possible, remedy any breach and compensate the landlord in respect of any irremediable breach. If the breach is in respect of a negative covenant (i.e. an obligation to not do something), he must normally undertake not to be in breach of that covenant in the future. For other breaches, the party seeking relief must normally undertake to not commit the breach again.

Forfeiture for non-payment of rent

At common law, there must be a demand for payment of rent before forfeiture **17–16** is competent, but it is usual for the parties to contract out of the need for a formal demand. The landlord cannot forfeit the lease for non-payment of rent by the tenant, unless, as is normal, the lease contains a specific right to re-enter and to terminate the lease because of non-payment, or the obligation to pay rent is a condition of the grant of the lease. It is important to check whether service charge, interest, insurance premia and VAT are treated as "rent" because, if so, forfeiture for non-payment of these would come within the scope of the law of forfeiture for non-payment of rent.

Relief from forfeiture for non-payment of rent

Sub-tenants have a general right of relief against forfeiture for non-payment of **17–17** rent under s.146(4) of the Law of Property Act 1925. In addition, tenants can apply to the court for relief. Separately, a tenant may have a defence to forfeiture for non-payment of rent if his right of set-off has not been specifically excluded in the lease and if he has a valid claim for set-off. Relief for non-payment of rent applies not only to "rent", but also to other sums that are reserved as rent.

In order to obtain relief, the arrears will normally require to be cleared.

Leasehold Property (Repairs) Act 1938

If the lease was for a term of at least seven years and there were still at least **17–18** three years remaining at the time of service of a schedule of dilapidations, then the Leasehold Property (Repairs) Act 1938 applies where forfeiture is for failure to carry out repairs. The notice threatening forfeiture must provide that the tenant can serve a counter-notice claiming the benefit of the Act and must specify the circumstances in which such counter-notice can be served. However, this does not apply if the repairs clause merely provides for the landlord to be able to enter the premises and carry out the works at the tenant's expense.

In cases where it is competent for the tenant to serve counter-notice, he must do so within 28 days after service of landlord's notice. If such a counter-notice is served, no proceedings can be taken for forfeiture other than with the leave of the court, but this only applies where proceedings begin more than three years before expiry of the term.

If the tenant does not serve counter-notice, then the court's leave is not required for forfeiture.

Waiver of right to forfeit

17–19 If the landlord demands or accepts rent after he becomes aware of the circumstances that entitle him to forfeit the lease, he waives the right to forfeit on that ground. While this may not be of much significance in the case of continuing breaches, this is of great importance for one-off breaches.

CHAPTER 18

OTHER TERMINATION OF LEASES

Introduction

In the previous Chapter we focused on irritancy of leases. There are, however, **18–01** many different ways in which a lease can be terminated, not only by operation of law but also contractually. In this Chapter we examine these and then we look briefly at some ways of terminating leases in England.

A—SCOTLAND

Early termination option

The lease may contain the right in favour of one or both parties to terminate the **18–02** lease early; this is sometimes called a "break option". The lease will usually state how much notice of early termination is to be given and will impose a deadline for giving it. There is case law that time is not of the essence in a lease, unless it is stated to be of the essence, or unless there is a strong presumption against it not being of the essence because of the wording of a particular clause. It is thought here that if an early termination option is exercisable at a specific date by giving a specified period of notice then it is implied that time is of the essence. The option would then no longer be exercisable if notice is not given before expiry of the deadline.

Early termination options by the tenant are often made conditional on the tenant having paid all rent and other sums up to date, and sometimes also on the tenant having performed all the non-monetary obligations up to date. In revising a lease, a tenant should not accept conditionality on non-monetary obligations having been performed, as the landlord could quite easily defeat the exercise of the option by, for example, claiming that a minor repair has not been done.

In *Trygort (No.2) Ltd v UK Home Finance Ltd*[1] a lease contained a clause that the tenant could not exercise his early termination option if he had been in breach of any of his obligations. The court held that the commercially sensible interpretation of the clause is that a historic breach that has been made good before exercise of the option will not invalidate the option, but if there is a subsisting breach at the time of the option notice being served, then the tenant would lose his right to terminate. The court commented that it is possible to draft a clause that would render exercise of a break option invalid if there had at any time during the lease been any breach, but the wording would have to be clear and precise.

In *RPS Re II A LLP v CBS Outdoor Ltd,*[2] a tenant had exercised its early termination option, and the lkandlrod then served a secheule of dilpaidations.

---

[1] *Trygort (No.2) Ltd v UK Home Finance Ltd*, 2009 S.C. 100; 2008 S.L.T. 1065.
[2] *RPS Re II A LLP v CBS Outdoor Ltd* [2013] CSOH 7.

In terms of the lease, the tenant's notice would be invalid if there were any subsisting breach at "the time of termination". The landlord asked the court for an order that the option had not been validly exercised because of the dilapidations (i.e. the tenant had not kept the premises in good repair). The court dismissed the landlord's application, a sthe clause could be interpreted in three different ways, and it was un clear whether any of the landlord's proposed interpretatiosn would be arrived at by a reasonable person. The decision might possibly have been different if at the time of exercsiign the break option, there was an outstsanding and unimplemented schedule of dilpaidatons.

Renunciation (surrender)

18–03 In Scotland, unless there is an early termination option, one party cannot unilaterally terminate the lease unless there is a legal ground entitling him to do so. In *Salaried Staff London Loan Company Ltd v Swears & Wells Ltd*[3] a tenant repudiated a lease without the landlord's consent, and it was held that the landlord was entitled to enforce all of the tenant's obligations including the continued payment of rent.

It is always open to the parties to agree a renunciation of the lease, and in such a case, the tenant should always include a statement in the renunciation that the landlord discharges the tenant from all obligations with effect from the date of renunciation. The tenant should include, in the missives or agreement for renunciation, an obligation on the landlord not to serve any schedule of dilapidations.

Rescission

18–04 If either party is in material breach of contract the other can rescind the lease. In order to be successful, the rescinding party has to show that the other has been in material breach of the lease contract. The tenant has the same statutory protections against rescission as he has against irritancy (see Ch.17).

Frustration–rei interitus

18–05 At common law, a contract ends immediately if the purpose of the contract is frustrated. This happens if the subject matter of the contract is destroyed or if something happens that makes the contract impossible to perform after the contract has been entered into. As we have seen in Ch.3, if the property is destroyed or is so damaged as to be unfit for use or occupancy, the lease is terminated by the rule of rei interitus, unless the destruction or damage was wilfully caused by one of the parties.

Most commercial leases contract out of the common law rule of frustration/ *rei interitus*.

Bankruptcy or insolvency of the tenant

18–06 At common law the bankruptcy or insolvency of a tenant does not bring a lease to an end; the tenant's interest passes to the trustee in sequestration or to the liquidator. Many leases will include bankruptcy or the appointment of a liquidator as a ground for irritancy, although it is usual to soften this provision by allowing a period of time for the trustee or liquidator, etc. to be able to take on

---

[3] *Salaried Staff London Loan Company Ltd v Swears & Wells Ltd*, 1985 S.L.T. 326.

the lease and dispose of the tenant's interest, and the landlord usually revises this so that the concession is only available if the trustee or liquidator, etc. personally adopts the lease and assumes personal responsibility for all payments including arrears and for performing all other obligations. If the tenant is a limited company then the lease will automatically terminate if and when the company is wound up or struck off the Register of Companies.

In some cases, the receiver, administrator or liquidator may try to obtain payment from the landlord for a renunciation, or for allowing access to tradesmen, marketing agents or prospective occupiers to view the property.

Death of tenant

If a tenant dies the lease passes to his executor in terms of s.16 of the Succession **18–07** (Scotland) Act 1964. However, if the lease restricts assignation then the executor can only transfer the tenancy if the landlord consents in terms of the assignation clause.

Partnership—death of a partner or dissolution of partnership

The death or resignation of a partner terminates a partnership, unless there is **18–08** anything to the contrary in the partnership agreement, and of course there is no need to have any written partnership agreement at all. If there is a partnership agreement and this makes it clear that the death of a partner will not dissolve the partnership, then the lease will continue (*Gordon & Co Ltd v Mrs Mary Thomson Partnership*[4]).

Section 38 of the Partnership Act 1890, which applies in all cases, states that after the dissolution of a partnership the obligations of the partnership continue for as long as is necessary to wind up the partnership and to complete transactions that have begun but which have not been completed as at the date of dissolution. In *Lujo Properties Ltd v Green*[5] a partnership ended and a judicial factor was appointed. A lease had been granted to the partnership and to the partners and their successors as trustees for the firm. The lease could only be assigned if the landlord granted consent, which was not to be unreasonably withheld. The court said that the qualified right to assign the lease is the counter-balance of the partners of the firm having the personal obligation to pay rent and to perform all other obligations under the lease until its expiry or earlier assignation.

Termination at ish

The lease will not terminate at the ish (contractual expiry date) unless either **18–09** party has given notice for the required period before the termination date. This is dealt with fully in Ch.19.

B—ENGLAND

At common law a lease can be terminated by expiry, notice, surrender, merger, **18–10** enlargement, disclaimer or forfeiture. The doctrine of frustration may apply to leases.

---

[4] *Gordon & Co Ltd v Mrs Mary Thomson Partnership*, 1985 S.L.T. 122.
[5] *Lujo Properties Ltd v Green*, 1997 S.L.T. 225.

Expiry

18–11 A fixed-term lease expires automatically at the end of the term, subject to considerable statutory provisions; it is not necessary for either party to take any action to terminate the lease. If a lease is granted for a fixed term, but is subject to termination if a specified event happens, then the lease automatically ends when that event happens. Leases terminating on death or marriage are affected by statutory provisions requiring notice and do not terminate automatically.

Business tenancies continue beyond the end of the term if the tenant remains in occupation and will only terminate on the date specified in a s.25 notice issued by the landlord or a s.26 notice issued by the tenant. There is a statutory right in favour of the tenant to renewal unless this has been specifically and correctly contracted out of, or unless the landlord can defeat the tenant's right by using one of the specified exceptions.

Periodic tenancies

18–12 Periodic tenancies carry on from one period to the next until either party gives notice to the other that he does not want the arrangement to continue. If a fixed-term lease has an early termination clause, it is likely to specify what notice has to be given. For a weekly, monthly or quarterly lease, the relevant notice period is a full week, month or quarter respectively. A yearly tenancy can be terminated by half a year's notice expiring at the end of a year.

Surrender

18–13 The tenant gives up his lease to, and with the agreement of, the landlord. This releases the tenant from future liability under the lease but, subject to the terms of the agreement, the tenant remains liable for previous breaches. The landlord may be held to have waived his right to damages for breach on the tenant's part, depending on the circumstances. A surrender should normally be done by way of a formal deed.

Surrender can be implied by the landlord accepting return of the keys or marketing the premises, but it will not be automatically implied where the tenant unilaterally returns the keys. Surrender can be implied by law where the parties agree significant variations to the terms of the lease, such as adding in additional land to the premises or extending the term. In such cases the variation will take ffect in law by a deemed surrender of the lease being varied and the grant of a new lease. This applies even if the parties have entered into a deed of variation of lease. The taxataiona nd other consequences of this need to be carefully considered.

Merger

18–14 The lease is terminated by merger where the tenant acquires the landlord's interest, or where a third party acquires both the landlord's and the tenant's interests. This termination will be subject to derivative interests being preserved.

Disclaimer

18–15 This is usually by a trustee in bankruptcy or a liquidator, who can disclaim certain contracts under the 1986 Insolvency Act. A disclaimer releases the tenant from future liabilities under the lease. This is significantly different to the law of Scotland, where although an insolvency practitioner can disclaim a lease, he cannot thus unilaterally terminate a lease.

Forfeiture

The landlord can forfeit the lease in the event of breach by a tenant. See Ch.17 **18–16** for a full discussion of this.

Frustration

There is no equivalent rule in England to the rule of rei interitus in Scotland. **18–17**
   In *National Carriers Ltd v Panalpina (Northern) Ltd*[6] the court had to consider a 10-year lease of a warehouse where for a period of 20 months access was not possible because the street was closed by the local authority due to a dangerous building. The tenant could not use the warehouse and refused to pay rent, claiming that the lease had been frustrated. The court considered that in the circumstances it had not been frustrated because the interruption of 20 months in a 10-year term did not destroy the entire contract. However, the court did accept the principle that in exceptional circumstances the doctrine of frustration could apply to a lease, despite the fact it is more than a contract, as it creates an estate in land. In such a case the court has to consider whether any term is to be implied that would terminate the lease if such an event occurs.

---

[6] *National Carriers Ltd v Panalpina (Northern) Ltd* [1981] A.C. 675.

CHAPTER 19

TACIT RELOCATION AND RENEWAL OF LEASES

Introduction

19–01　In Scotland, tenants of commercial premises have no right to renew or extend their lease, apart from a limited right for up to a year at a time in respect of shops. A lease does not actually end on the specified termination date unless either party gives at the right time the requisite notification of termination and then acts on that notice, or unless the tenant in a separate document confirms that the lease will end, and that he will vacate, on the specified termination date. This Chapter considers the statutes and common law on termination of leases at the contractual expiry date, the limited protection for shop tenants, and finally the position in England.

A—SCOTLAND

Limited right of renewal of leases

19–02　In Scotland, there is no common law right of renewal of leases, and apart from a limited right in respect of shops, there is no statutory right of renewal of leases either. The parties to a lease can provide for an option to terminate early or to extend the period of the lease.

Tacit relocation

19–03　The rule of tacit relocation (or silent re-letting) is that a lease continues beyond its contractual termination date, unless either party gives the required period of notice to the other that the lease is to end on that date, and such notice is followed by the tenant giving that vacant possession to the landlord.

Although the landlord and the tenant have signed a lease that is to last for a stated period, it does not end when the period expires, unless notice has been given to stop tacit relocation operating and that notice is acted upon. If notice is not given in time then the lease continues at the same rent and on the same terms, and so on until and unless either gives notice. In *Commercial Union Assurance Co.*[1] the lease contained an option to renew on the same terms, but the expiry date had come and gone without the tenant exercising the option and without either party taking steps to terminate the lease. It was held the lease continued for a year by way of tacit relocation and that the option right was no longer enforceable.

A guarantor's liability is not extended by tacit relocation, unless the guarantee expressly provides for this.

---

[1] *Commercial Union Assurance Co.*, 1964 S.C. 84; 1964 S.L.T. 62.

Tacit relocation does not apply to seasonal leases that do not require notice of termination, such as a lease of land for less than a year for grazing or mowing, or a sporting lease for a season.

As the principle of tacit relocation is based on the implied consent of the **19–04** parties it should be possible for the parties to specifically agree to vary or to disapply the principle, but there is some doubt as to whether it is possible to contract out of tacit relocation. If it is competent to contract out of tacit relocation, to do so would require express and explicit provision in the lease or in a separate document; the provision that is commonly found in leases obliging a tenant to remove without warning or process of law is not sufficient. In *Cesari v Anderson*[2] it was held that if the tenant has bound himself to remove, then no notice is required by the landlord, and an action of removal can be raised at any time after the date of removal and within 12 months thereafter. However, the written obligation must be outwith the lease, as an obligation to remove contained in the lease is not sufficient.

In *MacDougall v Guidi*[3] the lease of a shop stated that it is not capable of renewal or continuation by tacit relocation. It was held this provision was effective to terminate the lease at the termination date, and that the landlord was entitled to remove the tenant, even though less than the normally required 40 days' notice had been given.

Leases commonly provide for an extension for a shorter period than tacit relocation would imply, in the absence of notice.

Notice of termination

If the lease does not specify the period of notice to be given prior to, or the **19–05** length of the continuation beyond the contractual termination date, then the period of notice depends partly on the type of premises let, and partly on the length of the lease.

Under the Removal Terms (Scotland) Act 1886, which applies to shops and to all other buildings that are let with or without land, the dates of removal and period of notice are regulated. If the removal terms are Whitsunday or Martinmas then, unless specified to the contrary, the tenant is to remove at noon on May 28 or November 28 respectively, or on the following day if the term day falls on a Sunday. The notice, however, must be given 40 clear days before May 15 or November 11, as the case may be. Therefore a landlord or a tenant wanting to actually terminate a lease that has its contractual termination date at Whitsunday has to give at least 40 clear days notice before May 15, although the tenant removes on May 28, and likewise, if the contractual termination date is Martinmas the notice must be given at least 40 clear days notice before November 11, although the tenant removes on November 28. Section 37 of the Sheriff Courts (Scotland) Act 1907 also provides for notice to be at least 40 clear days before May 15 for leases terminating on Whitsunday, and November 11 for leases terminating on Martinmas.

The Term and Quarter Days (Scotland) Act 1990 amends the Removal Terms (Scotland) Act 1886 so as to make all four Scottish quarter days more or less equally divided throughout the year, so that Candlemas is now February

---

[2] *Cesari v Anderson*, 1922 38 Sh. Ct Rep. 137.
[3] *MacDougall v Guidi*, 1992 S.C.L.R. 167.

28, Whitsunday is May 28, Lammas is August 28 and Martinmas is November 28, irrespective of whether the lease in question was entered into before or after the Act came into force, unless the lease defines these terms as being any other date, in which case that other date will prevail.

19–06 The Sheriff Courts (Scotland) Act 1907 provides different periods of notice for various premises/durations of leases:

- premises let for four months or longer—40 clear days' notice;
- premises let for less than four months—the notice is to be one-third of the term, subject to a minimum period of 28 days;
- land of more than two acres, let for three years or longer—at least one year and not more than two years' notice to be given;
- land of more than two acres held from year to year or under tacit relocation or any other period less than three years—the notice period is not less than six months; and
- buildings and land of not more than two acres, and land of not more than two acres let for a year or longer—a minimum 40 clear days' notice.

The notice has to be the "clear" period, and so in the case of a 40 days' notice, this means 41 days, and it is, of course, necessary to add on any period provided in the lease for service of notices. In *McLeod v George*[4] it was held that a notice period of exactly 40 days is not good enough. In *Signet Group Plc v C & J Clark Retail Properties Ltd*[5] the tenant had vacated the premises three months before the termination date, which was in breach of the keep-open clause, but the landlord took no steps to enforce the keep-open clause. The tenant issued a notice by fax to the landlord terminating the lease as at the contractual termination date, exactly 40 days before the termination date. The court held that although informal communication by the tenant that he intended to terminate the tenancy at the contractual termination date could displace tacit relocation, it is doubtful that actings alone by the tenant would ever be sufficient, that in any event the actings the tenant relied on in this instance were insufficient to constitute notice, and that the faxed notice issued 40 days before the termination date is not good enough as 40 clear days' notice is required in terms of the law.

The content of the notice must be clear and unconditional, so that the recipient knows exactly what his position is. The Sheriff Courts (Scotland) Act 1907 provides certain different styles of notice for different circumstances, and it is preferable to adhere as closely as possible to one of these styles. The notice should refer to the lease, the premises, the date of termination and the fact that the tenant is to remove and that vacant possession is to be given. It is not enough merely to say that the lease is coming to an end or that the landlord intends to resume possession.

19–07 The lease may provide for how notices should be given; if so it should say how and to where notices are to be given, and when they are deemed to have been given. The lease may say that notices must be given by a specified method, such as recorded delivery, in which case notices can only be validly given if

---

[4] *McLeod v George*, 1933 49 Sh. Ct Rep. 302.
[5] *Signet Group Plc v C & J Clark Retail Properties Ltd*, 1996 S.C. 444.

they comply with the requirements set out in the lease. Alternatively, the notice provision might just say that notice will be sufficiently served if a certain procedure is followed. In such a case, service by other means is not precluded.

Notice on its own is not sufficient. If the tenant fails to remove, the landlord has to raise a court action to have him removed. If he attempts to remove a tenant without raising a court action, he may be liable at common law in damages. If the landlord does nothing and allows the tenant to remain in possession, then he will be held to have abandoned his notice, and tacit relocation will operate. If the tenant has given notice, then he must remove from and clear the premises at the termination date or else he will be held to have abandoned his intention to terminate.

If there is more than one tenant, a notice of termination by one of them is sufficient to exclude tacit relocation as silence by them all is required to enable tacit relocation to operate.[6]

It is not so clear what the case is if there is more than one landlord, as it can **19–08** be argued that silence on the part of all parties to the lease is needed for tacit relocation to operate, but on the other hand, termination by a landlord is an act that needs action by all the parties that constitute the landlord, and so it is thought to be safe practice that notice be given by all joint landlords.

If there is a sub-tenant the landlord must give notice to the principal tenant and to the sub-tenant in order to stop tacit relocation operating. However, it is not necessary to give notice to a sub-tenant if the sub-letting is prohibited.

In *Gates v Blair*[7] it was held that if there is a lease of more than one property, the notice must cover them all.

Exclusion of tacit relocation

Even if tacit relocation has not been contracted out of, and a notice to quit has **19–09** not been sent on time, tacit relocation may be excluded by circumstances that are not consistent with continuation of the existing lease, for example where a new lease has been agreed between the parties. In *Morrison-Low v Paterson*[8] continued payment of rent and possession following negotiation for a renewal was deemed to be a new lease as opposed to tacit relocation, even though the parties believed that tacit relocation was operating.

Tacit relocation is also excluded if a tenant gives notice of intention to remove, but is then prevented from doing so due to illness and remains in possession.[9] It is also excluded by the parties entering into a new lease for a year or for a longer period, even if the tenant continues to pay the old rent.

A party can bar himself from relying on tacit relocation, such as where a tenant abandons his lease or takes some step to put it beyond the landlord's power to terminate the lease. In *MacArthur v MacMaster*[10] the tenant had started proceedings at the Crofters Commission, thus preventing the landlord from taking action to remove the tenant while these proceedings were ongoing.

A party can prevent himself from objecting to tacit relocation, such as where **19–10** a landlord notifies the tenant of termination, but then takes no further action,

[6] *Smith v Grayton Estates Ltd*, 1960 S.C. 349; 1961 S.L.T. 38.
[7] *Gates v Blair*, 1923 S.C. 430.
[8] *Morrison-Low v Paterson*, 1985 S.L.T. 255.
[9] *Tod v Fraser* (1889) 17 R. 226.
[10] *MacArthur v MacMaster* (1894) 2 S.L.T. 137.

and allows the tenant to remain in possession; the implication is that the parties have agreed to depart from the notice and to allow tacit relocation to operate. Prolonged delay in enforcing a decree for recovery of possession may have this effect, but not a delay of only a few weeks. If a tenant gives notice but continues in possession without disturbance by the landlord, the parties are presumed to have allowed tacit relocation to operate. Either party is barred from trying to say that tacit relocation does not apply if rent is paid or accepted for a period after termination of the lease.[11]

If a party occupies premises without having a lease or other occupancy right, then the landlord can seek a court order to have him removed and can claim compensation for unauthorised occupancy; the amount will usually be equivalent to rent that would have been payable had there been a lease in existence. This payment is called "violent profits".

Tenancy of Shops (Scotland) Acts

19–11 The Tenancy of Shops (Scotland) Act 1949 and the Tenancy of Shops (Scotland) Act 1964 allow some security of tenure beyond termination date for shop tenants.

A tenant of a shop can apply, within 21 days of the landlord's notice to remove, to the sheriff court for renewal for a period of up to one year on such terms as the sheriff considers reasonable, no doubt bearing in mind the existing terms of the lease. Any renewal is deemed to be a new lease, and the tenant is entitled to further renewals, as previous applications are disregarded. If the sheriff does not consider that he can dispose finally of the application before the notice to quit takes effect, he can make an interim order allowing occupancy for up to three months on such terms as he thinks fit, or if greater hardship would be caused by continuing the tenancy, he can refuse to do so.

Many of the cases on the Acts were in the few years following the 1949 Act coming into force, and these mainly dealt with the meaning of "a shop" and the question of whether greater hardship would be suffered by one or other party if the lease were renewed.

A shop is defined in s.74(1) of the Shops Act 1950 as any premises where any retail trade or business is carried on; this includes hairdresser, sale of refreshment or alcohol, lending books or periodicals when carried on for profit and retail sales by auction. The character of the business itself (as opposed to the character of the area occupied) is of importance in determining whether the premises are a shop.

The 1949 Act provides[12] for various circumstances where the court must not grant the tenant's application. These are;

- where the tenant is in breach of any condition of his tenancy which in the sheriff's opinion is material;
- if the individual tenant is bankrupt, or if a company tenant is unable to pay its debts;
- where the landlord has offered to sell the premises to the tenant at a price which may be fixed by an arbiter, in the absence of agreement;

---

[11] *Milner's Curator Bonis v Mason*, 1965 S.L.T. (Sh. Ct) 56.
[12] Tenancy of Shops (Scotland) Act 1949 s.1(3).

- where the landlord has offered the tenant alternative accommodation, which in the sheriff's opinion is suitable for the purposes of the tenant's business, and is on terms and conditions which the sheriff considers are reasonable;
- where the tenant has previously given notice of termination of the tenancy, and as a consequence, the landlord has contracted to sell or let the premises or has taken any other steps which would mean that he would be seriously prejudiced if he could not then obtain vacant possession of the shop; or
- if, having regard to all the circumstances in the case, greater hardship would be caused by granting a renewal of the tenancy than by refusing to renew it.

Case Law on the Tenancy of Shops Acts

In *Loudon v St Paul's Parish Church*[13] the landlord issued notice to terminate **19–12** the lease because he could not agree a price with the tenant. The tenant refused to increase his offer when the landlord told him of a higher offer that had been received. The court held that the price offered by the landlord to the tenant was fair and that there would be greater hardship to the landlord if the application for renewal of the lease were granted.

In *Hunter v Bruce* 1949[14] the landlord served notice to terminate a lease and offered to sell the premises to the tenant at a price to be agreed, or determined by arbitration. The parties agreed to have the proposed price reviewed by arbitration. The arbiter said the landlord's price was reasonable. The tenant had wanted to pay a lower price. The tenant applied for renewal of the lease to preserve his rights, but the court held that the application be refused because the landlord had been willing to sell at a reasonable price.

In *Green v McClughan*[15] the premises were an open yard with two small wooden huts and traded as a building contractors. The main trade was to manufacture precast concrete fittings with occasional supply of cement by retail sale to the public and very occasional sale of the pre-cast concrete fittings. Held: the premises were mainly a builders yard and were not a shop.

In *Golder v Thomas Johnstons Bakers Ltd*[16] premises were used as a blacksmith's, mainly for wholesale but occasionally for retail sales. The premises were in a yard, and were not visible from the street and there was no counter or shop fittings. The court held the premises were not a shop.

In *Hill v McCaskills Trustees*[17] a lease had already been renewed for one year under the 1949 Act. The landlord served notice to terminate the renewed lease. The tenant did not make application under the Act but argued that he was entitled to continue occupying under tacit relocation. The court held that the notice to terminate under the original lease was sufficient to terminate the renewed lease at its expiry and therefore no new notice was necessary. The original notice became operative on the expiry of the renewed tenancy and there was no room for tacit relocation, and decree of ejection was granted.

---

[13] *Loudon v St Paul's Parish Church*, 1949 S.L.T. (Sh. Ct) 54.
[14] *Hunter v Bruce*, 1949 S.L.T. (Sh. Ct) 57.
[15] *Green v McClughan*, 1949 S.L.T. (Sh. Ct) 59.
[16] *Golder v Thomas Johnstons Bakers Ltd*, 1950 S.L.T. (Sh. Ct) 50.
[17] *Hill v McCaskills Trustees*, 1951 S.L.T. (Sh. Ct) 41.

In *Temperance Permanent Building Society v Kominek*[18], the landlord served notice and then entered into negotiations for a new ten year lease, but the negotiations fell apart. The tenant did not make any application under the 1949 Act because he believed that a lease would be entered into. The court held that the parties had not gone beyond the negotiation stage, and as the 21-day period had elapsed since the landlord's notice had been received, the tenant was too late to make any application. In this case the tenant should of course made application within 21 days of service of the notice so as to preserve his right.

In *Thom v British Transport Commission*[19] the court considered a lease of premises which were a garage, mostly used for garaging and repairs but with a frontage of two large windows displaying items for retail sale, and which also had three petrol pumps for retail sale of petrol. The court held the premises were a shop.

In *Ashley Wallpaper Co Limited v Morrisons Associated Companies Ltd*[20] a lease had previously been renewed under the Act. No notice of termination of the new lease was given to remove, and the tenant had remained in occupation. The landlord objected and called on the tenant to remove and the tenant applied to the court for a renewal. It was held that tacit relocation applies to leases granted under the Act.

In *Wallace v Bute Gift Co Ltd*[21] a lease had already been the subject of two renewals under the 1949 Act and the tenant applied for a further renewal. It was held that each application for renewal must be seen as a separate item, without reference to previous history. The court observed that over a period of years the refusal of possession to the landlord may become a question of hardship and reasonableness.

In *Mowat v Cockburn Hotel (Edinburgh) Company Ltd*[22] a landlord had served notice to terminate the lease. The landlord owned shares in a neighbouring garage which wanted to expand into the leased premises, and claimed hardship to him as landlord would be greater than hardship suffered by the tenant if the tenant were allowed to stay on in the premises. The court held the landlord's argument was relevant and the tenant's application failed.

In *Scottish Gas Board v Kerr's Trustees*[23] a lease had been renewed for a year by the court, following the tenant's application. The following year the tenant applied for another renewal, even though the landlord had not served any further notice. The court held that as the original notice to remove had lapsed when the original lease was renewed, it was not necessary for the landlord to serve any further notice and the application was incompetent and was refused. (Although the case does not mention this, the tenant may have been able to continue to occupy under tacit relocation.)

In *King v Cross Fisher Properties Ltd*[24] the court held that a sub-post office was a shop within the meaning of the Act.

---

[18] *Temperance Permanent Building Society v Kominek*, 1951 S.L.T. (Sh. Ct) 58.

[19] *Thom v British Transport Commission*, 1954 S.L.T. (Sh. Ct) 20.

[20] *Ashley Wallpaper Co Limited v Morrisons Associated Companies Ltd*, 1952 S.L.T. (Sh. Ct) 25.

[21] *Wallace v Bute Gift Co Ltd*, 1954 S.L.T. (Sh. Ct) 55.

[22] *Mowat v Cockburn Hotel (Edinburgh) Company Ltd*, 1954 S.L.T. (Sh. Ct) 76.

[23] *Scottish Gas Board v Kerr's Trs*, 1956 S.L.T. (Sh. Ct) 69.

[24] *King v Cross Fisher Properties Ltd*, 1956 S.L.T. (Sh. Ct) 79.

In *White v Paisley Co-operative Manufacturing Society Limited*[25] the land-lord, which was a co-operative society, required the premises back in order to extend their business. They gave over a year's prior notice before the end of the lease, and the tenant applied for renewal. The court held that the hardship to the tenant would be greater than the hardship to the landlord if the lease were not renewed and the application was granted. The court did, however, make the statement that over a period of time the continued exclusion of the landlord from the premises could become a hardship.

In *Stenhouse v East Kilbride Development Corporation*[26] the landlord of a newsagent's shop served notice of termination of lease, and the tenant applied for renewal. The landlord had been willing to re-let at an increased rent of £400 instead of the then £300. The tenant applied for renewal because of the hard-ship that would be caused to him, by what he considered was an unreasonable increase in rent. The court held that the rent sought by the landlord would be obtainable in the open market and the court refused the tenant's application.

In *Craig v Saunders & Connor Ltd*[27] the court considered an optician's where no sales were made. The tenant said he was unlikely to obtain other premises for anything up to a year, and would then have to rebuild his practice. The landlord wanted premises back, as he maintained the whole building, and the remainder was empty. It was held that the optician's was indeed a shop within the meaning of the Act, and there would be greater hardship on the tenant if the lease were not renewed. In this case the court allowed a six month renewal at an increased rent.

In *Oakes v Knowles*[28] premises were used for repair of boots and shoes with ancillary minor sales of items. The court held that the premises were a shop. Section 3(2) of the 1949 Act says that "A shop includes any shop within the meaning of the Shops Acts 1912 to 1936". In the various cases relating to the Tenancy of Shops Act the Shops Act 1950 is used as the reference point rather than the earlier Shops Act.

In *Boyd v A Bell & Sons Ltd*[29] the court pointed out that s.74 of the Shops Act 1950 defines a shop as "any premises where any trade or business is carried on—retail trade or business includes baker/hairdresser, sale of refreshments/intoxicating liquors, lending books and periodicals for profit, retail sale by auction but not the sale of programmes and catalogues and other similar sales at theatres and places of amusements". In this case, which dealt with a criminal offence in a dry cleaners it was held that a dry cleaners is not a shop, because in terms of criminal statutes, retail trade or business implies a sale of goods.

In *McMahon v Associated Rentals Ltd*[30] the court hearing was held after the contractual expiry date of the lease. The tenant had not asked for an interim order under s.1(5) of the 1949 Act. The court granted the tenant's application, and the lease was renewed for a year. It was held that s.1(2) states that a new lease is deemed to be entered into as a new statutory tenancy, as opposed to being a renewal of an old lease. Section 1(2) says the parties are deemed to

[25] *White v Paisley Co-operative Manufacturing Society Ltd*, 1956 S.L.T. (Sh. Ct) 95.
[26] *Stenhouse v East Kilbride Development Corp.*, 1962 S.L.T. (Sh. Ct) 35.
[27] *Craig v Saunders & Connor Ltd*, 1962 S.L.T. (Sh. Ct) 85.
[28] *Oakes v Knowles*, 1966 S.L.T. (Sh. Ct) 33.
[29] *Boyd v A Bell & Sons Ltd*, 1969 S.L.T. 156.
[30] *McMahon v Associated Rentals Ltd*, 1987 S.L.T. (Sh. Ct) 94.

have entered into a new lease, therefore if the old lease had ended by the date of the hearing it is immaterial.

In *Robertson v Bass Holdings Limited*[31] a brewery disposed of their least profitable outlets and took on direct management of the more profitable ones, in response to the Supply of Beer (Tied Estate Order 1989). They accordingly refused to renew the lease of a pub and instead offered the tenant the option of becoming a licensed house manager and senior bartender, purchasing an outlet accepting compensation or leasing an alternative tied outlet. The tenant applied for renewal of tenancy under the 1949 Act, and argued that taking up appointment as a licensed house manager and senior bartender would involve a reduction in income, that the alternative outlets offered were not comparable to the existing one and that the compensation offered was inadequate. The court held that, although alternative accommodation had been offered by the landlord, they had failed to establish facts and circumstances justifying dismissal of the tenant's application and accordingly the tenant's lease was renewed for one year.

B—ENGLAND

19–13 This book relates only to leases of commercial premises, and therefore any provisions relating to leases of residential or agricultural premises are not considered.

Non-business tenancies terminate at expiry

19–14 Unless the lease is a business tenancy under Part 2 of the Landlord and Tenant Act 1954, then if it is a lease for a specified period of time, rather than a periodic lease, for example from year to year, it ends automatically at the end of the contractual term without any requirement for notice, and the tenant must give up possession unless he has a statutory right to remain. The grant by the landlord of a valid new lease to the tenant is a surrender by the operation of law of the old lease where the new lease is to start during the currency of the old lease.

A business tenancy under Part 2 of the Landlord and Tenant Act 1954 does not end unless terminated in accordance with the provisions of Part 2. The Act gives a tenant who occupies premises for business or professional purposes the right to a new lease, provided he follows the required procedures and keeps to the prescribed time limits. If the tenant is entitled to a new lease but this is not granted, then he is often entitled to receive compensation. The landlord can avoid having to grant a new lease if he can establish one or more of the specific statutory grounds of opposition. While the application is pending, the existing tenancy is likely to remain in force, but the landlord can apply for an increased rent during this time. If the landlord does establish one or more of the grounds of opposition then the tenant might be entitled to compensation.

The following must be satisfied to fall within Part 2 of the 1954 Act: there must be a lease of premises (buildings and/or open land) occupied by the tenant for the purpose of a business carried on by the tenant; and the lease must not fall within any specific exclusion. The protection of the Act does not apply to licences.

---

[31] *Robertson v Bass Holdings Ltd*, 1993 S.L.T. (Sh. Ct 55).

The tenant does not lose the protection of the Act merely because he is not physically occupying the premises; they may be empty because of the need for structural repairs or another similar reason, but if the tenant voluntarily vacates the premises, then the protection disappears. There are various types of lease that are excluded.

There are provisions for terminating a lease that falls within the ambit of the Act.

Contracting out of the Act

A lease of premises for business or professional purposes is either governed by the Landlord and Tenant Act 1954 or it is contracted out of the Act. If a lease is governed by the Act, it is impossible to agree to restrict or prohibit the tenant from applying for or requesting a new lease under the Act. **19–15**

If the parties enter into a lease that is not to be governed by the Act, the tenant is not entitled to security of tenure or to compensation if the tenancy is not renewed.

Tenancies to which Pt 2 of the 1954 Act apply continue automatically until or unless terminated by special notice or until other specified matters occur.

If the parties agree to the grant of a new lease of the premises on terms and from a date specified in the agreement, then the current tenancy will continue until that date but no longer, and the current tenancy ceases to have the protection of Pt 2 of the Act.

Holding over

The phrase "holding over" commonly refers to the period of statutory continuation of a business lease pending its termination. This type of holding over is perfectly legal. **19–16**

The tenant is liable for failure to give complete possession of the premises at the end of the lease, even if an under-lessee wrongfully holds over and refuses to quit. The tenant is liable only for the period of the holding over, as opposed to being liable for a full year's rent. If the tenant holds over after termination of the lease, he is liable to pay mesne profits, i.e. damages for trespass. He may also be liable for damages payable by the landlord to someone to whom the landlord has re-let or sold.

Where a tenant holds over after termination of the lease, it is presumed, unless the contrary can be proved, that mesne profits will be calculated with reference to the amount of rent last payable. If the landlord expected an increased rent and the tenant knew of this and did not argue, then the landlord may be entitled to compensation at a rate higher than the old rent. If the parties were silent, then it is assumed the old rent remains payable, but if there was disagreement then the court can fix the rent payable.

CHAPTER 20

GUARANTEES

Introduction

20–01 When negotiating a lease, the landlord might not be satisfied that the tenant has sufficient financial resources to pay the rent, insurance premia, etc. and to pay for repairs and other non-monetary obligations under the lease. The landlord can obtain comfort by either having a performance deposit (see Ch.24) or by having a guarantee from a third party.

In this Chapter, we consider the main aspects of guarantees in commercial leases, and we also briefly examine the position of leases of English premises.

A—SCOTLAND

The tenant's financial strength

20–02 There is no definition of a "financially sound tenant"; the tenant will usually have assets and other liabilities, but the amount of these will fluctuate continuously. There is a view, which is far from universally held, that many landlords should find a prospective tenant to be satisfactory if he can show for the last three years he has made pre-tax profits of at least three times the proposed rent, and/or the tenant's net asset value for each of the previous three years has been at least three times the amount of annual rent, but every property and every tenant are different.

The landlord should be aware that if he is dealing with a tenant that is a limited company, the lease may be taken in the name of one company in a group while the main trading activity or assets are in the name of another member of the same group.

Even if the landlord is satisfied with the financial strength of the tenant at the start of the lease, he may still want to provide a guarantee clause so that there is an agreed text of a guarantee that would be given if a guarantee is required in respect of any assignee. However it is more common to provide for landlord's consent to a proposed assignation to be not unreasonably withheld and for the landlord, acting reasonably, to be entitled to require a guarantee to be given in terms acceptable to him. In that case, the wording of the guarantee would be adjusted if and when a guarantee is needed.

Missives of lease

20–03 If a guarantee is to be provided, the landlord's offer to enter into a lease should provide for the tenant's obligations in the missives to be guaranteed and for the missives to be entered into between the landlord on the one part and the tenant and the guarantor on the other. The guarantee will be in respect of the tenant's obligations under the missives and will also ensure that the guarantor will sign the lease as guarantor.

Foreign tenants and guarantors

If the tenant is a company registered outwith the UK, then it is desirable to **20–04** have a guarantor that is registered in the UK. If the tenant and/or guarantor are a non-UK entity, then the landlord should consider whether it is possible and if so how easy it would be to enforce the lease and the guarantee. There are enforcement treaties between the UK and many other jurisdictions, but the landlord should consider the practicality and cost of enforcement.

Power to grant guarantee

The landlord should check that the guarantor is entitled, in terms of its memo- **20–05** randum and articles of association, to grant a guarantee. If the guarantor is a non-UK entity, its constitution should be checked to ensure it has the power to grant a guarantee and that there is nothing in its home territory law that prevents it from guaranteeing the obligations of the tenant. An opinion letter should be obtained from a law firm in the guarantor's jurisdiction confirming: (a) the guarantor is properly constituted; (b) the guarantor has the power to grant the guarantee; (c) whether there are any stamp duty or registration requirements in the jurisdiction that are required to be complied with so as to make the guarantee enforceable; and (d) how the guarantor should sign documents. The letter should also give the result of whatever searches are available against the guarantor

Whose obligations are guaranteed?

The tenant will usually revise the lease so that the guarantee is in respect of **20–06** only the first named tenant. If this is not done, the guarantee may, in fact, be in respect of each and every tenant during the period of the lease if the guarantor's obligation is in respect of performance by "the tenant", and the definition of "the tenant" is "the original tenant and its assignees and successors".

What is guaranteed and for how long?

The landlord may require payment of all rent, insurance and other sums and **20–07** the performance of all other obligations in the lease to be guaranteed throughout the whole period of the lease. This is very onerous on the guarantor, especially as the purpose of the guarantee in the first place was to give the landlord some security and peace of mind in respect of a specific tenant that does not have a sufficient financial track record. It is reasonable that once the tenant has established a good financial track record, the guarantor should be released. Many tenants will insist that the guarantee is only in respect of rent and other sums, or they may require to limit the guarantee to say one year's rent or for the guarantor to be entitled to a discharge of its obligations once the tenant has shown a sufficient financial performance such as three years of consecutive trading that produces a pre-tax profit of at least three times the then current rent.

In order to ensure that a guarantee by a corporate guarantor is valid, the landlord should check that the guarantor is obtaining some commercial benefit from granting it.

The guarantee should be included within the lease document or, alternatively, set out in a separate document.

Death or termination of guarantor

20–08 If the guarantee is by an individual guarantor, the lease should provide what is to happen on his or her death. If a corporate guarantor is provided, the lease should say what happens if the guarantor goes into liquidation or ceases to exist. The easiest way is to allow the landlord to irritate the lease in the event of the guarantor's death or liquidation or cessation, but this is unlikely be acceptable to the tenant. A fair compromise would be for the tenant to notify the landlord of the event, and to be obliged to provide, within a specific period of time, an alternative guarantor who is reasonably acceptable to the landlord. On the grant of that new guarantee, the estate of the original guarantor can be released.

The lease should contain an option in favour of the landlord to terminate the lease as a matter of contract, with specific reference to such right not being irritancy, if the tenant fails to provide a suitable replacement guarantor in time. The reason for providing for a contractual termination right (as opposed to it being an event of irritancy) is that for non-monetary breaches a landlord can only irritate if, in the circumstances, a fair and reasonable landlord would seek irritancy. The landlord might not find it easy to pass this test, if at the time, there is no breach by the tenant, and there has been no breach during the term.

Insolvency or cessation of tenant

20–09 Landlords are concerned that a corporate tenant will cease to exist, which of course would happen if the tenant were struck off the Register of Companies for failing to lodge accounts or annual returns, or would eventually happen after the company is placed into liquidation. If the lease was granted to an individual, there should be wording that states that there is continuing liability on the executors of the individual, or on the trustee if the tenant is sequestrated (made bankrupt).

At common law, if a tenant ceases to exist, he cannot have any future liability to the landlord. A guarantor's liability runs with the liability of the tenant, and so the guarantor would have no further liability where the tenant ceases to exist. Most leases that contain guarantee clauses do provide that the guarantee continues to apply notwithstanding that the tenant may have ceased to exist. These provisions usually also state that the guarantor is joint principal debtor along with the tenant, and so this protects the landlord against the tenant ceasing to exist.

In *Kingston Communications (Hull) Plc v Stargas Nominees Ltd*[1] a lease contained a provision allowing the landlord to terminate if the tenant went into receivership. The tenant's receiver was entitled to "save" the lease if, within 21 days of his appointment, he accepted personal liability for performance, in which case he would be allowed six months within which to dispose of the lease. The tenant did go into receivership, but the receiver did not accept personal liability. The receiver sold the tenant's business to a third party and notified the landlord that the purchaser was occupying the premises under an occupancy licence. The receiver paid the rent, but said he was not adopting the

---

[1] *Kingston Communications (Hull) Plc v Stargas Nominees Ltd*, 2005 S.L.T. 413.

lease and was acting without personal responsibility. The landlord accepted the payment but called on the receiver to adopt the lease. The receiver refused to do so. The landlord wrote to the guarantor saying the guarantee would be enforced against him, and he called on the guarantor to enter into a new lease. The guarantor argued that the purchaser was legally occupying the premises, and the landlord could not offer vacant possession or require the guarantor to accept a lease. The court held that the guarantor had failed to show that the circumstances implied that the landlord had renounced the lease, and so the guarantee obligations remained in place.

Can the guarantor be called on to take a new lease?

Unless specifically contracted for, a landlord has no right to call on a guarantor **20–10** to take a lease of the premises for the remainder of the term in the event of the tenant ceasing to exist or if a liquidator, etc. disclaims the lease.

Many guarantee clauses provide for the landlord to have the right to call on the guarantor to take a new lease of the premises if the tenant goes into receivership, administration or liquidation, or is wound up or struck off. Guarantors will try to limit this provision so that the landlord can only make this call within, say, six months after the date of appointment of a receiver, etc. The lease is still in existence if the tenant goes into receivership, administration or liquidation as the tenant still exists, and although the receiver, etc. may disclaim the lease, this does not terminate the lease. Therefore, the lease should be renounced or irritated if a new lease is to be granted to the guarantor.

If there is a very short period after the appointment of a receiver, etc. within which to call on the guarantor to enter into a new lease, it is possible that the landlord may not know of the appointment until it is too late, especially if rent is payable quarterly and the appointment is made very soon after the last payment. The new lease will be on the same terms as the original lease but will run for the then remaining duration and will be granted at the then current rent. The landlord should be aware that he will not be entitled to call on the guarantor to remove any alterations or other works that had been carried out by the tenant, as these are works that were carried out under the "old" lease, unless the new lease were to specifically provide for this. The landlord would have no right to require the new lease to provide for this, unless there is specific wording that allows him to do so.

Matters that can invalidate a guarantee

If the landlord does something that is prejudicial to the rights of the guarantor, **20–11** then the guarantee might be extinguished. For example, if the landlord postpones to a later date the obligation on the tenant to pay rent, or if he accepts rent at a lower rate, postponing the balance to a later time, then this might release the guarantor. It has been held in England that if the landlord delays in enforcing against the tenant the payment of rent and other sums that are the subject of the guarantee, the guarantor may be discharged if there is implied or express agreement that the payment would be demanded on a certain date.[2]

---

[2] *Lawrence v Walmsley* (1862) 31 L.J.C.P. 143; *Bank of Ireland v Beresford* (1818) 6 Dow 233. In these two cases the debtor had become insolvent during the period of non-enforcement by the creditor, leaving the guarantor without any remedy that was worthwhile.

Therefore the guarantee should be stated to apply, despite any time or indulgence granted by the landlord to the tenant, or any neglect or forbearance on the landlord's part in enforcing the lease.

Any variations of the terms of the lease will discharge the guarantor unless he consents to these. A guarantor entering into a guarantee obligation should understand his potential liability for more than he intended to guarantee, if the clause says that the guarantee continues notwithstanding that the lease may have been varied by agreement between the landlord and the tenant. If the guarantee does say this, the guarantor's obligations could increase without his knowledge. From the landlord's point of view, the clause should state that the guarantee continues to apply to the rent as increased in terms of any rent-review provisions; otherwise it will be necessary to take the guarantor along with the tenant as party to each and every rent-review agreement.

Notices to tenant, minimising guarantor's loss

20–12   The guarantor should revise the guarantee to provide an obligation on the landlord to give a copy of all notices that are served on the tenant to the guarantor at the same time as serving them on the tenant. The guarantor could consider adding in a right (but not an obligation) for him to require the tenant to assign the lease to him in the event of tenant default, and for the landlord to consent automatically to such an assignation. This then allows the guarantor the opportunity to limit his liability by carrying on business at the premises and/or marketing the lease so as to get out of his future liability.

Joint and several liability

20–13   If the guarantor consists of more than one person or entity (for example a husband and wife, or two companies, etc.), it is normal to provide for liability of each of these to be joint and several, so that the landlord can choose whether to proceed against both or all of them or only one or some of them, for the whole amount.

Assignation of guarantee

20–14   If the landlord sells a property with a lease in place where there is a guarantee of the tenant's performance, it is good practice to assign the benefit of the guarantee, unless the terms of the guarantee are clearly stated to be in favour of the original landlord and his successors as landlord in the lease.

If the guarantee is clearly in favour of only a named party who happens to be the landlord, then the guarantee is not assignable except with the consent of the guarantor. In *Waydale v DHL Holdings (UK) Ltd (No.2)*[3] a lease contained a guarantee by the tenant's parent company in respect of rent and all other sums and the performance of all other obligations, and if the original landlord called on the guarantor in writing to do so, the guarantor would pay or perform any amount or obligation due. The property was sold, and the new landlord sought to enforce the guarantee. The original landlord assigned the guarantee to the purchaser. The court held that the guarantee was in terms sufficient to allow it to be assigned to the new landlord, that the primary obligation appeared to be a

---

[3] *Waydale v DHL Holdings (UK) Ltd (No.2)*, 2001 S.L.T. 224.

guarantee of due performance under a particular contract rather than a guarantee in favour of a particular creditor, and in the absence of clear language in the ancillary provisions, it would be inappropriate to read the primary obligation more restrictively than its own terms justified. The court also said that if the guarantee had been construed as only being in favour of the original landlord, it would not be assignable except with the guarantor's consent.

B—ENGLAND

Effect of variation of lease on guarantee

A guarantor will not be bound by any variation in the terms of the lease made **20–15** without the guarantor's consent, for example surrender of part of the premises. The unintended effect of the variation may, in certain circumstances, be to release the guarantor from his obligations.

Time bar on claims re former tenant's performance

Section 17 of the Landlord and Tenant (Covenants) Act 1995[4] provides that a **20–16** guarantor of a former tenant's obligations is not liable for rent due by a former tenant, unless within six months from the date on which the money becomes due, the landlord serves notice on the guarantor that the money is due and that he intends to recover the amount from the guarantor. It is not necessary for the landlord to serve notice under the Act on the former tenant before claiming against the guarantor.

Authorised guarantee agreement

The Landlord and Tenant (Covenants) Act 1995 abolished privity of contract **20–17** for leases granted on or after January 1, 1996 (it remains in place and enforceable for leases granted before that date). The Act also introduced the concept of the authorised guarantee agreement (AGA). An outgoing tenant, and in some cases his guarantor, can, in certain situations, be asked to grant an AGA to guarantee the performance of the relevant covenant by the assignee.

Guarantor's right to an over-riding lease

If the guarantor makes full payment with any interest payable, he is entitled in **20–18** terms of s.19 of the Landlord and Tenant (Covenants) Act 1995 to have an over-riding lease granted to him of the premises. This allows the guarantor to then enforce against the tenant the payment of rent and other sums and performance of obligations under the existing lease. It allows the guarantor to take some control of the situation, rather than remaining passive and waiting for further demands from the landlord. It also means that the guarantor becomes the landlord's tenant. The landlord needs to consider this carefully before enforcing the guarantee.

The over-riding lease must to be for at least three days longer than the existing lease and should contain the same obligations and terms.

Very similar considerations apply if the landlord wishes to collect arrears from a previous tenant.

---

[4] Landlord and Tenant (Covenants) Act 1995 (c.30).

Expiry of term of lease

20–19   The guarantee ceases on termination of the lease, even if a new lease is granted to the tenant. If a lease is forfeited for non-payment of rent, a guarantor has been held liable for damages due to the tenant's failure to leave the premises in accordance with his obligations to do so.

Insolvency of tenant

20–20   If the tenant goes into liquidation, the lease can be disclaimed by the liquidator, but the guarantor remains liable until the landlord retakes possession of the property. If the insolvent tenant is the original tenant, the guarantor remains liable.

CHAPTER 21

NOTICES

Introduction

In this chapter we focus on the law and practicalities of serving notices relating **21–01** to leases of property in Scotland. It would be rather self-righteous to say that all that is involved in serving notices is to do it correctly! There are many pitfalls awaiting those who attempt to serve notices, and while it is very easy for one of the parties to a lease to instruct a solicitor or surveyor to serve a notice, it is somewhat more difficult to ensure that it is done 100 per cent correctly. The questions to consider are how, when, by who, on whom, and the content.

Does notice have to be in writing?

If the lease says that notices are to be in writing, then there is no discussion **21–02** about the matter—the notice absolutely has to be in writing. The common law position on notification to prevent tacit relocation operating, is that such notification can be verbal or in writing. The only problem with verbal notification is the difficulty of proving the notification has been given. It is strongly recommended that all notifications be given in writing.

How are notices to be served?

The lease may say that notices have to be served in a certain manner and, if this **21–03** is the case, then the provision is mandatory and must be followed. If the lease says that a notice is sufficiently served by, for example, recorded delivery post, then it is thought that that is an acceptable means of service, and it does not preclude other means of service such as personal service by a sheriff officer.

In *Muir Construction Ltd v Hambly Ltd*[1] a building contract contained a provision that the contractor may terminate the contract by notice given by registered post or recorded delivery to the employer or architect. The contractor served a warning notice on the employers seeking payment under an interim certificate, and as no payment was made following that notice, the contractors issued a second notice terminating the contract, and this was served by hand delivery. The Court held that the notice of termination was invalid, as the precise words of the clause were intended to have a precise effect. The clause was very clear as to how the notice was to be served, and the procedure had not been followed.

In *L Batley Pet Products Ltd v North Lanarkshire Council*[2] a head lease required all notices to be in writing. In terms of a licence for works agreement

---

[1] *Muir Construction Ltd v Hambly Ltd*, 1990 S.L.T. 830.
[2] *L Batley Pet Products Ltd v North Lanarkshire Council* [2012] CSIH 83.

between the mid- landlord and the sub-tenant, consent was given for the works, subject to the sub-tenant having to remove the works and reinstate the premises at the end of the lease if so required by the head landlord. In terms of the sub-lease, the notice provisions in the head lease were incorporated into the licence for works. The head landlord only gave verbal notice to the mid-landlord that it required removal and reinstatement in respect of the works. An extra division of the Inner House held that the head landlord had failed to give written notice as was required in terms of the head lease, and so the sub-tenant was not required to remove and reinstate the works.

There is a special statutory provision for serving a pre-irritancy notice (See para.21–04).

Pre-irritancy notices

21–04   In terms of s.4 of the Law Reform (Miscellaneous Provisions) (Scotland) Act 1985 a notice threatening irritancy of a lease must be served by recorded delivery post; there is no alternative means of service that is competent. However, if the tenant does not have, or has not given to the landlord, an address for service in the UK, then there is no requirement to serve a pre-irritancy notice or an irritancy notice itself by recorded delivery.[3] It is therefore important, in order to obtain maximum statutory protection, for a non UK based tenant to provide a UK address to the landlord for service.

In *Ethel Austin Properties Holdings Ltd v D & A Factors (Dundee) Ltd*[4] the landlord served a pre-irritancy notice dated November 9, 2004, by recorded delivery. The following day he served the notice again, also bearing the date November 9, 2004, but this notice was served by Sheriff Officers. Neither of the notices made reference to s.4 of the Law Reform (Miscellaneous Provisions) (Scotland) Act 1985. This section specifies that any pre-irritancy notice must give not less than 14 days following service of the notice for payment of outstanding sums[5]. The notices both provided for the tenant to pay outstanding rent "within 14 days of today's date". The lease itself provided for notices served by Recorded Delivery to be deemed served 48 hours after the date and time of posting.

The court held that s.4 of the 1985 Act contains mandatory provisions for specific information in any pre-irritancy notice, and in particular s.4(3) states that the period specified in any notice must be not less than 14 days immediately following service of the notice. The main difficulty for the landlord was the service of two identical notices by different modes on different dates. The only notice that was effective, was the one served by recorded delivery, but it fell short, because it did not state in its own terms that the recipient had until midnight on November 25 to pay. The notices were deemed invalid.

In *Kodak Processing Company Ltd v Shoredale Ltd*[6] the landlord served a pre-irritancy notice by sheriff officers. This was because there was industrial action by the Post Office at the time. The tenant paid a lower sum than the outstanding rent that was due, and the landlord served a further notice saying

---

[3] Law Reform (Miscellaneous Provisions) (Scotland) Act 1985 s.4(5).
[4] *Ethel Austin Properties Holdings Ltd v D & A Factors (Dundee) Ltd* Unreported June 21, 2005, sheriff court.
[5] Law Reform (Miscellaneous Provisions) (Scotland) Act 1985 s.4(3).
[6] *Kodak Processing Company Ltd v Shoredale Ltd* [2009] CSIH 71.

that the lease had been irritated. The 1985 Act requires service by recorded delivery in respect of a pre-irritancy notice, and the landlord argued that this did not mean this was restricted to only recorded delivery offered by Royal Mail, and that, as the notice had been served by sheriff officers delivery, its delivery had been "recorded". The court held that the terms of the lease which said that certain notices are sufficiently served if sent by recorded delivery are of no assistance in deciding this matter, because it comes down to statutory interpretation. The court held that since 1962, when recorded delivery mail was introduced, the expression "recorded delivery" has been understood as a reference to the Royal Mail recorded delivery service and that the words used in s.4(4) of the Act can only mean that. The court also said that s.4(4) provides for notices to *be sent by* recorded delivery, and this implies that recorded delivery is a mechanism of service; it went on to say that if Parliament had intended any means of service that resulted in creation of a record of service, they would have used other language. The court said that the landlord could have still sent the notice by recorded delivery, and have intimated a copy to the tenant by other means, with an explanation as to the possibility it might be received late, and if this happened then there would have been no confusion caused.

See para.17–09 for more information and case law on pre-irritancy notices.

Proving service of a notice

In *Chaplin v Caledonian Land Properties Ltd*[7] a tenant served by recorded **21–05** delivery post a notice exercising a right to terminate a lease early, but could not prove it had been signed for, and the post office record had been destroyed. The tenant could prove it had been sent, whereas the landlord could not prove it had *not* been received. The court held that a notice is presumed to have been received unless the (supposed) recipient can prove it has not been received.

Notice given to the wrong landlord

In *Ben Cleuch Estates Ltd v Scottish Enterprise*[8] the Inner House of the Court **21–06** of Session held that, due to the particular circumstances of the case, a notice exercising an early termination option that was served on the "wrong" landlord was still effective, due to the true landlord being personally barred by his own actings from disputing that the notice has been received.

The lease included an option in favour of the tenant to terminate the lease early at a specific date by giving at least one year's prior written notice of termination, which could be given or served personally or sent by first class recorded delivery post to the landlord's registered office. Just over two years before the deadline for serving the early termination notice, the property was acquired by a company called Pacific Shelf 1145 Limited, and the change of ownership was notified to the tenant. The new landlord subsequently changed its name to Ben Cleuch Estates Limited but the change of name was not notified to the tenant.

Ben Cleuch Estates Limited was a subsidiary of Bonnytoun Estates Ltd, and both companies had the same registered office address and managing director. The first rent invoice issued by the managing agents was issued as "acting as

---

[7] *Chaplin v Caledonian Land Properties Ltd*, 1997 S.L.T. 384.
[8] *Ben Cleuch Estates Ltd v Scottish Enterprise* [2008] CSIH 1.

agents for Bonnytoun Estates Ltd" and below the word "tenant" it gave the tenant's name and then said "whole property, Ben Cleuch Estates" followed by the property address, and then it repeated "whole property, Ben Cleuch Estates". Subsequent rent invoices omitted the words "whole property, Ben Cleuch Estates" below the word "tenant".

18 months after the change of ownership took place, the tenant's surveyor requested landlord's consent for works, and in the application for consent they referred to the landlord as Bonnytoun Estates. Consent was duly granted.

The following year Bonnytoun Estates Limited issued e-mails to the tenant saying they were going to issue proposals for the tenant to not exercise the break option. Subsequently, the landlord's managing agents issued a letter containing the proposals, and this was issued on behalf of Bonnytoun Estates Limited via Ben Cleuch Estates Limited.

The tenant's solicitors issued a letter to Bonnytoun Estates Limited at its registered office exercising the early break option, and sent a copy to their solicitors.

At the original case, the Outer House of the Court of Session held that the early termination notice was not valid because it was issued to the wrong landlord. The court rejected the argument that notice was given to Bonnytoun Estates Limited as agent for Ben Cleuch Estates Limited. The tenant appealed to the Inner House, which held:

(a) The early termination notice was ineffective as it was given to the wrong landlord.

(b) Notice had to be given to the landlord. The fact that the notice was sent to the correct address but to the wrong landlord, does not constitute notice being given to the landlord.

(c) As the notice was invalid (having not been addressed to the correct landlord), the stage was not reached of considering how the notice would be understood by the recipient.

(d) The definition of personal bar that had been given in various previous cases which were discussed in the judgement is "where A by words or actings justifies B in believing a certain state of facts exists, and B acts on this belief to his prejudice, then A cannot claim against B that a different state of facts existed at the same time". The court said that personal bar applies where a reasonable man regards something as intended to be believed and relied on.

(e) The notice of change of ownership specifying Pacific Shelf 1145 Limited, and the subsequent invoices naming Bonnytoun Estates Limited as landlord, would lead anyone to assume that Pacific Shelf 1145 Ltd had changed its name to Bonnytoun Estates Limited. The landlord had never notified the change of name to the tenant and had never said why invoices represented Bonnytoun Estates Limited as landlord. The court said that, although the proposal for the tenant giving up its right to terminate the lease early was on behalf of Bonnytoun Estates Limited via Ben Cleuch Estates Limited, which would lead one to believe that Ben Cleuch Estates Limited is the actual landlord (otherwise what would be the reason for mentioning that company), everything else had used the name Bonnytoun Estates Limited. Therefore, in this particular case, the tenant was able to terminate the lease early and the notice survived.

In *Batt Cables plc v Spencer Business Parks Ltd*[9] the lease allowed either party to terminate at specific dates by giving not less than six months' prior notice in writing, with notices being deemed sufficiently given if sent by first class recorded post. After the lease had been granted, the original landlord sold the property to Spencer Business Parks Limited. The new landlord's associated company, Spencer Holdings plc, wrote to the tenant to introduce themselves, and to explain that the tenant was now a tenant of Spencer Business Parks Limited. The tenant issued a notice exercising the early termination which it addressed to Spencer Holdings plc at its registered office, which was the same registered office address as Spencer Business Parks Limited. The landlord rejected the notice as having been served on the wrong party. The tenant said that the only mandatory part of the clause was that it was to be in writing, and served on the landlord, and that there was no mandatory requirement for it to actually be addressed to the landlord. There were two issues to consider. First, whether the notice that was given is valid as being given to the landlord, and secondly, whether it is valid if it were given to an agent of the landlord specifically authorised for that purpose.

The court said that the lease imposed four requirements: (a) for the tenant to give notice, (b) for it to be given to the landlord, (c) for it to be in writing, and (d) and for it to be given on time. The court held that the notice had not been given to the landlord and therefore, on the surface, is not valid as such. However, there is then the question of service on an agent of the landlord. For a notice to an agent to be valid it is necessary to establish that the agent has authority to receive it for the principal. The court held that where an agent receives a notice (as opposed to giving a notice), it is sufficient to show the principal has empowered him to receive correspondence, and if so, then this would include the power to receive a break notice from a tenant of the agent's principal. The court said that it is important to note that, in contrast to the person who gives the break notice that terminates the lease, the recipient of a valid break notice has no discretion to prevent the termination, and therefore the break notice was valid.

However, it is important to appreciate that these cases turned on the very specific facts, and the behaviour of the landlord in inducing the tenant to believe that Bonnytoun Estates Limited was the true landlord. It is safer to assume that if a notice from a tenant to the landlord is not addressed to the correctly named landlord, then the notice will fail.

Properties frequently change hands during the lifetime of a lease and it is good practice to check on Companies House website whether there has been a change of name and/or registered office address, and to do a search in the Property or Land Registers and application record, to find out if there is a new landlord, before serving a notice exercising an option to terminate a lease early. If the search shows that the property has changed hands, it is worth giving notice to the old and the new landlords.

Notice from wrong tenant

In the case *AWD de Vere Wealth Management Ltd v Melville Street Properties* **21–07** *Ltd*[10] the tenant's solicitors issued a notice on behalf of the tenant exercising an

---

[9] *Batt Cables plc v Spencer Business Parks Ltd* [2010] CSOH 81.
[10] *AWD de Vere Wealth Management Ltd v Melville Street Properties Ltd* [2009] CSOH 150; 2010 S.C.L.R. 521.

option to terminate the lease early. The notice referred to a former name of the tenant (whose name had changed before the lease was entered into), and the body of the termination notice named a company that was an associated company of the actual tenant and which at no time had been the tenant. Unsurprisingly, the landlord argued that the notice is ineffective. The court held that the argument on the effectiveness of the notice, turns on whether a reasonable landlord would have understood the notice, as being sent on behalf of the actual tenant, or whether the error in naming the tenant introduces such uncertainty into the mind of the reasonable landlord, that he could not safely rely on the notice. The court said that the letter from the solicitors confirmed that they act for the current tenant of the property (albeit erroneously named), and they are exercising the right to bring the lease to an end as provided for in the lease. Therefore, the only possibilities are that there has been an assignation of the lease, or that the issuing solicitors made an error in identifying the tenant. The court held that a reasonable landlord, who knew the terms of the lease, would know his consent is necessary before any assignation could take place, and that he had not been asked for consent. Therefore, the fact the tenant is wrongly named was clearly an error. The court held that the letter was therefore an effective notice to terminate the lease early, despite the error in naming the tenant. However, in each case, the specific facts require detailed analysis, and it is not recommended to rely on a case where facts are similar but not the same, to predict an actual outcome.

Notice given by only one out of two joint tenants

21-08	In *Prudential Assurance Company Ltd v Exel UK Ltd*[11] one of the two tenants gave notice to the landlord terminating a lease at an early termination date. The court held this was not a valid notice, because there was genuine doubt as to whether the notice was also served on behalf of the tenant company that had been omitted.

Period of notice to be given

21-09	In *Esson Properties Ltd v Dresser UK Ltd*[12] a lease allowed the tenant to terminate the lease early by serving notice not less than nine months before a specified date. The notice was served on October 31, 1995 to terminate the lease at July 31, 1996, which was of course exactly nine months later. The court held that the words "*not less than*" meant that the first and last day are excluded when computing the period, and so the notice was void. For the notice to have been valid, it would have needed to have been served on or before October 29, 1995.

Error in notice

21-10	In *Mannai Investment Co. Ltd v Eagle Star Life Assurance Co. Ltd*[13] two leases allowed the tenant to terminate early, by giving not less than six months prior written notice to the landlord or its solicitors to expire "on the third anniversary of the term commencement date". This right was contained in

---

[11] *Prudential Assurance Company Ltd v Exel UK Ltd* [2009] EWHC 1350 (Ch).

[12] *Esson Properties Ltd v Dresser UK Ltd*, 1997 S.L.T. 949.

[13] *Mannai Investment Co. Ltd v Eagle Star Life Assurance Co. Ltd* [1997] A.C. 749; [1997] 2 W.L.R. 945; [1997] 3 All E.R. 352.

clause 7(13) of the leases. The leases ran for a term of ten years from and including January 13, 1992. The tenant issued letters terminating the two leases on January 12, 1995.

The House of Lords was far from unanimous, with three of the judges considering the notice was valid, despite the error, while the other two disagreed. The court held that the reasonable recipient of the notices would understand them as exercising the early termination right, and that a reasonable person with knowledge of the terms of the leases and of the third anniversary date (January 13, 1995) would have been in no doubt that the tenant wanted to terminate the leases on that date, but had wrongly described it as January 12, 1995. The court held that, accordingly, the notices were effective to terminate the lease.

Lord Goff (who was one of the two dissenting judges) said that, under a clause such as the break clause in question, it is not necessary to specify the date of expiry as such in the notice, and that it is good enough to say that the lease is to expire in accordance with the terms of the clause. Therefore, if the tenant had given notice saying that the lease will terminate on the third anniversary of the commencement date, that would have been sufficient to make the notice good. He cited the case *Gardner v Ingram*[14] as authority for this. He also said that if the issuer of the notice specifies the actual date, and being cautious, also specifies in the alternative the end of the period at which the notice is to take effect, the alternative will be effective to save the notice, if the actual specified date proves to be a mistake. He cited *Sidebotham v Holland*[15] as authority for this.

In *Mannai*, Lord Stayn said "the facts are simple. Crediting a reasonable recipient with knowledge of the terms of the lease and the third anniversary date (13 January) I venture to suggest that it is obvious that a reasonable recipient would have appreciated that the tenant wanted to terminate the leases on the third anniversary date of the Leases but wrongly described it as the twelfth instead of the thirteenth. The reasonable recipient would not have been perplexed in any way but the minor error in the notices. The notices would have achieved their intended purpose". In this case the notice stated at the outset that it is given "pursuant to clause 7 (Thirteen)—which was the relevant break option clause. Lord Clyde said this was a precise reference to the particular provision under which the notices were each being sent as distinct from some general reference to the agreement between the parties."

In *Scrabster Harbour Trust v Mowlem plc (t/a Mowlem Marine)*[16] the contractor in a building contract served notice on the employer, requiring a matter to be taken to arbitration. In terms of the relevant clause, any reference to arbitration was to be "conducted in accordance with the Scottish Arbitration Code". The notice did not comply with art.1.3(g) of the Code, as it did not propose the name of an arbiter. The court held that, although it was the intention of the parties to include the Code in its entirety, it did not therefore follow that, in order to be valid, a notice requiring arbitration had to comply with all of the provisions of art.1.3. It went on to say that, looking at the relevant article by itself and in the context of the contract as a whole, the parties could not have

[14] *Gardner v Ingram* (1889) 61 L.T. 729; [1886–90] All E.R. 258; (1889) 54 J.P. 311; 6 L.T.R. 76.
[15] *Sidebotham v Holland* [1895] 1 Q.B. 378.
[16] *Scrabster Harbour Trust v Mowlem plc (t/a Mowlem Marine)* [2006] CSIH12; 2006 S.C. 469.

intended that compliance in particular with art.1.3 (g) should be a formal requirement for the validity of a notice requiring a dispute to be referred to arbitration.

In *Lay v Ackerman*[17] a counter notice from "the landlord" in respect of an English lease was held to be valid, even though it named the wrong person as landlord, because a reasonable person receiving the notice as tenant would have been in no real doubt that the counter notice had been served by the actual landlord. The test is "reasonable person" as opposed to whether the actual tenant himself was in no real doubt. The court decided that the correct test to be applied was that laid down in *Mannai*, which is discussed above.

In *Capital Land Holdings Ltd v Secretary of State for the Environment*[18] a lease allowed the tenant to terminate early by written notice to the landlord to be sent to its registered office, unless the landlord had requested that notice be served on its agent. The tenant gave notice in time but sent it to a place of business of the landlord and to two of the landlord's agents. An extra division of the Court of Session held that the requirement for notice to be served on the landlord at his registered office was a provision that was conceived in favour of the recipient of the notice, and because of the wording of the lease, the recipient knows where he has to look for any notices that are being served on him, and does need to make arrangements for look for notices at any other business address he may have. The court also said the parties made specific provision for where notices are to be sent, and are entitled to hold each other to that, and that as the notice had not been served on the landlord at its registered office, it was not valid.

In *Lemmerbell Ltd and Matthew Fraser Ltd v Britannia LAS Direct Ltd (formerly LAS Direct Ltd)*[19] the tenant under a lease had the right to terminate the Lease early by serving not less than six months' and not more than twelve months' notice. The tenant company was part of a group generically known as Life Association of Scotland, and there was also a company called Life Association of Scotland.

The tenant's solicitors issued the notice in time, but it wrongly described the tenant as Life Association of Scotland Limited as the tenant in succession to Britannia LAS Direct Limited (formerly LAS Direct Limited). They sent a copy of the notice to the landlord's solicitors, and asked them to confirm that the notice was accepted as valid. The solicitors did not give this confirmation. After the deadline for giving the break option had expired, the landlord informed the tenant's solicitors that the break clause had not been operated.

The Court of Appeal held that, if a notice is given by someone who is not the tenant without stating that the issuing party is an agent, the court will only imply that it was given by an agent if the circumstances suggest that the recipient could act on the notice safely, knowing that the principal would be bound by it. Evidence produced to the court showed that "Life Association of Scotland" was a blanket name used by companies in the group of which both the correct tenant and the mistakenly named company were members. The court also decided that when using the blanket name, they had not intended to

---

[17] *Lay v Ackerman* [2004] EWCA Civ184; [2004] L. & T.R. 29.
[18] *Capital Land Holdings Ltd v Secretary of State for the Environment*, 1995 S.C. 109.
[19] *Lemmerbell Ltd and Matthew Fraser Ltd v Britannia LAS Direct Ltd (formerly LAS Direct Ltd)* [1999] L. & T.R. 102.

refer specifically to the Life Association of Scotland Limited, and that in the circumstances the landlords could not have safely acted on the notices from the Life Association of Scotland Ltd, and therefore the notices were not valid. The court also said that the reasonable recipient of notices describing the Life Association of Scotland Ltd as the tenant in succession entitled to L.A.S. Direct Limited would not know whether the lease had been assigned without landlord's consent or whether the original tenant remained in place. They said it was not obvious from the notices that there was an error in the name of the tenant, or that the solicitors who gave the notice was authorised to give it anyone other than Life Association of Scotland Limited. It was therefore impossible to cure the defect in the notices by substituting the correct tenant for the wrong one.

CHAPTER 22

PERSONAL AND CONTINUING LEASE OBLIGATIONS "INTER NATURALIA"

Introduction

22-01 This chapter deals only with the position in Scotland.

A lease is a contract that regulates and defines the relationship between the landlord, as one party, and the tenant as the other party, in respect of the tenant's exclusive occupation and use of property that is owned by the landlord. The contract operates on a personal level between those two parties, and all obligations contained in the lease are enforceable as between these two original parties. The landlord can always assign his interest, but the tenant is likely to have restrictions placed on his right to assign.

In addition to being a contract, the lease is also an interest in land, and so far as the main aspects of a lease are concerned, bind the landlord and tenant from time to time of the property. The landlord's interest in the lease is a beneficial incident of ownership and passes automatically upon transfer by the landlord of the subject of the lease: *Hall v M'Gill*[1] and *M'Gillivray's Exrs v Masson*.[2]

However there are some provisions in leases that may well be intended to run with the leasehold interest, but which in fact are only personal to the initial contracting parties, and thus are not enforceable against anyone who succeeds to the landlord's interest. These non-continuing provisions include exclusivity clauses (particularly in shopping centre leases), and options to purchase (particularly in leases of industrial or factory units).

Lease obligations—personal or continuing?

22-02 In Scotland, the continuing liability of the parties for obligations in the lease only applies to "ordinary and normal" conditions; these conditions are called "*inter naturalia*". A successor landlord to the original landlord is bound to honour the lease and all its "ordinary or normal" conditions. These conditions are enforceable between the landlord and the tenant for the time being of the property, not just the original contracting parties.

However, any conditions in the lease that are not "ordinary and normal" conditions, will not be enforceable against successors.

If the tenant's interest in a lease is registered in the Land Register, this does *not* imply that all of the landlord's and tenant's obligations in the lease are enforceable against parties who succeed to the landlord's interest. This is because lease obligations have to satisfy the same test as title conditions and

---

[1] *Hall v M'Gill* (1847) 9 D. 1557 at 1566.
[2] *M'Gillivray's Exrs v Masson* (1857) 19 D. 1334.

real burdens. In order for these to be valid and enforceable they have to comply with strict rules that affect their content and constitution.[3]

Therefore, we need to identify which of the conditions or obligations in a lease are personal, and which are real. It is only the real conditions in the lease which will bind successor landlords to the original contracting landlord. We have to make a distinction between what is, and what is not, *inter naturalia* of the lease we are looking at. This is because only "ordinary and normal" obligations will continue to be enforceable, once a party disposes of his interest in the lease.

The key test as to whether or not the obligation in question is "ordinary or natural", is if you can say or prove by evidence, that it is one that is common and customary in the type of lease in question. In *Montgomerie v Carrick*[4] the tenant in a mineral lease was granted a right to sink a further pit in addition to the two he already used on the land let to him in terms of the lease, the location of the further pit being subject to landlord's approval. The tenant applied for approval, and this was refused by the successor landlord. At arbitration, it was found that the tenant was entitled to enforce the right contained in the lease as being *inter naturalia* because evidence was produced that such a right was common practice in such leases.

Therefore, if an obligation is to remain enforceable after one or both of the original parties has disposed of their interest in the lease, it will be necessary to show that the obligation is within the class of ordinary or normal lease obligations. In the case *Advice Centre for Mortgages v McNicoll*[5] Lord Drummond Young said that an option to purchase that is contained in a lease is prima facie personal to the parties and does not transmit, and that if a party claims an otherwise personal obligation is to transmit to successors, then he needs to aver this (and support these averments with evidence).

Obligations that do continue

Common law obligations, such as giving possession, continuing peaceful **22–03** possession, payment of rent, repair, damages for disrepair, all continue to be enforceable against successors.

In addition the following obligations are considered to be enforceable by and against successors:

- Repairing obligations of both parties.
- The landlord's obligation not to derogate from the grant by, for example, carrying on damaging operations on neighbouring land that he owns unless he has reserved specific rights to do so.[6]
- An agreement for a permanent change in the method of paying rent.[7]
- The right to review the rent.
- The tenant's obligations to comply with all title obligations and statutory requirements.

---

[3] *Tailors of Aberdeen v Coutts* (1840) 1 Rob. 296; and ss.1, 2 and 3 of the Title Conditions (Scotland) Act 2003.

[4] *Montgomerie v Carrick*, 1849 S.C. 274.

[5] *Advice Centre for Mortgages v McNicoll*, 2006 CSOH 58.

[6] *Huber v Ross*, 1912 S.C. 898.

[7] *Baillie v Fraser* (1853) 15 D. 748.

- The landlord's obligations to compensate the tenant for improvements carried out by the tenant.[8]
- Service charge cap, unless stated to apply to only a specific tenant.
- Rent deposit obligations, provided these are contained in the lease, and the definitions and terms are sufficient. However, if the rent deposit is dealt with by way of a separate document, then it is necessary to make sure that its terms make it clear that a successor landlord is to benefit from it.
- Guarantees. If (a) the guarantee is contained in the lease itself, (b) the lease is signed by the guarantor, and (c) the wording of the guarantee makes it clear that the guarantee is available for the benefit of successor landlord, then the guarantee runs with the lease.[9] However, if the guarantee is contained in a separate document, then the definitions should include successor landlords, and the terms of the guarantee should make it clear that assignation of the right to the landlord's successors is intended.

Grey areas

22–04
- **Break options**. If these are set out in the lease document itself, and if the definitions of landlord and tenant clearly include successors of either party, then there is a wide school of thought that says that these will bind successor landlords. It is of course essential that the break option is not just contained in the missives or a back letter; it needs to be in the lease, or in a document that varies the lease. Back letters do *not* vary leases.
- **Use clauses**. The right granted to a particular tenant to change the use, may or may not bind successors; it all depends on the wording.[10]
- **Options to renew or extend**. If the option is to *extend* the lease for a specified period, at a rent set out in the lease, or at a rent ascertainable from a specified mechanism set out in the lease, then it may bind a singular successor of the original landlord, but only if possession is taken under the new lease. Case law suggests the position may be slightly different if the option is to *renew* the lease. If the lease is a 1449 Leases Act possession real right lease, and if the new landlord has completed his purchase before the option to renew is exercised, then it is unlikely that the option will be binding on the new landlord. This is because, if the option to renew comes at termination of the original lease, then at the point of transfer the successor landlord is only bound by the term of the lease going on at that time.

There are old authorities which say that options to renew are binding on successor landlords.[11] More recently, s.22A of the Land Registration (Scotland) Act 1979 gives the tenant under a long lease which includes a right to renew, a

---

[8] *Purvis v Traill's Trs*, 1914 S.L.T. 455.
[9] *Waydale Ltd v DHL Holdings (UK) Ltd (No 1)*, 1996 S.C.L.R. 391; and *Waydale Ltd v DHL Holdings (UK) Ltd (No 3)*, 2001 S.L.T. 224.
[10] *B.P. Oil Ltd v Caledonian Heritable Estates Ltd*, 1990 S.L.T. 114.
[11] *Wright v Hopetoun* (1763) Mor 10461; and *Scott v Straiton* (1772) 3 Pat. 666.

right to apply to the Sheriff for renewal if the landlord does not honour the obligation to renew as set out in the lease.

Note that an option to renew a lease is different to an option to purchase; see para.22–08 below.

- Exclusivity clauses; see para.22–06 below.

Rights and obligations that do not continue

The following rights and obligations are personal, and do not transmit to **22–05** successors:

- Provisions that are clearly stated in the lease to be personal to one or other of the parties, provided the drafting is clear on this.
- Option to take a lease of another property.
- Rent reduction provisions given in relation to services rendered by a tenant to a landlord, or to cover circumstances personal to an individual tenant.
- A clause allowing a tenant to retain rent in satisfaction of a private debt owed by the landlord to the tenant, for a matter not connected with the lease.
- A right for a tenant to use another part of the landlord's property which the landlord no longer owns.
- Buy back rights.
- Pre-emption rights.

Exclusivity clauses

In the case of *Davie v Stark*[12] a landlord owned two adjacent shops. He used **22–06** one himself, and leased the adjacent one to a draper. In the lease, he undertook not to sell or allow to be sold in his other shop items commonly found in a draper's store. He subsequently sold both properties to one person, who started to use the unlet shop as a general store, and he displayed items that were commonly sold in a drapery. The tenant withheld rent and moved out, and the landlord then sued him for rent. The court held that the use restriction of the landlord's adjoining shop was *inter naturalia* of the type of lease concerned, and therefore given that the landlord was in material breach of the lease, the tenant was entitled to remove, and to receive damages for loss of profit.

The outcome might not have been favourable to the tenant if the original landlord had sold the two shops to different people, unless he imposed the use restriction as a title condition on the vacant shop, in favour of the leased shop.

In *Optical Express (Gyle) Limited v Marks & Spencer plc*[13] a back letter was given by the original landlord to the tenant saying that his unit would be the only opticians in the shopping centre. The shopping centre was subsequently sold, and although the purchaser knew about the back letter, he subsequently let another unit to one of the tenant's competitors. The back letter did not require the original landlord to obtain a back letter in the same terms from any

---

[12] *Davie v Stark* (1876) 3 R. 1114.
[13] *Optical Express (Gyle) Limited v Marks & Spencer plc*, 2000 S.L.T. 644.

purchaser. Optical Express sought an interdict and cancellation of the lease to the competitor.

The court held that, as the exclusivity was in a back letter granted at the same time as the lease, there was an implied intention that the back letter was not to form part of the lease itself. The court also decided that the exclusivity clause, as drafted, did not bind a singular successor of the landlord as a back letter is, by its very nature, collateral to the lease. It also held that, even if the exclusivity clause had been in the lease, it would be a private agreement between the original landlord and original tenant setting out how the landlord would deal with his other property.

However, there is a conflicting decision in the later case of *Warren James (Jewellers) Limited v OvergateJP Ltd*[14] where an exclusivity clause contained in the lease itself was held to bind successor landlords. In that case there was no argument about the point as such, and the court may not have followed the correct test for identifying real conditions. The case was concerned with which rules of interpretation should apply—the normal contract rules, or the real conditions rules. There was an implicit acceptance by the parties involved in the case that an exclusivity clause was a real condition, and therefore transmitted to singular successors. But the decision was reached without the benefit of argument, as the point was conceded. It is therefore safer to rely on the *Optical Express* position at this stage, i.e. that exclusivity clauses do not bind singular successors of the original landlord to the lease.

Does the original landlord remain bound by the terms of the obligation?

22–07   The authorities indicate that the answer to this is probably "yes". The lease is, after all, a contract between the original landlord and tenant, with each obliging themselves to perform obligations. On a sale by the landlord, the original landlord impliedly assigns the right to receive rent, and he substitutes the purchaser in his place as owner to perform the various common law obligations. But personal obligations remain personal to the original landlord. However, as the original landlord will not be in a position to actually perform his obligations, he can only compensate the tenant for his breach by paying damages. The landlord may no longer be around, or solvent.

An argument against this is based on the effect of s.2 of The Registration of Leases (Scotland) Act 1857 as amended by The Land Tenure Reform (Scotland) Act 1974 and the Land Registration (Scotland) Act 1979. These Acts provide for the registration/recording of a long lease (over 20 years in duration) as a means of obtaining a real right. The Acts state clearly that, on registration or recording of the Lease, it will bind singular successors. However, this has to be subject to the common law rule about *inter naturalia* exception, which has been around since *Bissett v Magistrates of Aberdeen*[15] in 1898. Under the 1979 Act then, if the lease in question appears on the Land Certificate and therefore its conditions are included, the singular successor should be bound by its terms whatever they are. The argument about what is a competent title condition arises again. The difficulty is that the matter is undecided by the senior courts. Of course, the question of enforceability has still got to be dealt with: see para.22–02 above.

---

[14] *Warren James (Jewellers) Ltd v Overgate JP Ltd* [2010] CSOH 57.
[15] *Bissett v Magistrates of Aberdeen* (1898) 1 F. 87.

Tenant's option to purchase

There may be several reasons why a landlord and tenant would enter into a **22–08** lease with an option in favour of the tenant to buy the property after a certain period of time. One example is where the landlord wants to preserve his right to claim industrial buildings allowances when disposing of industrial (including storage or distribution) premises. These have a 25-year maturity period after the date of qualifying expenditure, and these run with ownership of the property. It has been common practice, for at least the past 30 years, for long leases to be granted of industrial premises so as to preserve the landlord's right to claim, and for many of these leases to include the tenant's right to purchase the landlord's interest once the allowance period has expired. The lease would be granted in exchange for a premium (equivalent to the sale price), and there would usually be a nominal rent of £1 per annum if asked only.

The general view is that an option to purchase that is specifically set out in a lease does not bind singular successors of the original landlord who granted the right to the tenant.[16] It is thought that even if the option does state that successor landlords will be bound, they cannot as a matter of law be so bound, as an option to purchase is not generally *inter naturalia* of a lease. In the *Advice Centre* case, Lord Drummond Young said that such an option is not *inter naturalia* of a lease, unless there is law and practice to the contrary. The question of an option to purchase that is contained in an industrial buildings allowance scenario, has not been tested in the courts.

The "off side goal rule", where a purchaser of property who is aware of a prior arrangement between the seller and the tenant, and of the seller's obligation to take the purchaser bound by that arrangement, puts the buyer in bad faith, if at a given point in the future he denies the existence of the arrangement. This point was taken in the *Advice Centre for Mortgages* case,[17] where an option to purchase was mentioned in the missives of let which had, in fact, not been concluded, and was not mentioned in the lease. A formal lease was never signed, and entry was taken on the basis of the unconcluded missive. The court considered whether the option in the unconcluded missives followed by possession could trigger the rule, as the purchaser was aware of it, and decided this was *not* available, as there was no right in favour of the tenant to prevent the original landlord from selling the property. The general principle which is thought to apply to application of the off-side goals rule is that the pre-existing personal right in respect of which the subsequent grant in breach of that right must, of itself, be a personal right which is capable of being made a real right.[18]

Using a standard security to protect purchase options and non-continuing obligations

The tenant should consider obtaining a standard security over the landlord's **22–09** interest, to protect his option to purchase and other non-continuing obligations. However, this only allows the tenant to sell the property if the landlord is in

---

[16] *Bissett v Magistrates of Aberdeen* (1898) 1 F. 87; and *Advice Centre for Mortgages v McNicol*, 2006 CSOH 58.

[17] *Advice Centre for Mortgages v McNicoll*, 2006 CSOH 58.

[18] *Advice Centre for Mortgages v McNicoll*, 2006 CSOH 58.

breach, and the tenant could only obtain title if having tried to sell the property, no purchaser is found, and the tenant seeks, and is granted, a decree of foreclosure.

It is recommended that in order to give the tenant as much protection as reasonably possible in respect of a purchase option (or other non-continuing obligation):

- The option or obligation should be in the lease itself, as opposed to being in a back letter or simply in the missives.
- The lease should state that the option or obligation is binding on the landlord, and on all successors of the landlord.
- The lease should require the landlord to take its successors bound by the terms of the option or obligation.
- The lease should require the landlord to have its successors enter into an agreement with the tenant whereby the successors bind themselves to comply with the option or obligation.
- A standard security should be granted in favour of the tenant over the landlord's heritable interest.

However, a standard security will not protect the tenant if any prior charge-holder enforces their charge. Also, the grant of the standard security could possibly be challenged as an unfair preference by the landlord's creditors.

The standard security gives the right to the grantee to sell the property but does not give him the right to acquire title, unless the property is exposed for sale at auction and it is not sold, in which case the grantee can ask the court for a degree of foreclosure. If granted, this will transfer the title to the security holder

The following wording is suggested for insertion into the lease in order to address the problem of successors being bound:

> "The Option and the terms and conditions of [*specify clause* numbers] shall be binding upon the said [*original landlord*] and on all successors and disponees in respect of the Landlord's interest in the Premises. In addition to and without prejudice to the foregoing, the Landlord shall be obliged, prior to the completion of any sale, lease or other disposal of the Landlord's interest, to procure that its successors or disponees (i) enter into an agreement with the Tenant [and the Guarantor], in such form as the Tenant, acting reasonably, shall require in terms of which such successors or disponees bind and oblige themselves (and their successors and disponees) to comply with the terms of [*specify clause numbers*], and to grant to the Tenant a standard security to secure against the Landlord's interest the obligations contained in [*specify clause numbers*]."

This should achieve a nuisance value, so that when the landlord comes to sell and deal with any question that the landlord or his successors are bound by the relevant provisions. The selling landlord will have to obtain a discharge of the security to give a good title.

One could also consider obtaining some additional comfort, by attempting to obtain a defective title indemnity policy to protect against non enforceability of the option or other obligation.

CHAPTER 23

STAMP DUTY LAND TAX, LAND AND BUILDINGS TRANSACTION TAX, AND VALUE ADDED TAX

Introduction

In this Chapter, we examine the main provisions of stamp duty land tax and **23–01** value added tax on transactions involving commercial leases. Stamp duty land tax ("SDLT") and value added tax ("VAT") law is basically the same in Scotland and England although the application of SDLT can be difficult in Scotland, due to the differences in the underlying property laws. We also consider very briefly the proposed land and buldings transaction tax, which is to come into effect in April 2015, to replace stamp duty land tax in Scotland.

The law does change frequently in respect of these taxes, and this Chapter states the position as at April 30, 2013.

A—STAMP DUTY LAND TAX

Background

SDLT on transactions was introduced on December 1, 2003, and it replaced **23–02** stamp duty on documents. Stamp duty on leases was really a voluntary tax—if the tenant wanted to record or register his lease in the Register of Sasines or the Land Register of Scotland, he had to pay stamp duty on the lease document; if the landlord wanted to register the lease for execution in the Books of Council and Session so he could carry out summary diligence (fast track enforcement of financial obligations), he had to have had the lease stamped.

SDLT is a mandatory tax on transactions (as opposed to being a tax on documents). The responsibility is on the tenant to complete and submit an SDLT return and to pay any SDLT due. The tax is payable by the tenant on the grant of a lease, or by the sub-tenant on the grant of a sub-lease, and occasionally by the grantee on an assignation, surrender or renunciation of a lease.

The main provisions governing lease transactions are set out in ss.77 and 77A and Schs 5 and 17A of the Finance Act 2003 (as amended), although there are other relevant provisions scattered throughout the legislation and contained in various guidance notes and technical guides.

The effective date

(a) Leases
The effective date is the date of substantial performance which, for SDLT **23–03** purposes, can arise in one of a number of ways such as the last date of execution of the lease or the date entry is given to the premises or rent is paid or, in some cases, when missives are concluded.

When completing the SDLT return, one must be careful not to confuse the effective date with the start date of the lease.

(b) Other types of transaction

23–04 The effective date for other types of transactions such as variations and extensions of leases is the date the minute of variation/extension is signed, even where the variation/extension is a future event.

Notification

23–05 The obligation is on the tenant of a lease (or the sub-tenant of a sub-lease, or the grantee of an assignation or renunciation) to complete and submit an SDLT Return, where one is required, and to pay any SDLT that is due, within 30 days after the "effective date". This is called "notification".

In Scotland, there must always be a rent payable under a lease, even if the amount of rent is only £1 per annum if demanded. In England, it is not necessary to have rent payable in the form of money; leases have traditionally been able to be granted for a rent of one peppercorn.

Consideration payable in leases and other types of transactions

(a) Rent payable in leases

23–06 SDLT is payable on the net present value ("NPV") of the rent. The statutory formula for calculating the NPV is found in Para.3 of Sch.5 of the Finance Act 2003. The NPV is calculated by adding up the rent payable and discounting the rent at three per cent per annum over the duration of the lease. This is done by using the highest rent payable in any consecutive 12-month period within the first five years to calculate the rent for the remainder of the term, no matter what the amount of rent is for the remainder of the term. Any initial rent-free period will therefore be taken into account. In calculating the NPV, any rent reviews after the first five years may be ignored. Any rent reviews (other than RPI increases which can be ignored for the purposes of calculation of the NPV) within the first five years must be estimated using a reasonable estimate. In a lease of non-residential property, the first £150,000 is charged at nil, and then the remainder is charged at one per cent.

Where a VAT option to tax has been made before the effective date of the lease, SDLT is payable on the VAT-inclusive rent. Any option to tax made after the effective date of a transaction, however, has no effect on the amount of consideration chargeable for SDLT purposes.

There is a calculator facility on the SDLT section of the HMRC website (*http://www.hmrc.gov.uk/* [accessed April 2, 2013]) that will calculate the amount, if any, of SDLT payable. It should be noted that the HMRC's lease calculator will not take account of any decreases in rent and therefore it may be worth carrying out a manual calculation of tax where the lease provides for known rent decreases after the first five years (as sometimes happens in utility/windfarm leases).

(b) Premia—All transactions

23–07 SDLT will be chargeable on the premium at the same rates as SDLT is charged on the price in a purchase transaction, with the same bandings, so that, in a lease of non-residential property,:

- a premium of less than £150,000 is not chargeable to SDLT;
- if the premium is £150,000 up to £249,999 then SDLT is payable on the whole premium at one per cent;
- if the premium is £250,000 up to £499,999 then SDLT is payable on the whole premium at three per cent; and
- if the premium is £500,000 or more, then SDLT is payable on the whole premium at four per cent.

In certain cases involving non-residential properties, where a premium is paid for the grant of a lease and the annual rent is £1,000 or more then the nil-rate band threshold is withdrawn and SDLT is charged at one per cent on the premium ("the £1,000 rule"). For residential properties, regardless of what rent is paid, the normal thresholds will have effect to any premium paid.

(c) Effect of VAT on SDLT—all transactions
If the granter is charging VAT on the rent or on the premium, then SDLT is **23–08** payable on the sum of the total payment including the VAT; therefore tax is being paid on tax.

If no VAT was chargeable on the rent at the effective date, then SDLT is calculated only on the amount of rent. If the landlord subsequently opts to charge VAT in respect of its property interest and thus makes the rent chargeable to VAT, then this is ignored for the purpose of SDLT.

(d) Payment by tenant of landlord's legal costs
If the tenant pays the landlord's legal costs for granting the lease, this is not **23–09** chargeable to SDLT. However, payment of costs on the assignation or renunciation of a lease does count as chargeable consideration for the transaction.

(e) Works
The carrying out of works might be a consideration for the grant of a lease, and **23–10** this should be borne in mind when considering whether fitting out works carried out by the tenant or the landlord, and paid for by the tenant, are consideration.

(f) Other lease obligations not chargeable to SDLT
Schedule 17A, Para.10 of the Finance Act 2003 sets out the various obligations **23–11** contained in leases that do not amount to chargeable consideration for SDLT purposes, including the following:

- any undertaking by the tenant to repair, maintain or insure the leased premises;
- any undertaking by the tenant to pay any amount in respect of services, repairs, maintenance or insurance or the landlord's costs of management;
- any other obligation undertaken by the tenant that is not such as to affect the rent that a tenant would be willing to pay in the open market;
- any guarantee of the payment of rent, or the performance of any other obligation of the tenant under the lease;
- any penal rent, or increased rent in the nature of a penal rent, payable in respect of the breach of any obligation of the tenant under the lease;

- in England, liability of a tenant for certain statutory costs (in terms of the Leasehold Reform Act 1967 or Leasehold Reform, Housing and Urban Development Act 1993); and
- any obligation to transfer payments under the single payment scheme on termination of a lease.

The assumption or release of any of the obligations mentioned above also does not amount to chargeable consideration, nor does the payment made in discharge of such obligation.

Where a new lease is granted in consideration for the surrender of an existing lease between the same parties, the surrender does not amount to chargeable consideration for the grant of the new lease,[1] nor does the grant of the new lease amount to chargeable consideration for the surrender of the old lease.

(g) Dilapidations

23–12   Payment by the tenant for dilapidations is not treated as consideration for SDLT purposes.

(h) Reverse premia

23–13   A reverse premium is where the granter of a deed pays money to the grantee. The following are examples of a reverse premium:

- a landlord pays money to a tenant in order to enter into a lease;
- an existing tenant pays money to an incoming tenant to take an assignation of a lease; or
- where the tenant pays money to the landlord to renounce a lease.

Reverse premia are not chargeable to SDLT.

However, if the grantee pays money to the granter, this is a premium and is (potentially, subject to the relevant thresholds) chargeable to SDLT.

(i) Market value consideration where "purchaser" (tenant/grantee) is a connected company

23–14   The provisions of s.53 of the Finance Act 2003 impose a deemed market value consideration on transactions in certain cases where the tenant/grantee is a company, and either (1) the landlord/granter is connected to the tenant/grantee or (2) some or all of the consideration for the transaction consists of the issue or transfer of shares in a company with which the landlord/granter is connected. There are exceptions from the deemed market value rule in s.54 of the Finance Act 2003.

Rent increases

(a) RPI reviews

23–15   Where the lease provides that the rent is to be reviewed based on RPI, the effect of these reviews can be ignored altogether when calculating the NPV of a lease.

---

[1] Finance Act 2003 sch.17A, para.16.

(b) Stepped rents

If the lease provides for rent increases by known amounts, these are used in the **23–16** initial calculation. The highest known rent in the first five-year period is used as the rent for every year after year five.

Any known increases after year five are therefore ignored unless these fall foul of the abnormal rent increase provisions (see below for further information on this).

(c) Rent reviews

(i) Rent increases at review within the first five years of the lease:

- If there is a rent review that affects the rent payable before the end of **23–17** the fifth year of the lease, it has to be taken into account in calculating the SDLT payable by the tenant on the grant of the lease.
- If a rent review (other than RPI reviews) occurs within the first five years of the lease, then, when calculating the SDLT at the outset, a reasonable estimate must be made of the rent following review. This is then used for the purposes of the NPV calculation.
- At the end of the fifth year, or if earlier when the outcome of the rent review is known, the tenant must re-calculate the NPV calculation in order to substitute the revised rent following the rent review.
- If at the end of the fifth year the rent is still uncertain, perhaps because the rent review is still not complete at this date, the revised NPV should be based on the revised estimates of rent for periods for which accounts have not been finalised. The amount of the highest rent should also be revised as necessary.

(ii) Lease for less than five years with rent reviews:

if the lease is shorter than five years and includes provision for rent review **23–18** (again, other than RPI reviews), then SDLT is initially payable within 30 days of the outset, based on a reasonable estimate of the rent for the term. An additional return has to be made within 30 days of the earlier of the dates the reviewed rent is determined and at the end of the term when any additional tax will be payable or any refund claimed.

If the reviewed rent is not known at the end of the term of the lease then a further return requires to be made within 30 days of the end of the term based on a reasonable estimate of the rent. In this case, a third return should then be made within 30 days of when the rent is finally determined.

(d) Turnover rents and contingent rents

If the rent is wholly or partly based on the tenant's turnover at the premises or **23–19** is in some other way contingent, then the calculation of the NPV and submission of returns can be complicated from the tenant's point of view.

(i) Turnover/contingent rent leases for a term of five years or more:

SDLT is payable at the outset on a reasonable estimate of the rent for the first **23–20** five years. A reasonable estimate must be given of the turnover rent at the start of the lease.

If the lease provides for a rent which is still uncertain after five years, then an additional return has to be made at the end of the five-year period when any additional tax will be payable or any refund claimed. This return will be based on the NPV of the actual rent paid in the first five years, and after that the highest actual rent paid in the first five years for any consecutive period of 12 months will be used.

(ii) Turnover/contingent rent leases for a term of less than five years:

23–21 if the lease is for a term of less than five years then SDLT is initially payable within 30 days of the start on a reasonable estimate of the rent for the term. An additional return has to be made within 30 days of the end of the term when any additional tax will be payable or any refund claimed.

If the turnover rent is not known at the end of the term of the lease then a further return requires to be made based on a reasonable estimate of the rent. In this case, a third return should then be made within 30 days of when the rent is finally determined.

The abnormal rent increase provisions (until abolished) apply to SDLT turn-over/contingent rent leases.

What to notify

Grant of a lease

23–22 A lease for a term of seven years or more does not require to be notified where any chargeable consideration, apart from rent, is less than £40,000 and where the "Relevant Rent" is less than £1,000.

"Relevant Rent" is defined[2] as either (1) the "Annual Rent" in relation to the transaction in question or (2) if the transaction is one of a number of linked transactions for which the chargeable consideration consists of or includes rent, then the total of annual rents in relation to all of those transactions.

"Annual Rent" is defined[3] as either:

1. the average annual rent over term of lease or, if there are:

    (a) different amounts payable for different parts of the term; and
    (b) those amounts are ascertainable at the effective date of the transaction,

    then it is the average annual rent over the period for which the highest ascertainable rent is payable; or
2. for partnership transactions, the relevant chargeable proportion of annual rent calculated in accordance with the partnership rules.[4]

The grant of a lease of less than seven years requires to be notified where SDLT is payable, including where it would be payable if a relief were not being claimed.

---

[2] Finance Act 2003 Sch.5, para.9A(6).
[3] Finance Act 2003 Sch.5, para.9A(7).
[4] In terms of Finance Act 2003 Sch.15, paras 11 or 19.

Other types of lease transactions, e.g. assignations and renunciations.
Transactions such as assignations or surrenders of leases involving leases for a **23–23**
term of seven years or less no longer have to be notified unless SDLT is payable
or would be payable if a relief were not being claimed.

Other such transactions involving leases for a term of seven years or more
no longer have to be notified where any chargeable consideration other than
rent is less than £40,000.

When to notify

The "effective date" for a lease may arise sooner than might be anticipated. **23–24**
This should be borne in mind when dealing with cross-border transactions as it
may be that a notification point arises earlier in Scotland than it might in
England due to the different laws relating to constitution of leases in the two
countries.

"Substantial performance" for leases has varying meanings, including the
date of last execution of the lease, the date of entry, the date rent is paid and, in
some cases, the date of conclusion of the missives. It is possible in Scotland for
missives of lease to actually constitute the lease itself, so that no formal lease
document is granted after the missives have been entered into. This is all
explained in more detail in the following brief guide to some notification
points that may arise in practice.

1. For leases in Scotland, the legislation differentiates between:

- missives of let themselves constituting the lease, i.e. they are not to be **23–25**
  followed by a formal lease. These missives of let are treated as the
  grant of a lease; and
- missives of let (or agreement for lease) to be followed by a lease.
  These missives of let are treated as a contract.[5] This means that
  substantial performance of the missives of let (or agreement for lease)
  will be treated as the grant of a notional lease with the effective date of
  that notional lease being the date of substantial performance. The
  subsequent grant of the lease is then covered in that the notional lease
  is treated as if it was surrendered at that time.[6]

2. Early access and missives of let/lease
It is often the case that entry is taken early to the property, either because the **23–26**
clients have agreed this informally or in terms of the missives, to enable the
tenant to carry out fitting out works. Sometimes the solicitors are not aware
this has happened.

(a) missives of let without provision for formal lease and entry has been taken **23–27**
or rent has been paid:
when early access occurs the SDLT position will depend on whether or not the
missives have been concluded. If there are agreed terms but no concluded

---

[5] Finance Act 2003 s.44.
[6] Finance Act 2003 Sch.17A, para.19(4).

missives then, on taking entry, the tenant has, at best, an informal lease for up to a year.

For tax purposes, if the lease term is uncertain (though it is difficult to see how that could be the case in Scots law other than perhaps a lease for a fixed term then month-to-month thereafter) then there is an implied term of a year.[7]

A return would only therefore be required where the rent paid by the tenant results in an NPV of an amount on which tax is due (or would be but for a relief), or where there is a premium exceeding the nil-rate band, or where the nil-rate band is disapplied and the premium is taxed (see above).

At the point the missives are entered into, notification will be required in the usual way. Depending on whether the original verbal lease was notifiable and tax was paid, and whether the start date of the lease is backdated to cover the original period of occupation (for more see below), these missives may be linked to the original verbal lease.

23–28 *(b) missives of let (or agreement for lease) constituting a lease with provision for a formal lease, and entry has been taken or rent paid:*
again, when early access occurs, the SDLT position will depend on whether the missives have been concluded. If there are agreed terms but no concluded missives then, on taking entry, the tenant has at best an informal lease for up to a year. A return would only therefore be required where the rent paid by the tenant results in an NPV of an amount on which tax is due (or would be but for a relief), or where there is a premium exceeding the nil-rate band, or where the nil-rate band is disapplied and the premium is taxed (see above).

When missives are concluded, notification will be required in the usual way. Depending on whether the original verbal lease was notifiable and tax was paid, these missives may be linked to the original verbal lease.

If, as usually happens, the formal lease is backdated to the date on which entry was taken, the grant of the lease is not notifiable as, when the formal lease is granted, there is a deemed surrender of the notional lease (the missives). Overlap relief will be available and will reduce the chargeable consideration for the formal lease–if this overlaps exactly then the chargeable consideration will be reduced to zero–and therefore the formal lease will not be notifiable.

3. Missives of let/lease—where no early access is taken or rent paid

23–29
- Missives of let constituting a lease without provision for a formal lease, where entry has not yet been taken and rent has not yet been paid, are notifiable and tax is to be paid, subject to the relevant thresholds, within 30 days of the date of conclusion of the missives.

    If, at a later date, a formal lease is signed (even though this is not intended at the outset), overlap relief would apply. The effect of this is that a credit is given for the tax paid on the missives against the tax due on the formal lease. Assuming the two are exactly the same, there is no tax payable under the formal lease, so this is in effect a lease for no consideration and is therefore not notifiable.

---

[7] Finance Act 2003 Sch.17A, para.4(1)(a).

- Missives of let constituting a lease with provision for a formal lease, and no entry/rent paid, are notifiable at the earlier of (1) substantial performance of the missives, i.e. entry being taken or rent being paid and (2) the lease being signed.[8] At this point, the missives of let are treated as a notional lease. Later, when the formal lease is signed, the notional lease is treated as being surrendered and the second, formal lease is treated as "overlapping" with the first. The lease is therefore notifiable and tax requires to be paid, subject to the relevant thresholds, within 30 days of the date of last execution of the lease.

4. Lease only and no entry/rent paid

Where a lease is entered into without missives (and before access is taken or **23–30** rent is paid) then notification must take place within 30 days of the last date of execution of the lease.

5. Lease only and early entry/rent paid

When early access occurs the SDLT position will depend on whether the lease **23–31** is executed or not. If there are agreed terms but no executed lease then, on taking entry, the tenant probably has, at best, an informal lease for up to a year at the point of entry.

A return would therefore only be required where the rent paid by the tenant results in an NPV of an amount on which that tax is due (or would be but for a relief)–or where there is a premium exceeding the nil-rate band or where the nil-rate band is disapplied and the premium is taxed (see above).

At the point the lease is executed notification of the lease will be required in the usual way. Depending on whether the original verbal lease was notifiable and tax was paid, and whether the start date of the lease is backdated to cover the original period of occupation, this lease may be linked to the original verbal lease.

Registration of lease

If a lease transaction is notifiable, and the landlord wants to register the lease **23–32** in the Books of Council and Session, or the tenant wants to register it in the Land Register of Scotland, then an SDLT 5 Certificate is needed. This is issued by HMRC following submission of the appropriate SDLT return.

There may be cases where there is consideration in the lease which is not a chargeable consideration for SDLT purposes (for example in some partnership transactions)–in other words, on the face of the document, an SDLT 5 Certificate would appear to be required for registration purposes but, in fact, is not. In this case, a letter should be provided to the Registers, on behalf of the tenant, confirming that the consideration is not a chargeable consideration, in order to allow them to accept the lease for registration.

Assignations

Assignations of leases for zero consideration do not need to be notified to **23–33** HMRC even where the original lease was notifiable, unless the assignation is

---

[8] Finance Act 2003 Sch.17A, para.19(2).

between connected companies, where market value rules will apply. If therefore there is a market value to the assignation (i.e. the rent is less than market
value) then this will need to be notified even where the actual consideration is
zero.

Otherwise, assignations of leases for a term of seven years or less no longer
have to be notified unless SDLT is payable, or would be payable but for a
relief. Assignations of leases for a term of seven years or more no longer have
to be notified where any chargeable consideration other than rent is less than
£40,000. This has inadvertently made assignations for no consideration
notifiable.

There is no SDLT charged on the rent in an existing lease that is assigned,
unless there was no SDLT payable at the initial grant of the lease because there
was a relief such as group relief or charities relief. In this case, the assignation
is treated as the grant of a new lease for the remaining term of the lease, and
the incoming tenant has to make an SDLT return and pay any tax chargeable.
It is therefore important that the assignee makes enquiries as to the status of the
original lease to ascertain whether SDLT was paid and if so how much, or
whether there was any relief granted.

Extensions of leases

23–34   There is an anti-avoidance provision that "linked leases" will be chargeable to
SDLT. The HMRC guidance is that leases are not deemed to be linked just
because the tenant decides to take another lease at the end of the first lease, nor
if the tenant or landlord exercises an option to renew the lease.

It seems that in order for leases to be linked there requires to have been an
intention at the start to enter into a lease for the longer period, which is broken
down into shorter leases. If leases are linked, then the result is that these leases
are treated as a single lease covering the whole of the period of all of the leases
taken together. A lease that was not notifiable because the rent was below the
threshold could become retrospectively notifiable by being linked to a later
lease even if that later lease itself is not over the threshold. Interest will run on
any sums of tax payable or on any additional sums from 30 days after the date
of the grant of the initial lease.

Where a lease is a linked lease, only one nil-rate band is applied across the
entire length of the linked leases. A re-calculation, taking into account the original NPV and tax paid, is therefore required in order to calculate the correct
amount of tax due for the linked leases.

Tacit relocation

23–35   Leases that were granted on or after December 1, 2003 and which continue by
tacit relocation[9] are subject to SDLT. The lease is treated as a "growing"
lease.[10]

The lease is first of all treated as being for its original term, say five years.
When it is extended by tacit relocation it is treated as being for a total period of
one more year than the original term, so it becomes a six-year lease. Where
additional tax is payable on a "growing" lease the payment date for interest

---

[9]   Tacit relocation is dealt with in Ch.16.
[10]   Finance Act 2003 Sch.17A, para.3.

purposes will be determined by the date it grew and not the date of original grant. Tenants should be aware that leases which originally were not notifiable may become notifiable if they "grow" sufficiently.

These rules only apply to leases that were granted on or after December 1, 2003. There is no SDLT chargeable if a lease that was granted before December 1, 2003 continues by tacit relocation.

Options

Options to extend or to terminate a lease early are ignored for the purpose of **23–36** calculating SDLT; it is assumed that the options will not be exercised. However if the option to extend the term is exercised, this may create an additional charge to SDLT at the time of exercise.

Variation of lease

A variation to extend the period of a lease is treated for SDLT purposes as **23–37** the grant of a new lease starting on the day following the original expiry date of the lease. The effective date is the date of signing of the variation, even though the new lease may not start until sometime in the future. Notification and payment of tax, subject to the relevant thresholds, must take place within 30 days of signing. The relevant threshold rates of tax and exemptions are those applying at the effective date, i.e. the date of signing of the Minute of Variation. In calculating the NPV of the period of extension (deemed new lease), the start date of the deemed new lease is used. For example if a lease terminates on November 27, 2014 and the parties agree to extend the term by 10 years and the variation deed is signed on April 15, 2013, the effective date is April 15, 2013, and the SDLT return and any tax must be submitted by May 14, 2013, but the SDLT is calculated on rents payable over the 10 years commencing November 28, 2014, using present-day SDLT rates.

Where instead of doing a deed of variation, the existing lease is renounced and a new lease is granted, then SDLT is payable on the NPV of the new lease, but the amount of rent is reduced during the overlap period by the rent already taken into account for SDLT purposes. If the original lease was granted before December 1, 2003 (i.e. under the stamp duty regime), then there is no overlap relief and no reduction of rent of the new lease.

A variation to reduce the term of the lease is an acquisition of an interest by the landlord and is notifiable by the landlord where notification is required.

Renunciations

A renunciation is an acquisition of an interest by the landlord and if money is **23–38** payable by the landlord then SDLT is payable by the landlord, subject to the relevant thresholds.

If the tenant pays the landlord for the renunciation, then this is not chargeable because it is a reverse premium.

Reliefs

1. Sale and lease-back
If a property is sold, and as part of the deal a lease is granted by the purchaser **23–39** in favour of the seller, then SDLT will be payable by the purchaser on the

purchase price, but the lease-back part of the transaction will not be charge-able. In order to obtain this concession, the consideration for the sale must have been payment of money or the assumption or discharge of a debt, and the sale must not be a sub-sale, and the parties must not be group companies.

The market value of the sale leg will depend upon whether there was a written agreement, at the time of the sale, for the lease-back leg to be entered into. If there was, then the market value of the sale leg should take this encum-brance into account (and value any rent obtainable from the leaseback leg). If there is no such agreement, then the market value of the sale leg should be the unencumbered value.

Sale and lease-back relief applies in circumstances where the sale is effected by the grant of a lease followed by an sub-lease back.

There is no particular requirement for a lease-back to be in consideration of only one sale, or for one sale to be in consideration of only one leaseback for the relief to apply. It is possible to have one sale with multiple leasebacks and also to have several sales with only one leaseback.

HMRC has also confirmed that the SDLT treatment on a sale and leaseback (which is effectively an exchange) remains unchanged following the Finance Act 2011 changes insofar as calculation of the market value element. Therefore, the market value of the "superior interest" (heritable interest) acquired will be its market value encumbered by the obligation to grant the lease back. Under the changes to the exchange rules introduced in 2011, the chargeable consid-eration is the greater of the market value of the (encumbered) interest acquired and the consideration given.

2. Group relief and charities relief

23–40 Reliefs, such as group relief and charities relief, may be available if the criteria in the Finance Act 2003 are fulfilled. Care should be exercised as reliefs are liable to withdrawal in certain circumstances.

Group relief is not available if a transaction is not for bona fide commercial reasons, and accordingly may not be available in, for example, inter-company leases. There is guidance on the HMRC website setting out the situations in which group relief will not be denied.

Disclosure requirements

23–41 There are SDLT disclosure requirements for transactions involving commercial property with a value of over £5,000,000. From November 1, 2012, the disclo-sure rules were extended to cover schemes intended to be used for non-residential and/or residential property of any value, subject to certain exceptions. This needs to be borne in mind when providing advice, as certain routine transactions would, if the value is high enough, require notification to HMRC.

B—LAND AND BUILDINGS TRANSACTION TAX ("LBTT")

23–42 The Land and Buildings Transaction Tax Bill was introduced in the Scottish Parliament on November 29, 2012 to introduce Land and Buildings Transaction Tax to replace Stamp Duty Land Tax in Scotland with effect from April 2015. A new body, "Revenue Scotland", has been created and will be responsible for collecting the tax.

The Land and Buildings Transaction Tax Bill does not contain (at this stage) detailed provision for non residential leases, but Section 55 imposes the obligation on the Scottish Ministers to provide for the tax on non-residential leases by order. However, the detailed provisions may appear in a later stage of the Bill. Like SDLT, LBTT will be a tax on transactions as opposed to a tax on documents.

C—VALUE ADDED TAX

Background

Sales and leases of land and buildings are exempt from Value Added Tax **23–43** ("VAT"), unless the owner or landlord has opted to charge VAT in respect of its interest in the property, or unless the sale takes place within three years after the earlier of (a) the issue of the certificate of practical completion for the building and (b) the date it is fully occupied. There is no VAT on the rents payable in leases that are granted of a "new building" unless the landlord opted to charge VAT in respect of the property.

The landlord opts to charge VAT by submitting the appropriate form to the VAT Office saying that he wants to charge VAT on his rents for a particular property. The VAT option can not be back-dated by more than 30 days. Property owners can submit a Real Estate Election, which covers all properties that they acquire in the future.

Opting to charge VAT has advantages and disadvantages for the owner or landlord. He can set-off or reclaim all VAT that he pays in respect of the property, and he gets a cash-flow benefit of having the use of VAT paid to him by the tenant from the date of payment until he has to account to HMRC for that VAT. The disadvantages are that some tenants are not able to claim back the VAT they pay because of the nature of their business, such as insurance companies, banks and building societies. Therefore if one of these parties who cannot claim back VAT is a tenant in a property where they have to pay VAT on the rent, they are effectively paying extra rent to occupy the premises and are being penalised. The other disadvantage is that the owner or landlord will be involved in more VAT paperwork.

If the lease is silent about VAT

If the landlord has opted to charge VAT before entering into the lease itself (or **23–44** before entering into an obligation to grant a lease), and if the lease is silent about VAT being payable on rent and other sums, the rent and other sums are deemed to be inclusive of VAT. The landlord then has to account to HMRC for the VAT element. It is therefore important that the lease should state that the tenant must pay all VAT that is or that may be payable on rents and all other sums payable from time-to-time under the lease.

If the landlord has not opted to charge VAT before entering into the lease, and then proceeds to opt to do so at some time after the lease starts, and if the lease is silent about VAT, then the landlord is not prejudiced. The act of opting to charge VAT is considered by HMRC to be a change in the law, and so the tenant then has to pay all VAT on the rents after the date of the landlord's option to tax.

Premium on new lease and on assignation

23–45 If a tenant pays a capital sum to a landlord for the lease to be granted to him, this is a premium. If the landlord opted to charge VAT, then he must charge VAT on the premium.

If a tenant who has opted to charge VAT in respect of his leasehold interest is assigning his lease, and charges a premium to the assignee, then he must charge VAT on the premium.

Reverse premium on new lease and on assignation

23–46 If a landlord pays money to a tenant to enter into the lease, there is no supply for VAT purposes. However, if the tenant does more for the landlord than just entering into the lease, such as carrying out works to improve or repair the building, then there would be a supply that is likely to be standard-rated.

Money paid by a tenant to a prospective assignee to accept an assignation of the lease, or to a prospective sub-tenant to accept the grant of a sub-lease (subject to the proviso in the preceding paragraph), is not chargeable to VAT.

Rent-free period

23–47 If a landlord allows a rent-free period to the tenant, and nothing is done or received in respect of the rent-free period, then as far as that period is concerned, no supply is being made, and no VAT is payable.

Renunciations

23–48 If a landlord pays a tenant to renounce (surrender) his interest then that is a supply by the tenant and is generally exempt, unless the tenant has opted to charge VAT in respect of his leasehold interest.

If the tenant pays the landlord to let him out of the lease then this is exempt, unless the landlord has opted to tax.

Dilapidations

23–49 If the tenant pays for dilapidations, this is seen as a payment of damages by the tenant for breach of his obligation to repair. Dilapidations payments are not chargeable to VAT.

Parking facilities

23–50 If facilities are provided for parking vehicles, the supply will normally be standard-rated, such as a lease or licence of a garage or of designated parking spaces, and so VAT must be charged. However, it will be exempt if land is let with no specific reference to parking vehicles, unless the property is a lock-up or other garage.

Chapter 24

PERFORMANCE DEPOSITS

Introduction

If the landlord is not satisfied with the financial strength of the tenant, the **24–01** parties may agree that a performance deposit should be put in place, so as to have a fund available for rent and for other sums payable by the tenant if the tenant defaults. Performance deposits are more common in leases of secondary or tertiary properties and are an easy, and from the landlord's viewpoint, attractive alternative to guarantees. The attraction lies in the fact that the deposit is "money on the table", whereas, with a guarantee, the landlord has to demand and enforce payment against the guarantor.

Many landlords prefer to retain control of the deposit without being bound by any formal deposit agreement, and they may undertake in the missives (which may expire before the lease does) to refund any unused part of the deposit at termination of the lease. Some tenants, particularly if they are receiving good advice, will insist that the parties enter into a deposit agreement stating the amount of deposit paid, what is to happen to the money if the tenant pays his rent, etc. on time, what is to happen to the interest earned on the money, and how and when the rent deposit and accrued interest are to be paid back to the tenant. The deposit agreement should also provide a procedure for the landlord to use money in the deposit if the tenant is in breach, and for the tenant to be required to make up the funds so as to become a full deposit again within so many days after demand.

The tenant will want the deposit to be released at the earliest possible time, and for interest earned on the deposit to be accounted for to the tenant on a regular basis, especially as he will have to pay tax on the interest.

If the deposit money is merely handed over to the landlord, then it becomes part of the landlord's own funds, with a personal obligation, enforceable against the landlord, to pay back the deposit when provided for in the agreement. However, if in the meantime the landlord becomes insolvent, then the tenant will only be treated as an ordinary creditor as against the landlord, and if the lease is disposed of by the receiver, administrator or liquidator, then the tenant will have no claim against the new landlord for return of the deposit.

Providing for the deposit

The missives or agreement for lease will provide for payment by the tenant to **24–02** the landlord of a sum of money to be held as a deposit, which can be drawn against if the tenant fails to pay rent or other sums due under the lease. If there is no provision for the deposit to be placed in a separate account, the deposit will merely become part of the landlord's own funds, and the deposit will remain a purely contractual matter between the original tenant and the original landlord. The Property Standardisation Group has a style deposit agreement available on its website: *http://www.psglegal.co.uk* [accessed April 2013], which contains full provisions regarding what should happen to a deposit and various protections for the tenant. Most tenants will require some sort of deposit agreement to be entered into with the landlord so as to give certain protections to the tenant, and the draft agreement should be annexed to the missives. There should also be provision for this to be signed and registered, and a copy given to the tenant contemporaneously with the lease itself.

Amount of the deposit

24–03 Many landlords will require a lump sum that may be equivalent to rent for a specific period. This may be to cover the landlord while he is enforcing the lease against the tenant, or the landlord may see the deposit as covering him for the time he thinks it will take to irritate the lease and re-let the premises. If the intention is that the deposit should equate to the amount of rent for a period of time, the landlord should consider whether the amount of the deposit is to be increased from time to time to reflect increases agreed or determined at rent review, and if this is indeed required, then it needs to be provided for in the deposit agreement. By the time that the first rent review occurs, the missives are likely to have terminated.

If the landlord has waived VAT exemption in respect of the property, and is thus charging VAT on the rents, the deposit should be for the amount of rental equivalent required, plus a sum equivalent to VAT on that amount. The purpose of the deposit is that there be money available for the landlord to use if the tenant fails to pay, and if VAT is payable on rent and other sums, then the landlord should be able to take the required amount plus VAT. The actual payment of the deposit by the tenant to the landlord does not itself attract VAT, as there is no service being given by the landlord in return for the payment.

Duration of the deposit

24–04 The parties should consider whether the deposit is to remain in place for the whole term of the lease, or whether it is to be in place for a specific period of time or until the tenant has proven that he is financially sound, for example by producing three years' accounts showing a pre-tax profit and/or net asset value to a minimum specified amount.

Holding the deposit

24–05 The missives and the deposit agreement itself should both provide for the tenant to have to pay the deposit to the landlord at the date of commencement of the lease. The deposit agreement should impose on the landlord the obligation to lodge the deposit into a separate account, which should be in the landlord's name. If the account were in joint names of the landlord and the tenant, then the tenant would, depending on how the account is set up, probably be entitled to draw on the account, which is of course not what is intended. The agreement may require the landlord to lodge the money in the highest interest account available from one of the clearing banks, or there may be some other standard imposed.

The agreement should state that so far as not used by the landlord, the deposit is to be held by the landlord in trust for the landlord and the tenant on terms that allow the landlord to withdraw from the account, and that allows the tenant the right to receive interest, and the right to receive the deposit or any balance remaining at the end of the deposit period. This right protects the tenant against insolvency of the landlord. From April 6, 2013 it is no longer necessary to register the rent deposit agreement as a charge against a corporate tenant.[1]

Interest earned on the deposit

The deposit agreement might provide that interest will belong to the tenant, so **24–06** that the tenant is liable for tax on the interest, but for the interest itself to be left in the deposit account during the whole period of the deposit. The tenant will usually, however, want the right to receive payment of the interest from time to time, and many deposit agreements will provide for this right to be exercisable only once a year. The landlord should not have to pay the interest if, at the date of request from the tenant, there are any arrears due by the tenant, or if the withdrawal would result in a reduction in the main amount required as the deposit.

The agreement should state that the tenant is responsible for accounting for the interest to HMRC, and that the landlord is entitled to notify HMRC of the name and address of the tenant and of the amount of interest.

Withdrawals from the deposit account

The deposit agreement should say that if the tenant fails to pay rent or any **24–07** other amount due plus VAT (if applicable), the landlord is entitled to withdraw the arrears from the deposit. The landlord should also be entitled to withdraw money from the deposit in order to be reimbursed or to pay for the cost of making good any breach by the tenant of his repairing and other obligations under the lease.

Top-up payments

The deposit agreement should provide for the tenant to be required to top up **24–08** the deposit within 7 or 14 days after demand if the landlord has had to make a withdrawal from the account. If the deposit is to be equivalent to rent for a specified period of time, there should also be an obligation on the tenant to top up the deposit to reflect any increase at rent review.

Forfeit of the deposit

The landlord will usually want the deposit agreement to provide that he is enti- **24–09** tled to uplift and keep the whole of the money in the deposit account, including interest earned to date, if a receiver, administrator or liquidator is appointed in respect of the tenant, if the tenant is wound up or ceases to exist, or if the lease is irritated for any reason. The tenant is likely to resist this, but the landlord can argue that the money will cover part of his expense of dealing with an insolvency practitioner or re-letting the premises.

---

[1] Companies Act 2006 s.859A(6)(a).

If the landlord chooses not to use money in the deposit account for paying the rent that is outstanding or any other money that is outstanding, then the landlord can choose to irritate the lease and then take the deposit money.

Landlord's sale of the property

24–10   The agreement should provide that if the landlord sells or disposes of his interest as landlord under the lease, then he should have to transfer the whole amount, including interest accrued to date, in the deposit fund to the party to whom he disposes, and he should take that party bound by all obligations in the deposit agreement.

Landlord's remedies

24–11   A clause should be inserted in the deposit agreement that any breach by the tenant of his obligations in the agreement will be deemed to be a breach of the tenant's obligations in the lease, allowing the landlord to exercise his irritancy and other rights of enforcement under the lease. However, the irritancy clause in the lease should also provide that breach of the deposit agreement constitutes a breach of the lease itself and is grounds for irritancy of the lease. There should also be a statement that the landlord's rights in the agreement are in addition to his rights under the lease and are without prejudice to these rights.

There should be a statement in the agreement that the fact that the deposit is in place is no defence to an action for declarator of irritancy of the lease, nor to any court action for payment of arrears. The effect of this is that the landlord can choose whether to enforce payment by any of his remedies under the lease, or he can alternatively draw on the deposit.

Return of deposit

24–12   The landlord should return the deposit, or rather, the balance left or credit in it, together with accrued interest, to the tenant on completion of any permitted assignation of the tenant's interest, on renunciation by the tenant of his interest under the lease with landlord's agreement or on termination of the lease, provided the tenant has complied with its obligations. Therefore, if the landlord serves a Schedule of Dilapidations shortly before termination of the lease, and the tenant has not complied with the Schedule, then the tenant is not entitled to return of the deposit until the works have been completed. The parties may agree that the deposit can be returned prior to termination of the lease, for instance after a certain period of time or once the tenant has produced audited accounts that comply with a specific standard.

CHAPTER 25

EXTENSIONS AND VARIATION OF LEASES

Introduction

In Scotland it has always been possible to extend or shorten the period of a **25–01** lease, or to vary the actual terms of the lease by way of a deed between the parties who at that time are the landlord and the tenant (and guarantor, if any). The lease remains intact, and the Minute of Variation is a document that changes the terms of the lease. In England an extension or reduction of the term of a lease, or a significant variation, is sometimes carried out by a surrender and re-grant, but will often be dealt with by way of a deed of variation of the lease, which has the effect of constituting a surrender and re-grant at law.

Variation by back letter

A back letter, which is sometimes called a "side letter", is a personal arrange- **25–02** ment between the granter and the grantee that does not vary the terms of the lease so as to be binding against future landlords or in favour of future tenants, unless the letter says that it is a variation of the lease or states that its terms are binding on all future landlords and all future tenants. In such a case it will, in fact, be a variation of the lease.

Most back letters are granted for the benefit of the tenant in favour of whom they are granted and to whom it is addressed, and they are usually declared to be non-assignable. In *Optical Express (Gyle) Ltd v Marks & Spencer Plc*[1] the original landlord gave a "solus undertaking" back letter to the tenant, saying that while the centre was its original size, the tenant's premises would be the only optician's, and if the centre were extended in the future, there would be no more than one additional optician. The back letter did not provide for the granter to obtain a letter in the same terms from any future landlord. The original landlord sold the centre, and the new landlord granted a lease to another optician. The tenant sought interdict against the new landlord and the competitor to prevent the competitor from trading as an optician in the centre, and to have the lease to the competitor cancelled. The court held that the fact that the exclusivity provision was in a back letter meant that it was collateral to the lease and was not a variation of the lease as such, and it was therefore not binding on anyone to whom the landlord conveyed the property. The tenant therefore lost the case and was not granted interdict.

---

[1] *Optical Express (Gyle) Ltd v Marks & Spencer Plc*, 2000 S.L.T. 644.

Extension of the term

25–03 Landlords sometimes seek to extend the duration of the lease so as to ensure an income stream from the property for a longer time. The tenant may agree to enter into such an extension in exchange for payment of a capital sum. By extending the term, the landlord enhances the value of his investment, as there is a longer period of income available, and this usually also enables the landlord to obtain more favourable lending terms over the property. There are stamp duty land tax (SDLT) implications in that an SDLT return may have to be lodged and more SDLT paid by the tenant at the time the extension is entered into, even though this may be many years before expiry of the original term. The SDLT provisions change frequently, so the current provisions should always be checked.

If the term is being extended then it is important to consider what is to happen with rent reviews; the Minute of Extension and Variation may well need to provide for rent reviews to take place at additional dates, and there may be a deemed notional duration of the lease in question, which may need to be reconsidered.

Shortening of the term

25–04 If the parties want to agree to shorten the period of the lease, they should sign a deed that varies the lease accordingly. This deed should be signed in the same way as the lease itself, and should be expressed as being a variation of the lease.

Addition or reduction in the leased premises

25–05 If the tenant is being given extra space or additional premises, or if the tenant is giving up part of the premises, then the parties should set this out in a deed that varies the lease. If the transaction is to add to the extent of the premises, the document should expressly state that the landlord is leasing to the tenant the additional premises.

If the existing and the additional premises are adjacent, but divided by a wall which is to be removed, then the premises will be increased so as to include not only the space "on the other side of the wall", but also the space that was occupied by the wall itself. The deed should provide for who is removing the wall, and for all necessary consents to be obtained. These consents will be building warrant and possibly planning permission and listed building consent. If either of the premises are part of a larger building, then the consent of the other owners of the building will probably be required for the removal of the wall.

The deed should also specify what is to happen at rent review. If there is a division wall between the original and the additional premises, the space that the division wall occupied should be taken into account in calculating the area. It is possible that the tenant might be able to argue for a "quantum" allowance so as to obtain a reduction in any increase otherwise achievable, because the overall area of the premises is now larger. If at rent review the intention is that the works that join the original and the additional premises are to be disregarded, then what will be reviewed is premises that are separated and that have two separate entrances. Valuation advice should always be obtained from a rent-review surveyor in such an instance.

If the variation of the lease is to extend the premises by removing a wall from the original premises in order to allow the tenant to enjoy the original and additional premises as one whole entity, then reinstatement provisions may need to be inserted. The landlord should be made aware that if the tenant becomes insolvent and the lease terminates, there is likely to be no right to have the works completed by the administrator, etc. If the lease is irritated, then the likelihood is that the tenant will not be in a financial position to carry out any reinstatement works.

If the tenant also leases adjoining premises from another landlord and wants to knock through so as to make one larger unit, there should be a tri-partite agreement among the tenant and both landlords. This should impose on the tenant the obligation to remove the wall in a good and workmanlike manner, and on termination of either of the two leases to reinstate the wall, to separate the services to the units and to form a separate entrance into each of the unit(s). It is possible that the tenant may default on his obligation to reinstate, and so the agreement should allow each landlord to enter the premises of the other in order to carry out the reinstatement works and to recover one-half of the cost of the works. These costs should not be limited to just the construction of the new division wall, but should also include separation of services, creation of a new entrance and if relevant a new shopfront. However, such a tri-partite agreement is merely contractual among the parties, and in order to give the fullest protection, the reinstatement obligations that would apply in the event of tenant default should be created as reciprocal real burdens affecting both titles in a deed that would be registered in the Land Register of Scotland, or in the case of unregistered property, in the Register of Sasines.

Variation of clauses

Parties often agree to vary certain clauses in a lease, especially in respect of **25–06** assignation and sub-letting, use, insurance, etc. If the landlord seeks to vary the lease as a condition of allowing an assignation or a sub-lease, or of the tenant carrying out works, then the landlord will be deemed to be acting unreasonably in this position if the lease provides that consent is not to be unreasonably withheld. Any variation of the terms of the lease should be contained in a deed that states that the lease is varied as provided for in the deed, but is otherwise confirmed, so as to make it clear that the only variation involved is contained in this deed. The variation can, of course, be included in an assignation document.

Position of guarantees

Some guarantee provisions will provide that the guarantee will stand, and will **25–07** not be affected by any variation of the terms of the lease or by any agreement or award in respect of scheduled rent reviews in the lease. Otherwise, the guarantor's consent should be obtained to any variations of the lease and in particular any extension or reduction in the duration of the lease, and the guarantor should be party to the deed of variation.

Registration of the deed of extension or variation

The landlord will want to register for execution the deed that varies or extends **25–08** the lease, so as to be able to do summary diligence, i.e. fast-track enforcement,

of the lease as varied. If the tenant's interest in the lease was registered in the
Land Register of Scotland, or becomes registrable because the original term as
extended is more than 20 years, then the tenant should register the lease as
varied in the Land Register of Scotland so as to obtain a real right, i.e. a good
leasehold right against everyone.

CHAPTER 26

ENFORCEMENT OF COMMERCIAL LEASES IN SCOTLAND

Introduction

The Scottish law of commercial leases is radically different to that of England, **26–01** and there are different remedies available for tenant default.

The best remedy in any case will depend on what the landlord is looking to achieve. This will vary according to market conditions, as a landlord would think very carefully before terminating a lease on the ground of tenant breach if he anticipates it would be difficult to find another tenant.

In this Chapter, we address the remedies available in commercial leases of premises in Scotland, and then we look very briefly at some of the remedies available in England.

A—SCOTLAND

Remedies available for tenant breach, not directly against the tenant

If the tenant has provided a performance deposit, the landlord will usually be **26–02** entitled to draw against the money lodged to satisfy any unpaid rent or other sums. Depending on the actual wording of the deposit provisions, the landlord may not be required to draw on the deposit if he does not want to, allowing him to choose another remedy instead.

If there is a guarantor in respect of the tenant's obligations, the landlord will usually be able to enforce against the guarantor, again depending on the actual wording of the guarantee.

If (unusually) the lease contains joint and several liability on the tenant and his successors and assignees, the landlord can choose to enforce against one or more of the current tenant and/or any previous tenant(s).

Court action for debt

If the tenant is late or fails to pay rent or other money due, and any period of **26–03** grace for payment has expired, the landlord can raise a court action for payment of money. The size of the debt will determine in which court the action can be appropriately raised. If the matter is particularly complex or if there are significant arrears, an action can be raised in the Court of Session. Otherwise, the action should be raised in the sheriff court. Once the action is concluded, whether by an out-of-court settlement or after a decision by the court, a decree will be issued, which can be enforced. If a landlord raises court proceedings and is not successful, then he will usually have to pay the tenant's judicial expenses as well as his own legal expenses. If the landlord is successful, then the tenant will usually be liable for the landlord's judicial expenses, but there will always be a shortfall between judicial expenses and the total amount of legal fees, VAT and outlays. Judicial expenses are generally around half to two-thirds of the actual legal fees incurred while, by contrast, in England the successful party is usually awarded his full costs. In some Scottish leases, there is a clause that allows the landlord to recover from the tenant all costs in enforcing breach of lease. This should allow the landlord to recover all costs, and not just judicially awarded costs.

Fast-track enforcement–payment of arrears

26–04 Leases of Scottish property are usually registered in the Books of Council and Session. Registration can be for "preservation", which merely involves the original of the document being retained at the Register and an "extract" being issued, which is treated in the same way as the original. Landlords often register the lease for preservation and "execution". Registration for execution means that fast-track enforcement ("summary diligence") can be carried out against the tenant for ascertained, i.e. known amounts such as rent, without needing to go to court.

The extract lease is given to sheriff officers with instructions to "arrest" or to "serve a charge".

Arrestment is the freezing, up to the amount owed to the landlord, of the tenant's bank accounts or of debts due to the tenant by third parties (such as customers of the tenant). If funds are caught by the arrestment, the party holding them is required to release them to the landlord 14 weeks after the date of service of the arrestment.

26–05 A charge is an order to pay within 14 days, failing which the tenant can be sequestrated (made bankrupt) or put into liquidation, or (if the amount owed is over £3,000) the tenant's assets can be made the subject of an attachment order, as detailed in para.26–08 below. A tenant who is not a limited company can ask the court to grant a "time to pay order" allowing payment by instalments, and if that order is granted, then the tenant must pay the instalments on time, or else the whole balance becomes immediately payable.

If a charge is served on the tenant (whether the tenant is an individual, a firm or a company) and the amount due is not paid in full within 14 days of it being served, then, unless a time to pay order has been granted by the court, the landlord can present a bankruptcy or liquidation petition to the court in respect of the tenant. This is on the basis that the failure to comply with the charge is evidence of the tenant's inability to pay his debts as they fall due

Statutory demand for payment of arrears

26–06 A statutory demand can be served in respect of a specific amount of at least £1,500, requiring payment within 21 days under threat of bankruptcy or liquidation. This method is not appropriate if the amount of debt is able to be, or is actually, disputed because the landlord will then need to prove the debt, and so the process would not really be accelerated. By serving a statutory demand or indeed a charge the landlord is not actually bound to proceed to liquidation or bankruptcy of the tenant.

Hypothec

26–07 Hypothec is a right of security over the tenant's goods in the leased premises, which is available in respect of all unpaid rent. It is not available in respect of any items that a third party, acting in good faith, has acquired from the tenant. If the landlord chooses to exercise his right of hypothec, then he becomes personally liable for up to one year's arrears of PAYE and for construction industry sub-contractor's deduction payments due by the tenant to HMRC (if any). The hypothec can only now be enforced where the tenant is in liquidation. As it is a form of security, it allows the landlord to rank higher than any unsecured creditors in any distribution of moveable assets. It is a useful remedy if the tenant company has valuable moveable assets within the leased premises, but the potential liabilities mean that it is a seldom-used remedy.

Attachment order

If the lease has been registered for execution, or if the landlord has a court **26–08** decree against the tenant for payment, and the amount owed is more than £3,000, the landlord can proceed with an attachment, following service of a charge that has expired. The attachment affects moveable goods and objects owned by, and in the possession of, the tenant. Attachment prevents the tenant disposing of the property affected. A schedule of attachment detailing the attached property is served on the tenant and others who have an interest in the attached property. If the amount due is not paid, the landlord can apply to the court for an order authorising him to satisfy the debt out of the attached property by way of an auction sale.

A special application to the court is required in the case of residential property, which may include mixed-use property, for example a shop with a flat above it. In such cases, the landlord would require to demonstrate "exceptional circumstances" justifying the use of attachment for a residential property.

Third parties who have transacted in good faith in respect of the attached property will be protected. An attachment prohibits any dealings with the attached property except by order of the court, and breach of the prohibition is treated as contempt of court.

Enforcing keep-open clauses

Many leases impose an obligation on the tenant to occupy and trade from the **26–09** premises throughout the duration of the lease, and sometimes there are stipulated minimum hours each day on which he must trade. If the clause is in clear terms leaving no doubt as to what the tenant is to do in terms of both trading and hours of opening, the courts will usually grant an order of specific implement. This is an order that requires the tenant to comply with his obligations under the lease, essentially forcing the tenant to occupy and trade. Most keep-open clauses relate to units in shopping centres or a parade of shops, where the existence of an empty unit may have a detrimental effect on the capital value of the whole investment. However, they are also present in leases of single units or shops, and if the clause is clear in its terms, the courts will generally enforce it.

If the keep-open clause is not sufficiently precise as to the obligations on the tenant, the court is unlikely to grant the "keep open" order. As an alternative the landlord may be entitled to damages, but only for any loss the landlord has actually suffered as a consequence of the tenant not trading. The award of damages may be minor, or even zero, if it would make no real difference to the landlord's interest whether or not the tenant trades from the premises (for example in the case of a stand-alone property). The tenant may be continuing to pay rent and to perform his other obligations, in which case the landlord is unlikely to have suffered any real loss, unless he sells or tries to sell a leased, but vacant, shop or unit.

It is always easier to prevent a tenant from leaving than to try and compel them to re-enter. The remedy of specific implement in this situation compelling the tenant to perform his obligations is usually combined with an interdict, which prevents the tenant from leaving. The topic of keep-open clauses is further discussed in Ch.8.

Dilapidations

26–10　A schedule of wants of repair (usually called a schedule of dilapidations, as in England) is a list of repair works that the tenant is to carry out in order to comply with his obligations in the lease. Normally, in a commercial lease, most, if not all of the common law repairing liability is transferred to the tenant, but at common law any liability that is not transferred on to the tenant will remain with the landlord.

If the tenant fails to carry out the works that are his responsibility in terms of the lease, the landlord may, depending on the wording of the lease, be entitled to carry out the works himself and reclaim the cost from the tenant. Alternatively, if the lease has not come to an end, the landlord may be able to obtain a court order of specific implement ordering the tenant to do the work. If the lease comes to an end before the works are carried out or are completed, the landlord's only remedy is to claim damages from the tenant for the tenant's failure to have complied with its obligations in the lease. The damages are quantified as being the amount of the loss suffered by the landlord, and this is usually, but far from always, the cost of doing the works. If the landlord is prevented from selling or letting the property for a time while the tenant's failure is made good, then the landlord may be entitled to damages to compensate for loss of use of the property for that time.

Landlords should take care where refurbishments are planned before a new tenant takes occupation, or if they intend selling the property, as the outgoing tenant may claim that if the landlord intended to sell, refurbish or re-develop, there is no purpose to be gained by the tenant doing the works, and that the landlord has therefore suffered a smaller or zero loss. See Ch.14 for a full discussion of dilapidations.

Irritancy

26–11　Irritancy is termination by the landlord of a lease due to breach by the tenant (known in England as forfeiture). If the tenant is in administration, the landlord cannot irritate the lease or obtain a court order for possession of the premises, except with the consent of the administrator or the permission of the court. Irritancy is fully covered in Ch.17.

A tenant can never lawfully be removed from premises except with a court order.

If the landlord does get a court order of irritancy, he cannot sue the tenant for damages for early termination of the lease or for breach of contract; furthermore, he is not entitled to any rent in respect of the period after which the lease is irritated. If the tenant remains in occupation the landlord may have a claim for damages against him.

If a lease is irritated or renounced, the landlord will become liable for half of the rates payable after three months, or even immediately if the tenant vacated more than three months before the lease was terminated, unless the property is industrial or is a listed building, in which case the landlord will have no liability for rates if the property is unlet and unoccupied.

Liquidation

A landlord who is owed rent or other arrears, e.g. service charge, and who **26–12** holds a decree or an expired charge against a tenant, may seek to put a corporate tenant into liquidation. If the tenant is insolvent, the landlord will be unlikely to be able to recover the costs of the liquidation petition. In some situations it can be a useful tool against a tenant who does have funds, but refuses to pay. This remedy should not be used oppressively, as the courts take a dim view of threatening liquidation as a matter of course, particularly where the debt is disputed.

Remedies available to the tenant against the landlord

If the lease does not contain a statement that the tenant must pay rent without **26–13** retention, deduction or set-off, then the tenant has a right to retain or set-off rent against unperformed landlord's obligations. This does not cancel the obligation to pay the rent, but merely delays it until the landlord has performed his obligation. This is the most effective remedy a tenant has, though the lease usually prevents the tenant from using this remedy.

The tenant can sue the landlord for damages for breach of obligation, such as an obligation to pay fit-out costs, to carry out common repairs or maintenance, to provide services that he has contracted to provide or to make good insured risk damage.

In certain situations the tenant can seek an order of specific implement against the landlord.

The tenant can seek interdict against the landlord to stop him doing some- **26–14** thing that prevents the tenant having full use, occupancy and enjoyment of the premises, or if the tenant believes the landlord is about to do such a thing. This is derogation from the grant and is dealt with more fully in Ch.3. The tenant can seek interim interdict, which is an immediate stop order that is usually granted on the statements of the party seeking the order; however, if the order is wrongly sought, the tenant could be found liable in damages to the landlord.

In extreme circumstances, where the landlord acts in such a way as to strike at the root of the lease contract, the tenant would be entitled to bring the lease to an end through rescission. This happens very rarely. Rescission by the landlord is competent where the tenant fails to take occupancy of the premises; the tenant can rescind where the landlord fails to provide premises reasonably fit for the purpose let. Either party may be entitled to rescind if the other is in serious breach of his repairing obligations under the lease or at common law and if this failure has lasted a considerable period of time.

B—ENGLAND

Rates liability

If a lease is terminated by forfeiture or otherwise, the landlord immediately **26–15** becomes liable for payment of rates.

"Distress" and recovery of rent

26–16 The Tribunals, Courts and Enforcement Act 2007 provides for the abolition of the remedy of distress, and its replacement by a new Commercial Rent Arrears Recovery procedure.

Distress for rent was a remedy that enabled a landlord to seize goods from the leased premises and sell them to raise money to cover arrears of rent due by the tenant. The remedy could be exercised without giving prior notice or warning, and the court's permission was not required unless the tenant was (or may shortly have become) insolvent. Distress was available to recover arrears of rent and also insurance, service charge, VAT and interest on late payments. The verb deriving from "distress" is "to distrain".

The relevant part of the Act relates to arrears due in respect of commercial premises. The Act replaces distress with a new procedure for recovery of commercial rent arrears. Distress against an immediate tenant will no longer be competent. Under the new procedure, the landlord will have to give notice before seizing goods. Regulations will specify the minimum period of notice required. The new procedure applies to all legal and equitable written leases of commercial premises, but it is not available where there are arrears relating to occupancy by a tenant who remains in occupation after his lease has expired, and where the landlord has not confirmed that he is willing for the tenant to remain.

26–17 The new procedure only applies to leases, and it therefore does not apply to occupancy licences.

There are specific provisions that apply where there are arrears due under a lease that has terminated.

The Act provides that "rent" does not include rates, service charge, repairs costs, maintenance or insurance, even if the lease includes these items in the definition of "rent". The new procedure therefore differs from, and is less landlord-friendly than, the old remedy of distress. If the lease provides for an inclusive rent, only the part that is reasonably attributable to possession and use of the premises is recoverable under the new procedure. The Act does not make any special provision for leases with a turnover rent.

There will be a minimum amount, to be prescribed in regulations from time to time, in respect of which the landlord can enforce this remedy. This amount will exclude interest, VAT and any other amount the tenant is entitled to deduct or set-off.

It is, of course, open to the landlord to sue the tenant for payment of arrears of other sums through the courts.

Forfeiture

26–18 The remedy of forfeiture is fully dealt with in Ch.17.

Specific performance

26–19 "Specific performance" is an equitable remedy granted at the court's discretion. The courts may grant an order compelling the tenant to carry out repairs or any other positive obligation where the obligation is clearly defined in the lease, where it would not be unjust or oppressive to grant the order and where damages would not be an appropriate remedy. However, the landlord will usually have an adequate remedy in damages, so such an order is uncommon.

If a tenant has breached a "keep open" obligation in the lease, the court will not grant an order requiring him to trade from the property, but will award damages if appropriate.

Self help for repairs

In many commercial leases, if the tenant defaults in carrying out his repairing **26–20** obligation, there will be a right reserved to the landlord to enter the premises to carry out repairs and to then recover the cost from the tenant.

CHAPTER 27

TENANT INSOLVENCY

Introduction

27–01 This chapter deals with tenant insolvency in respect of leases of commercial premises in Scotland, and covers individual as well as Scottish and English registered companies.

In this chapter we consider the legal remedies and practicalities surrounding tenant insolvency; it is not a full commentary on insolvency law, as such is not appropriate for a book of this nature. When faced with a tenant who is insolvent, the landlord will want to know what he can do and how quickly he can do it.

Insolvency practitioners will often issue a letter disclaiming the lease, or stating that they have no intention to perform the obligations, but in Scotland such a notification does not bring the lease to an end.

Guarantees

27–02 The landlord may be able to look to other parties to pay sums and to perform obligations under the lease. If a guarantee has been granted, then the landlord should be able to look to the guarantor to pay and perform. The detailed wording of the guarantee should be checked, as it may be limited in amount or time. It may also contain a provision that the guarantor is bound to accept a new lease on identical terms for the remainder of the period of the existing lease, but there is often a short period of time within which the landlord can call on the guarantor to accept such a new lease and, if he fails to give notice correctly and in time, he will lose the right to have the guarantor take on a new lease.

Rent (performance) deposit

27–03 The mere fact that the landlord has a rent or performance deposit from the tenant does not mean that he is entitled to keep it or to use that for arrears. If the tenant is an individual and is granting or has granted a protected trust deed, then it all depends on the specific wording of the trust deed itself. If the tenant is a company that is applying for or has entered into a creditors' voluntary agreement (a "CVA"), then the permission of the court may be required before the landlord can use the deposit.

If the deposit is held in a separate account in trust for the tenant (whether an individual or a company), then the landlord is unlikely to be able to use the money, except with the consent of the insolvency practitioner. This is because the deposit money will form part of the tenant's assets. The landlord, of course, has a claim as creditor, but may rank behind others to whom the tenant owes money.

Joint and several liability

It is unusual nowadays, but there are some instances where a lease imposes **27–04** joint and several liability on the original tenant and each assignee for payment of rent, and also in some cases, for non-monetary obligations. If the lease in question does contain such a provision, and the current tenant is not the original tenant, then the landlord can choose to recover arrears etc from the original or any successor tenant, leaving that party to claim back from the current tenant.

Effect of insolvency

If the tenant is a limited company and goes into administration, receivership or **27–05** liquidation, the insolvency practitioner cannot unilaterally terminate the lease. If the insolvency practitioner sends a letter saying he disclaims the lease, that does not terminate the lease. Therefore the lease will continue in force despite the insolvency practitioner having been appointed, and is likely only to come to an end if (a) the landlord obtains a decree of irritancy from the court, or (b) the landlord accepts a renunciation (surrender) of the Lease. There is no requirement on a landlord to actually accept a surrender, and he does not even need to act reasonably if he is requested to accept a surrender of the lease.

It is probable that a lease is not terminated if the tenant company is dissolved, following a winding-up. This is because the lease is an asset of the company, as well as being a liability, and as such, falls to the Crown. The Queen's and Lord Treasurer's Remembrancer will often grant a renunciation if requested to do so.

Effect on sub-leases, etc. if head lease terminates

If the head lease is terminated by irritancy, then any sub-lease or other occu- **27–06** pancy right that has been granted by the tenant will also be terminated. However, this does not apply if the head lease is surrendered, as any sub-lease is, in that instance, likely to continue. Nor does it apply if the head lease is renounced, or if the landlord and tenant's interest in a head lease become vested in the same entity[1] if the head lease is itself an interposed lease.[2]

In many instances a head landlord will have entered into an irritancy protection agreement in favour of the sub-tenant, which imposes on the head landlord the obligation to grant a new lease directly to the sub-tenant if the head lease is irritated or terminated for any other reason. Separately, head landlords will often grant security of tenure to a sub-tenant either expressly or by implication, by being party to the sub-lease itself.

Irritancy

The lease will invariably have an irritancy clause that gives details of the **27–07** various circumstances in which the landlord can irritate the lease. These usually include the insolvency of the tenant, but it is common to find a saving provisions for insolvency practitioners in the lease so that the insolvency practitioner is allowed a period of time (which is usually anything up to a year) in

---

[1] *The Howgate Shopping Centre Ltd v Catercraft Services Ltd*, 2004 S.L.T. 231.
[2] Land Tenure Reform (Scotland) Act 1974 s.17(2).

which to dispose of the tenant's interest in the lease. Such a right is often quali-fied by applying *only* if the insolvency practitioner accepts personal responsi-bility for performance of all obligations under the lease from the date of appointment of the insolvency practitioner, and for arrears arising before his appointment. Many landlords will insist on such a proviso, with a time limit of anything from 14 to 28 days for the insolvency practitioner to give this written confirmation.

If the lease is irritated due to failure to pay monetary sums, then any saving provisions for insolvency practitioners will not assist – these only help if the landlord is seeking to irritate the lease because the tenant has become insolvent. This is different to seeking to irritate because the rent etc. has not been paid.

Administration

27–08   If the tenant is a limited company and goes into administration then the land-lord is not allowed to raise any court proceedings again the tenant, except with permission of the court or the consent of the administrator. In many cases the administrator will want to continue trading from the premises for some time to obtain the best position for the insolvent tenant's creditors. However, this is likely to be a short term situation, and the administrator will often resist accepting personal liability for all arrears and for rent, and other obligations going forward from the date of appointment. In many instances the adminis-trator will "play for time" while he continues to trade.

The court's permission or the administrator's consent is needed not only for the landlord to seek a Court Order granting decree of irritancy but also for any other proceedings including a court action seeking payment of arrears and also attempting to do summary diligence such as freezing bank accounts, etc.

Rent as an expense of administration

27–09   In *Cheshire West and Chester Borough Council v Springfield Retail Ltd (In Administration)*[3] a tenant went into administration, following which the admin-istrators traded for a short period of time, and then sold the business. The admin-istrators granted a licence to occupy in favour of the purchaser, and this was in clear breach of the terms of the lease, but the administrators anticipated that the purchaser would take an assignation of the lease subject to obtaining the consent of the landlord. The administrators told the purchaser to pay rent directly to the landlord, but no rent was paid. The occupancy licence ran for six months, but the purchaser did nothing to try to obtain an assignation of the lease. The court held that the administrators were liable to the landlord to pay the rent as an expense of the administration. The court decided that (a) it was irrelevant that the administrators themselves had not been trading from the premises, and (b) they were bound to pay the rent by virtue of having granted the licence to occupy as this had been granted for the purposes of the administration.

In *Goldacre (Offices) Ltd v Nortel Networks UK Ltd (in administration)*[4] the court held that, where administrators occupied a small part of the property to

---

[3] *Cheshire West and Chester Borough Council v Springfield Retail Limited (In Administration)* [2010] CSOH 115.
[4] *Goldacre (Offices) Ltd v Nortel Networks UK Ltd (in administration)* [2009] EWHC 3389 (Ch.).

carry out their duties as administrators, they had to pay the rent for the whole premises as an expense of the administration. However, this should be treated with some caution, as the administrator does not have to pay the rent immediately that it is due if he does not have sufficient funds.

Landlord's hypothec

The old Scottish common law remedy of landlord's hypothec remains avail- **27–10** able for all rent arrears, as security in favour of the landlord; this includes the situation where a tenant becomes insolvent. The common law rules were changed significantly by s.208 of the Bankruptcy and Diligence, etc. (Scotland) Act 2007.[5] This provides for the hypothec to continue as a right in security over moveable items (contents) kept in the leased premises. However, it is not available for any property that is kept in residential premises, nor is it available for any property that is owned by a person other than the tenant in commercial premises.

Another important change that was introduced by the 2007 Act is that the remedy of sequestration for rent has been abolished. However, the hypothec can provide the landlord with a preferential ranking in the tenant's insolvency.

Where a property is owned in common by the tenant and someone else, the right of hypothec is available only to the extent of the tenant's ownership of the items in question. If there are arrears of rent in respect of the period before the date of appointment of the insolvency practitioner, the landlord can secure, by way of hypothec, any items owned by the tenant where these items are stored in the property.

Any items that are subject to retention of title or which are leased to the tenant by a third party do not fall within the hypothec.

It is not totally clear whether hypothec is available to the landlord for new goods brought into the premises after the date of appointment of the insolvency practitioner. Although hypothec is available for all arrears of rent whether before or after the insolvency practitioner's appointment, the arrears are subject of course to the five year time-bar rule of prescription which still applies, so as to prevent recovery of debts that are more than five years old.

Violent profits

At common law, the owner of a property in Scotland is entitled to seek payment **27–11** from an unauthorised occupier to pay an amount equivalent to rent for his occupancy of the premises. This is called "violent profits". It is unlikely that the landlord would be entitled to demand violent profits from a party who a tenant has let into the premises without the landlord's consent, as the tenant still has the right to occupy the premises while the lease is still running, and who remains liable for the rent under the lease. However, the landlord is entitled to seek a court order to remove an unauthorised occupier directly, and this right is not affected by the restriction on raising court actions against a tenant who has entered into administration.

---

[5] Bankruptcy and Diligence, etc. (Scotland) Act 2007.

Business rates

27–12 In Scotland, business rates are payable by the party who is entitled to possession of the premises. If the tenant has become insolvent, and the insolvency practitioner has "disclaimed" the lease, the tenant is still in existence (even if the tenant is put into liquidation), as is the lease, and therefore the Local Authority would only be able to pursue the tenant in administration for unpaid rates. If the landlord accepts a surrender of the lease, or if the landlord obtains a decree of irritancy or if the tenant ceases to exist because it is dissolved, then the landlord will become liable for rates.

Practicalities—What should the landlord do?

27–13
    (a) Check whether any of the possibilities covered in paras 27–02 to 27–04 are available.

    (b) The landlord should check the detailed wording of the lease so as to find out what, if any, saving provisions there are for insolvency practitioners in the event of tenant insolvency. The relief provisions in respect of irritancy that are contained in the Law Reform (Miscellaneous Provisions) (Scotland) Act 1985[6] do not give any assistance to insolvency practitioners to prevent the lease from being irritated on the grounds of the insolvency practitioner being appointed in respect of the tenant. If there is a saving provision, he should also check what if any period is allowed for the insolvency practitioner to save the lease. If there is any such provisions this may well be subject to the insolvency practitioner giving written notification that he accepts personal liability for arrears due and for payment of all sums going forward from the date of appointment and for performance of all other obligations.

    (c) The landlord should consider whether there is security of tenure available for any sub-tenants or other occupants.

    (d) If the landlord wants the premises back, so that he can then re-let or sell, etc. he should allow a sufficient period of time to negotiate and obtain a surrender, or (subject to any necessary permission from the court or an administrator) to obtain a decree of irritancy. He should also remember that, with effect from three months after the lease terminates, he will start to become liable for business rates for the property.

    (e) If the landlord is going to seek irritancy of the lease he should check the wording of the irritancy clause as there may be a requirement for him to provide a separate notice or a copy of any notice to the holders of any standard securities or floating charges over the tenant's interest. There may also be a saving provision in favour of the holders of any standard security allowing them a period of time to dispose of the lease.

    (f) Remember that the landlord cannot just change the locks, and cannot generally commence any irritancy or removal proceedings except with the consent of the court or, in some cases, the insolvency practitioner.

---

[6] Law Reform (Miscellaneous Provisions) (Scotland) Act 1985.

CHAPTER 28

PROPERTY MANAGEMENT AND MANAGEMENT TRANSACTIONS

Introduction

In this chapter we look, from a legal viewpoint, at managing a property or a **28–01** portfolio of properties as well as considering management transactions such as rent reviews, assignations, sub-leases, licences for works, schedules of dilapidations, insurance and notices to quit.

The all important person is always, of course, the client, who wants to be looked after by his professional team, without any matters falling into "black holes". The solicitor puts the lease in place but generally is not expected or required to remind the client of impending rent reviews, approaching expiry dates or break/extension options unless he specifically undertakes to do this in his letter of engagement or otherwise. The property owner should therefore diary forward for the appropriate dates and/or appoint a managing agent to deal with all matters of property management.

Managing agents

Ideally a management contract should be entered into between the property **28–02** owner and the managing agent setting out the various duties and costs. If the property is self-contained and the lease is full repairing and insuring then the landlord's only "duties" are to collect the rent (which may in any event be paid by Standing Order) and to insure the property, and collect the insurance premium from the tenant. In such an instance it is not always easy to justify imposing on the tenant a management charge.

However, if the property is part of a portfolio of properties then some management issues may well arise in respect of insurance. The owner may have a "block policy" which covers all of his properties. If the property is part of a larger building there may be a common insurance policy for the whole building with premiums being recharged to the tenants on a proportionate basis. If the property forms part of a larger building where there are various ownerships, then it possible that there is a co-proprietors' insurance policy organised by the factor (managing agent) for the building. In such an instance there will be two lots of management charges—one for the managing agent of the building, and the other for the landlord's portfolio of properties.

If the property is "multi-occupancy", i.e. a large entity where the landlord lets out separate units/floors, then management can be intensive, and may involve service charge administration.

Management charge

28–03 Traditionally landlords have passed on to the tenant all charges of the managing agents; typically the fees charged by managing agent in the past have been five per cent of the passing rent. There are no longer any scale fees, but most landlords would expect to pay managing agents a charge of five per cent of the rent. Many landlords will self-manage, often through an associated company and this way the landlord would hope to achieve 105 per cent of rent! If it is a standalone property, then the tenant will often resist paying any managing charge at all, on the basis that managing is very straightforward. If it is a multi occupancy situation with service charge, many tenants will try to limit their liability for management charges to say 10 per cent of their service charge liability in any year, so that it is not in any way linked to the rent.

Assignations

28–04 It is important to obtain instructions from the client as soon as possible, because the lease will very often provide for consent not to be unreasonably withheld, and any significant delay in dealing with an application for consent, could be prejudicial to the existing tenant, who may lose his deal if there is unreasonable delay. His loss could be considerable as he would continue to pay rent and all other sums to the landlord, and would continue to have responsibility for rates, repairs and other obligations under the lease if the deal is lost. It is important to check with the client and the managing agents as to their respective requirements. If there is a standard security affecting the property, then although possibly not strictly needed, it is sensible to apply for consent from the security holder. The loan documentation may contain a specific prohibition against the grant of consent to any assignation except with the lender's consent.

It is worth finding out from the assignor whether the incoming tenant intends doing any alterations, and if so to obtain details of these.

In any assignation transaction, the landlord should check the following points:

- Is the covenant (financial strength) of the proposed assignee acceptable? It is possible for a grandiose named company to merely be a shell, even though it contains a "household name" in its title.
- Ask for a copy of the last three years' audited accounts.
- Ask whether there is any premium or reverse premium payable to or by the assignor/assignee.
- Ask if there any back letters are being granted in respect of the lease as between assignor and assignee.
- If in terms of the lease the tenant's interest is to be noted on the insurance policy, make sure that this happens in respect of the new tenant.
- Consider what effect the assignation may have on any rent deposit, guarantee or back letters.

Make sure that not only the landlord's solicitors' fees, but also managing agents' fees and the fees of any secured lender are to be paid by the tenant whether or not the transaction proceeds.

Sub-letting

It is important to obtain instructions from the client as soon as possible, because **28–05** the lease will very often provide for consent not to be unreasonably withheld, and any significant delay in dealing with an application for consent could be prejudicial to the existing tenant, who may lose his sub-tenant if there is unreasonable delay. His loss could be considerable as he would not have any rent coming in, whereas he would continue to pay rent to the landlord.

It is important to check with the client and the managing agents as to their respective requirements. If there is a standard security affecting the property, then although possibly not strictly needed, it is sensible to apply for consent from the security holder. The loan documentation may contain a specific prohibition against the grant of consent to any sub-lease except with the lender's consent.

If the proposed sub-lease is of part of the premises as opposed to the whole premises, the lease should be checked to ascertain whether partial sub-letting is totally prohibited.

It is worth finding out from the tenant whether the sub-tenant intends doing any alterations and if so to obtain details of these.

In any assignation transaction, the landlord should check the following points:

- Is the covenant (financial strength) of the proposed sub-tenant acceptable? It can be argued, of course, that the landlord should not be overly concerned about the sub-tenant's strength, but if there is any irritancy protection agreement or clause in place to protect a sub-tenant, then this point becomes very significant.
- Ask whether there is any premium or reverse premium payable to or by the tenant/sub-tenant.
- Ask if there any back letters are being granted in respect of the lease as between the tenant and sub-tenant.
- Consider what effect the sub-lease may have on any rent deposit, guarantee or back letters.

It should be noted that any existing Back Letters are likely to continue unless these are specifically linked to the tenant's personal occupancy. Make sure that not only the landlord's solicitors' fees, but also managing agents' fees and the fees of any secured lender are to be paid by the tenant whether or not the transaction proceeds.

Rent reviews

The lease may provide for a trigger notice to be issued to start the rent review **28–06** process. Many such clauses specify that the landlord must actually specify the amount of rent he is seeking to be paid from the rent review date. The lease should be checked carefully for any specific provisions, as well as for any prescribed timetable and procedure for serving notices. It is worth checking with the managing agent as to where, and for whose attention, they send the invoices. It is also important to check Companies House website to make sure that you have the current as opposed to historic registered office address of a company or limited liability partnership, and that they have not changed their name. The lease should be checked to determine whether the expenses of any rent review agreement are payable by the tenant or whether each party pays their own.

If there is a guarantor in place then the guarantor should be party to the rent review agreement, or else the guarantee's enforceability could be prejudiced.

Licence for works

28–07   If the tenant wants to carry out fitting out works or other alterations, then the lease may provide for landlord's consent to be needed. Some leases say that non structural internal works can be carried out without needing landlord's consent, but in some instances the tenant has an obligation to notify the landlord of the proposed alterations. A question arises as to whether works done which are stated as not requiring landlord's consent are, or are not, to be disregarded at rent review. If the lease says that landlord's consent is not required for internal non structural works then in strict terms the landlord has not consented to these and therefore it could be argued these should not be disregarded at rent review. In such a case the tenant is paying twice for these; he is paying to have the works done in the first place and then he is then paying rent on them.

The normal position in a commercial lease is that works carried out by the tenant with landlord's consent are disregarded at rent review. It should be remembered that there is a difference between disregarding the works *as such* on the one hand, and disregarding *any effect on rent value* of the works on the other. In the first instance, the disregard of the existence of the works could be prejudicial to the landlord. For example, if a shop consists of retail space on the ground floor and has historically had storage space on the first floor, but the tenant creates a staircase that is usable by the public and which complies with all building regulations, and starts selling from the first floor, then disregarding the existence of the staircase disqualifies the first floor from being reviewed as retail space. However, if all you are disregarding is *the effect on value* of the existence of the staircase, the landlord can obtain rent for retail use of the first floor (although in that instance you would certainly want to include a statement that there is access for the public so as to enable the first floor to be used for retail). In other words, in the first case you disregard the fact the staircase is there, but in the second, you accept there is an actual staircase, but disregard the actual staircase that is in place. It all comes down to the specific wording.

As the tenant is applying for consent, he should have to pay the expenses of the landlord, the managing agents and the secured lender. PSG (Property Standardisation Group) has a good style of licence for works document that includes obligations in respect of the construction, design and management regulations, indemnity, obtaining local authority consents, etc. The question of reinstatement of the works at termination of the lease should be considered: should the landlord have the right to require the tenant to do all, none or some reinstatement. It should be noted that it can be very costly and difficult to remove say heavy cooking equipment, etc. Once again the guarantor's consent should be obtained in respect of a licence for works.

Schedules of dilapidations

28–08   The detailed wording of the repair clause and the obligations at terminations clause should be checked so as to ensure that all common law obligations of the landlord have been passed on to the tenant. Common law obligations are dealt with in Ch.3 and dilapidations are treated in detail in Ch.14. The lease should be checked for any timetable or deadline by which schedules of dilapidations are to be served and for procedure for serving notices. There should be dialogue between the solicitor and the building surveyor to ensure that the schedule of dilapidations does not contain irrelevant material. The tenant could argue that items in the schedule of dilapidations that are in fact not the tenant's responsibility of themselves form a schedule of dilapidations served on the landlord and enforceable by the tenant.

Insurance

The landlord should check that the risks that he is undertaking to insure in **28–09** terms of the lease are indeed included in his insurance policy. He should also check these risks do not conflict with any insurance arranged by the factor (managing agents) of the building, title obligations or obligations to the lender. It is possible that, if the building is owned by various different parties in different parts, there is likely be a co-proprietors' insurance policy, and the lease will need to cater for this, as the landlord will not be in control of the insurance and would thus not be able to do certain things that he would be able to do if it was his own insurance policy.

If the landlord insures for loss of rent, and if there is a service charge regime in place, the loss of rent insurance should also include loss of service charge for the same period as loss of rent. If the property is a listed building then the normal three-year period for loss of rent and service charge insurance may not be sufficient, and perhaps a five year, or other, period may be more appropriate.

The lease should not require the landlord, as an absolute obligation, to have the tenant's interest noted and/or to obtain a waiver of subrogation rights from the insurers, and all that should be given is an obligation to use reasonable endeavours. In any event any obligation needs to be performed.

CHAPTER 29

SERVICE CHARGE IN MULTI-OCCUPANCY LEASES

Introductory

29–01 If the owner grants separate leases of different parts of his property, he will not let out any part of the structure or of the entrance, passages, stairs, etc. but will grant to each tenant a right in common to use these items. The landlord will undertake to look after these common items, and will recover the cost by way of a service charge.

In this Chapter, we look at the concept, set up, and accounting and payment aspects of service charge, and we examine the points that landlords and tenants should bear in mind when negotiating service charge provisions in leases. England differs from Scotland in that there is a separate non-compulsory service charge code for premises in England.

"Service charges" in single occupancy leases

29–02 If the landlord lets out all that he himself owns or leases at a location, and this is a stand-alone building or forms part of a larger building or of an estate, then he will usually pass on to the tenant the obligations contained in the title deeds, as well as those imposed by statute and by common law in respect of repair, etc.

Another scenario is that the landlord owns various units, shops or offices at one location, but the remainder of the entirety is owned by other proprietors. In such cases there is likely to be a deed of conditions that deals with appointment of managing agents, co-proprietors' common insurance, etc. Once again, the landlord will pass on to the tenant the obligations that are imposed on the landlord under the titles, etc.

Multiple-occupancy leases

29–03 If the owner of an entire building or of the entire property is granting separate leases of parts of the building/property, he will use a multiple-occupancy lease. The principle behind such a lease is that the tenant has exclusive right to the actual premises and has a right to use the "common parts" in common with the landlord and all other occupants, etc. The definition of the "common parts" will usually include the structure, including the roof, foundations, outside walls (apart from shop fronts) and the gable walls, and also the service media, heating, ventilation and air conditioning, fire alarm and security systems, passages, stairs, car park, service yards, lifts, stairs, entrance hall and other structural and common items.

Although the tenant is responsible for repair, maintenance, etc. of the premises, this is really only air-space and inner surfaces, and so the repairing obligation is not particularly onerous. The landlord is responsible for repair, maintenance, renewal, rebuilding, etc. of the common parts, which of course includes the whole structure. He will recover the cost of this from the various tenants through the service charge.

The landlord will insure the entire building or estate as the case may be, and will insure against loss of rent and service charge in respect of premises let to separate tenants. He will recover the cost of the insurance either as a separate charge or through the service charge.

It is normal for the lease to provide for services to be performed by the landlord, with recovery by way of service charge from the tenants.

How service charge works–overview

Having defined the "common parts", and having granted to the tenant the right **29–04** to use these in common, the lease will contain a list of services which the landlord will usually undertake to provide. The tenant will be required to pay his share of the cost of the provision of these services, and there will be provision for an accounting.

The services

"The services" will be defined as a list that will vary depending on the actual **29–05** building or entity involved, but will usually include:

- maintenance, repair and when necessary renewal, rebuilding, reinstatement and replacement of the common parts, which includes the actual structure of the building;
- lighting of roads and footpaths and other common parts;
- servicing, maintenance and operation, and where necessary, replacement and renewal of boilers, central heating systems, air-conditioning plant, lifts and escalators, etc.;
- landscaping and gardening;
- engaging and paying for managing agents to manage the whole property;
- heating the common parts, including toilets, reception area, entrance hall, etc.; and
- the cost of financing the services.

There will invariably be a "sweep-up" item, allowing the landlord to provide additional services from time to time. It is sensible to have this, as legal requirements, expected standards and technology all change from time to time, and it is important for the landlord to have some flexibility.

It is important to check whether the definition of "the services" is the actual list of items that are specified, or whether it is "such of the following that are from time to time provided by the landlord". If it is the latter, then the list of services is nothing more than a menu, from which the landlord can choose to provide none, some or all of the listed items.

The landlord's obligations

The tenant should check that the landlord has an absolute obligation to provide **29–06** the main items within the list of services. Nothing is achieved for the tenant if the lease merely states that the landlord is obliged to provide such of the services that he chooses to provide from time to time.

However, there will be times when the landlord is prevented, through no fault of his own, from performing fully all of the services, and the lease should provide for the landlord to be free of liability to the tenant for such failure, as long as the landlord is required to take all reasonable steps to resume providing the service as soon as possible.

Most tenants would agree there are certain core services that are necessary for the tenant's beneficial use and occupancy, while other services are not important, and can be provided if the landlord so chooses. There may not be much scope for revising the service charge provisions, as the landlord will, understandably, argue that he needs uniformity in the service charge provisions for all leases in the larger entity. If the lease has been drafted in a fair and reasonable manner, there should not be any need for the sensible tenant to revise the clause. However, there is always a first tenant, and there is always a first major, or anchor, tenant in to any development, and these tenants should take the opportunity to revise the lease so that it is fair and marketable from the tenant's viewpoint, as one day that tenant will probably seek to sub-let or to assign.

Who pays how much?

29–07 If the property is divided into units of equal size, and these are all being used for the same or similar purposes, then it is easy to see that each tenant should pay exactly the same. However, if the property has different sized units and these are used for different purposes, then the tenants who benefit more from the services should pay more for these. For example, a restaurant has more rubbish to dispose of and may have longer opening hours than retail units.

It is of the utmost importance to the landlord that he achieves 100 per cent recovery of service charge, although it has to be said that some landlords do take an unconventional approach to arithmetic and achieve 105 per cent or more recovery!

Some leases specify the actual percentage payable, and that way, the tenant knows where he stands so far as proportionate liability is concerned. The landlord will usually provide for apportionment to be made on the basis of the proportion of the floor area of the unit in question to the floor area of all the units in the property. This is generally fair, but it is important that there is consistency in the approach to determining floor area. Shops and offices are generally dealt with on a net internal area basis, while retail warehouses and industrial buildings are usually dealt with on a gross internal area basis. Complications can therefore arise if there is a mixed use development! Often, there is provision for the landlord to vary the percentages in a fair and equitable manner.

The tenant of a very large unit may demand that his service charge be on a stepped basis to give him a quantum allowance, so that for example the first 5,000 square feet are charged at the full rate, the next 3,000 square feet at a lower rate, and so on. The important thing to bear in mind is that every concession that is given to a tenant has to be paid for, either by the other tenants or by the landlord.

A somewhat old-fashioned way of apportioning service charge among tenants is to use the respective rateable values of the premises, but this creates difficulty if rating appeals are made by any tenants and are successful, as it throws out the existing apportionment each time.

The landlord of a development will usually want to have flexibility to increase or decrease the common parts and the size of the development, without denying the tenants beneficial use and occupancy of their particular unit and necessary common parts enjoyment. If there is no reserved right in favour of the landlord to carry out works or to change the common parts, etc. then he would be derogating from the grant, and exposing himself to a claim for damages or rescission of the lease by the tenant, as seen in Ch.3. If an extra unit is created, then the service charge liability matrix would need to be amended so as to reduce the existing tenant's proportions, although this should happen automatically if service charge is on a floor area basis.

Many leases will allow the landlord, acting in a fair and equitable manner, to vary the proportion payable by the tenant from time to time, and this is generally acceptable to tenants, as the landlord has to demonstrate that he is acting reasonably.

Payment and accounting

Some leases will provide for the landlord to be able to call on the tenant to **29–08** reimburse the landlord for the cost of services as and when these costs are incurred, or on the immediately following rent payment day. The more usual scenario is for the tenant to be required to pay "advance service charge", being a sum of money, usually paid quarterly on the rent payment days, to account of the service charge in advance, and for the landlord to have to provide a budget of service charge expenditure and annual statements of actual expenditure. The tenant should ensure the lease provides for the advance service charge to be payable by equal quarterly amounts based on a reasonable estimate of likely cost. The landlord should provide for the advance service charge to be payable at the same rate as the previous year's payments if the budget for the coming, or actual, service charge year has not yet been produced, so as to ensure continuity of cash flow.

There is also usually provision for any balance due by the tenant to be payable within 14 or 21 days after production of the annual statement, and for any surplus to be carried forward to the next year.

Case law

The lease will usually provide for the statement or certificate of expenditure to **29–09** be issued by the landlord's surveyor. In *W.W. Promotions (Scotland) Ltd v De Marco*[1] a lease contained a clause that the amount payable by the tenant was to be determined by the certificate issued by the landlord's surveyor, "whose decision shall be final". The tenant argued that there is an implied term that the service charge should be calculated on a reasonable basis. The court held that the parties had never intended that either of them would be able to question the terms of the certificate to determine whether the certifying surveyor had made an error. The court did, however, say that there is indeed an implied term that service charge costs have to be reasonably incurred, and that the parties to the lease could not have intended to give the landlord the right to incur costs that are inordinate and extravagant.

---

[1] *W.W. Promotions (Scotland) Ltd v De Marco*, 1988 S.L.T. (Sh. Ct) 43.

Commercially, if a landlord has a major tenant whose lease is about to expire, he may choose to accelerate work not yet needed and carry out that work before that lease ends, so as to recover a significant proportion of cost from the tenant.

In *Scottish Mutual Assurance Plc v Jardine Public Relations Ltd*[2] a three-year lease provided for the tenant to reimburse the landlord for the cost of repairs to the building, and the landlord sought to recover the whole cost incurred in the final year of the term of substantial renewal of the roof. The court held that the works were repairs, but it would not be reasonable for the tenant to have to pay the whole cost, as the roof would have a life expectancy way beyond the remaining term of the lease, and the court determined that the tenant should pay just under 40 per cent of the cost of the works as being a fair proportion.

Fixed and capped service charge concessions

29–10 In the same way as landlords sweeten a deal for tenants by allowing rent-free periods, they also sometimes (but perhaps more rarely) allow service charge concessions. These come in various forms, are invariably for the benefit of only the first tenant and are usually granted in the form of a personal back letter. These concessions include any of the following: allowing a service-charge free period; a fixed amount being payable for a certain period; a maximum amount being payable each year for a period of time; and a limit on annual increases payable by the tenant. If the tenant sub-lets, the concession will usually remain in place, but if he assigns, it will usually cease to apply, depending on the wording of the concession.

Sinking fund (provision for future expenditure)

29–11 A sinking fund is a fund that is built up in order to pay for the replacement of specific major items, such as a flat roof, lifts, escalators, boilers, etc. The sinking fund may not be called a "sinking fund" as such, but may be disguised as "provision for expenditure in respect of replacement or renewal of plant and machinery and other items". Although most tenants would not readily choose to put money aside on a regular basis for the landlord to spend in the future, it may be preferable to spread the cost of major items as opposed to having to find a large sum of money at once.

Note that a sinking fund is radically different to money paid in advance in respect of estimated expenditure for the year in question. If the tenant has no option but to go along with a sinking fund, then there should be a provision that the sinking fund is held separately from the landlord's other funds and is to be held by trustees, and that, if and when the landlord disposes of the property, the sinking fund will be transferred to trustees on the same basis for the new land-lord. The tenant should try to get contributions to the sinking fund capped, and if at all possible to achieve return of unused contributions at termination of the lease. He is unlikely to be successful with this argument.

If the tenant assigns the lease during the term then a deal should be done with the assignee to take account of contributions that the tenant has already made towards the sinking fund.

---

[2] *Scottish Mutual Assurance Plc v Jardine Public Relations Ltd* [1999] All E.R. (D.) 305.

The service charge code (optional)

The RICS introduced a Scottish edition of the code of practice for service charges **29–12** in commercial leases in September 2007, and this was updated with a second edition of the Code in June 2011. the Scottish Code is similar to the code of practice used in England. The code is not mandatory, and it is not implied into leases. If the parties to a lease want to follow the code, they should insert appropriate drafting into the lease. The intention of the code is to provide a service charge regime that is fair to both parties. Some of the provisions of the code are as follows:

- The tenants have the right to be able to reasonably challenge the need for expenditure.
- The landlord should monitor standards of services and should regularly review quality and cost.
- The landlord should communicate continuously, give good advance warning of proposed major expenditure and provide a summary of the results of tenders and the process that has been gone through, with full information on the programme of works, timing and likely cost.
- Where service charge payments paid in advance are kept in a separate account, interest earned should be credited back to that account.
- The tenants should not be required to pay, through service charge, for improvement or the equipping of any building,
- The charge should be shown to be fair and reasonable.
- The service charge should not be run at a profit, or indeed at a loss. However, the landlord is allowed to impose a reasonable management charge.
- The services provided should be beneficial and relevant to the needs of the property and its owner, occupiers and customers.
- The aim is to achieve value for money and effective service rather than always going for just the cheapest price.
- Service charge should not include initial design, construction or provision costs, nor any improvement costs over and above cost of normal maintenance or replacement. (Many landlords would resist this.)
- Apportionment of service charge should be fair and reasonable and should be applied consistently throughout the property having regard to the size, nature of use, benefits and use by the occupier.
- Any sinking, replacement or reserve funds should be held in an interest-bearing account held in trust for the occupiers of the property and separate from the landlord's own money. The landlord should act reasonably in estimating the amount of contributions to the fund, which should relate to specific items such as roof, boiler, plant, lift, etc. rather than just unidentified future expenditure. A clear explanation should be provided in calculating the fund contribution, having regard to a realistic assessment of the anticipated life of the item in question. The owner should be required to pay into the sinking or reserved fund account the amount due for vacant premises.

Drafting and revising service charge provisions–landlord's position

Matters referred to in the service charge code may or may not be taken into **29–13** account when drafting the lease. Quite separately, there are various points to consider when acting for a landlord in drafting and negotiating the service charge clauses in multi-occupancy leases:

- The landlord should only be required to do a bare minimum by way of services, but should have that the right to do additional specified services, and also a discretion to do other services. His obligation to do services must be subject to there being no external preventing factor such as strikes, unavailability of materials, etc.
- The landlord should have the right to carry out any additional services that he considers appropriate from time to time—this is the "sweep-up" clause.
- The landlord should be entitled to recover service charge on a floor area or other specified basis, but there should be the ability for the landlord to vary the basis of charging so long as he acts fairly and reasonably; it can be dangerous to put in specific percentages.
- There should be flexibility so that the landlord can vary the service charge allocation if the larger entity grows or shrinks.
- There should always be full recoverability from the tenants in respect of service charge, hence the need for the landlord to be able to vary the basis of charging.
- There should be provision for penalty interest to be charged on advance service charge and on the payment of deficit in service charge following year-end accounting, from the due date until paid.
- There should be no right in favour of the tenant to withhold, retain or set-off any advance service charge payments.
- The landlord will want to have the right to insure the whole entity, with recoverability from the tenants in respect of insurance premiums that may or may not be apportioned in the same way as service charge. Premiums in respect of loss of rent and service charge insurance should be separate for each of the premises and should be payable by the tenants within a short time after demand.
- All leases of parts of the whole entity must be consistent in respect of service charge so as to avoid impossibility of performance, or arguments from one tenant that he is paying for services that are not appropriate or applicable to his premises.

Each concession to one tenant is a liability either on the other tenants or on the landlord himself.

Drafting and revising service charge provisions—tenant's position

29–14   If acting for the tenant, or for a prospective assignee or sub-tenant, the following matters should be considered:

- There should be a positive and absolute obligation on the landlord to carry out what the tenant considers to be the essential services; failure on the landlord's part to perform due to circumstances outside his control (or force majeure) is usually an acceptable exclusion, provided he undertakes to perform as soon as possible.
- Replacement, renewal and rebuilding are only to be done if an item is beyond economic or viable repair.

- The sweep-up clause is qualified so that any additional non-specified services are only provided for the benefit of the tenants as a whole, and are services that are normally provided in other similar entities in the same general locality.
- Check that the additional specified services are sensible and reasonable.
- There should be an obligation on the landlord to act reasonably and in the interests of economy in providing services.
- Try to cap the service charge liability for each year of the lease (or failing that at least for the first few years) so as to limit the tenant's maximum expenditure.
- Estimates of advance service charge are to be reasonable. The tenant should try to limit these annual increases to a small percentage increase (for example linked to the CPI, consumer prices index) above the previous year's actual service charge expenditure.
- Annual service charge accounts should be produced within a specific period of time after each service charge year, and the tenant should have the right to inspect vouchers.
- Beware of potentially extravagant items to improve amenity or to provide entertainment, other than where such cost is reasonable and is clearly to promote, for example, a shopping centre.
- Exclude from the service charge all expenditure in respect of the original construction of the entity, initial provision of services and initial landscaping.
- Exclude any expenditure for improvements, unless this is a necessary consequence of a replacement of something that is beyond economic or viable repair, and is of similar quality.
- Exclude expenditure in respect of provision and accommodation of staff relative to management of the entity.
- Exclude the amount of service charge that is payable for vacant premises let, or intended or able to be let.
- Exclude expenditure arising from damage or destruction by any of the insured risks.
- Exclude costs of enforcement of or proceedings relative to all leases.
- Exclude any expenditure in respect of financing and interest incurred by the landlord in respect of service expenditure. If the lease provides for advance service charge then there should be no need for financing charges.

CHAPTER 30

LEASES OF CARE HOMES

Introduction

30–01 The care home industry in Scotland is large, and is likely to grow further, despite the recent high profile failures among some of the main providers of care. Care homes provide care for the elderly, the young, those with, e.g. dementia, and others needing residential care. Many of the care homes, whether purpose-built, or converted Victorian houses, are leased.

There are various aspects of care home leases that are unique, and which require attention, whether acting for the property investor buying a care home with an income producing lease in place, a lender, an assignee, or indeed a landlord or tenant negotiating a new lease. The starting point is that the lease of a care home is a commercial lease of commercial premises.

A shop or other building in a high street of a town can be let to a new tenant in various sectors of the market, subject to any required planning permission being obtained. An industrial unit or an office in a business park will also have a wide pool of potential tenants. Many of the larger care homes have been purpose built or have undergone extensive refurbishment so as to be suitable for use, and many smaller care homes which were traditional houses etc. have also been adapted for use. There is a much smaller pool of prospective tenants for care homes than for other commercial properties.

Statutory regulation

30–02 In Scotland the current legislation is the Public Services Reform (Scotland) Act 2010, and various regulations and orders made under that Act. Before the 2010 Act came into force, the relevant legislation was the Regulation of Care (Scotland) Act 2001. The current Act regulates care, social work and child protection services, as well as regulating care homes. The inspection and regulatory body in Scotland is the Social Care and Social Work Improvement Scotland ("SCSWIS") but this is colloquially known as the "Care Inspectorate". This body does the equivalent job as the Care Quality Commission does in England and Wales. SCSWIS is responsible for registration and periodic inspection of care homes in Scotland.

What makes care homes different?

30–03 Although a care home is a commercial business, operating from commercial premises, there are significant differences to businesses carried on in the high street, an industrial estate or an office environment. When it comes to care homes, a lot of emotion is involved, as relatives of the residents of the care home are concerned that there is a good standard of care given, and are understandably worried if the business is sold, in particular as to whether standards will be maintained (or improved).

Generally in Scotland, care homes will have privately funded residents, as well as those who are paid for by the Local Authorities. Unless a care home is registered, and continues to remain registered, then it cannot trade.

If the tenant goes into administration or liquidation, the insolvency practitioner may try to sell the business and appoint a manager to run the business in the meantime. The manager will need to comply with the statutory and regulatory requirements until a buyer is found and the buyer becomes registered.

Typical specialist provisions in care home leases

The larger operators of care homes have over the past 10 to 15 years entered **30–04** into leases of a comparatively longer duration than found in leases of other commercial premises. 25 years is the norm, and in some cases 30 or 35 years. It is common to find an option in favour of the tenant to extend a care home lease by up to 25 years. This is because care home tenants are in business for the long run, and want to operate from a specific location.

It is usual to find provision for rent to be payable monthly in advance, as opposed to quarterly, and for rent reviews to take place every year as opposed to every five years. It is rare to find rent reviews based on open market rental values, and instead the care home industry has accepted rent reviews on the basis of a fixed increase each year (such as 2.5 per cent), or inflation linked, sometimes with a maximum and minimum percentage increase each year. Such annual review provisions have been attractive to property investors, and also to lenders in the past.

VAT

There is no Value Added Tax chargeable on the provision of services found in **30–05** care homes. Therefore it would be significantly adverse to a tenant if the landlord were to waive VAT exemption in respect of the property, as this would require the landlord to charge VAT on the rent, and the tenant would not be able to recover or set off that VAT. Accordingly, it is common to find in care home leases a clause that prohibits the landlord from doing anything to make VAT payable on the rent. Some leases go further and state that, if the landlord does register the property for VAT (waive VAT exemption in respect of the property), then the landlord will indemnify the tenant in respect of the VAT payable by virtue of such exemption, and in some cases the tenant is allowed to acquire the landlord's interest for an agreed consideration.

Tenant's financial covenant obligations

The concept of EBITDAR, frequently found in the world of accountancy, is **30–06** introduced into commercial leases of care homes. EBITDAR stands for earnings before interest, tax depreciation, amortisation, and rents. The landlord who enters into a care home lease wants to ensure that the tenant has sufficient financial strength throughout the term and might impose on the tenant an obligation to ensure that EBITDAR each year is disclosed to the landlord, and that if this falls below a specified ratio relative to rent then the landlord has various remedies. This can be used in order to trigger an option contained in the lease for the landlord to require the tenant to grant a renunciation, which is useful to the landlord if he finds another party who would be more profitable and thus enhance his investment value. It can be used to trigger an increase in rent once profitability has reached a certain level. EBITDAR is often used as a measure for assessing the financial strength of a prospective assignee.

Leases often provide for the tenant to comply with various financial covenants such as maintaining a net asset value of at least a minimum amount, maintaining a ratio of current assets to current liabilities (for example 1.2 to 1) and to maintain a ratio of cash flow to rent of for example 1.25 to 1.

Some care home leases also prohibit the tenant from incurring additional debt unless the ratio of cash flow to debt service is at least 1.5 to 1, and from making distributions in any accounting period which in aggregate are more than a proportion (for example half its net profit).

Although many leases that contain such financial covenant obligations say that any breach of these will entitle the landlord to seek a court order of irritancy, it is thought that irritancy may not work as a remedy, as the reasonableness test may not be passed, especially if, at the time, the tenant is up to date with rent, etc. payments. See para.30–09 below.

Rent review

30–07 In addition to fixed annual uplifts it is common to find rent reviews linked to inflation. Sometimes, rent will comprise two elements—a basic rent and a top-up rent—possibly linked to the tenant's EBITDAR or turnover, with the base rent being reviewed to the highest or average total rent over the preceding period of years.

Example wording for rent review involving fixed increases, inflation linking and maximum and minimum increases, are as follows:

Fixed increase

"At each Review Date, the annual rent payable hereunder shall be the amount of the annual rent payable immediately before the Review Date multiplied by 1.025"

This achieves a 2.5 per cent increase in rent each year.

Annual Inflation Increase (wording for maximum and minimum increase is in *italics*)

"As at each review date the yearly rent payable hereunder shall be increased to an amount (herein called "the revised rent") being the annual rent payable immediately before the relevant review date increased by a percentage equivalent to the increase in the General Retail Prices Index for the year preceding the Review Date, *[subject to a minimum increase of [1]% per annum and a maximum increase of [4]% per annum]* and declaring that any change in the said General Retail Prices Index commencement date or it being rebased, shall not prejudice or affect the rent review provisions herein contained and further declaring that in the event of cessation of said index or if it is otherwise impossible to ascertain the increase in the index then such index as shall replace the said General Retail Prices Index will be used and if no replacement is provided or available then such index as shall be agreed upon between the landlord and the tenant will be used, and failing agreement on same, such other index as shall be determined by an arbitrator appointed and acting in accordance with arbitration provisions contained in this lease. If for any reason the arbitrator is unable to or otherwise fails to determine any such index then the rent will be increased to the open market rental value of the

premises at the review date as such expression "open market rental value" is
defined in clause [ ] hereof."

Tenant's obligations re statutory regulation

A care home lease should provide for the following obligations on the tenant, **30–08**
for as long as the premises are used as an establishment requiring registration
under the Public Services Reform (Scotland) Act 2010[1] (or any replacement of
that Act):

- To obtain and keep in place all necessary registrations, and to comply
  fully with all relevant legislation and with the requirements of the
  relevant authorities.
- To manage and control the Premises properly so as to not prejudice the
  registration.
- To provide the landlord with details of all changes in the registration
  made pursuant to the Act.
- To give the landlord a copy of all inspection reports and correspondence from the registration authorities, and to comply fully with these.
- At termination of the lease, to co-operate with the landlord to facilitate
  the continuation of the business.
- To irrevocably appoint the landlord as attorney of the tenant to do
  everything necessary to facilitate the registration of any future owner
  or occupier of the premises.

Tenant default

The ultimate sanction is of course irritancy, but in a care home situation this **30–09**
may not be attractive to the landlord. It is necessary to be registered under the
relevant Act in order to operate the care home and, as it is the tenant who is
actually running the business, it is he who necessarily has this registration. If
the lease is irritated, then the landlord's investment could be prejudiced, as the
value of the property will decline if it is not trading. For non-money breaches,
it may not be "fair and reasonable" in terms of the Law Reform Miscellaneous
Provisions (Scotland) Act 1985[2] for the landlord to irritate the lease.

Irritancy of a lease does not automatically transfer ownership of the moveables to the landlord. The moveables are likely to be very valuable and are of
course absolutely essential to the continued running of the business.

Landlords may attempt to get round the difficulties with irritancy, by
including a contractual provision that the landlord is entitled to terminate the
lease if certain events happen. This is really irritancy by the back door, as the
trigger event is a breach of an obligation of the tenant. It is impossible to
contract out of the tenant protection provisions in the 1985 Act, and so it is
thought that such a provision could be struck at by a tenant or an insolvency
practitioner.

For this reason, landlords of care homes will often require a standard security from the tenant (if the lease is for longer than 20 years) and/or a floating

---

[1] Public Services Reform (Scotland) Act 2010.
[2] Law Reform Miscellaneous Provisions (Scotland) Act 1985.

charge (available for any duration of lease) over the tenant's assets. It is generally considered to be easier to enforce a standard security or a floating charge than to enforce irritancy. However, the standard security only enables the landlord to serve a notice of default, or to call up the security, and then to market the tenant's interest, or to enter into possession of the property. Of course, if the landlord enters into possession of the property he still has to overcome the problems about registration under the 2010 Act. Obtaining a standard security or floating charge is not a cure all. There may be a prior ranking standard security, so that the tenant can obtain funding to operate its business. If the landlord is obtaining a standard security over the tenant's interest in the lease then the following matters should be catered for:

- Provide for the creditor (landlord) to insure at the debtor's (tenant's) cost; this is because the lease will usually provide for the landlord to insure at the tenant's cost.
- As the standard security represents a contingent obligation on the tenant, the tenant's statutory right of redemption should be contracted out of.
- In order to avoid conflicts between the lease and the standard security, there should be a statement that the lease will prevail in the event of any conflict between the two.
- The standard security should be to secure the tenant's obligations to pay all sums from time to time under the lease, and to perform all other obligations under the lease. It may be easier for the landlord to enforce the standard security than to enforce the irritancy clause.

If the landlord wants to rely on the floating charge instead of the standard security, he can appoint an administrator of the tenant if the tenant is in breach. The administrator would then run the home until a buyer is found.

Restricting the use

30–10 Because a care home has to be registered under the relevant Act, the permitted use should be as a care home that is registered under the Act. The landlord may well want to specify the number of registered beds for each category if the registration covers more than one category – some categories may attract higher weekly occupancy fees and therefore it will be in the landlord's interest to ensure this allocation continues. The clause could be expressed so as to prohibit any change in the number of registered beds in total, and also the number of registered beds in any particular category. The clause could also totally prohibit any change of use. As many care home leases have rent reviews that are fixed or inflation linked, this will not be detrimental to the landlord at rent review in such cases. However, if rent reviews are based on open market value, a very strict use clause will be adverse to the landlord at rent review.

Alterations

30–11 For larger properties, the landlord is likely to allow more discretion to the tenant to carry out alterations without requiring consent, subject to the usual obligation to reinstate if so required by the landlord at termination of the lease. The lease should contain a provision that any alterations to the premises that are needed in order to comply with statutory regulations of care homes should not require landlord's consent.

Alienation

If a property investor owns a large number of care homes he may want to try to **30–12** control who is the actual tenant of any of these, so as to ensure that he does not have too much exposure to one particular tenant in the care home industry. It is therefore quite common for care home leases to include a definition of "prohibited assignees". These leases are also likely to contain a stricter test of financial strength, possibly with reference to EBITDAR, than leases of other properties, and are also likely to impose on the outgoing tenant the obligation to procure that an incoming tenant grants a standard security and/or floating charge to the landlord, if the existing tenant has granted these.

The care home operator obviously has to enter into contracts with the individual residents or in the case of Council funded occupants, contracts with the Local Authority, and this must be allowed in the lease.

Tenants will often want to have the right to have members of the same group of companies occupying parts of the premises, on the basis that no tenancy rights are acquired by such occupant. This is particularly the case in respect of specialist services provided by different divisions of a group. In addition, care home operators are increasingly offering ancillary services such as hairdressing, beautician etc. and these are often by way of concession occupancies to the providers of such services, no tenancy rights being created.

Change of control of tenant

The landlord may have great faith in the existing management of the tenant. **30–13** Change of control of a registered operator of a care home requires a new registration with the authorities, and therefore the landlord has an interest in restricting change of control. Irritancy is unlikely to be appropriate, as the tenant itself has done nothing wrong. it is only the shareholders who change. However, the landlord could include an obligation in a standard security or floating charge that the tenant must not undergo any change of control except with the landlord's consent and that a breach of the obligation would entitle the landlord to call up the standard security or to appoint an administrator.

Moveables

The landlord has a right of hypothec over all moveables in the premises from **30–14** time to time, but only so far as these are owned by the tenant. Therefore any moveables that are leased to the tenant by third parties, or that are subject to retention of title, or owned by any concessionaire, etc. will not be included in hypothec. Hypothec no longer allows the landlord to sell these items, but it does give the landlord a higher degree of ranking than merely being an ordinary creditor.

The main thing about the moveables is that they are very specialist in nature and are often very expensive to replace. They are absolutely essential to the proper running of the care home. Many leases will contain a provision that on termination of the lease the tenant's trade and other fixture and fittings, beds and other furniture, nurse call systems, fire alarm and security system, and all other items in connection with the running of the business carried on at the premises will, without any payment being due or payable in respect thereof be transferred to and will belong to the landlord or will be sold to the landlord for a nominal consideration. However, if the tenant has granted a floating charge to any other party, these items will be subject to the charge, and can be disposed of by the chargeholder.

There are two suggested ways of dealing with the problem:

(1) The tenant transfers ownership of the moveables to the landlord on the date of grant of the lease, and the landlord leases these as well as the premises to the tenant. This has the effect of retaining ownership of the moveables in the landlord. However, that only deals with the moveables as at the date of the grant of the lease; in order to fully protect the landlord, the tenant would need to transfer ownership of all items acquired and in the premises during the lease on each occasion this happens. Being realistic, this is unlikely to happen!

(2) The tenant signs a declaration of trust that all moveable items in the premises from time to time are held by the tenant in trust for the landlord, and these are deemed to be delivered to the landlord by their physical presence in the premises, and that at termination of the lease, for whatever reason, these will be left in the premises for the landlord to use, retain or dispose of as the landlord sees fit.

Obviously it is necessary for the landlord to be aware of which moveables are owned by the tenant and which are leased or are subject to retention of title.

CHAPTER 31

GREEN LEASES

Introduction

Green leases, which started life in Australia, and were subsequently adopted **31–01** with enthusiasm in Canada. Awareness of these has been growing in the UK, and they do make their presence felt in some new developments, and increasingly in the public sector. They encourage the landlord and tenant to work together by creating environmentally friendly policies, which enable the increase of a building's energy efficiency, by reducing its energy consumption, water usage and waste production and by other environmentally-focused actions.

However, landlords are reluctant to make their leases even more onerous on tenants at a time when many tenants are economically fragile, and when it is difficult to fill empty properties. Landlords and their tenants do not want to spend money on carrying out works to bring premises up to an enhanced standard of environmental performance.

If some of the environmental provisions are now contained in statute, then a simple obligation on the tenant to comply with all statutory requirements will be sufficient. There is a generally accepted desire to improve sustainability, not least because government and other public tenants have sustainability very high up on their agenda.

The Better Buildings Partnership, which is a group of some of the major commercial property owners in London, published its green lease tool kit in 2009. Public sector tenants are enthusiastic about the idea of green leases.

Landlords and investors are unwilling to incur capital costs to improve the energy, water and waste efficiency of a building unless they can recover the cost of these improvement works through savings in service charge. It is the tenant who will benefit through lower energy and waste bills. However, the landlord may experience an increase in demand for a building that costs less to run. He may also see this same reward when it comes to negotiating a new lease, at which point there may be more of a market available to the landlord because his building is more energy efficient.

There are various degrees of sustainability that can be contained in a lease – there can be a very soft commitment that the parties agree to co-operate to try to save energy and to use sustainable materials. A stronger approach can be achieved by prescribing that any alteration works or repairs must use sustainable materials where these are available, as well as setting general obligations and the most extreme fashion would be to set specific targets with legal commitments and rewards/sanctions. However, for as long as the market remains subdued, green leases are not going to be at the top of the agenda. Having said that, corporate social responsibility is more of a significant factor, and the public sector is very keen on sustainability and energy saving.

Green leases are thought to be beneficial to both the landlord and tenant, not only for environmental reasons, but also because they bring with them certain commercial advantages for each party. This Chapter looks at the environmental background and the legislation introduced in Scotland (similar requirements have been introduced in England) relating to provision of energy performance of buildings, and the main aspects that are provided for in green leases.

Background

31–02   The growth of environmental awareness and the increase in energy prices have led to building owners and occupiers becoming more aware of energy efficiency. European legislation requires member countries to cut greenhouse gas emissions, a significant amount of which is produced by buildings consuming energy.

The EU Energy Performance in Buildings Directive requires Member States to introduce energy performance certificates ("EPC") for buildings. In Scotland, the relevant provisions are contained in reg.6.9 of the Building (Scotland) Amendment Regulations 2006.[1]

Although it is clearly possible to design new buildings to be more energy efficient, this usually comes at an increased cost; it is also possible to alter existing buildings to make them more energy-efficient, but this is likely to involve quite considerable cost. The expense involved in providing a new building or converting an existing property to make it more environmentally friendly can in fact be economically worthwhile for both parties.

31–03   Leases of commercial property have previously not addressed any environmental issues. Green issues are increasingly influencing the commercial leasing market in the UK, starting with the overall desire that buildings should be "sustainable". Environmentally concerned tenants have been pressing landlords to improve the sustainability of buildings, and some environmentally concerned landlords have been persuading tenants to adopt more sustainable behaviour in occupying buildings.

In short, a green lease includes an agreement between the landlord and tenant as to how the property is to be used, managed and occupied in an environmentally friendly way. Green leases impose obligations on the tenant to increase the energy efficiency of a building by decreasing consumption, water usage and waste production, and by increasing recycling.

Before a landlord offers a green lease, he should have an environmental audit done in respect of the building to determine what energy efficiency measures can be put in place and to assess the costs; any energy efficiency targets need to be realistic. A little improvement is better than none, and there is no point in parties entering into obligations that cannot realistically be performed.

Energy Performance Certificates

31–04   An Energy Performance Certificate ("EPC") is needed for all commercial buildings unless the building:

- has an intended life of two years or shorter;
- does not use fuel or power to control internal temperature;

---

[1] The Building (Scotland) Amendment Regulations 2006 (SSI 2006/534).

- is a place of worship, such as a church;
- is a temporary building in use for less than two years, such as a portacabin;
- is a low energy demand building, such as an outbuilding; or
- is a stand alone building less than 50sq m.

The EPC is produced by an accredited energy assessor, and is issued with a recommendation report, which includes advice and suggestions on improvements. There is a fine of up to £1,000 imposed as a civil penalty for failure to provide an EPC, but there is at present no sanction for failing to improve energy performance or to implement recommendations contained in an EPC.

The EPC measures the energy performance of a building based on its design; the certificate needs to be renewed every 10 years, and it must be produced when selling or granting a new lease or a renewal of a lease of the building. An EPC gives information about the estimated energy consumption of a building, based on the energy efficiency of the building itself rather than on the appliances inside it; this allows investors and occupiers to determine a building's green credentials at the time of purchase or of entering into a lease. The certificate will also take into account the age, location, size and condition of the building when providing the rating.

Display Energy Certificates

Public buildings, i.e. public sector buildings regularly visited by the public, such **31–05** as sports centres, libraries, schools, hospitals, concert halls, theatres and some local government offices, need to have and display a Display Energy Certificate ("DEC"), which shows the energy consumption of a building and its Operational Rating, and enables the public to see the energy efficiency of a building. This is based on the energy consumption of the building as recorded by gas, electricity and other meters. The DEC should be clearly displayed at all times so as to be clearly visible by the public. DECs have to be renewed on an annual basis, and they apply to buildings with a usable floor area greater than 1,000 sq. m.

Provision of certificates

From January 4, 2009, an EPC has been needed for the sale or lease of any **31–06** commercial building in Scotland, unless the building falls within one of the exemptions detailed in para.31–04 above.

Although there is no sanction at present for failure to implement recommendations contained in an EPC, it is possible that in the future there could be sanctions introduced in the form of taxation on energy inefficiency and waste.

The applicable date for introduction of EPCs for commercial buildings in England was October 1, 2008.

In conducting a lease transaction, the tenant's solicitors need to check whether a building has got an EPC or a DEC.

Green leases—design issues and benefits for the parties

In deciding to go along the "green" route, the landlord should consider what **31–07** environmental and energy saving benefits he is willing to provide. There is clearly much more scope for effective measures when a large multi-occupancy entity is being designed for construction, rather than where an old building is being leased. The landlord may be constructing a shopping centre or business park that can be heated and powered by renewable or recycled energy sources. An extension to the existing public transport network could be negotiated by the developer to allow easy access to and from the property, and the landlord could provide cycle racks and internal estate cycle paths. For new and existing multi-occupancy buildings, the landlord can undertake to provide as efficient a boiler, air conditioning, water heating, and other services, etc. as reasonably possible in the circumstances. This will make the property more attractive to tenants, and will achieve an energy cost saving for tenants.

From the tenant's point of view an environmentally friendly property has the advantages of reduced energy costs and reduced service charges, and increased marketability of the tenant's interest, as prospective tenants or sub-tenants will like the cheaper running costs and the fact that the building "measures up" environmentally. An added attraction is the possibility of carbon emission trading schemes for medium-size energy users. Employees are increasingly aware of their well-being at work, and environmentally friendly buildings can help attract and retain staff, improve productivity, reduce absenteeism and enhance the tenant organisation's reputation.

From the landlord's point of view, the benefits of a building that is environmentally friendly are likely to be recognised in property valuations, and the property is likely to be more marketable, due to higher demand from tenants for a building with low environmental impact. Property lenders will also prefer to lend in respect of a property that ticks all the right environmental boxes, as the property is then more marketable for purchasers and for prospective tenants. Tenants will not want to sign up to a lease of a building that is going to cost more to run than a non-environmentally friendly building.

31–08   The landlord should modify buildings, plant and equipment to improve energy efficiency and produce lower operating costs. He should instigate a green management plan, setting realistic targets rather than setting out obligations, and should ensure that all plant and equipment, and in particular air conditioning systems, operate to maximum efficiency. He should also arrange an annual independent audit of the building's performance level.

Where potential tenants are proposing to fit out premises, the landlord may want some control over the design and materials used, so as not to adversely affect energy efficiency. Tenants would therefore have to comply with the landlord's specific fit-out policy, and would need to factor in any additional cost of compliance.

Provisions that can be included in the green lease

31–09 Green lease provisions can be grouped together in a schedule or, perhaps preferably, can be slotted in to the relevant parts of the lease, so that the parties know what obligations are imposed in respect of each relevant aspect of the lease.

Matters that could be inserted into a new lease, or indeed by way of mutual agreement into an existing lease, include the following:

- Provision for independent regular audits of the building, to assess whether there has been compliance. There needs to be a dispute resolution procedure.
- Depending on the degree of "green" involvement, there can be provision for a tenant handbook/environmental policy/energy management

plan. The landlord would produce a handbook or information pack, which can contain the current data, targets and information on the availability of grants, loans and support schemes.

- For multi-let buildings, the landlord is to separately meter the water, gas and electricity consumption of each tenant.
- In drafting the clauses that deal with tenant's works and alterations:

  (a) there should be a requirement that any works that are carried out by the tenant should use recycled materials or those that can be recycled if at all practicable;
  (b) tenant's alterations should be energy neutral or should provide energy savings;
  (c) the tenant should be required to use the cleaning and waste removal services of the landlord, if provided;
  (d) the tenant should not be allowed to install partitioning that makes the air conditioning system less efficient or that leads to a greater use of energy;
  (e) there should be a prohibition against carrying out any alterations that materially impact adversely on the environmental performance of the building, including any adverse effects on the ratings contained in the EPC/DEC; and
  (f) if the tenant wants to change the use of the premises, and this involves any alterations to the layout, etc. of the premises, the landlord should be deemed to be acting reasonably in refusing consent if such change would adversely affect the energy efficiency of the building.

- The tenant should observe and perform the landlord's green management plan, and should give back the premises with at least the same energy rating as applied at the beginning of the lease.
- There are some significant points in respect of rent review:

  (a) because an EPC needs to be produced on a sale or a new lease, there should be an assumption at rent review that the property has a current EPC and that all recommendations in it have been implemented.
  (b) at rent review it should be assumed that the energy rating has remained the same, or has improved, if that is the case.
  (c) if the tenant has paid for green improvements, these should be ignored, as he gets the benefit; however, if the landlord has paid for green improvements, these should be rentalised, as the tenant is getting a benefit for which the landlord has paid.

- Recycling bins should be provided as part of the services and the tenants should have to use these.
- The landlord is entitled to carry out repairs and alterations to the property to improve energy efficiency. (The tenant may object to this as being unfair, as the landlord could unilaterally cause an increase in any uplift achievable at rent review by adding value to the premises. However, the tenant will benefit by cheaper running costs.)
- On assignation or a sub-lease, an obligation is to be given by the assignee or sub-tenant to the landlord to comply with the landlord's environmental policy for the building/estate.

- If the premises are part of a larger entity controlled by the landlord, then he should be required to have all the buildings or estate systems operate to maximum efficiency levels as certified by an appropriate professional. If the premises are all that the landlord owns at that location, the obligation should instead be imposed on the tenant.
- The landlord should be required to monitor energy consumption and to lower levels where appropriate in order to meet efficiency targets.
- Co-operation by the landlord in implementing environmentally friendly travel to work policies such as bicycle racks.
- Service charge–the landlord could reserve the right to adjust the service charge payable by each tenant to reflect their respective environmental impact, and to reward "good" tenants.
- Obligation to provide to the landlord full details of the tenant's energy and water use, including all meter readings and monitoring data, and to allow the landlord access to inspect as well.
- There can be provision for a building management committee; this can include energy representatives from both sides.
- Obligation on both parties to produce energy and sustainability performance reports from time to time.
- Dilapidations: if the energy efficiency shown in the EPC/DEC is worse at any time during or at the end of the term than at the beginning, there should be an obligation on the tenant to carry out or contribute to the cost of carrying out any works required or recommended to restore the energy rating to what it should be. (The tenant would, however, probably seek to exclude from his responsibility any works required due to advances in technology.)
- The tenant should not be required to reinstate or remove alterations that helped to achieve energy efficiency measures or targets.
- There could be provision for the tenant to get rent rebates or a service charge reduction if the landlord fails to perform agreed obligations in respect of energy efficiency improvements, or to meet the required energy efficiency rating for the building.
- Any maintenance contracts for services need to be performed so as to not reduce the energy rating of the building.
- There should be a dispute resolution procedure and provisions for development of a remedial action plan where energy efficiency and sustainability targets have not been met.

It should be remembered that if there are too many clauses that are onerous on the tenant, there will be an adverse effect on the landlord at rent review. However, as green leases become more common, a suite of generally acceptable clauses will evolve, and these will become the market norm, thus avoiding any detriment to the landlord at rent review.

Green lease buildings—an emerging market?

31–10 If buildings that are not environmentally friendly are less attractive to tenants, they will command a lower rent than those that are sustainable. They will also take longer to re-let and they will have higher running costs, especially for energy. If property investors start to select their investments on the basis of sustainability or at least taking that into significant account, then owners of older or "non-compliant" stock could find that they are in a second-class market.

Institutional investors will feel a responsibility to invest in environmentally friendly/sustainable properties.

Landlords may find higher tenant demand for a building that has a low environmental impact and lower running costs; they may also find that property lenders may well prefer to lend in respect of a property that ticks all the right environmental boxes.

Many corporate and government occupants in the UK will choose not to occupy a new building that does not meet their sustainability criteria–it is also a factor that is taken into account when they are taking older or "non-compliant" stock for occupancy. Low running and maintenance costs for buildings are an incentive for tenants to go in. The investment community is starting to focus on sustainability.

Perhaps the environmental improvement of properties will come as a result of commercial pressures, as opposed to being the result of an environmental enlightenment.

Carbon reduction Energy Efficiency Scheme

The CRC Energy Efficiency Scheme is mandatory and has been introduced to **31–11** improve energy efficiency in large public and private sector organisations. Details of the scheme are available on the Department of Energy and Climate Change's website address, *https://www.gov.uk/crc-energy-efficiency-scheme* [accessed April 2013]. There are some issues for landlords and tenants. A landlord may find that the cost of participation in the scheme that is attributable to a property may not be recoverable from the tenant in terms of the lease. An existing tenant will not have much of any incentive to vary his lease so as to sign up to pay yet another overhead. Even where a new lease is being negotiated, a strong tenant may simply refuse to accept liability for the CRC participation. Even if he is willing to contribute, he may refuse to pay all or part of the landlords cost of registration and reporting.

A tenant should be aware of the extra cost involved if he is liable for the costs of the landlord's CRC commitment. This extra cost may have the effect of making the lease less attractive to a prospective assignee. The tenant will also need to be aware of any increase in service charge costs arising from the landlord putting in place energy saving initiatives so as to improve its CRC performance. These initiatives could include repairs or improvements to the common parts or to plant and machinery.

CHAPTER 32

THE SHORT FORM MISSIVE OF LEASE

Introduction

32–01 Property owners often want to let out their property on the basis of a simple and straightforward lease for a relatively short term, maybe only for a month, especially in the run-up to Christmas. They want the transaction to be quick and cheap. This Chapter addresses the short form of lease, which is in the form of missives, so as to avoid the need to adjust and enter into a separate lease document, and thus the missives and the lease document are rolled into one. A style of short form missive of lease is provided starting at para.32–18, and a further copy is included on the CD supplied with this book.

The style is very much weighted in the landlord's favour, and therefore tenants should revise it so as to soften the obligations that are imposed.

The style includes provision for the tenant to contribute towards the cost of repairs, etc. of common parts of a larger building. It also contains a full rent-review clause and can be adapted for different premises. If there are to be no rent reviews, then the whole rent-review clause can be omitted. This Chapter contains a commentary on the style, but the reader should bear in mind this is merely a style and that it should be adapted to take account of the particular premises and transaction.

The RICS Scottish Branch has issued an even briefer document for use in leases of retail shops for short term lettings.

Initial paragraph

32–02 The initial paragraph sets out the parties and the premises. If the premises form part of a larger building, it is necessary to give the tenant a right in common to use the "common parts". A suggested definition is provided, but this will need to be amended to take account of the specific characteristics of the common parts in question.

Clause 1

32–03 This says that the lease rests on the missives, i.e. the missives will be the lease itself.

Clause 2—duration

32–04 This sets out the duration of the lease. If there is to be any option to terminate early then this should be included here and the option should be clearly worded, so as to say who can exercise it, and when and how it can be exercised. For example

"notwithstanding the foregoing the Tenant is entitled to terminate the Lease as at [date] by serving not less than [three] months prior written notice to that effect on the Landlord, such notice being able to be served by fax and/or recorded delivery post."

Clause 3—rent

This sets out the rent and provides for quarterly instalments in advance. The **32–05** amount payable at entry is three months' rent, and then at the end of that three-month period, the amount of rent from that day until the day before the next quarterly rent payment day is payable. This is calculated by dividing the annual rent by 365 (or 366 in a leap year) and multiplying by the number of days from that day until the day before the next quarter day inclusive. The landlord has the right to have rent paid by bankers order. (VAT on rent is dealt with in clause 4.1 of the style.)

If there is a rent-free period then this should be included in clause 3. Of course, if there is a rent-free period granted in any lease, the tenant is still responsible for other payments such as insurance, rates, etc. from the start of the term.

Clause 4—statutory notices and other payments by the tenant

The tenant is to comply with any statutory notices affecting the premises. **32–06**
The tenant is to pay:

- VAT (if payable) on rent and all other sums;
- local rates and all utilities charges;
- insurance premia in respect of the premises and for loss of three years' rent; if the premises are part of a larger entity, the tenant is to pay the amount reasonably determined by the landlord;
- if the premises are part of a larger entity, the tenant is to pay the proportion reasonably determined by the landlord of repairs, etc. to the common parts;
- interest at four per cent above base rate on rent from the due date, and on all other sums from the date of demand;
- stamp duty land tax and registration costs; and
- enforcement costs, and also the cost of schedules of dilapidations.

Clause 5—tenant's non-money obligations

This contains obligations on the tenant as follows: **32–07**

- to use the premises for a specified purpose. Landlord's consent to change of use is needed, but is not to be unreasonably withheld;
- to not do anything to cause nuisance or disturbance;
- this is a very strong repairing, etc. obligation, in which the tenant accepts the premises and the common parts as being in good repair, and undertakes to put and keep the premises in good repair, to keep them wind and watertight and to renew and rebuild as necessary, even if this is due to any latent or inherent defect. Many tenants will not accept such an onerous repairs clause in a short-term lease (if at all), and will insist they only have to keep the premises in no worse condition than when they take entry, and for them to not be responsible for

fair wear and tear. In a short-term letting, the landlord may accept the tenant's position as he is getting rent for the short period of the lease;

- not to assign, sub-let, share or allow possession, except with landlord's consent, which is not to be unreasonably withheld in the case of assignation or sub-lease of the whole. Everything else is prohibited;
- not to carry out alterations or additions except with landlord's consent, which is not to be unreasonably withheld. See cl.6 of the style for optional reinstatement;
- to notify the landlord if any damage occurs to the premises. The landlord has an interest in making sure that the property is not damaged or destroyed and he may not know if there is a problem unless the tenant tells him;
- to comply with all statutory requirements relating to the premises. This is a compliance with standards matter, and is different to an obligation to comply with statutory notices, which is an enforcement issue;
- not to do anything that increases the insurance costs or which endangers insurance cover remaining in place; and
- to allow the landlord, on not less than three days' written notice (except in emergencies), to inspect and to carry out works or repairs not only to the premises but also to adjoining property. The landlord must make good any damage he causes in exercising this right.

Clause 6—tenant's obligations at termination

32–08 The tenant is to leave the premises in good condition and must remove his fixtures and fittings at termination. The obligation on the tenant to vacate the premises at termination of the lease is not good enough to actually terminate the lease and allow the landlord to recover possession, as tacit relocation will operate unless requisite notice is given by either party or unless the tenant has given to the landlord a separate document undertaking to vacate the premises at the contractual termination date of the lease. See Ch.19.

Clause 7—irritancy, indemnity and notices

32–09 If rent or any other money is not paid in time, or if there is any other breach of tenant's obligations or if the tenant becomes insolvent, the landlord can seek an order terminating the lease. The statutory protection applies whereby a tenant is to be given at least 14 days' prior written notice threatening termination on the grounds of monetary breach and the opportunity to save his lease, and the landlord can only seek termination for non-monetary breaches if in all the circumstances a fair and reasonable landlord would seek termination.

The tenant indemnifies the landlord in respect of any loss, expense or claim arising from the state of repair or the use made of the premises and any breach by the tenant or any permitted occupant

Notices are to be in writing, and if addressed to the tenant, they are to be sent or delivered to the premises. If sent by recorded delivery post, they are deemed served at the premises 48 hours after posting.

Exclusion of landlord's obligations

32–10 Clause 7 also says that the landlord does not require to carry out any works whatsoever. This is a very important clause because the landlord would have an obligation to carry out certain works by virtue of common law if this clause were not inserted.

The warranties implied by common law that planning permission exists for the permitted use from time to time and that the premises are fit for the purpose let, are specifically excluded.

Fast-track enforcement

Clause 7.6 contains the tenant's consent to registration for execution and there- **32–11** fore the tenant is agreeing that summary diligence (fast-track enforcement) can be carried out by the landlord to obtain payment of known amounts of money due by the tenant.

Clause 8—lease continues in force

This clause contracts out of the common law rule of *rei interitus*, so that, if the **32–12** premises are significantly damaged or destroyed, the lease will continue in full force, subject to the termination provisions in clause 10.

Clause 9—rent review

If there are to be no rent reviews then this clause should be omitted. **32–13**

This is a typical rent-review clause and provides for upward only rent reviews. Review is to market value, and there is a list of assumptions and disregards, and provision for the review to be determined by an independent surveyor acting as an expert, if the review is not agreed by the review date. Interest runs on any uplift in rent at one per cent above base rate from the review date (or relevant quarter) until the quarter day after the review is agreed or determined. The subject of rent review is fully dealt with in Chs 10 and 11.

Clause 10—landlord's obligations—insurance and rent abatement

The landlord is required to insure the premises (or the building) against a list **32–14** of risks and for three years' loss of rent, taking into account potential increases at rent review, all at the cost of the tenant. The style provides for the landlord to have the right to choose, following damage or destruction caused by any of the insured risks, either to make good or to terminate the lease. The tenant will be excused from paying rent according to the degree of damage until three years after the insured risk damage or destruction, or until the premises and common parts have been made good, or until the loss of rent insurance proceeds have run out, whichever is the earliest. If he chooses to make good the insured damage, either party can terminate the lease if the damage has not been made good within three years. This clause can be tailored to fit in with whatever position is desired or negotiated; some landlords are happy to omit any obligation on their part to insure or to make good insured damage, but they are keen to include the obligation on the tenant to pay the insurance premium!

Clause 11—stamp duty land tax

If the lease is notifiable to HMRC then the tenant is to submit the SDLT return, **32–15** and is to produce the SDLT certificate so as to enable the landlord to register the lease.

Clause 12—deadline

32–16 This is the deadline for acceptance of the offer.

Other matters

32–17
- There is no element of conditionality in respect of the landlord being satisfied with the tenant's financial strength (or covenant).
- There is no conditionality on consent being obtained from the landlord's secured lender or floating charge holder.

Style short missive of lease

32–18 This style is drafted so as to be strongly weighted in favour of the landlord. Tenants should revise the document so as to water down some of the obligations that are imposed on the tenant.

Dear Sirs

On behalf of and as instructed by our clients, [*name*] (hereinafter referred to as "the Landlord") we hereby offer to lease to your client, [*name*] (who, and whose successors as tenant in the Lease including sub-tenants where the context so admits, are hereinafter referred to as "the Tenant") the property subjects comprising [*specify*] [shown outlined in red on the plan annexed and signed as relative hereto], (hereinafter referred to as "the Premises") [forming part of the building ("the building") known as *specify*], [together with a right in common with the landlord and all other occupants of the building to use the "Common Parts", being the solum, the foundations, the roofs of the building, the outside walls, and mutual gables so far as belonging to the building, all other structural parts of the building, and all other items from time to time used in common by more than one occupant of the building], and that on the following terms and conditions:

1. The lease (hereinafter referred to as "the Lease") of the Premises shall rest on the missives of which this offer forms part.
2. The period of this Lease shall be for the period of [*specify*] from and including [*date*] ("the date of entry") until and including [*date*].
3. The rent shall be [*number*] THOUSAND POUNDS (£ [*amount*]) Sterling per annum [subject to review as provided for in Clause 9 hereof] all payable by the Tenant quarterly in advance on the Scottish quarter days of 28th February, 28th May, 28th August and 28th November by equal instalments, by bankers order if so required by the Landlord, without retention, set-off or deduction, commencing the first payment being three months rent on the date of entry, and will pay on the date being three months after the date of entry rent apportioned on a daily basis as a fraction of a year from such date until the next occurring rent payment day specified above, and thereafter quarterly in advance.
4. The Tenant:
   4.1 shall pay to the Landlord value added tax and any other tax that may from time to time be payable on the rents and other sums

payable hereunder such Value added tax and other tax aforesaid being due and payable contemporaneously with payment of said rents and other sums.

4.2 shall pay to the appropriate authorities or bodies all local rates exigible in respect of the Premises during the Lease and all electricity, gas, water and telephone charges incurred during the period of the Lease.

4.3 shall comply with all statutory notices from time to time affecting the Premises.

4.4 shall reimburse to the Landlord on demand the cost incurred by the Landlord in insuring the Premises, [or the proportion determined by the Landlord acting reasonably, of the cost of insuring the building] for full reinstatement value as determined by the Landlord, third party liability and for insuring loss of rent in respect of the Premises for three years, [taking into account potential increases at rent review].

4.5 shall pay or reimburse the Landlord on demand the amount, determined by the Landlord acting reasonably, payable from time to time by the Landlord in respect of the Premises in respect of the cost of maintenance, repair, renewal, reinstatement, factoring and managing the building of which the Premises form part.

4.6 shall pay to the Landlord on demand:

4.6.1 interest on rent and on other sums of money payable to the Landlord at "the Prescribed Rate" being the rate of 4 per cent per annum above the base lending rate from time to time of The Royal Bank of Scotland plc or of such other clearing bank as is from time to time nominated by the Landlord, (a) in the case of rent the date when the same became due and (b) in the case of all other sums, the date of demand until payment thereof.

4.6.2 the cost of registration of the Lease in the Books of Council and Session and of obtaining two extracts.

4.6.3 The cost of enforcing any of the Tenant's obligation in the Lease, of making good any breach on the part of the Tenant, and of preparation and service of all schedules of dilapidations.

4.7 The Tenant agrees that a Certificate by the Landlord or by its Agents shall be conclusive evidence of the amount due in respect of rent or other sums of money due to the Landlord by the Tenant hereunder.

5. The Tenant:

5.1 shall use, and continuously during the Lease occupy, the Premises as [*specify*] and for no other purpose, except with the Landlord's prior written consent, which consent will not be unreasonably withheld.

5.2 shall not do anything which, in the opinion of the Landlord, may be or tend to become a nuisance or disturbance or inconvenience to the Landlord or to neighbours.

5.3 accepts the Premises [and the Common Parts] as being in good tenantable order and repair and shall, at the Tenant's expense put and keep the Premises in good order and repair and wind and water-tight, and in a clean and tidy condition and clear of all rubbish, and will if necessary reinstate, renew, replace or rebuild the Premises, irrespective of the cause of any damage, deterioration or destruction.

5.4 shall not at any time assign, sub-let or otherwise dispose of or, for any purpose in any way, deal with the Tenant's interest in or part with or share possession or occupation of the whole or part only of the Premises, except with the Landlord's prior written consent, which consent will not be unreasonably withheld in the case of a proposed assignation of the whole of the Lease or of a proposed sub-lease of the whole of the Premises.

5.5 shall not at any time cut, divide, alter or damage the Premises nor make any additions thereto, except with the Landlord's prior written consent, which consent will not be unreasonably withheld.

5.6 shall give immediate notice to the Landlord of any damage to the Premises.

5.7 shall comply in all respects with all statutory requirements relating to the Premises.

5.8 shall not do anything which increases the cost of insuring the Premises or of the building, or which prejudices the insurance.

5.9 shall permit the Landlord and its agents with or without workmen on not less than 3 days notice, except in emergencies when no notice is required, to enter the Premises to inspect the same or to carry out any repairs or alterations or improvements to the Premises or any adjoining or neighbouring property which the Landlord may deem necessary, subject to the Landlord making good any damage thereby caused to the Premises, and shall further permit all persons authorised in writing by the Landlord to view the Premises at all reasonable hours.

6. On the date of termination of the Lease the Tenant shall:

6.1 remove from and leave vacant and clear the Premises in good repair and condition, and freshly painted in a workmanlike manner to the Landlord's reasonable satisfaction.

6.2 replace or pay to the Landlord the replacement cost of any articles, fixtures or fittings which may have been broken or otherwise damaged, lost or stolen during the lease.

6.3 remove all of the Tenant's fixtures and fittings, machinery, equipment and effects from the Premises making good all damage caused by such removal.

6.4 except to the extent otherwise notified in writing by the Landlord to the Tenant, remove all alterations and additions made by the Tenant and reinstate and make good any damage caused in so doing.

7. The Tenant acknowledges and agrees that:

7.1 if the rent or any other money or any part thereof due by the Tenant under this Lease shall at any time be in arrears or if there shall be a breach of any of the other obligations undertaken by the Tenant under this Lease or, if the Tenant shall become apparently insolvent or is sequestrated or made bankrupt, or if a receiver, administrator or liquidator is appointed in respect of the Tenant, or shall make any arrangement with creditors or shall suffer any diligence to be levied on the Premises or the contents thereof, then and in any such case it shall be lawful for the Landlord by notice to the Tenant to bring this Lease to an end forthwith and to re-possess the Premises subject to the provisions of Sections 4, 5 and 6 of the Law Reform (Miscellaneous Provisions) (Scotland) Act 1985 but without prejudice to and reserving any right of action or remedy of the Landlord in respect of any previous breach of any of the obligations of the Tenant hereunder.

7.2 it shall indemnify the Landlord against loss, claim or expense arising from use or the state of repair of the Premises or any breach of the Tenant's obligations under the Lease by the Tenant and/or by any permitted occupant and/or of its or their employees, agents, customers or others.

7.3 any notice by the Landlord to the Tenant shall be deemed to be sufficiently served if sent to or delivered at the Premises. Any notice shall be in writing and shall be deemed to be received at the expiry of forty eight hours after posting if sent by recorded delivery post.

7.4 the Landlord does not require whether in terms of the Lease or at common law or otherwise to carry out any repairs or other works to the Premises or the building of which the Premises form part and that the Landlord shall at no time become liable to the Tenant for any loss, injury or damage which the Tenant may sustain from a deficiency in any part of the Premises or the building of which the Premises form part.

7.5 the Landlord gives no representation or warranty that (a) the use permitted hereunder is or will be or will remain a permitted use within the provisions of the Planning Acts, or (b) the Premises are fit for the purpose let.

7.6 it consents to the registration of this Lease and of any certificate hereunder for preservation and execution.

8. Subject to the termination provisions contained in Clause 10 hereof, the Lease will not be terminated in the event of any damage to or destruction of the Premises or of the building of which the Premises forms part.

9. Rent Review

9.1 As at [*specify*] in the years [*year*], [*year*] and [*year*] (each such date being called a "relevant date of review") the yearly rent payable hereunder shall be increased to an amount (hereinafter called "the revised rent") which shall represent the market rental value (as hereinafter defined) of the Premises at the relevant date of review.

9.2 Valuation

The "Market Rent "of the Premises at the relevant date of review shall be such an amount as may be agreed between the Landlord and the Tenant or determined in accordance with Sub-Clause 9.3 hereof as representing the market rent of the Premises for the period of this Lease on the open market as between a willing landlord and a willing tenant without payment of grassum or premium by the tenant and with vacant possession for a period equivalent to the then remaining term and upon the supposition (if not a fact):

(a) that all parts of the Premises are then available and able to be used for the purposes herein permitted;

(b) that the Landlord and the Tenant have complied with all their respective obligations imposed by these presents (but without prejudice to any rights of the Landlord in regard thereto);

(c) that no work has been carried out to the Premises by the Tenant or any permitted sub-tenants (notwithstanding that the Landlord may have granted consent thereto) which has diminished the market rent of the Premises;

(d) that the Tenant is registered for VAT purposes and is able to fully recover all input VAT (whether or not such is indeed the case); and

(e) that (without prejudice to the Landlord's control thereof in terms of this Lease) the Landlord will give consent to a change of use or assignation or sub-letting,

and taking no account of:

(i)   any goodwill attributable to the Premises by reason of any trade or business carried on therein by the Tenant or any sub-tenant or any predecessor in title to the Tenant's interest hereunder;

(ii) any effect on rent of any works or improvements to the Premises (to which the Landlord shall have given written consent) carried out by the Tenant or any sub-tenant or any predecessor in title to the Tenant's interest hereunder otherwise than in pursuance of an obligation to the Landlord;

(iii) the destruction of or damage to the Premises or the Building or any part thereof;

(iv) any effect on rent of the fact that the Tenant or any sub-tenant or any predecessor in title to the Tenant's interest hereunder may have been in occupation of the Premises;

(v)   the amount of rent payable under, and the terms of, any sub-lease of the Premises or any part thereof;

(vi) any rent free period, reverse premium or other financial inducement granted (a) to the Tenant at the commencement of the period of this Lease or when the Tenant took entry to the Premises or (b) to tenants of comparable subjects;

(vii) any restriction on use or on assignation or sub-letting herein stipulated;

and in all other respects on the terms and conditions of this Lease (excluding the actual amount of rent payable hereunder but with provision for upward only rent reviews on the same terms and with the same frequency as herein provided).

9.3 Decision on Market Rent

If the Landlord and the Tenant have not agreed on the amount of the market rent as aforesaid by the relevant date of review then on the election of either the Landlord or the Tenant the same shall be decided by a Surveyor who for at least five years prior to the relevant date of review has been either a partner or an associate partner or Consultant in a firm of Surveyors and is experienced in the letting and valuation of subjects similar to the Premises, to be agreed upon by the parties whereto or in the event of failure so to agree such Surveyor to be nominated at any time at the request of the Landlord or the Tenant by the Chairman or Senior Office Holder or his deputy for the time being of the Scottish Branch of the Royal Institution of Chartered Surveyors and which Surveyor, acting as an expert, will determine the Market Rent as aforesaid and the decision of such Surveyor shall be binding on both the Landlord and the Tenant; Within one month of the date upon which such Surveyor is agreed upon or appointed as aforesaid the Landlord and the Tenant shall each be entitled to submit to such Surveyor written valuations, statements and other evidence relating to or supporting their assessment of the market rental value, in which event they shall, at the same time, deliver to the other party a copy of all such valuations and others submitted as aforesaid; such Surveyor shall, if so requested by written notice from one party (a copy of which shall be served on the other party) received within six weeks of such last mentioned date, hold a hearing at which both parties may be heard and, if present, cross examined and that at such time or times and such place or places as such Surveyor shall appoint for that purpose; Declaring that the parties hereby agree that the yearly rent hereinbefore reserved will be subject to review on the relevant date of review and that any right to have such rent reviewed will not be lost or abandoned by reason of any delay in attempting to agree and/or in requesting such Surveyor or arbitration to settle the rent review and/or acceptance by the Landlord of rent at the then current rate as at or after the relevant date of review. Provided always that if such Surveyor dies or is for any other reason unable to act before he shall have given his decision then either party hereto may request the Chairman or Senior Office Holder or his deputy aforesaid to nominate a further Surveyor to act on the terms of this sub-paragraph. The fees payable to any such Chairman, Senior Office Holder and any such Surveyor shall be borne and paid by the Landlord and the Tenant in such shares and in such manner as such Surveyor shall determine and failing any such decision and subject thereto in equal shares.

9.4 Upwards Only

Notwithstanding the decision of the Surveyor hereinbefore referred to in no event shall the rent payable by the Tenant after each relevant date of review be less than the rent payable by the Tenant immediately before such relevant date of review.

9.5 Payment after Date of Review

In the event that by the relevant date of review the amount of the revised rent has not been agreed between the parties in respect of the period of time (hereinafter called "the said interval") beginning with the relevant date of review and ending on the quarter day immediately following the date upon which the amount of the revised rent is agreed or determined as aforesaid the Tenant shall pay to the Landlord in manner hereinbefore provided rent at the yearly rate payable immediately before the relevant date of review and at the expiration of the said interval there shall be due as a debt payable by the Tenant to the Landlord as arrears of rent an amount equal to the difference between the revised rent and the rent actually paid during the said interval and apportioned on a daily basis in respect of the said interval together with interest at three per cent below the Prescribed Rate from time to time on the said difference between the revised rent and the rent actually paid calculated from the beginning of the said interval until the end of the said interval, (which said difference plus interest aforesaid is hereinafter referred to as "the Balance") declaring that interest at the Prescribed Rate will be due on the Balance from the end of the said interval until paid (as well before as after any decree or judgment).

9.6 Statutory Restriction

In the event of the Landlord being prevented or prohibited in whole or in part (in part meaning anything less than the whole) from exercising his rights under this Clause and/or obtaining an increase in the rent at the relevant date of review by reason of any legislation, governmental decree or notice (increase in this context meaning such increase as would be obtainable disregarding the provisions of any such legislation and others as aforesaid) then and upon each and every occasion on which such event shall occur, if the occurrence gives rise to a total prevention or prohibition, the date at which such review would otherwise have taken effect shall be deemed to be extended to permit and require such review to take place on the first date or dates thereafter (each of said dates being hereinafter referred to as "the substitute review date") upon which such rights or increase may be exercised and/or obtained in whole or in part and when in part, on so many occasions as shall be necessary to obtain the whole increase (meaning the whole of the increase which the Landlord would have obtained if not prevented or prohibited as aforesaid) and if there shall be a partial prevention or prohibition only, there shall be a further review or reviews (as the case may require) on the first date or dates as aforesaid and notwithstanding that the rent may have been increased in part on or since the last occurring relevant date of review, provided always that (i) the provisions of this subclause are without prejudice to the Landlord's rights to review the rent on any relevant date of review as specified in the foregoing paragraphs of this Clause and (ii) it is expressly understood that any increase in rent arising at the substitute review date shall only affect the rent for the period arising after the substitute review date.

9.7 Memorandum

As soon as the amount of rent payable after a date of review has been agreed or ascertained in accordance with the terms hereof (and if required by the Landlord so to do) the parties hereto will at the Tenant's expense forthwith execute a memorandum specifying the amount of the revised rent.

10. Landlord's Obligation to Insure and Rent Abatement

    10.1 Subject to the Landlord being able to obtain and maintain at reasonable commercial rates insurance cover, and subject to such insurance cover not being invalidated, diminished or excluded by any act or omission of the Tenant, any sub-tenants or authorised occupant or (apart from the Landlords) by any other party, the Landlord will insure in the name of the Landlord and at the expense of the Tenant:

        10.1.1 against property owners liability for such amount as shall be deemed necessary by the Landlords;

        10.1.2 the Premises and the Common Parts against the Insured Risks, namely, loss or damage by fire, in peace time aircraft (and aerial devices or articles dropped therefrom), explosion, malicious damage, riot and civil commotion, storm, lightning, earthquake or tempest, bursting or over-flowing of water tanks, apparatus or pipes, flood and impact, and at the sole option of the Landlords, terrorism and/or subsidence/landslip, and such other risks as the Landlords may from time to time consider appropriate, for such sum as the Landlords may consider to be the cost of completely reinstating the Premises and the Landlords' plant, equipment and fixtures therein and the Common Parts, together with an amount sufficient to cover inflation and the fees of all architects, engineers, surveyors and other professional advisers, the cost of temporary hoarding, and other temporary works, removal of debris, disman-tling or demolishing and shoring up or propping and all Value Added Tax on such costs and others;

        10.1.3 against loss of rent for a sum equal to three years' rent of the Premises to take into account any potential increase in rent in pursuance of Clause 9 of this Lease.

    10.2 In the event of any damage or destruction to the Premises or any part thereof or to the Common Parts or any part thereof caused by any of the Insured Risks the Landlord will be entitled to choose to either (a) (subject to obtaining all necessary statutory consents) make good such damage or destruction, declaring that any excess in the insurance policy will be payable by the Tenant on demand or (b) terminate the Lease by written notification of same to the Tenant.

    10.3 Save to the extent that the insurance monies shall be rendered wholly or partially irrecoverable solely by reason of any act or default of the Tenant or those for whom they are responsible in law, or due to the Premises being left unoccupied, the rent or a fair proportion thereof according to the nature and extent of the damage shall be suspended until the earliest of (i) the date when the Premises are again fit for occupation and use for the purposes herein permitted (ii) the expiry of three years following such damage or destruction or (iii) the date on which the Landlord terminates the Lease as provided for in Clause 10.2 hereof.

10.4 If the Landlord has not exercised its option to terminate the Lease as provided for in Clause 10.2 hereof, and if the Landlord has not within a period of three years from the occurrence of such damage or destruction caused by any of the Insured Risks reinstated the Premises and the Common Parts it shall be in the option of the Landlord and/or the Tenant to terminate the Lease by giving one month's written notice, and on the expiry thereof neither party shall be in any way liable to the other except that such termination shall be without prejudice to any claims competent to the Landlord or the Tenant against the other party in respect of any breach prior to the expiry of such notice of any of the obligations of such party under the Lease. The Premises shall be deemed to have been reinstated and to be fit for occupation and use in terms of the foregoing provisions if the Premises and any Common Parts necessary for the reasonable enjoyment thereof have been rebuilt or reinstated or repaired and rendered fit for occupation and use to provide in respect of the Premises substantially the same comparable premises to the Premises (with substantially the same usable floor area as there was at the date of such damage or destruction) notwithstanding that the layout of the Premises and/or the Common Parts is not identical to that as existing before such damage or destruction.

11. If the transaction contemplated by the Lease is notifiable for stamp duty land tax purposes, the Tenant will submit to the Inland Revenue within 7 days of the effective date of the transaction a completed and signed SDLT1 form (with the Agent's address selected as the response to Question 58) together with any applicable supplementary forms and the stamp duty land tax (if any) arising from the Lease. If prior to the issue of a Land Transaction Return Certificate (SDLT5) the Inland Revenue rejects the Tenant's SDLT application, the Tenant will without delay (i) provide the Landlord with a copy of any such rejection and other relevant correspondence and (ii) correct the application and resubmit it and a remittance for the correct amount of the stamp duty land tax to the Inland Revenue. Within 7 days of receipt from the Inland Revenue, the Tenant will deliver to the Landlord's solicitor the Land Transaction Return Certificate (SDLT5) issued by the Inland Revenue. The Landlord will, within 7 days of receipt of the SDLT5 from the Tenant, submit the Lease and the SDLT5 to the Books of Council and Session for registration for preservation and execution and will obtain two extracts thereof. Within 7 days of receipt, the Landlord will return the SDLT5 to the Tenant, and one extract of the Lease. The Tenant acknowledges that if they breach the terms of their obligations in this Clause, they will indemnify the Landlord in respect of loss suffered by the Landlord by virtue of such delay.

12. This offer unless previously withdrawn, shall remain open for acceptance to be received in this office by [*date*], failing which it shall be held to have been withdrawn.

Yours faithfully,

CHAPTER 33

GROUND LEASES AND INTERPOSED LEASES

Introduction

In Scots law a lease of land includes the infrastructure under and on the land as **33–01** well as all buildings erected from time to time on the land. The name "ground lease" is generally used to describe a lease of open ground, where the intention usually is that the tenant will build on that ground, but only has to pay rent for the ground itself, ignoring the value for rent-review purposes of any buildings or other works carried out on the land. The phrases "head lease" and "ground lease" are often used to mean the same thing. A head lease is held from the owner of the property, and the premises leased by it may be ground plus buildings. Having said that, just because a document is called a "ground lease", it does not follow that the premises are merely ground, as the lease may well be of land and buildings from time to time thereon.

There is, in effect, no difference between a lease and a ground lease. The same common law rules apply to all leases, except to the extent these are contracted out of.

An interposed lease is granted when the landlord in an existing lease wants to create a new lease in favour of a third party so that the third party becomes the landlord under that existing lease, and will thus receive the rent payable under that lease.

In this Chapter, we consider various aspects of ground leases and interposed leases, such as rent review, repairs, insurance, alienation and irritancy. We then look very briefly at leases of the reversion in English law.

A—SCOTLAND

Duration

Traditionally, ground leases were of very long duration, often for periods of **33–02** 999 years, but since June 9, 2000, the same 175-year maximum duration applies to new ground leases, in the same way as it does to every other lease and sub-lease of commercial property. This means that any lease granted after that date and which is stated to run beyond a date that is 175 years after the start, will automatically terminate after 175 years, unless the lease is granted in implement of an obligation entered into before June 9, 2000. Longer leases that were granted prior to that date are still valid.

Ground lease as an alternative to sale

Ground leases are often used as an alternative to straightforward sale, with the **33–03** premium payable for the grant of the ground lease being the same as the price if it were a sale transaction. Such ground leases would still need to reserve a rent, even of £1 per annum (if demanded), and would otherwise be very soft, with no obligations imposed on the tenant, no restriction on assignation, sub-letting or granting charges, no restriction on use, and there would be no irritancy clause. An actual ground lease may, or may not restrict assignation or sub-letting, but it may restrict the grant of charges over the tenant's interest, and therefore the landlord's consent may be required for the grant of a standard security or floating charge.

Interposed leases

33–04   Interposed leases are used as an alternative to a straight sale where there is in place an existing income-producing lease, and the seller is disposing of the property with the benefit of that lease. An interposed lease is often used in order to preserve industrial buildings tax allowances, as these run with owner-ship, and they have a 25-year life, with the owner obtaining the tax benefit at the end of that period. Such a lease is also used where the seller has other prop-erty nearby and wants to preserve some element of control over what happens to the premises that he has "sold". The interposed lease will be for any period up to 175 years, and will be granted subject to and with the benefit of the existing lease. There must be a rent payable, and there must be a defined or an ascertainable termination date.

There must be a rent payable, and there must be a defined or an ascertainable termination date.

As the seller (who is the landlord in the interposed lease) will eventually have no interest in the premises, he will often grant an option in favour of the tenant in the interposed lease to buy the landlord's interest after a certain time. The tenant in the interposed lease needs to consider four matters if such an option is to be granted. First, the option should be contained in the interposed lease itself, as opposed to being in missives, because missives only bind the original landlord, and missives have a relatively short lifespan. Secondly, there may well be stamp duty land tax payable in respect of the option. Thirdly, the tenant should ensure that any standard securities over the landlord's interest are discharged, and finally, the landlord should grant to the tenant a standard security over the landlord's interest, in order to secure the obligation to convey his interest to the tenant in terms of the option.

Tenant's works and ground leases

33–05   If the tenant provides infrastructure and/or buildings, these items will become part of the heritage and will thus belong to the landlord, and the tenant there-fore has no right to remove these items at any time. This is to be contrasted with the tenant's right to remove at any time (unless the lease provides other-wise) tenant's trade fittings and fixtures, so far as these are not heritable.

There is no provision at common law for the tenant to receive compensation for works or improvements carried out during the term of the lease, and at the end of the lease the tenant must leave the property without any compensation being payable to him.

Although the infrastructure and buildings become part of the landlord's property, they do not become part of the premises, unless the lease specifically provides for this to happen. If the lease is silent about any additions or improve-ments to the ground, then the landlord's common law obligations in respect of repair, etc. will not apply to any infrastructure or buildings, as these do not form part of the premises leased to the tenant. There will be no obligation on either party to make good any damage or destruction of these things.

Rei Interitus

In the normal commercial occupational lease, the premises let will often **33–06** comprise a building or part of a building, while in the ground lease situation, the premises will usually be a piece of ground without any buildings. At common law, the rule of rei interitus (or "frustration") applies to all leases, whereby if the premises let are damaged or are destroyed such that they cannot be used and occupied, then the lease comes to an end immediately, and neither party has any obligation to the other. Therefore, given that in the ground lease the premises let are usually open ground, it is of no relevance for the purposes of this rule whether or not the buildings on the ground are damaged or destroyed; the lease will continue in force.

Repairing obligation

Ground leases may impose initial construction obligations on the tenant, such as **33–07** putting in infrastructure and erecting buildings; the intention is usually that the tenant should comply with these obligations very early in the duration of the lease. Such leases are likely to impose on the tenant the obligation to repair and maintain, and if necessary to renew and rebuild, the infrastructure and buildings.

A landlord of a ground lease will quite often want to impose strict controls in the ground lease, especially if he has an interest in the site and in the buildings being kept in good repair, and wants to be comfortable as to who his tenant is from time to time (so as to preserve marketability if rent under the ground lease is geared to occupational sub-lease rents). This will be more likely in the case where the landlord has a continuing interest in the premises, such as where a local authority grants a ground lease for development of a town centre, or where the rent under the ground lease is calculated with reference to rents payable under the occupational sub-leases. Such a ground lease then becomes more than just an ordinary ground lease, and adopts some of the characteristics of the normal occupational FRI lease.

Buying the tenant's interest in a ground lease

The incoming tenant should ask to see written confirmation from the landlord **33–08** confirming that initial construction obligations have been performed according to the terms of the ground lease. He should, of course, also ask to see all planning permissions and building control documentation.

The lease may contain an option to terminate or to extend, or indeed for the tenant to acquire the landlord's interest or vice versa; this option may have a deadline way in the future, but that does not mean that the option has not been exercised.

Rent review implications

The first thing to consider in respect of rent reviews is what is actually being **33–09** reviewed. It is important to know whether, for the purpose of rent review, the premises are merely an area of ground, or the ground with infrastructure, services, utilities and buildings. The difference in value can be very significant.

If the lease contains an obligation on the tenant to construct buildings, etc. at the start of the period of the lease, there should, from the tenant's point of view, be an assumption at rent review that this obligation has been complied with, and that the buildings, etc. are in good repair.

If the rent-review clause contains a statement that the rent is to be valued on the basis of the existing lease, then one-off obligations contained in the ground lease in respect of initial construction will be deemed to apply at rent review, and this would be prejudicial to the landlord, as being an onerous obligation on the tenant. If the lease is silent about the hypothetical lease at rent review being on the same terms as the actual lease, then it will be assumed that the terms of the actual lease are to apply, and so once again the onerous obligation problem arises. If the lease tries to negate any adverse effect by disregarding the onerous obligation, this in itself could be seen as onerous, and so on. From the landlord's point of view, and without being unfair to the tenant, it is probably safer to include an assumption that the one-off construction obligations have been performed but to specifically exclude any effect on value of these obligations having been performed. The "pure" ground lease is, of course, a lease of only an area of ground, and it is normal to say that at rent review the value of any buildings is excluded. But one should also consider whether to exclude any effect on value of the provision of infrastructure and services.

If the lease specifies that the site is to be valued without buildings, then it should address the question of what, if any, type of building development is to be assumed. There may be a statement in the rent-review clause that the existence of any planning permission or of any certificate of lawful use is to be taken into account, or that it is to be disregarded. If effectively it is to be implied that the premises are sterile in respect of planning permission, the result could well be that the premises attract a nil or almost nil value, as they could be deemed unable to be used for any purpose other than vacant ground on which nothing can happen. The landlord would not be happy with this.

Please see the text and reported case at para.11–26.

There may be a difficulty with lack of comparables at rent review, i.e. similar leases of similar properties. There may also be a difficulty due to the provision of a lengthy interval between rent reviews; some ground leases have rent reviews only every 21 years.

In *Norwich Union Life Insurance Society v British Railways Board*[1] a lease for 150 years contained obligations on a tenant not only to repair the premises, but also when necessary to rebuild, reconstruct or replace them. At arbitration a reduction of over 20 per cent was made by the arbiter to take account of these obligations. The court held that the arbiter was correct, as clearly in a 150-year period of time, a building is likely to need to be rebuilt or replaced at the end of its natural life.

The ground lease may contain obligations to remove, at termination, any works carried out on the premises, and this could therefore involve the tenant in very expensive demolition at the end of the term. This can therefore reduce any uplift that would otherwise be achievable at rent review, even if the review is on the basis of valuing only the ground, ignoring the existence and value of any buildings.

Options and obligations to develop

33–10 An option or an obligation contained in a ground lease (or an occupational lease for that matter) for the tenant to build, or to have the landlord build, any new or

---

[1] *Norwich Union Life Insurance Society v British Railways Board* (1987) 283 E.G. 846; (1987) 2 E.G.L.R. 137.

additional premises can give rise to problems with funding and marketability. If the landlord has effectively achieved a sale by granting the ground lease for a full market-value premium with only nominal rent, the landlord has thus really washed his hands of the property, and he will not be concerned about what the tenant does. In such a case, there is unlikely to be any construction obligations. However, if the landlord has any continuing financial or other interest in what happens on the property, the lease is likely to impose construction and repairing obligations on the tenant.

The worry for a lender and for the other party is what will happen if construction works are started but not completed, or if they are done badly; the property could become a mess and could be difficult to dispose of. Care and attention are needed to ensure that there is no adverse effect at rent review arising from the right to have construction works done and/or the fact they are ongoing as at review date or that they have been done. This is true not only in actual fact (i.e. what has happened on the ground), but also in terms of the hypothetical lease being considered at rent review.

Rent gearing to occupational sub-leases

If the grant of the ground lease (or interposed lease) was effectively a sale **33–11** transaction, then in all probability a large premium will have been paid at entry, and there will be only a nominal rent of, say, £1 per annum if demanded. However, if the landlord has a continuing financial interest, then the ground lease may well involve a market rent or a geared rent. If the rent is the going rate at the start of the lease, then the rent-review clause will provide for periodical reviews of the rent payable.

The landlord may instead want to receive rent based on what his tenant receives, or should receive, from the occupational sub-leases. There can be unfortunate results in tethering head-lease rent to sub-lease income. There is a difference between rents receivable on the one hand, and rents received on the other. A sub-tenant may fail to pay or may become insolvent. If the ground-lease rent is based on rents receivable from sub-tenants, then the mid-landlord would lose out in such an instance.

Vacant premises need to be considered; if part of the property is not sub-let, does the head landlord lose out? Some ground leases provide for a notional sub-rent for vacant parts, and this may be the amount that was last payable for these parts, or it may be an average of the remainder of the entity. If the lease does not prevent the grant of sub-leases to connected parties of the tenant, a mid-landlord might grant sub-leases of vacant areas to associated companies at a very much reduced rent so as to avoid a greater loss by having a notional value attributed to the void.

Separately, if rents are based on sub-lease rents receivable, and if there is no restriction against granting sub-leases to connected parties, the mid-landlord could minimise the amount payable to the head-landlord by putting in place some sub-leases at concessionary rents to connected parties, then having these connected parties grant full rent sub-under-leases to occupational tenants at full-market rent.

Inter-relationship of head lease and sub-lease

If the head lease contains a rent-review provision, the tenant and also the sub- **33–12** tenant may be concerned that the result in one rent review is prejudicial to the other. If the sub-lease provides that the rent payable will be whatever rent is payable after review in the head lease, the sub-tenant will be worried that the tenant might not try as hard as he could to keep any head-lease rent review to a minimum increase, and the sub-tenant should therefore demand input. This can be achieved by prohibiting the tenant in the head lease from agreeing a rent review or appointing a third party to determine the rent review, except with the prior consent of the sub-tenant, and by providing for the sub-tenant to be allowed to feed into representations and submissions made by the tenant to the third party.

If the head lease provides for the head landlord to provide services, then it is important that the occupational sub-leases allow full recovery from the sub-tenant of money paid by the tenant under the head lease.

Insurance

33–13 While the tenant under a ground lease is usually in control of insurance, this is not always the case, and if insurance is controlled by the head landlord, there may not be scope for having occupational sub-tenants' interests noted on the policy. There could also be problems in respect of obtaining funding in respect of the ground lease interest if the tenant, i.e. the borrower, does not have control over (or any input into) the insurance of the property.

Irritancy (forfeiture)

33–14 If a ground lease or any other lease is irritated, then at common law all sub-leases flowing from that will fall away. There is an important exception provided by s.17(2) of the Land Tenure Reform (Scotland) Act 1974, whereby if the lease that is irritated is an interposed lease, the sub-lease (which of course had originally been the head lease) survives. For all other situations, in an ideal tenant's world, there should be a statement in the head lease to the effect that the head landlord will offer to take on the sub-leases as if they were head leases in the event of irritancy of the head lease. This of course gives the sub-tenant a right, but not any obligation, to enter into a new lease with the head landlord. From the landlord's point of view, it may be desirable to have a right in favour of the landlord to call on the sub-tenant to enter into a new lease with him. This may not be attractive to sub-tenants, who may instead want to state that, if the head lease is irritated, the sub-tenant has the right for the sub-lease to become a head lease.

In any event, sub-tenants will be nervous of any irritancy clause that there may be in the head lease because there is no obligation at present for the landlord under a lease to notify sub-tenants or indeed security holders of any threatened irritancy of the lease. They will therefore ask for the head landlord to enter into an irritancy protection agreement, so as to impose on the head landlord the obligation to grant a new lease directly to him, if the head lease is irritated or rescinded. The head landlord may insist that the agreement require him to grant such a direct lease only to the named initial sub-tenant, as he will want to know that the party that could be his direct tenant one day is someone to whom he would want to lease the property. This understandable concern on the part of the head landlord creates an uncertainty for the sub-tenant. This is because, if he ever wants to assign the sub-lease, he will need to find an assignee who is acceptable to the head landlord. One could introduce an element of reaosnableness into the matter, but the head landlord may not be willing to entertain that. This is, of course, also a concern for the sub-tenant's lender, who will see the personal concession to the sub-tenant as an obstacle to disposing of the sub-tenant's leasehold interest in the event of loan default by the sub-tenant.

It will be difficult to obtain funding in respect of a leasehold interest if there is no provision in the irritancy clause requiring the landlord to notify security or charge holders of a breach and threatened irritancy, and in particular allowing the security or charge holder the opportunity to save the lease. Many landlords will agree to insert a "warning" notification to lenders so as to enable the existing head-lease tenant to obtain funding.

The irritancy clause should contain a saving provision allowing heritable creditors, receivers, administrators and liquidators the opportunity to pay any outstanding sum or to perform any other obligation, and to save the lease from being irritated in the event of tenant insolvency. This should be conditional on such party accepting personal responsibility for the performance of the tenant's obligations including arrears, and allowing such party a realistic period of time in which to dispose of the tenant's interest in accordance with the lease.

B—ENGLAND

Building leases

A building lease is granted where the landlord lets premises to the tenant for **33–15** the purpose of carrying out building, alteration or improvement works. There is no maximum duration of a lease in England.

Lease of the reversion

These are sometimes known as concurrent or over-riding leases. It is always **33–16** open to the landlord in an existing lease to grant a lease of the reversion, i.e. to grant a lease to a third party, whereby that third party becomes the immediate landlord of the existing tenant. A lease of the reversion usually runs for at least three days after the contractual expiry date of the existing lease, but of course it can run for a considerably longer period.

Effect of termination of head lease on sub-leases

If a head lease is terminated by forfeiture, or if the tenant terminates the head **33–17** lease by exercising an early termination option, while the sub-lease is still running, the sub-lease terminates immediately, leaving the sub-tenant with only a claim of damages against his immediate landlord. In the case of forfeiture, the sub-tenant can ask the court to have a new lease created in his favour for a period up to (but not longer than) the then remaining term of the sub-lease. This is how relief from forfeiture operates in the case of a sub-lease. It is at the court's discretion whether or not to grant relief. The sub-tenant will have to pay any arrears due by the tenant.

If the head lease terminates because the tenant has acquired the head landlord's interest, or a third party has acquired both the landlord's and tenant's interests in the head lease (this is called "merger"), then the sub-lease continues in existence. Similarly, if the tenant surrenders his leasehold interest, the sub-lease remains in place.

A lease of the reversion will continue when the pre-existing lease (now relegated to the position of a sub-lease) terminates, as that lease was already in existence and does not depend on the new lease of the reversion.

INDEX

Instructions for Use of CD

These notes are provided for guidance only. They should be read and inter-preted in the context of your own computer system and operational procedures. It is assumed that you have a basic knowledge of WINDOWS. However, if there is any problem please contact our help line (tel. 0845 850 9355 or email trluki.techsupport@thomsonreuters.com) who will be happy to help you.

CD Format and Contents

To run this CD you need at least:

- 133 MHz or more Pentium microprocessor (or equivalent).

- Windows 2000, XP, Vista or Windows 7

- 64 megabytes (MB) of RAM recommended minimum. 32 MB of RAM is the minimum supported. 4 gigabytes (GB) of RAM is the maximum.

- A 2 GB hard disk that has 650 MB of free space. If you are installing over a network, more free hard disk space is required.

- VGA or higher-resolution monitor.

- Keyboard.

- Mouse or compatible pointing device (optional).

- CD drive or DVD drive

The CD contains data files of the clauses in this book. It does not contain soft-ware or commentary.

Installation

The following instructions make the assumption that you will copy the data files to a single directory on your hard disk (e.g. C:\W.Green\Commercial Leases in Scotland).

Open your **CD ROM drive**, select and double click on **setup.exe** and follow the instructions. The files will be unzipped to your **C drive** and you will be able to open them up from the new **C:\W.Green\Commercial Leases in Scotland** folder there.

LICENCE AGREEMENT

Definitions
1. The following terms will have the following meanings:
"The PUBLISHERS" means W. Green, 21 Alva Street, Edinburgh EH2 4PS Part of Thomson Reuters (Professional) UK Limited (Registered in England & Wales, Company No.1679046. Registered Office and address for service: Aldgate House, 33 Aldgate High Street, London EC3N 1DL), (which expression shall, where the context admits, include the PUBLISHERS' assigns or successors in business as the case may be) of the other part (on behalf of Thomson Reuters (Legal) Limited incorporated in England & Wales under the Companies Acts (Registered No.1679046) whose registered office is 100 Avenue Road, London NW3 3PF)
"The LICENSEE" means the purchaser of the work containing the Licensed Material;
"Licensed Material" means the data included on the disk;
"Licence" means a single user licence;
"Computer" means an IBM-PC compatible computer.

Grant of Licence; Back-up Copies
2. (1) The PUBLISHERS hereby grant to the LICENSEE, a non-exclusive, non-transferable licence to use the Licensed Material in accordance with those terms and conditions.

(2) The LICENSEE may install the Licensed Material for use on one computer only at any one time.

(3) The LICENSEE may make one back-up copy of the Licensed Material only, to be kept in the LICENSEE's control and possession.

Proprietary Rights
3. (1) All rights not expressly granted herein are reserved.

(2) The Licensed Material is not sold to the LICENSEE who shall not acquire any right, sale or interest in the Licensed Material or in the media upon which the Licensed Material is supplied.

(3) The LICENSEE, shall not erase, remove, deface or cover any trademark, copyright notice, guarantee or other statement on any media containing the Licensed Material.

(4) The LICENSEE shall only use the Licensed Material in the normal course of its business and shall not use the Licensed Material for the purpose of operating a bureau or similar service or any online service whatsoever.

(5) Permission is hereby granted to LICENSEES who are members of the legal profession (which expression does not include individuals or organisations engaged in the supply of services to the legal profession) to reproduce, transmit and store small quantities of text for the purpose of enabling them to provide legal advice to or to draft documents or conduct proceedings on behalf of their clients.

(6) The LICENSEE shall not sublicense the Licensed Material to others and this Licence Agreement may not be transferred, sublicensed, assigned or otherwise disposed of in whole or in part.

(7) The LICENSEE shall inform the PUBLISHERS on becoming aware of any unauthorised use of the Licensed Material.

Warranties
4. (1) The PUBLISHERS warrant that they have obtained all necessary rights to grant this licence.

(2) Whilst reasonable care is taken to ensure the accuracy and completeness of the Licensed Material supplied, the PUBLISHERS make no representations or warranties, express or implied, that the Licensed Material is free from errors or omissions.

(3) The Licensed Material is supplied to the LICENSEE on an "as is" basis and has not been supplied to meet the LICENSEE's individual requirements. It is the sole responsibility of the LICENSEE to satisfy itself prior to entering this Licence Agreement that the Licensed Material will meet the LICENSEE's requirements and be compatible with the LICENSEE's hardware/software configuration. No failure of any part of the Licensed Material to be suitable for the LICENSEE's requirements will give rise to any claim against the PUBLISHERS.

(4) In the event of any material inherent defects in the physical media on which the licensed material may be supplied, other than caused by accident abuse or misuse by the LICENSEE, the PUBLISHERS will replace the defective original media free of charge provided it is returned to the place of purchase within 90 days of the purchase date. The PUBLISHERS' entire liability and the LICENSEE's exclusive remedy shall be the replacement of such defective media.

(5) Whilst all reasonable care has been taken to exclude computer viruses, no warranty is made that the Licensed Material is virus free. The LICENSEE shall be responsible to ensure that no virus is introduced to any computer or network and shall not hold the PUBLISHERS responsible.

(6) The warranties set out herein are exclusive of and in lieu of all other conditions and warranties, either express or implied, statutory or otherwise.

(7) All other conditions and warranties, either express or implied, statutory or otherwise, which relate in the condition and fitness for any purpose of the Licensed Material are hereby excluded and the PUBLISHERS shall not be liable in contract, delict or in tort for any loss of any kind suffered by reason of any defect in the Licensed Material (whether or not caused by the negligence of the PUBLISHERS).

Limitation of Liability and Indemnity
5. (1) The LICENSEE shall accept sole responsibility for and the PUBLISHERS shall not be liable for the use of the Licensed Material by the LICENSEE, its agents and employees and the LICENSEE shall hold the PUBLISHERS harmless and fully indemnified against any claims, costs, damages, loss and liabilities arising out of any such use.

(2) The PUBLISHERS shall not be liable for any indirect or consequential loss suffered by the LICENSEE (including without limitation loss of profits, goodwill or data) in connection with the Licensed Material howsoever arising.

(3) The PUBLISHERS will have no liability whatsoever for any liability of the LICENSEE to any third party which might arise.

(4) The LICENSEE hereby agrees that

(a) the LICENSEE is best placed to foresee and evaluate any loss that might be suffered in connection with this Licence Agreement,

(b) that the cost of supply of the Licensed Material has been calculated on the basis of the limitations and exclusions contained herein; and

(c) the LICENSEE will effect such insurance as is suitable having regard to the LICENSEE's circumstances.

(5) The aggregate maximum liability of the PUBLISHERS in respect of any direct loss or any other loss (to the extent that such loss is not excluded by this Licence Agreement or otherwise) whether such a claim arises in contract or tort shall not exceed a sum equal to that paid at the price for the title containing the Licensed Material.

Termination
6. (1) In the event of any breach of this Agreement including any violation of any copyright in the Licensed Material, whether held by the PUBLISHERS or others in the Licensed Material, the Licence Agreement shall automatically terminate immediately, without notice and without prejudice to any claim which the PUBLISHERS may have either for moneys due and/ or damages and/or otherwise.

(2) Clauses 3 to 5 shall survive the termination for whatsoever reason of this Licence Agreement.

(3) In the event of termination of this Licence Agreement the LICENSEE will remove the Licensed Material.

Miscellaneous
7. (1) Any delay or forbearance by the PUBLISHERS in enforcing any provisions of this License Agreement shall not be construed as a waiver of such provision or an agreement thereafter not to enforce the said provision.

(2) This Licence Agreement shall be governed by the laws of England and Wales. If any difference shall arise between the Parties touching the meaning of this Licence Agreement or the rights and liabilities of the parties thereto, the same shall be referred to arbitration in accordance with the provisions of the Arbitration Act 1996, or any amending or substituting statute for the time being in force.

DISCLAIMER

Styles material in this publication may be used as a guide for the drafting of legal documents specifically for particular clients, though no liability is accepted by the publishers or authors in relation to their use. Such documents may be provided to clients for their own use. Styles may not otherwise be distributed to third parties.